CONTESTED TERRAIN

Contested Terrain

*Reflections with
Afghan Women Leaders*

SALLY L. KITCH

UNIVERSITY OF ILLINOIS PRESS
URBANA, CHICAGO, AND SPRINGFIELD

© 2014 by the Board of Trustees
of the University of Illinois
All rights reserved
Manufactured in the United States of America
1 2 3 4 5 C P 5 4 3 2 1
∞ This book is printed on acid-free paper.

Library of Congress Cataloging-in-Publication Data
Kitch, Sally.
Contested terrain : reflections with Afghan women leaders / Sally L.
Kitch.
pages   cm
Includes bibliographical references and index.
ISBN 978-0-252-03870-9 (hardcover : alk. paper) —
ISBN 978-0-252-08027-2 (pbk. : alk. paper) —
ISBN 978-0-252-09664-8 (e-book)
1. Feminism—Afghanistan. 2. Feminists—Afghanistan.
3. Women—Political activity—Afghanistan. 4. Leadership in women—
Afghanistans. 5. Women—Afghanistan—Social conditions. I. Title.
HQ1735.6.K56   2014
305.409581—dc23   2014013016

To Jamila Afghani, Marzia Basel,
and the women of Afghanistan whom they have served.
May they be heard.

CONTENTS

Acknowledgments   ix

Introduction: Journeys through Contested Terrain   1

PART I. HOPE (2002–2005)   19

1. Working for Women in "Postconflict" Afghanistan   25
2. Two Strong Voices: The Making of Women Leaders in Afghanistan   44
3. Constructing Women's Rights in Afghanistan   62

PART II. REALITY (2005–2010)   77

4. The Basics of Change   83
5. The Political Is Personal   98
6. Afghan Marriage Practices   114
7. Marriage Hits Home   130

PART III. UNCERTAINTY (2010–2013)   151

8. Addressing Afghanistan's Problems   157
9. Fast-Forward   181
10. Future Prospects   204

Afterword: The Clock Is Ticking, 2014   229

Notes   235

References   247

Index   255

ACKNOWLEDGMENTS

My thanks go to many people and organizations for their support of the Afghan Women's Leadership Project from which this book evolved. First and foremost, I thank Margaret Mills, my collaborator and partner in that project from 2001 to 2006. Together we organized the conference at Ohio State University that brought Marzia Basel and Jamila Afghani into my life. I also wish to thank the Mershon Center for International Security Studies at OSU, the American Institute of Afghanistan Studies, the Asia Foundation, the National and Ohio League of Women Voters, the Columbus Council on World Affairs, OSU's Critical Difference for Women program, and the Ohio State University Office of International Affairs for their support of that initial project over several years. Since my production of this book spanned my employment at two universities, it has been my good fortune to have the research and administrative support of graduate assistants at both OSU and Arizona State University over the years. They include Melanie Maltry and Dong Li from OSU and Aundrea Snitker, Abigale Vercauten, and Michelle Spiegel from the Gender Studies Ph.D. program at ASU.

Research and sabbatical leaves and research funding provided by Arizona State made my immersion in this book project possible. I am also grateful for the ongoing support and intellectual camaraderie of ASU's Center for the Study of Religion and Conflict. I especially thank the center's director, Linell Cady, for including me in the center's Ford Foundation– and Luce Foundation–funded seminars for ongoing discussions from 2007 to 2012 about religion, politics, and gender as well as women's rights in an international framework. I also thank Yasmin Saikia, Hardt-Nichachos Chair in Peace Studies at ASU, for including me in her seminar on women, Islam, and peace building in 2011.

Finally, I wish to thank my editor at the University of Illinois Press, Larin McLaughlin, for believing in this project and supporting it through the editorial and publication process. I am grateful, too, for the critiques of thoughtful reviewers whose observations and guidance have enhanced and strengthened the book. Of course, all errors that may remain are mine alone.

INTRODUCTION

Journeys through Contested Terrain

My first in-person meeting with women leaders from Afghanistan occurred in the wee hours of a stormy November morning in 2005 at the Port Columbus International Airport in Columbus, Ohio. Seven of them were coming to Ohio State University from Afghanistan, as well as from New York City and Washington, D.C., to participate in the first conference ever held in the United States to feature so many Afghan women in leadership positions. The full group included a deputy in the Ministry of Information and Culture, a judge, a medical student and children's advocate, a gender specialist for the Asian Development Bank, and leaders in international nongovernmental organizations (NGOs) focused on peace, democracy, and women's education, health, and economic capacity building. Five were coming that night from Kabul, and two would arrive from their U.S. locations the next day. My Ohio State colleague Margaret Mills and I had been planning the conference for more than three years, and we were very excited to see the women at last. We were concerned because the group we had been waiting for since 11:00 p.m. had faced a three-hour delay on the last leg of their journey, from New York to Columbus, after traveling from Kabul via London for well over twenty-four hours. It was now after 2:00 a.m.

When the plane finally arrived, Margaret and I were not initially worried as a crowd of passengers emerged from the concourse and passed through the security gate where we were waiting with no sign of our visitors. We knew the women might bring up the rear because one of them, Jamila, had trouble walking. Because we could not persuade the lone security guard on duty to take a wheelchair to meet the flight, we expected the group to make a slow and halting exit. The guard's claim that he could not leave his post, since he was alone, or allow Margaret or me to enter the secure concourse to deliver the chair, because we could not be screened, had struck us as one of many inhumane unintended consequences of our country's post-9/11 vigilance. But as the minutes ticked by, we grew more impatient to see for ourselves that the women were all right. We increasingly expected to receive a haggard clutch of weary travelers, dazed and worn from their traumatic travel experience. We even wondered if they could possibly recover from their ordeal in time for the upcoming schedule of panel presentations and interviews.

What happened next only increased our anxiety. Before we saw any sign of our Afghan visitors, the pilots of the plane—both women, as it happened—passed through the security gate where we were waiting. The pilots were talking to one another about how bad the weather had been and how glad they were to have completed the landing, after aborting the first attempt. Because pilots seldom complain about weather conditions, their comments got my attention. I became doubly convinced that our Kabul contingent would be traumatized, worn-out, and possibly resentful about their ordeal.

So, when we heard happy laughter coming from the concourse, just beyond where we could see, I assumed it must be the cleaning crew. Instead, when the cheery group came into view, we saw our five visitors from Kabul enjoying a joke together or possibly appreciating the absurdity of their situation as they helped Jamila navigate the long walk. They displayed no anxieties about travel or weather. They even looked fresh and energetic. Several were wearing fashionable and colorful Western clothes and high-heeled shoes. (None was wearing a sufficiently warm coat, though, which we quickly had to remedy.) Only Jamila was wearing *hijab,* but her lovely face beamed from the wimple of scarf that framed it and covered her hair. Her smile belied what must have been acute physical pain from her swollen legs and lopsided gait—caused, I later learned, by untreated childhood polio—as she labored down the concourse. Instead of complaining about the lack of a wheelchair or the long trip, as she was perfectly entitled to do, however, Jamila was hugging us and making instant friends with her American hosts. The other women were also greeting us with the characteristic three-kiss Afghan embrace, with no mention of fatigue or hardship.

That was my first personal lesson in the famed Afghan spirit of generosity, which includes both giving material gifts and giving one's best self to others, especially to strangers. I immediately felt small-minded and very American for expecting the women to express their discomfort and fatigue. I happily allowed the glow of their kindness and selflessness to dispel my own exhaustion and worry.

As Margaret and I escorted the women to their hotel that night, I had no inkling that the conference we had been planning for so long would only be the start of an amazing personal journey for me that would culminate in *Contested Terrain.* Nor did I realize that I would develop an ongoing relationship with two of those women, Jamila Afghani, founder and director of an Afghan-based educational NGO then called the Noor Educational Center (NEC), and Marzia Basel, the judge and founder of the Afghan Women Judges Association.[1] Nor did I foresee that those two would ask me to write about their personal stories and political perspectives on Afghan women's tumultuous and contested opportunities and responsibilities, a request I would do my best to honor as the core and inspiration of a book. I certainly did not realize that our journey together—more metaphorical than literal but also involving much travel and change of scene—would take us over such contested terrain.

Back to the Beginning

That November morning at the airport in 2005 was an important milestone in what has been for me a riveting connection with one of the most compelling gender issues of my lifetime. Although it has taken me years to know just how to characterize the issue, it was first manifested to Western audiences in the late 1990s as the horrific specter of Afghan women struggling under Taliban rule. I have learned that such a characterization was only a partial truth, but it served for many Americans, including me, as a point of entry into a distant, unknown, but politically important geopolitical flash point. As a career-long women's studies scholar and professor, whose work focused on U.S. social history and gendered social structures, I was perhaps more interested—but not necessarily much better informed—than many of my fellow Americans in understanding what Taliban rule meant, how it had come about, and why it had happened when and where it did. I also wanted to know more about the Afghan women who were subject to that rule.

Media coverage and U.S. governmental dispatches about the situation called on such terms as *burqa, Islamic brutality, Taliban, feudal, backward, clash of cultures,* and *saving* as they represented the situation. Together those terms contributed to public narratives that ran something like this: *Afghan women suffer from the brutality of the Islamic fundamentalist Taliban regime, which has imprisoned them in* burqas *and taken their country back to the Middle Ages, from whom Western powers should save them so they can share in Western-style women's liberation, which is a centerpiece of true democracy.*

Some U.S. celebrities, feminists, and celebrity feminists jumped on the bandwagon of Afghan women's plight. Mavis Leno was among those who came forward to offer their help. "'I firmly believe we are their last hope,'" she declared about Afghan women in October 1998 at a fund-raiser for the cause, while her husband, Jay, beamed his approval of her philanthropy (quoted in Khan 2001, 3). The Feminist Majority Foundation (FMF) had selected Mavis to head its ongoing Afghanistan campaign, which worked with Afghan activists and organizations. One of those organizations, the Women's Alliance for Peace and Human Rights in Afghanistan (WAPHA), had organized conferences as well as demonstrations and rallies and had sent its president, Zeiba Shorish-Shamley, to testify three times before the U.S. Senate and House of Representatives (Khan 2001, 13).

The Feminist Majority's lobbying against U.S. support of the Taliban was instrumental in influencing President Bill Clinton to withdraw support from a $2.5 billion pipeline from the gas fields of Turkmenistan through Afghanistan to Pakistan as an alleged peace-promoting project. The project's contractor, UNOCAL

Corporation of California, actually cited the Feminist Majority's revelations about and protests against Afghan women's treatment under the Taliban in announcing its withdrawal from the project in 1998 (Khan 2001, 11). Although later criticized for its imperialist Western biases, the FMF's approach in the 1990s lulled many Americans into thinking the United States could make a difference for Afghan women.[2]

Then came September 11, 2001. As New York City's World Trade Center towers collapsed in a cloud of toxic smoke that sunny morning, and another 125 people perished at the very seat of U.S. military might, the United States looked less powerful, more deluded, and less on top of global politics than many of its citizens had thought (or hoped). The links between the plot's mastermind, Osama bin Laden, al Qaeda, and the Taliban seemed unmistakable, if not altogether clear. By November 17, however, the George W. Bush administration had worked it all out. In a historic radio address, First Lady Laura Bush justified the administration's military attack on Afghanistan a few weeks before on the grounds that such action would liberate Afghan women from their "brutal oppression by terrorists." Mrs. Bush thereby conflated the Taliban with the 9/11 attackers and reassured the country that "recent military gains in much of Afghanistan" meant that Afghan "women are no longer imprisoned in their homes. They can listen to music and teach their daughters without fear of punishment. . . . The fight against terrorism is also a fight for the rights and dignity of women," she concluded (quoted in Abu-Lughod 2002, 784).

That speech jolted me and other feminists around the world to attention. After noting the convenient conflation of "enemies" and Mrs. Bush's focus on freeing Afghan women to play conventional feminine roles, my first thought was for the impact of more war and bombing on a country that had by then been at war for decades. How could military action improve Afghan women's lives when it was they who suffered most from the deaths of husbands, fathers, sons, and other male relatives on whom their own and their children's livelihoods depended? Had anyone in the Bush administration consulted with any Afghan women to see if attack by the United States was the best way to improve their lives? And what would happen to the Afghan women the United States ostensibly "saved"? What would their lives be worth?

Next I wondered where the allegedly gender-sensitive Bush administration had been since their election in the ongoing struggle for women's rights in the United States. What did it mean that these faraway women were suddenly attracting conservative Republican attention when feminist causes and gender equity had been absent from their platform and legislative priorities throughout the campaign and first nine months of their term?

With the help of other observers and scholars, the answers to those questions started becoming clearer. Mrs. Bush's logic reflected not a new position on gender for her husband's administration but rather a holdover from colonialism, which had often been justified in the name of "saving" women. The British were frequent perpetrators of that excuse: Indian women needed saving from sati (widow burning) and child marriage; Egyptian women needed saving from the veil (Abu-Lughod 2002, 784).

But the United States had also played the same game. From my work on the gendered foundations of racial distinctions and hierarchy in the United States, I knew that our country's colonization of Puerto Rico, for example, had been justified in part by Puerto Rican women's need to be saved from excess childbearing, an allegedly racial characteristic that was blamed for dragging down the Puerto Rican economy. That goal actually helped to justify a program, lasting from February 1948 through October 1949, that imported young Puerto Rican women to train as domestic servants in the homes of white families living in Scarsdale, New York (Kitch 2009, 216). The racism inherent in such colonizing moves was patently obvious: the prevailing norm of white people (or "the right kind of women . . . white and innocent") rescuing brown women from brown men (Jabbra 2013, 236). Of course, getting low-cost household help was another plus for U.S. moneyed interests.

At the heart of such "about them without them," white-father-knows-best colonial thinking is the idea of culture clash, which blames intransigent cultural actors instead of historical geopolitical relationships for political and military conflicts. The rhetoric of culture clash soon began appearing in administration and popular-press explanations for the attacks of 9/11. Its message was, "We have reason; they do not. We are located in modernity; they are not. Significantly, because they have not advanced as we have, it is our moral obligation to correct, discipline, and keep them in line" (Razack 2005, 15). It was not coincidental that the culture-clash argument pitted Western values against Muslim ones, since the notion of Western innocence and progress versus "Muslim savagery" and stagnation had characterized Orientalist thinking in Europe and the United States from the nineteenth century on, through "an instant chain of associations (the veil, female genital mutilation, arranged marriages, etc.)." Those associations reinforced "the declared superiority of European [and U.S.] culture, imagined as a homogeneous composite of values, including a unique commitment to democracy and human rights, and to the human rights of women in particular" (Razack 2005, 14; Yeğenoğlu 1998, 98). Such a view completely ignored, among other things, the long and torturous path to full citizenship that U.S. women did not achieve until 1934.[3]

It was also timely in 2001 that, finally, in the decade since most evils in the world could be blamed by U.S. politicians on the Soviet menace of the Cold War period, there was a new set of "cultural monsters . . . the Taliban-and-the-terrorists . . . who want[ed] to, as [Mrs. Bush] put it, 'impose their world on the rest of us.'" We, on the other hand, were among the "'civilized people throughout the world,'" she said, whose hearts break for the women and children of Afghanistan. In blending "the enemy" into a single force, Mrs. Bush not only manipulated some key facts but also blurred the separate causes of Afghan women's continuing malnutrition, poverty, poor health, "and their more recent exclusion under the Taliban from employment, schooling, and the joys of wearing nail polish" (Abu-Lughod 2002, 784).

Moreover, situating the United States firmly in the paragon position, there was little opportunity or need for self-critique, for seeing clearly the kind of gender issues activists and gender scholars had long struggled with in U.S. culture: the violent prostitution industry, high numbers of rape and sexual homicides (many times those in countries such as India), sexual harassment, relationship violence, and sex trafficking, among others. By fixating on the evils and suffering of the "other," the administration effectively reinforced U.S. culture's "heroic status" and ignored the motes in American eyes (Franks 2003, 146).

The culture-clash rhetoric after 9/11 also overlooked important facts about the historical interconnections of colonist and colonizer, abject and powerful, superior and inferior, and conveniently obscured the long-standing role of the United States in the crisis in Afghanistan, including the oppression of Afghan women and the rise of the Taliban. Even a cursory understanding of recent history should have cautioned U.S. officials to admit at least some responsibility for the role of the U.S.-backed mujahideen in creating opportunities and providing weapons for the Taliban in the 1980s and 1990s (Khan 2001, 12–13). The administration's silence on that U.S. role kept intact the idea, promulgated by President Reagan, that the mujahideen were "freedom fighters" and "'the moral equivalents of America's founding fathers'" (Jalalzai and Jefferess 2011, 11).

Such judgments persisted despite evidence that the mujahideen "government in exile" in Peshawar, Pakistan, had issued Taliban-like decrees in 1990, stating that "women were not to wear perfume, noisy bangles, or western clothes. Veils had to cover the body at all times and clothes were not to be made of material which was soft or which rustled. Women were not to walk in the middle of the street or swing their hips; they were not to talk, laugh, or joke with strangers or foreigners" (Moghadam 2003, 264). Those same mujahideen had often attacked families that allowed women to work with foreigners, go to school, or shop without a *mahram* (male relative) (Barakat and Wardell 2002, 921–22).

Digging a little deeper into the historical record, it was also clear that U.S. interests during the Cold War had prompted several American administrations to oppose promised reforms for Afghan women, especially those promoted by the People's Democratic Party of Afghanistan (PDPA), a communist-affiliated party supported by many Afghans before the Soviet invasion in 1979 (Moghadam 2003, 247). U.S. Cold War imperatives sacrificed such reforms to the overarching goal of thwarting Soviet interests in Afghanistan's contested terrain, perhaps even "allowing Islam to crystalize as the major ideology of resistance groups" (Khan 2001, 9).

Such a historical perspective would have made keen observers of the situation in 2001 skeptical that the removal of the Taliban would transform Afghan women's lives overnight to reveal women who wanted to be "just like us" or root out the causes of Afghan women's oppression. There was no doubt that restrictions, especially on urban Afghan women's opportunities and mobility, had become much harsher under Taliban rule, but the seeds of such restrictions—some of them welcomed by women themselves—were deeply planted, in part by world powers that had repeatedly backed or created backlash from the most conservative political and religious elements of Afghan society.

Afghan women's own activism and agency were also obscured by the culture-clash rhetoric and the construction of Afghan women as mute victims in need of Western saviors. U.S. media and government paid little attention—and gave no support—to the Revolutionary Association of Women of Afghanistan, the Organization for the Liberation of the People of Afghanistan, the Organization for Liberation of the Working Class of Afghanistan, the Afghanistan Liberation Organization, the Afghanistan Women's Council, the Afghan Institute of Learning, and the Muslim Women Society, all of which were then struggling for Afghan women's rights and equality in one way or another.[4] Nor did they provide support for the nongovernmental organizations headed by women such as Marzia and Jamila, who had spent their adult lives working for Afghan women's educational opportunities and legal rights. Replacing such support and deep investigation of Afghan women's situation was an obsessive focus in the United States on removing the *burqa,* as if a bare female face were the sine qua non of freedom.

Mrs. Bush's speech was a catalyst not only for my and many others' anger but also for my decision to try to act in some way that might support an alternative vision of the U.S. government's responsibilities and obligations to Afghan women. In late 2001, I helped to assemble a group of OSU colleagues to discuss what actions by academics at a major research university in the United States might be appropriate in response to the administration's use of Afghan women's welfare to justify military invasion. Among the participants was Margaret Mills, professor in the Department of Near Eastern Languages and Cultures (NELC) and an internationally recognized expert on Afghan culture, history, and folklore, with by then a thirty-year track record of scholarship about and interaction with Afghans. I would later learn that her 1991 book, *Rhetorics and Politics in Afghan Traditional Storytelling,* which won the Chicago Folklore Prize in 1993, was considered groundbreaking in her field because it extended narrative theory in new directions, bridged anthropology and folklore, and revealed "an 'etiquette of indirectness'" in the narrative patterns of Afghan storytelling (Caton 1991, 330; Edwards 1994, 1124). Margaret's work also focused on gender, as illustrated by her many articles on female tricksters and misogynist proverbs.[5] Her fieldwork in Herat, Afghanistan, had given her access to women's worlds as well as to their stories, and she was an astute observer of communication patterns among them as well as of the exigencies and joys that shaped their lives.

Luckily for me, Margaret also wanted to work on crafting an appropriate response to U.S. policy toward Afghan women. She would lend her experience and expertise in Afghanistan to the project, as I continued to learn about Afghan history, politics, and traditions. I hoped to lend my expertise in gender and feminist and cultural theory, which included analysis of sometimes hidden gendered social structures and women's strategies of resistance to them, mostly in the United States in the nineteenth and twentieth centuries. By the end of the academic year, we had hatched a plan. We decided that our best contribution under the circumstances would be to provide a rare opportunity for at least some Americans to do what our government had not done—listen to Afghan women instead of tell them what was best for them or their country.

We were persuaded through our consultations over the next year with other experts who had worked with groups of Afghan women, including Mahnaz Afkhami, executive director of the Sisterhood Is Global Institute and author of many books on Muslim women, that our original plan to bring rural women to speak at the conference (through translators) was misguided and would be too jarring an experience for them. We decided that both our project and our collaborators would be better off if we worked with those who could express themselves directly, preferably in English, and had already worked on behalf of Afghan women and gender issues in their country. We recognized that that choice put another layer of representation between us and grassroots women's needs and desires, but it still seemed a valid option for our goals. In addition, it allowed us to explore a little-recognized group of women activists, whose experience and perspectives were significant in their own right.

To further our newly named Afghan Women's Leadership Project, we set about identifying the women we could bring to our campus, and by the summer of 2003, we had located and invited eleven women from those who met our criteria, which included relative fluency in English. The list included the first female provincial governor in Afghanistan, the current minister for women's affairs, college professors, doctors, and gender advisers for various multinational companies and institutions. Margaret met with most of the eleven in Kabul that summer. In the end, five of those women serving in Afghanistan were able to obtain visas and permission to leave their jobs and families. Two others were already working in the United States. Most were in their twenties and thirties, a sad reminder that short life expectancies force those who can to get a head start on their life's work.

Those who argue that our selection of these women played into U.S. government policies for Afghanistan might be interested to know that we were rebuffed by the government agencies we approached to help fund the conference.[6] The administration was not interested in hearing "Afghan Women Leaders Speak" about "Conflict Mitigation and Social Reconstruction," as we titled our conference. From 2002 to 2005, government agencies were primarily financing U.S. contractors to build schools, roads, and clinics and to offer short-term training programs for Afghans, including women, in business or technological skills. The websites of the Departments of State (including the United States Agency for International Development [USAID]) and Defense revealed no funded projects that entailed listening to Afghans' views about their own or their country's needs and priorities or about U.S. policy or actions.

Unprompted, several of the women at the conference would later reinforce our perception that the U.S. presence in Afghanistan through 2005 (and probably beyond) consisted mostly of our citizens speaking and doing *to* Afghans rather than *with* them. Conference attendees criticized the failure of international donors, including the U.S. government, to consult with Afghan people or to provide long-term capacity building that would further the agencies' good work after the foreigners left Afghanistan. Our project was a small attempt to correct that failure.

Ultimately, Margaret and I had to depend on Ohio State's Mershon Center for International Security Studies for most funding for the conference. The center's director, Richard Hermann, understood how important gender issues were to questions of international security and peace. He and many of the center's associated faculty were eager to provide a forum for our visitors. While planning the conference, Margaret and I became scholars in residence at the Mershon Center and spent two years meeting and consulting with experts on and dignitaries from Afghanistan and other countries in the region. We also obtained support from the American Institute of Afghanistan Studies, the Asia Foundation, the National and Ohio League of Women Voters, and the Columbus Council on World Affairs, as well as seven other Ohio State University offices, including the OSU Coca-Cola Critical Difference for Women program.

During those planning years, Ohio State's Office of International Affairs also provided funds for a lecture series on women in Islam, Afghan history, and Afghan women, through which we brought three speakers on Afghanistan and gender politics, with whom we also consulted for the leadership project. In addition, we identified appropriate readings and cotaught a graduate seminar on transnational feminism, the possibilities and complexities of Islamic feminism, women's rights in Islam, and ethnographic accounts of Afghan women's lives. We were particularly interested in exploring prospects for cross-cultural understanding and action. By the time we greeted the women for the conference, our collaboration had greatly enhanced my understanding of Margaret's part of the world and our collective understanding of the gendered geopolitics of U.S.-Afghanistan relations.

When the "Afghan Women Leaders Speak" conference ended, after five intensive days of panel presentations and individual interviews, we had a fascinating video record of a historic event. Audiences of between forty and eighty people per day had listened as our visitors expressed their views about current conditions for Afghan women, women as agents of conflict resolution, the effects on women of U.S. occupation of their country, and the role of Islam in women's status, among other topics, and presented information about their own projects for women.[7] Marzia had also given an eye-opening lecture to a large community audience about Afghan women's legal rights and the judicial system.

By 2006 Margaret and I had published two articles together. We also discussed next steps, which included a follow-up grant from the Mershon Center. And then I accepted a job at Arizona State University and moved from Columbus in June 2006. As the geographic basis for our collaboration evaporated, Margaret and I decided that we would each pursue our own interests in the Afghan material. Writing a book was the furthest thing from my mind, but I still hoped to do something with the conference transcripts and bring attention to this little-known group of activists. I had struck up a particular relationship with Marzia and Jamila during the conference, so I continued exchanging e-mails with them and trying to keep up with their evolving life and work situations.

In addition, even though I was consumed with my new job as the founding director of the Institute for Humanities Research at ASU and deep into an unrelated book project, I became involved in the work of ASU's Center for the Study of Religion and Conflict, which over the next several years attracted significant grant funding from the Ford and Luce Foundations to advance knowledge about gender issues in religious and political conflicts in Muslim regions, including South Asia and the Middle East. Through those grant-funded projects, I participated in seminars with historians; political scientists; international law, South Asia, and human rights specialists; religious studies scholars; and other gender scholars discussing extensive readings about religion and secularism, gender and Islam, religion and women's rights, religious fundamentalism, gender and human rights, and the history of women's status in Muslim countries. Through the seminars I was also able to interact with guest speakers from around the world on many aspects of those topics.

When my research funding at ASU permitted in 2009, I asked Marzia and Jamila if they would be interested in meeting me again to continue in person our conversations about their life experiences and political and cultural perspectives. We selected dates in early September 2010 for a meeting in Istanbul. I underwent the proper institutional review board (IRB) training and review for continuing my research with them.[8] Although I had hoped that Margaret could join us and use the opportunity to further her own research, she was unable to do so. Therefore, as I approached the meeting, I was guided by my own expanded circle of collaborators and knowledge about Afghanistan, Afghan women, and women's status in Islam, which further informed my long-term scholarly interest in the structures of gender relations, gender symbolism, visions for feminist social change, and transnational feminist theory and activism.[9]

Although my original plan for the Istanbul meeting was simply to update my knowledge of the women's views and of their activist work, Jamila and Marzia quickly made clear that they wanted me to help them disseminate their perspectives on and experiences of Afghanistan's social, political, and economic conditions. As I began recording our interviews in Istanbul, Marzia volunteered that "this research is very important for Afghanistan. . . . It should be done. . . . We want our voices to reach out throughout the world; that is the purpose why we are here." Jamila agreed. We decided together that the women's hopes could be realized only through a full-length book project, devoted not only to their ideas about Afghanistan but also to their life experiences, which so aptly and poignantly represent the struggles and possibilities for a subset of professional urban women in Afghanistan, who often remain invisible in international discussions of the country's future.

Further, a book project would allow me to consider some of the larger questions Marzia and Jamila raised about gender and Islam, women's education and civic participation, family life, and Afghanistan's history and prospects. It would also provide an opportunity to reflect on the history of women's rights in Afghanistan and on transnational feminist perspectives on the possibilities and hazards of working on women's issues across daunting boundaries of geopolitical history, contemporary politics, religion, and traditions.

Transformative Passage

The women leaders' stories that unfold throughout *Contested Terrain,* especially those of Marzia and Jamila, reveal transformative changes in personal and professional relationships that can be understood as both actual and figurative journeys. The figurative changes include my professional move toward a greater global awareness of gender issues, with all the challenges to some of my own and my culture's preconceptions and priorities such a change necessarily entails. In embarking on that professional journey, I have become increasingly aware of the embarrassing history of Western women's roles in imperial cultures and in exoticizing the veiled woman as a fantasy against which their own lives could be judged superior. I have also come to understand differences among women less as products of immutable cultures than as results of geopolitics and "differently structured desires . . . different ideas about justice," and different visions of the future—what Lila Abu-Lughod terms "personhood . . . in a different language" (2002, 788).

The book's stories also include actual travel. Some of that involved meetings between Marzia, Jamila, and myself, including the 2005 OSU conference with the seven leaders in Columbus, my meeting with Jamila and Marzia in Istanbul in 2010, and Marzia's monthlong stay in Tempe, Arizona, in 2011 as a visiting fellow. On her own, Marzia traveled to Washington, D.C.; Ithaca and Buffalo, New York;

and Toronto, Canada. Jamila considered coming to Tempe and London to further her education, and she actually traveled twice to the United States—to Madison, New Jersey, to receive an award in 2011 and to New York City to participate in a retreat for peacemakers in 2013. Our collaboration on this project also entailed some "time travel," as we three struggled to communicate via telephone and e-mail across two or three continents and up to eleven time zones.

From our 2005 meeting through our collaboration on this book for the following eight years, our journey together has covered much contested terrain, also in actual and figurative ways. The physical dangers of the burned-over war zone of Afghanistan that Marzia, Jamila, and so many other Afghan women and girls—urban and rural—have faced over the past four decades are quite real, of course. To this day, complex historical and contemporary geopolitical forces make Afghanistan alarmingly dangerous territory for most women, as their behavior, demeanor, and dress remain indicators and symbols of conflicting political, ethnic, and religious interests. By 2010 those very real dangers had proceeded ever closer to Kabul, where Marzia and Jamila lived. The women's foreign travel (including to see me) and their virtual connection with me and other foreigners compounded the physical dangers they and their families faced in Kabul. I worried about that and offered to use pseudonyms and disguise the details of their lives in the book. That they declined my offer reflects the seriousness of their commitment to share their views of their country. They refused to let themselves be intimidated into inaction. I decided to trust their judgment and committed to get their approval for my depictions of their lives and views before publication.

Afghanistan itself is also literally contested terrain, of course, and has been for many centuries, as world powers have tried to utilize its "buffer zone" location for their own purposes and attempted (and mostly failed) to mold the country in their own images. This book project has opened my eyes to the centuries of meddling and manipulation by foreign powers, including the United States, and their interconnections and conflicts with the country's indigenous practices and values. It has also revealed how Marzia's and Jamila's leadership aspirations have been physically and emotionally contested throughout their lives, as their goals for themselves and their country have both merged and conflicted with family plans and local, national, and international forces.

My role in investigating and representing Marzia and Jamila can be seen as figuratively contested terrain, in part because of our different geopolitical and cultural locations and the power differentials between us in the contemporary world. After all, my country invaded theirs; American soldiers and politicians have called the actual and figurative shots that wounded them and their people. Furthermore, I reside in a relatively peaceful, prosperous cocoon in this war-torn world and have the privilege of making the two women the subjects of my research, while they do not (yet) have the same opportunity or privilege (although I would welcome that role reversal). Such inequities require a fine balance between recognizing absolute differences between us and seeing us as both "the same and different," since neither extreme is accurate. Even letting the "other" speak can reinforce a caricatured "otherness" of the speaker (Yeğenoğlu 1998, 104–5, 94).

Given such dangers and difficulties, some critics have asked whether it is really possible for a Western woman *not* to be "always and unavoidably the stooge of Orientalism and imperialism" (Yeğenoğlu 1998, 101–2; Lewis 2002, 218–19). Even when interactions like those in *Contested Terrain* are not designed to "dominate the Orient imperially," unconscious fantasies and desires are "always socially and historically located and hence part of power/knowledge relations," they claim (Lewis 2002, 215).

Further vexing the figurative landscape is the fact that I have never visited Afghanistan. That could also be seen as symptomatic of the power differential between us, although not visiting Afghanistan was a strategy we chose for safety reasons (mine and theirs). To be sure, I could have written a different book had I worked with Marzia and Jamila in Afghanistan, but I hope that the circumstances of this book's production nevertheless constitute a legitimate and worthy approach to its subject.

In establishing my authorial position, I have tried to fulfill what I consider my ethical and personal responsibilities to Marzia and Jamila. That has meant not positioning myself as a Western white woman who uses her own life as a normative measuring stick for judging Oriental others or of setting up either the West, the United States, or myself as the "universal subject of history" or as uniquely situated to produce truth about those others (Yeğenoğlu 1998, 92, 95–96). It has also meant not reenacting the dynamics that make non-Western peoples seem like "problems" for the world to solve and not buying into the proposition that transforming women is the key to a society's modernization. That proposition is objectionable in large part because it reinforces its opposite: restricting women's behavior and activities therefore becomes the best way to *resist* unwanted modern practices and values.

Fulfilling my responsibilities to my subjects has also meant recognizing the interconnections between my privilege and the oppression of other women. Indeed, my work on the gendered construction of racial difference and hierarchy in the United States has taught me well how white women's "liberation" has too often entailed subordinating marginalized women, just as male privilege has required imposing subservient roles on women (see Kitch 2009). I recognize how U.S. white women's career success in the 1970s and 1980s, for example, elevated middle-class women's aspirations above those of the poor African American or Latina women they depended on for child care and housekeeping.[10] Similar interdependencies still exist between the privileged and the marginalized around the world.

Another treacherous region for this project was its literary context, since my book would necessarily join the plethora of published narratives by and about subaltern or Third World women and intended for Western audiences that filled Western bookstores after 2002. Gillian Whitlock's *Soft Weapons* (2007) catalogs the myriad ways in which many such narratives produced "culturally other goods" for Western consumption and appealed to readers because their stories converged with readers' own autobiographical narratives, dreams, and desires.

In particular, many autoethnographies by Afghan women (often narrated by Western writers), which multiplied after 2003, were deliberately marketed as revelations from beneath the *burqa* that reinforced veiled women's need for salvation by the books' intended audience (shades of Mavis Leno?). While reinforcing the Western obsession with the veil, such narratives also obscured the "idioms of agency that are relevant" for their wearers (Butler 2004, 47, quoted in Whitlock 2007, location 714). Whitlock argues that many of those texts strengthened Western readers' desires to see all women as "just like us," exoticized differences between women, and obscured the power relations and community connections that constructed their subjects (see also Razack 2005, 26).

It is the bright side to this narrative explosion, however, that I believe positions *Contested Terrain* as a different kind of narrative. That is, like the best of Whitlock's examples, this book is intended to open an important outlet for previously silenced speakers, promote dialogue between cultures, make readers think beyond themselves, and allow some subaltern "others" to control and authorize their own self-representations and aspirations. In addition, freeing women from the *burqa* figures not at all in *Contested Terrain*.

At the same time, I recognize how the book's discussions about Afghan women's educational and career aspirations, increased mobility, and the other longings discussed by the leaders represented in this text might be misconstrued as promoting Western secular cultural ideals back to a Western audience (Whitlock 2007, location 348). I can also see that these leaders might be recognizable to Western readers precisely because they are not representative of the majority of Afghan women. It is perhaps inevitable that such possibilities will arise from this project's goal of listening to those Afghan women who can best be heard by the U.S. readers the women hope to reach, but they are not its intent.

My attempts to navigate the potentially contested aspects of this book's political terrain will become clearer throughout the text. For now I can reiterate that this narrative is intended to do different work than the "beneath the *burqa*" narratives, which elevate Western secular values and position their subjects as victims of their cultures just awaiting rescue by us. Thus, I have contextualized the women's experience through historical and political analysis, recognized (along with them) their unusual position in Afghan society, limited claims about who and what they represent, trusted Marzia's and Jamila's critiques of the book manuscript and their judgment that their true identities should be used, and made myself visible as a character in the narrative so that readers can judge my own "contaminations" as I ask questions and offer judgments, comparisons, or opinions (Yeğenoğlu 1998, 86). I have also done my best to listen to the subjects of this book and depict their views accurately, thereby also allowing readers to judge for themselves the women's motivations and self-representations.

I have further navigated the treacherous terrain of memory and representation itself. This narrative relies on the women's own accounts of their lives, experiences, and accomplishments, which I have taken at face value even though I know how human memory can distort facts and mold events into coherent or flattering narratives when the truth is more confusing, amorphous, and incoherent. Moreover, I could not control what my subjects disclosed or omitted or the conscious or unconscious spin they gave their actions and thoughts. I could, however, ensure the accuracy of my reports of the women's words and cross-check the information they gave me at different times with their own words and with public records. (I decided to ignore bits of gossip that came my way.) I could also recognize the role of our evolving personal relationships in my reception of the women's stories and in their selection of stories they wanted me to tell.

In the end, I hope that this book will be valuable to the women represented in it. I believe that after a decade of U.S. occupation of Afghanistan, Americans have a duty to hear what any Afghan women have to say. Marzia and Jamila in particular "deserve thoughtful representation and much wider attention for all that they have achieved and all they have to teach us about Afghan women's realities," as Margaret Mills says (e-mail, April 7, 2013). While their perspectives are no more definitive about their country than mine would be about the United States, they constitute an important and informed part of the "the rhizomic and multiple truths of Afghan life" (Heath 2011, 10). These women are a special case but still a worthy case study.

Jamila and Marzia hope that readers of *Contested Terrain* might become allies in realizing their visions for Afghanistan. I hope that their views might inform public perceptions of the U.S. government's long-term obligations to Afghanistan, even after troop withdrawal. Whether either of those things happens or not, Marzia's and Jamila's projects for Afghan women will benefit from any success the book achieves, because they will receive all royalties.

The three of us hope that *Contested Terrain* will benefit Western readers by expanding their knowledge about gender in Afghanistan and their understanding of what Judith Butler calls relevant images of agency from at least some Afghan women's perspectives. Those images do not derive from Western values in the view of the women leaders studied herein. Rather, they consider women's right to economic empowerment, education, and professional training, as well as to civil rights and to justice under the law, as Islamic as any prayer ritual or practice. Perhaps *Contested Terrain* will help Western readers to understand and recognize how "the desire for freedom and liberation is a historically situated desire whose motivational force . . . needs to be reconsidered in light of other desires, aspirations, and capacities" (Mahmood 2001, 223).

Book Structure and Organization

Contested Terrain is divided into three parts that reflect the changing political landscape in Afghanistan as well as Marzia's and Jamila's evolving personal and professional situations from 2005 to 2013. Part I, "Hope," captures a dominant affective theme of the OSU conference and the participants' relatively optimistic, forward-looking narratives in 2005, despite their recognition of dangers and blunders in the post-Taliban period.

Part II, "Reality," captures the more mixed picture for women and women's rights and opportunities in Afghanistan, especially after 2008, as the hardships of military occupation, constant skirmishes and bombings, and the resurgence of the Taliban were increasingly taking their toll on Afghans' security and on infrastructure and development around the country. My Istanbul interviews with Marzia and Jamila occurred in the midst of that downward spiral. Although they had certainly not lost hope, the women were becoming increasingly pessimistic about their own and their country's future, even as they reiterated their intentions to keep working to improve Afghan women's lives and to expand their capacity to exercise their rights.

Part III, "Uncertainty," captures the dramatic changes that occurred in Marzia's and Jamila's individual lives after 2010, which in turn reflect the more dramatic deterioration of the political and security conditions in Afghanistan and the final assessment of the country's future by 2014. "Uncertainty" also captures the future prospects for women's rights in Afghanistan.

Throughout the book, my overlapping roles as *witness, narrator,* and *participant* also evolve. The book begins as I began the project—as an "empathic" *witness* (Whitlock 2007, location 1080) to Afghan women's distant lives and a recipient of the views and information the visitors from Afghanistan offered at the OSU conference. I was grateful that those women had made the arduous journey to be heard, and I wanted to listen. I could not get to know them on their own terrain, but I could try to connect to them by taking my cues from more knowledgeable and experienced scholars, including Margaret, and by working to transcend the biases and preconceptions that a Western upbringing and feminist background might have instilled in me, despite my then twenty-five years of critiquing Western politics and values—from liberalism to neoliberalism, secularism to Christianity, slavery to genocide, racism to sexism—as a women's studies scholar. Indeed, I regarded this project as another lens for assessing my own country and culture in light of its historical and contemporary relationship with Afghanistan. In the process, I tried to understand the women and their priorities and views on their own terms while also relating to them through our shared humanity. I tried also to avoid imposing my own self-identification on their aspirations (Young 1997, 13, 48).[11]

I became more conscious of my role as *narrator* in Istanbul in 2010, as the two women asked me to share their perspectives and stories with the world. If as a witness I was watching waves hit the shore and deducing the ocean forces that produced them, as a narrator in part II, I moved closer to the actual storms at sea. I focused more intently on the experiences and perspectives of the two women, asked questions, sought meanings, and tried to understand the circumstances and structural conditions that constituted their identities and lives. I became increasingly aware of the gap—which Jamila, Marzia, and other women leaders recognized themselves—between their relatively privileged positions and those of the women they were trying to serve, as well as between their and my geopolitical locations and relative privilege. I hoped to make my representation of their stories "part of a continuous process of [Afghan] history" (Khan 2001, 16) and tried to navigate the contested terrain of speaking with and for others. As a narrator, I wanted to retain the flavor and tone of the women's expressive styles as well to report accurately their life stories, observations, and opinions, as much as possible in their own words.[12]

Finally, as our relationship evolved, I began to see that I was also becoming a *participant* in the women's lives and plans. That role, which is most evident in part III, was perhaps inevitable as our friendships deepened and my wish to address their needs, provide emotional support, and reciprocate their generosity increased. Even if I had wanted to limit my roles to witnessing and narrating, that would have become impossible as the women's survival became less certain and my geographical position and privilege took on new meaning. I realized I could never look away from their situations and would never want to look away.

PART I

Hope

(2002–2005)

Prologue: Preparing to Witness

The Afghan women leaders who arrived at Ohio State's Mershon Center on November 17, 2005, were emissaries from a shattered and complex country. Understanding where they had come from and what had happened to them in recent years was an important part of knowing how to hear what they had to say.

The most obvious fact about them was their status compared with that of most Afghan women. Even for Kabul-based urban elites, the five women from Afghanistan were unusually well educated, successfully employed, politically active, and economically privileged. They also had unusual levels of mobility and access to the international stage. Marzia estimated that there were probably no more than fifty or seventy-five women in all of Afghanistan who were like herself, Jamila, and the other women at the conference. As she explained, "Out of twelve million women, maybe we have fifty thousand educated, and not higher educated, just educated. And maybe one thousand of all the Afghan women [can] practice their rights" (see also Barakat and Wardell 2002, 917).

The lives of such women contrasted sharply with those of the majority of their sisters, who lived in seclusion from nonrelated men within their families and whose movements, behavior, dress, and occupations were restricted in order to protect family honor. In Afghanistan as in other Muslim countries, a woman typically embodies a man's honor, which is measured "through the reputation and behavior of his wife and daughters" (Moghadam 2003, 241). Most Afghan women lived in small villages and rural areas, where education for girls was minimal, poverty was common, and regional as well as ethnic mores (Pashtun, Tajik, Hazara, or other) shaped their lives.[1] Afghanistan's patriarchal social structure—which may hark back to pre-Islamic times—meant that most women were not only subject to the individual choices of their fathers, husbands, brothers, and other male family members but also regulated by the decisions of local *shuras*, or councils, which were typically male dominated. For most groups, the tribal structure (*qabila*) shaped Afghan communal relations (*quam*) so that women became the virtual property of men (Moghadam 2003, 233).

Equally important for all women's condition and status in 2005 Afghanistan, however, was the influence of decades of war, including the war waged by the United States and allied forces starting in 2001. Wars since 1979 had sent 3.6 million Afghans into exile in neighboring countries (primarily Iran and Pakistan), displaced 1.1 million people within Afghanistan, maimed an additional 1 million, and killed more than 2 million.[2] Women constituted "the most underprivileged group," according to human rights activist Sima Wali. With millions in abject poverty, women constituted the majority of the 22 million Afghans who relied on international assistance for survival. Their average life span in 2001 was less than forty years; by 2005 estimates placed it at only forty-six years. Children had a mortality rate of 25.7 percent before age five. Clampdowns on women by the mujahideen and the Taliban had left a generation of Afghan women malnourished, unhealthy, and uneducated. Without access to education, landownership, civil society, or paid labor, most Afghan women had few resources for escaping poverty (Wali 2002, 15–16; Ahmed-Ghosh 2006, 112).

Because so many men had died in war, which was still continuing, women constituted 60 percent of the Afghan population by 2005. That loss had thrust greater levels of responsibility on many of them—both at home and in refugee camps—while also making them more exposed and therefore more vulnerable (Barakat and Wardell 2002, 910). Approximately 70 percent of Afghan women were clinically depressed. In 2001 alone, 16 percent had attempted suicide, according to a report by Physicians for Human Rights (Ahmed-Ghosh 2006, 112).

Urban privilege could not fully protect the women at the OSU conference from such conditions. During the mujahideen and Taliban periods, the life conditions of women in Kabul, Mazar-e-Sharif, Herat, and other Dari-speaking urban centers had actually changed more dramatically than had those of rural women, whose family lives and traditional agricultural activities functioned more or less as usual (Barakat and Wardell 2002, 916). Many urban women, such as Jamila, had fled the country and spent time as refugees. Many of those who had stayed in Afghanistan, such as Marzia, lost employment, were forced to adopt the veil for the first time, suffered from untreated diseases, and missed educational opportunities.[3] Although conference attendees were the first to recognize gaps between their lifestyles and aspirations and those of the majority of Afghan women, their hardships during the preceding decade had brought their lives closer to those of their rural countrywomen than might otherwise have been the case. In times of strife, their role in family honor also became more pronounced, and they faced increased scrutiny for alleged sexual offenses. In addition, the country's dire straits had led urban activists to concentrate more directly on women in nonurban communities.

The conference attendees' commitment to activism also linked them to certain traditions in their country. There was actually a heritage of Afghan women's resistance going back to the early twentieth century, including in some of the more recent organizations mentioned in this book's introduction (which will be discussed more fully in chapter 3). There were also powerful models of active women in Islamic history. Some refugee women were reconnected with that heritage, as they experienced health care and schooling for the first time in camps outside of Afghanistan and realized that conditions they had considered immutable could actually be changed (Barakat and Wardell 2002, 922). Others recognized and rebelled against their loss of roles and opportunities in the camps, including education, which they considered their right. It was in a Pakistan camp that the underground Revolutionary Association of Women of Afghanistan was formed in 1977. The United States paid no attention to the group's complaints and instead supported one of the most intimidating and misogynist of the mujahideen warlords, Gulbeddin Hekmatyar (Moghadam 2003, 263–64).

Afghan women's heritage, even in traditional rural communities, also includes their roles in family and community decision making and leadership. Because of the kin-oriented wards in larger villages, many rural women are able to move freely between family units, and some older women even move between kinship sections. Such women may broker peace and mobilize (or demobilize) men for fighting. While fathers are family heads and sanctioned community leaders, who may decide to support one side or another in war, mothers usually decide whether their own sons should or should not go to the front lines. Moreover, the Qur'an teaches that a mother is the gateway to heaven, so a son needs his mother's forgiveness before he can enter Paradise. Mothers also typically choose their sons' wives and broker their marriages. Women are also expected to assume leadership roles in their families during times of war, hardship, and struggle. Such powers bring honor to traditional female roles and make being a sister or mother in Afghan culture worthy of respect (Barakat and Wardell 2002, 920).

The conference attendees' participation in economic activity was also more consistent with Afghan tradition than it might appear. Although typically prevented from keeping their wages, even rural Afghan women do work for money, which in some circumstances—as in profits from carpet weaving—may sustain a family. The need to keep girls and women working for money is often the reason that they are denied an education. Their work must finance men's education, marriage costs, and travel for economic purposes (Moghadam 2003, 233).

Thus, the kinds of leadership the conference attendees were exercising in contemporary Afghanistan did not necessarily contradict women's legitimate place in Islam or women's traditional family roles, nor did they inevitably eclipse the importance of family and community membership in women's identities, value systems, and survival. Indeed, based on the expectation that women will attend to their families' survival needs in times of crisis, Afghan women's leadership had flourished under the Taliban's very noses, as women's organizations and solidarity networks (some of them operating from exile) built grassroots support for girls' education and services for widows and poor women, even in rural areas. According to Palwasha Hassan, country director for rights and democracy in Afghanistan from 2007 to 2009, "The role of female agency and the efforts of women's organizations that focus on the practical needs of the rural majority [is seldom] given . . . credit . . . for producing long-term changes," even though "women's secret organizations and networks in Afghanistan were the only functioning organizations trusted by the community" during Afghanistan's wars (2010, 172; see also Rostami-Povey 2007, 32).[4]

It was too bad that the international community did not take advantage of the opportunity such existing organizations offered but rather sapped the spirit of volunteerism that was high in 2002 by luring some of the best voluntary talent into well-paying jobs in their organizations (Kandiyoti 2005, 8–11). That talent included a few of the women at the OSU conference, who took advantage of job opportunities in foreign-operated NGOs.

The conference attendees also hailed from an Afghanistan transformed since late 2001 by U.S. military and political occupation and by the Bonn Agreement of December 2001 that had mandated a new constitution and established the Hamid Karzai administration. Although those changes were celebrated in the West, they had many negative effects on Afghan women, despite the U.S. government's assurance that the departure of the Taliban would solve all of their problems.

Initially, many Afghans, including most women, did welcome the U.S. and international forces. They even rejoiced in the streets of Kabul. But it soon became clear that the troops' arrival would not produce security for women, as rapes, general violence, and abuses by the Northern Alliance, with which Karzai was affiliated, persisted (Wali 2002, 17–18). Indeed, many Afghan women regarded mujahideen warlords connected with the Northern Alliance—some of whom were now in power—as "equally atrocious villains" as the Taliban (Alvi-Aziz 2008, 175; see also Ahmed-Ghosh 2006, 114; 2003, 7).

By 2005 it had become clear that the Bush administration's "fast war, fast peace" approach to Afghanistan and quick turn to Iraq had squandered the two-year window when establishing democratic institutions and practices and reinforcing women's rights had a real chance (Jalali 2008, 32).[5] The missteps started with the Bonn Conference. First, organizers completely overlooked UN Resolution 1325, which requires member states to make women central in peacemaking and social reconstruction. Instead, they selected only three official female delegates out of a total of thirty-two (Sima Wali, the human rights activist, was one). And even though the Bonn Agreement required that women constitute 25 percent of delegates to the December 2003 constitutional Loya Jirga, established the Ministry of Women's Affairs, and appointed Sima Samar as the MWA's first minister and Suhaila Seddiqi as minister for public health, it contained no mechanisms for enforcing its requirements in the long run. That oversight had many consequences, most immediately for Sima Samar, who was forced for several years to pay her own expenses and work from her home. Hers was the only ministry without a building or staff (Armstrong 2002, 184–86).[6]

Second, neither the Bonn Agreement nor any U.S. requirement prohibited warlords from holding office in the Parliament, a problem Marzia repeatedly emphasized, or ensured that women representatives would be listened to or free from harassment (Abirafeh 2005, 7). As a consequence, the Parliament never prioritized women's rights. Members offered no support when Samar was forced out of her job for objecting to the role of warlords in the government and did not object when her replacement, Habiba Sarabi, was required to dismiss 150 of her female staff (Rostami-Povey 2007, 59). (Even today, Parliament is an unreliable partner for women's rights, as fewer than a dozen women now serving—of the total of ninety-seven in both houses—support them [Baker 2010, 1–2]).[7]

Third, instead of providing security and justice, the basic tenets of a successful state and of women's access to rights and opportunities, the handpicked Karzai government had become to many by 2005 a source of insecurity and injustice. Although chapter 3 contains a deeper investigation of his administration, suffice it to say that many observers believe that Karzai's selection as president in 2002 might have been the international community's biggest misstep if their goal was to advance women's rights and opportunities in Afghanistan. The concentration of so much power in a single man not only recalled the warlord past for many Afghans and disrupted what could have been a pure parliamentary system but also inevitably favored a particular ethnic group, which in Karzai's case was considered to be the Dorrani Pashtun.[8] That lineage had supplied nation-building rulers in the past, the last of whom was Daoud Khan, who was overthrown in 1978. Karzai's selection was intended to reinforce that tradition, while also allowing the Pashtuns who had initially supported the Taliban to save face and pacifying the primarily Tajik Northern Alliance in which Karzai played a leading role (Barfield 2010, 291–92). But it did not take women's rights into account.

Many of the international community's direct interventions in Afghanistan in the early years of the occupation were also misguided. They were based on false assumptions and miscalculations, including exaggerated confidence in technical solutions to complex social and economic problems, the use of aid for short-term political objectives that weakened longer-term political interests, the failure to recognize how modernization has historically fueled instability in Afghanistan, the failure to recognize the "zero-sum" mentality that makes nonrecipients of aid jealous, and the failure to staunch corruption in aid delivery (Crews 2010, 75–78).

In addition, in the early days, the Bush administration put too much stock in the power of the market, which resulted in some ludicrous efforts to improve women's status by implanting "free-market capitalism" in post-Taliban Afghanistan. On women's alleged behalf, one "reconstruction effort" built beauty salons and marketed makeup, supplied by top Western cosmetic companies. A new Coca-Cola bottling company added to the irony, since most Afghans couldn't afford—and didn't need—a single lipstick or bottle of Coke (Alvi-Aziz 2008, 171–75).[9]

The administration was also more interested in the trappings of democracy—a constitution, open elections, public school buildings—than in laying the complicated groundwork necessary to create a democratic society, especially to achieve grassroots involvement. Furthermore, to justify the occupation, the Bush administration also tended to exaggerate progress, thereby undermining Afghan confidence. They reported in 2003, for example that 4 million children were enrolled in school in Afghanistan and 5 percent of them (335,000) were girls. News sources, the United Nations International Children's Emergency Fund (UNICEF), and even the Central Intelligence Agency (CIA) could find only 2.9 million children in school and at most 201,000 girls. In addition, by 2005 both tertiary enrollments and the number of female teachers in Afghanistan had not yet reached pre-Taliban levels. The administration also failed to change course when, by 2006, half of the schools the United States built had burned down. Indeed, in that year alone, 200,000 Afghan children were deprived of schooling because of threats and intimidation. It is possible that at least some of the culprits were warlords, formerly in the Northern Alliance and now in the government (Alvi-Aziz 2008, 171, 173, 175).

All of this was in our minds as we welcomed the Afghan women leaders to OSU. As we shall see in chapter 3, this was only the tip of the iceberg of U.S. and Western culpability for the hardships we would hear about at the conference. We marveled that attendees still wanted to address a U.S. audience and that they remained optimistic about the prospects of increased international intervention in their land. Their discussions would reveal why Afghan women might be more welcoming of such intervention than Afghan men, but it would also show the pitfalls of placing additional confidence in that solution.

In chapter 1 we hear from the group as a whole about the conditions for Afghan women in 2005 and their ideas about ways to effect positive change. In chapter 2, we learn about the path to leadership for the conference women in general and for Marzia and Jamila in particular. Chapter 3 provides a more detailed look at the longer story of U.S. involvement in Afghan women's difficulties, which among other things prepares us for the recurrent and somewhat predictable realities revealed in part II.

1

Working for Women in "Postconflict" Afghanistan

Hope is a relative term, since it depends on expectations. So it was inspiring to see that, war-torn and battered as the OSU conference attendees and their country had been for so long, they still felt hopeful, even as they recognized that conditions at home were far from perfect. At least now, they seemed to say, problems can be aired, some progress has been made compared to the mujahideen and Taliban periods, and we can propose new solutions. Because these women were comfortable in the international arena, they were especially cheered by foreigners' interest in Afghan women's situation, despite the obvious blunders by foreign powers that had hampered true progress.

The conference began with sessions that addressed what the leaders in the room thought life was really like for ordinary Afghan women and how they as activists were trying to address those women's needs. All attendees spoke to that question from the perspective of their own work and interests, yet there was a surprising level of agreement among them.

Were things better for Afghan women since the Taliban had departed? Everyone thought yes. More women were getting educated. There were three female ministers (out of seven) in the Karzai government.[1] There was one female provincial governor, Habiba Sarabi, in Banyam Province. Women constituted 20 percent of the constitutional *jirga* in 2004. Women made up 25 percent of the lower house of Parliament in 2005. Since the defeat of the Taliban, women were at least technically able to work outside of their homes. Their clothing, shoes, and fingernails were no longer subject to constant scrutiny, although modesty in dress, family limitations on their activities, and the uncertain security climate remained powerful constraints on their lives.

Were there still problems for Afghan women? Unsurprisingly, everyone again said yes. This list was longer. Aziza Ahmadyar, a modestly dressed middle-aged woman who was then a deputy minister in the Ministry of Information and Culture, said that security was still a huge problem, especially for women working with international NGOs.[2] Maternal and infant mortality was still high. Early forced marriages were still implicated in violence against women. Eighty-two percent of women were illiterate.[3] As she ticked off these obstacles, she unconsciously pulled her light shawl over her hair, which suggested to me both modesty and mourning for the sad facts she recounted.

Masuda Sultan, a young Afghan raised mostly in the United States who was working in New York with the NGO Women for Afghan Women, said somberly that women's major problem was the cultural belief that they were the enemies of an Islamic society.[4] Women had internalized that idea, she said, and accepted men's judgments about their minimal worth, their continual threat to family honor, and their unruly emotions and desires. Until that actually un-Islamic belief changed, women would still be special targets of suspicion and abuse in Afghanistan. Masuda also pointed to the high maternal mortality rate (as high as 60 percent at the time) and the pathetically small amount of money targeting the problem (only $15 million). She reiterated the importance of working through Islam to solve Afghanistan's problems, and she warned that a failure to do so could actually make things worse for women.

Jamila Afghani emphasized the lack of female teachers, without whom girls could not get educated, and the continuing lack of consultation with women themselves as international donors and the Afghan government designed programs to meet their needs. She also lamented the recurring use of women as symbolic tools of fundamentalists' causes and Afghans' inability to distinguish between "Islam, culture, and politics." Of the self-immolations among young women that were burgeoning in parts of Afghanistan in 2005, Jamila said that the girls were expressing their "anger to be a woman." Without options, life looked unlivable to them. "Women need options."

Marzia Basel expressed the opinion that as exciting as it seemed, just having women in the Parliament did not mean that things would instantly improve for women. In fact, she said, things could get worse, because so many warlords had been elected and they would never work on behalf of women. They might even defame women in Parliament to better their own positions. In addition, there was no evidence that the Parliament was interested in working for women's rights at all, even the women parliamentarians themselves.

As speaker after speaker expressed her doubts as well as her hopes, each also explained the elements she thought might turn the tide. Among the women's suggestions were direct international aid to Afghan organizations or workers rather than payments to U.S. contractors, peace education for Afghans, a true democracy, basic skills training and microloans for women, a more robust civil society, more unity among women, an effective Ministry for Women's Affairs, a women's agency in every ministry, factories where women could work with family approval, improved health care, continued support from the international community, and more coordination among NGOs.

The women's extensive list of necessities seemed overwhelming. Although it was difficult to decide how to prioritize it, I found myself most impressed by the laser-like foci of Marzia and Jamila on the importance of legal reform and the need for more and better education and skill training. Both seemed fruitful paths through the complex and difficult tangle of Afghan women's needs.

Marzia: The Rule of Law

Of all of her accomplishments, Marzia was perhaps proudest of having founded the Afghan Women Judges Association (AWJA) in 2002. She was quick to point out that her organization not only was two years older than the British Women Judges Association but also involved all women judges in her country (a mere 7 percent of all judges in 2005, but growing). She did acknowledge, however, that the U.S. Women Judges Association was thirty-seven years old.

Marzia explained that the purpose of the AWJA was to promote the rule of law, help reform Afghanistan's legal and judicial system, create solidarity among female judges, expand the legal and professional rights of women judges, stand up for the rights of women and indigents, and increase all Afghan women's knowledge of their rights and standing under the law. The AWJA especially wanted to get at least one or two women appointed to the Afghan Supreme Court, which, like its counterpart in the United States, has nine members. Marzia's work with the AWJA had impressed upon her the importance of educating women about their rights. Her experience had taught her that women must demand their rights and not wait for others to bestow them. Women needed to know that Sharia law guarantees their rights to education and to economic independence, which are embedded in Islam's holy texts.

In a speech that Marzia gave to about 130 people at the OSU conference, she explained that security and the rule of law were the "key components that can bring changes in a country like Afghanistan." She felt positive about Afghan women's political participation in the 2004 election, both as voters and as candidates, and despite her concern about the prospects for change in the near term, she believed that such participation was central to "the rehabilitation and rebuilding of the rule of law" throughout the region. She found women's recent political participation "a good omen" for their increased political clout, but she repeated her worry that many women candidates "were supported by . . . strong power voters [warlords] whose legitimacy of power has been questioned by some [outside] civil society and international human rights groups." Still, "many women were securing their place in Parliament on their own merits." And that was a good precedent.

Marzia was also proud of the new Afghan Constitution's promise of gender equality and the government's promise "not to marginalize gender and . . . to observe international rules and regulations about human rights." She celebrated the constitution's guarantee that two women from each province be elected to the lower house of Parliament, the Wolesi Jirga, which would mean the election of sixty-eight women from across the country. By the same token, Marzia praised the constitution for requiring the president to choose women for half of the upper house of Parliament, the Meshrano Jirga, consisting of appointed elders and roughly equivalent in its powers to the U.S. Senate. Indeed, she noted, the election would make Afghanistan one of the top-twenty countries in the world with elected women parliamentarians, at least 25 percent.[5]

At the same time, Marzia's optimism was tempered by her long experience in Afghanistan through the mujahideen and Taliban periods. While legal guarantees from the national government were encouraging, the real political problem for women, she observed, was at the local or community level, "where most of the decisions impacting their lives are made by men." Decisions about whether a girl will attend school or go to work, have access to health services as well as justice, and have physical mobility are all made at the local or family level. Respect for national law also begins at the local level. Afghanistan's problem is not the lack of law but rather the lack of law enforcement. For example, child marriage is prohibited by civil law. But even though the minimum legal marriage age for girls is sixteen, families are still "selling their daughters at the age of seven, ten, twelve, or less than that." Unfortunately, "there is no provision in criminal law or penal code to criminalize this kind of action."

Moreover, women constitute more than 50 percent of Afghan society, but Marzia claimed that only twenty ("two zero") women out of twelve million had used the courts, as they are entitled to do, to adjudicate family problems, such as divorce or inheritance, because "going to the court is such a shameful thing that you will be rejected from society." And if a woman is arrested and jailed, often for defying a family or social norm for her sex, she is deprived of legal aid assistance unless she registers herself officially to the court and files a claim. "Do you know how long it will take for a woman who is in jail to make a document? Five days, with hundreds of Afghani [the currency] in bribes." In effect, then, women are deprived of the basic human right to legal representation.

The rule of law was also undermined by the history of Afghan power sharing. Marzia revealed, for example, that most Afghan judges at that time had no legal training whatsoever. "What would you think if I told you that the chief justice of Afghanistan has never gone to law school?"[6] He was a mullah, educated at a madrassa, and appointed chief justice for political reasons. Moreover, "the chief justice has appointed twenty-five family members, including his sons, including his son-in-law; they are head of the courts. All are highest-level decision makers in Afghanistan."

Indeed, Marzia explained, political parties, the judiciary, and certain government agencies "belong" to one tribe or one party in Afghan society. "For example, there are twenty-six ministries in Afghanistan; five are for this party, five for that party; it doesn't matter who you bring . . . they can get in the door without any particular qualification. . . . The prosecutor is given to one party, Supreme Court is given to another party, the Justice Ministry is given to the another party." (Thus, Marzia's own education, which included a master's degree from George Washington University [GW], was unusual, to say the least, among judges of either sex in Afghanistan.) Not only did merit have little to do with the appointment of officeholders, but the appointees were also always fighting with each other, especially prosecutors and judges.

Poor education in general and poor training in law and politics in particular also hampered Afghanistan's efforts to create a viable governing structure and reduced women's chances to exercise their rights. In the 2004 election, Marzia explained, "most of the educated people didn't go to vote; this is why the warlords came on board." She called on the international community to "support Afghans to have a fair and just Parliament." This is especially important for women, because corruption in the election process would likely bring more extremists, who oppose women's rights, into the system.

The competitiveness endemic to Afghan culture also limited women's ability to become full participants in the decision-making process at all levels because they had no models for collaboration and solidarity in their own cause. Marzia made a plea for help from the international community in getting women to work for one another's advancement. Because of the lack of education, "we do not build what we have sometimes," she said. Both she and the other women at the conference said repeatedly that the scarcity of resources and opportunities, coupled with the low esteem in which women are held, had created a toxic atmosphere among women. It starts in the family, where mothers-in-law learn from their own experience to be harsh and even tyrannical to their daughters-in-law, in part because such tyranny represents the apex of their social power. That model passes from generation to generation, fueled by a gossip culture among women who have little outside activity to occupy their minds and imaginations. Low levels of literacy feed the small-minded competition, until a woman's achievements become the target of other women's negative attention. Marzia and other panelists at the conference thought that education was the best antidote for this phenomenon, as schooling would increase every girl's potential to achieve something and reduce their jealousy about other women's accomplishments. "People with too little to do care too much about what other people are doing," Marzia said.

Equally worrying to Marzia, however, was the first article of the Afghan Constitution, which says, "Afghanistan is an Islamic country." As a devout Muslim, Marzia had no problem with that idea in principle, but she could support it only if Islam is properly understood. "*Islam* [is] a tricky word," she said. "It can be interpreted any way that people want. So if we have these extremists in Parliament, then anyone could go to extreme reasoning in interpreting our law, which is really bad." She reiterated the Afghan Women Judges Association's hope to get one or two women appointed to the Supreme Court. Because one of the Parliament's first tasks was to bring changes to the Supreme Court, the AWJA intended to pressure that body. Her audience was aghast when she expressed the hope that the seven illiterate members of the Court would soon be removed. We wondered how there could be illiterate judges in the first place. Marzia also expressed the hope that "some rich woman who knows about women's rights . . . will practice the women's right in Afghanistan." Alas, none of us knew who that could possibly be.

Jamila: Education

Jamila's hopes centered on the benefits of educating the population more broadly, especially its women. "We want to have a strong educated nation. And we believe that impartiality, unity, equality, and brotherhood will bring the changes in our community. . . . We want to empower widows, children, orphans, disabled [people] with different kind of programs like vocational programs and dependency programs." Making no reference to herself, she noted that handicapped women had a double disability, so they were especially in need of education. "We want to make technical, professional people, who are living outside or inside of Afghanistan to assist those people who are living inside Afghanistan," by teaching skills and increasing their professionalism. Such an effort, she asserted, could reclaim "the nation from the rich people . . . for the poor community, and divide it for the very needy people."

Jamila's Noor Educational Center was dedicated to those missions, including empowering the poor. In 2005 NEC had activities in Ghazni, Jalalabad, and Kabul. They had sixteen centers in Kabul. There were seven centers and three suboffices in Ghazni, together offering a total of eight literacy programs. Jamila reminded us that Ghazni, a mixed-ethnic area, is very restrictive, "creating lots of problems for women," as she well knew herself. NEC was also supplying food for widows, who have no place in Afghan culture and often starve. In addition, the center was providing human rights program training for women in Ghazni, as well as English courses and vocational training.

NEC gained the people's trust, even in conservative Ghazni, by training and hiring teachers from the local area and by starting with Qur'anic education and literacy training, which were seen as fairly noncontroversial topics. After joining those programs, the women became interested in lessons about "gender knowledge, gender information. . . . And we found inside the women [had] many conflicts, like domestic violence, family problems, especially [with the] mother-in-law." Those topics led to peace education, human rights education, and psychosocial training. The latter programs were especially well developed in Jalalabad. "Now they are well-aware women. Now they ask us, 'How should we sustain ourselves?'" So NEC began vocational training and self-dependency programs to enhance women's awareness of their own economic power. Jamila showed slides of women being trained in handicrafts, like flower making, as well as calligraphy and embroidery. "One of the important things we have in our program is our library. We are trying to promote the culture of reading books in Kabul, Ghazni, and Jalalabad." Courageously, NEC was also trying to persuade imams to use Friday prayers in the mosque "to condemn violence against women from an Islamic perspective."

In addition to these programs for adult women, NEC had created youth committees. Jamila believed that working with children would be effective in promoting peace, eliminating violence, and improving literacy. In 2005 NEC had six youth committees in Ghazni, three for boys and three for girls. In Jalalabad the youth committee included both boys and girls. They also had youth committees in their libraries. Members represented different age groups. During discussions in these committees, they discovered hidden problems. "We found that boys are afraid if their mother and sister are going out they will be teased by men outside." The girls said, well, of course they would be teased because men have been trained to jeer at women. But should that keep them from going outside? According to Jamila, NEC's programs were being well received. Even magazines and newspapers were giving them good coverage. "And even people now, if they have any family problem—everything from internal disagreements over money to divorce—they are coming to train at our centers to solve their problems."

Jamila repeatedly expressed her concern about the international media's waning interest in her country. She warned that the lack of international attention would leave Afghan women in the lurch. The successes since 2003 were wonderful but limited. They addressed only a small part of Afghan society. If we in the West were "thinking that the problems of Afghan women are finished," what with the new constitution, the presence of international organizations, and the increased numbers of girls and women going to school, we would be wrong. "We have a large number of women in [rural areas] that still are deprived of their basic needs and basic rights. And they don't know . . . their basic rights, and they consider [whatever happens to them] part of their fate and luck. And they are facing and suffering every day lots and lots of problems." We need to put aside the slogans about women's rights and human rights and pay attention to the "resistance on the ground."

She was delighted that there were more schools opening for women, and she understood that five million Afghan children—both inside Afghanistan and in nearby areas—were enrolled in school. She believed that international organizations had improved the curriculum, and she mentioned specifically new textbooks that had been published in May 2005 by UNICEF. "But of course, there is a big need to do more work." There were often long delays in getting registration for new schools, "sometimes years instead of days." The budgets for the schools were also being delayed by the government. The construction of schools was too slow. There was a shortage of professional teachers, especially female teachers.

Most important for girls was the difficulty of getting family members to allow their education. The girls were still getting married at early ages. They were mired in "traditional activities." And village leaders were "using the wrong name of Islam to create problems in the ways of women." In addition, a lot of women were being deprived of schooling "because their schools are built in a very far away area that women are not getting there." Moreover, international donors were "sitting on high levels and they're deciding and they're making plans instead of asking Afghan women what is their need or analyzing their situation." One example? Where to build schools in the first place.

Jamila also emphasized that education is only the beginning of social reconstruction in Afghanistan. Afghan women also had health and security problems, economic problems, and social participation problems. Even more depressing to her were the killings of women who were working outside of their homes. "Anybody is working outside, nobody can know that she will come back home in the evening or not." Those killings are also based on a misunderstanding of Islam. Instead of recognizing their religion as the source of democracy—as all the panelists at the conference did—most Afghans saw Islam only in terms of their own traditions. And the uneducated resented international organizations for creating new opportunities for women that the culture did not yet condone. Women were being used as political tools in the name of religion. "That is why sometimes we are locked in the walls and we are forced to wear *burqas*." Maybe, Jamila reflected, that was the reason for the awakened insurgency in Iraq in 2005. That too was coming "from the bottom of the grassroot."

Despite their positive outcome "on paper," the elections in 2004 ultimately discouraged many of the conference attendees about the prospects of voting their way to a new Afghanistan. Jamila had worked in the complaint office during the 2004 election, for example, and she saw firsthand the corruption and "big cheating inside the election." She saw a "full-fledged booklet of the voter registrations . . . sold to a special party." She saw ballot boxes that were so blatantly stuffed that "the numbers of the ballots were coming . . . just in serial number. Like from one hundred to five hundred, even they couldn't get the time to mix it up. It was just a number from one to the top for a particular person." Toward the end of the election season, one NGO realized too late that "they should develop some booklets which have some introduction about the candidates," but there was no time to get such a booklet to the villages so people would know "who's going for voting and who has what sort of background." She shared Marzia's view that despite good and honorable intentions, the election "was a total disappointment . . . really a pity."

Jamila still had hope for the future of Afghanistan, however. She celebrated women's increased access to education, including through her Noor Educational Center. She had worked from 2002 to 2005 "to promote other sisters, to give awareness to other sisters, to join social reconstruction, to build a peaceful community, in their house, in their society . . . to go for voting, to take their political participation actively." She also rejoiced in the women who took an active part in the Loya Jirga of 2002, which worked to establish the new government and helped to rewrite the Afghan Constitution that was ratified in 2003. Unlike the U.S. Constitution, it includes an equal rights clause.[7] As she spoke about this work in 2005, she also called on the government, civil society, and the international community to work together not only to complete their projects but also to increase the economic capacity of Afghan women in their small poultry farms and truck gardens, as well as by producing "the beautiful carpets they make with their beautiful hands," which Jamila believed could improve their own economic status and the economic condition of their families. She also hoped that international donors would play an active role in promoting a culture of peace through television and radio programming, which she considered more an effective educational outlet than a commercial venture.

Jamila also had high hopes that Afghans could promote security for one another. She acknowledged that this was problematic in the big cities, where they had to rely on the government for security, but she had a vision of mutual protection in villages, "because the community is for the aim of each other."

A Contentious Example

Outsiders attending the OSU conference caught a glimpse of the disagreements and complexities that lay beneath the otherwise harmonious surface of the leaders' assessments of Afghan women's past, present, and future needs in discussions of carpet weaving, for which Jamila showed some enthusiasm in her presentation. The topic arose again when one action team of Afghan participants, which like other teams was asked to prioritize one issue they would like to support back home, suggested creating new kinds of cooperatives to ensure women's access to the profits from their weaving. That suggestion caused a virtual uproar among the other leaders. Several complained about the side effects of carpet weaving, including the dust that the weavers and their small children must breathe as the rugs are produced in individual homes or in unventilated or unregulated cooperatives.

Marzia was the most outspoken. The women "give the NyQuil to the children to keep them asleep . . . just [because] they have to work and weave, weave, weave all the time. It's not an easy choice. And they all have their backs crooked like big, big hips on their backs, but do . . . people need luxurious rugs to just walk on? . . . Women suffer to make them. . . . If someone tells me to go to the hell or [to] weave a rug, . . . I will go to the hell."

Marzia and others noted that the economic rewards of carpet sales on the international market seldom trickled down to the women who produced them. "Do you know how much is the price here, and how much is the price there? It gets ten times more, even with [the kind of] unions" that the team at the conference was proposing. And whatever money does come back to Afghanistan is appropriated by husbands, who typically control all household income. To be fair, men do contribute to carpet weaving by raising and sheering the sheep, dyeing the wool, and marketing the rugs, although women spin and weave on their own (Barakat and Wardell 2002, 918). But in the end, Marzia noted, the husbands of most carpet weavers ask their wives how much they earned on a particular day and then take the money. "Then he gives her the exact money she needs for transportation. It's terrible. Women can weave very beautiful carpets, but then the money goes to the men."

A discussion followed about what products women could make that would result in good incomes for them. People wondered whether all traditional women's handicrafts should be discontinued. Marzia did not think so, but she suggested that only those that are easy for women, such as embroidery, should be retained. She admitted, however, that such crafts would never make the producers economically secure. Others talked about the pros and cons of microfinance for women, which allowed them to start small household businesses. One of the worst "cons" was the problem of success. One audience member pointed out that "the more you can get the money into the hands of women, the greater the pressure of the family on the woman to not stop doing" whatever the business is. The next step from there is drugging the children so the woman can keep her attention on the profitable activity.

It was then that Rachel Lehr, director of Rubia International (RI), who was a speaker at the conference, described how her embroidery cooperatives in Afghanistan worked and how they empowered women.[8] First, she said:

> We don't pay women a huge amount . . . because we don't want them to be under pressure, like in the rug industry, to drug their children. We also believe that . . . Afghan women have so much work they have to do anyway that it needs to be part of the whole family picture. Supplemental income is a much better way to structure things. I also feel very strongly in the work that I've done teaching women who've never had the opportunity to go to school or go to work before, that these are skills to learn how to work. Yeah, they know how to embroider, but they don't know how to embroider to a high standard, they don't know how to do it in a timely fashion, they don't know how to do it so it's clean in the end.

Thus, RI not only utilized the women's skills, building on traditional knowledge they already had, but also worked to elevate those skills to a more professional level. RI had gone through the certification process to ensure that their products never relied on child labor. RI also provided literacy instruction to their workers.

The discussion about how to empower women economically concluded with yet another conundrum. Because Afghan women's traditional skills are unlikely to produce great profits, they must produce luxury items that can be marketed abroad in order to make a better living. But the farther away their markets are, the less control of the profits women can exercise. Rachel's suggestion was to start with the skills women have and build to something greater, refusing to subject either women workers or their families to harsh conditions or impossibly long hours. She admitted that the exact application of that theory to things as they stood in 2005 was unclear.

International Intervention

Because all the leaders at the conference already had international connections, they were generally supportive of the presence of outsiders as "essential for the time being" in order to promote women's rights and support women's economic and political capacity building. But that did not mean they were uncritical about the quality of that intervention or unaware of some of its negative impacts on their country.

One criticism targeted the tendency of "internationals" to engage in short-term projects that did not meet larger goals, especially capacity building for Afghan women. Jamila suspected that internationals engaged in such projects "because they do not trust that Afghan women can work." Indeed, after three years of concentrated NGO activity in Afghanistan, Jamila observed, "we still don't have women professionals in different fields. Instead we have short-term projects for four months, six months, and after that there is nothing. . . . When [the internationals] depart Afghanistan, [Afghan women] should be able to continue with their work" so that "the international community would not be responsible for us forever."

Several speakers thought that a key problem was a lack of coordination among organizations. Marzia said that NGOs tended "to fund the same projects and remain ignorant of what other agencies are doing. They . . . compete rather than help us to bring changes." For her, "the worst is that they never share the ideas of the Afghans."

Jamila recited a list of things that Afghans needed from international supporters: housing, education, health facilities, national armed forces, police forces, highways. Afghanistan also needed help with implementing law and order, increasing security, reducing corruption in the government, enhancing media support for civil society, and providing shelter for refugees and displaced persons, especially for disabled women and widows. "Dear friends," she said at one point, "lots of Afghan women are widows today; lots of Afghan women are disabled today. But nobody has paid any sort of attention to them, or if there was attention, it was very minute."

Jamila added that international groups had actually exacerbated divisions between ethnic groups in Afghanistan. "Some of the donors are supporting Hazara, and some of the donors are supporting Tajik, and some of the donors are supporting Pashto. Even some of our neighbors are supporting different ethnic groups in Afghanistan, which is creating more and more problems . . ., especially for women." Jamila explained, "Before that it was not understandable. We were united." Even after the fall of the Soviets, "we were thinking that everyone is like the same." Only with the civil war and its international donors did Afghans find "wow, there is a big difference between us." Those newly exaggerated divisions, in turn, made assistance more difficult to give and accept.

The same was true for military affinities within the country. "Even in one family, a husband would support one of the military groups, and the wife would support another group, and then the son and daughter would go to another." There are different "classes" of mujahideen, just as Jamila had seen different types of Communists during the Soviet period. Given all of this division, she concluded, "We should have our own force of our own army, a strong government to look after their activities and responsibilities."

The conference attendees had hoped that the combination of Afghan and outside troops could improve security in Afghanistan, but those hopes had been dashed. There were robberies, kidnappings, and murders in the big cities, where people do not look after one another. Speakers explained that the administration of justice was inadequate, because people did not necessarily report cases and the military and police were hard to identify, even in uniform, as uniforms were widely available. Jamila was skeptical that women would become a big factor in law enforcement. "It will take time to develop such a capacity," she said.

Foreign soldiers who were in the country to train Afghans were also contributing to crime by creating a market for prostitutes. Because the soldiers were "paying big money" for the women, brokers had materialized to "introduce the women to the army forces," Jamila explained. As a result, "every week one or two dead bodies of women can be found in the garbage, dustbins of military forces." Jamila was aware that this situation was not unique. She recalled the transformation of whole cities, such as Pattaya, Thailand, into prostitution rings after years of military occupation. But "we should understand that it is very, very sensitive for the Afghan community," Jamila said. "Being a traditional and religious community . . . we are not wanting to digest that. . . . And the same thing of drinking wine, which is not permitted in this land." Yet soldiers were drinking alcohol. Foreigners "bring this business" and create havoc, she said.

Women as Agents of Social Reconstruction and Conflict Resolution

Some conference attendees were optimistic about women's future in Afghanistan because of their ability to help build a better Afghanistan. Yes, there were many problems the women considered endemic to their culture, but at the same time, as Jamila said, "we should not forget that we have some good culture as well which we can use . . . for promotion of women's rights in Afghanistan, and lots and lots from our religion. . . . Afghan women have a very important role being . . . more than half of the society. . . . Afghan women have taken a very important role from the beginning, and they have a very important role today."

Jamila's exile in Pakistan had revealed the possibilities: "We could see what the future life is like. And these were Afghan women who could make possible the victory of men for defeating the Soviet Union. . . . They were not caring about their self, about their family, about their children." Rather, they developed projects to help their countrywomen in Peshawar, Iran, and in other local areas where women were living. And even in Afghanistan, during the mujahideen and Taliban periods, "although they were all the time facing different risks, . . . women inside their house were taking many initiatives. They were running home schools, and they were helping each other. It was the help they were doing for Afghan women and their community that was really important for them."

Jamila was especially proud that the women returnees to Afghanistan, who were operating in unspeakable conditions and getting very little help from the government or from international donors, were throwing themselves into the support of their countrywomen who had stayed at home, especially in the area of education. "They are trying to bend up the level of education higher and higher. We have different sorts of programs, like home schools and literacy programs." She mentioned the Afghan Women's Network (AWN), which consisted of seventy-two women's organizations in multiple fields. But regardless of the focus of an organization's work—from domestic violence programs to training programs for home gardens and poultry farms to political participation workshops—"everybody has somehow a program about literacy in their projects. . . . Because we Afghan women understand the importance of education, we have literacy programs for our sisters." She acknowledged, however, that there were "many areas where we still need to work hard to help each other to build a better society."

Farida Azizi, manager of the Washington-based Afghanistan Program for Vital Voices Global Partnership, supported Jamila's view of women's possibilities for contributing to Afghan social reconstruction as well as peace building.[9] A young, petite woman in her early thirties, Farida's projects helped to build women's capacity for paid work in a peaceful reconstruction of Afghanistan.

She recalled rural women's historical role in maintaining alliances between families, tribes, and villages. She told a story about two villages that had been alienated from one another during the mujahideen and Taliban periods because men from each village had killed men from the other. After the wars, when Farida's organization offered midwife training in both villages, the women at first agreed. Farida explained: "We will start this training, but with one condition, that you . . . decide who will come from both communities. If you come with your one common interest or need, then we will implement [the training]; otherwise, we cannot do anything here. We have the money, we have the [tools], we have the [materials], but if you do not come with a common goal with each other, we cannot do this." Considering that challenge too daunting, the villagers decided that the training should start in one village and then move to the other. The training included peace education and literacy and history lessons.

In the middle of the training for the first village, an elderly woman in the midwifery class heard about a woman struggling in childbirth in the other village. She said, "That woman is having pain; she will die if I don't help her." Farida said, "What do you want? Do you want to take revenge, or do you want to help her to be alive?" The woman said, "I want to help her. It doesn't matter; whatever it takes, I have to help that woman." Farida explained that the woman then went to the other village without the permission of the male elders of her village. "She just went there to that village; she was an old woman. And she said, 'I can do this; I can [handle the] criticism.'" After she helped the woman deliver her baby, "what happened? This community that hated that other village . . . said, 'You know it is in our heart that we hated you, [but] you are not the person that we can hate you. We can love each other. See, you came and saved one of our women here. Even you hated us, but you saved the life of one woman here and delivered a child. So why . . . we are fighting, for what reason?' And then they decided to communicate with each other."

Like Jamila, Farida was also counting on the power of education to bring peace to Afghanistan. She was dismayed that the current textbooks in many schools in Afghanistan and in schools for refugees in Pakistan were filled with violence. Often they were supplied by Saudi Arabia and written in Arabic rather than the children's own language.[10] Political groups were trying to indoctrinate the children. "When they go back to their families, of course, if they have knowledge of such violence, it's very difficult to bring peace within one year or two years," Farida admitted. They see how easy it is to blow up school buildings. But if you can convince them that the schools could be used "for their own benefit," there will be a chance to educate them to promote peace. Women could be the agents of education for peace, Farida thought.

Marzia was less optimistic about women's ability to affect the reconstruction of Afghanistan or contribute to peace, however, because of the severe limitations placed on their mobility and social power. "Women are not the decision makers," she reminded us. The basic reason for women's social powerlessness was economic exclusion. Women simply do not command resources in Afghan society, even though they are supposed to have their own money according to Sharia law.

Marzia did have and control her own money, which she called her "economy," and she considered that the biggest difference between her and the majority of Afghan women. "My brother does not ask me, 'Why do you go to the United States?' because it is up to me to make my decision. This is my economic empowerment. Once you beg your husband for two dollars for transportation, then you are a slave for him. . . . What makes you have power in this part of the world . . . is your knowledge and your economy. Because you don't worry if you are married or not. . . . If I don't have income, I need protection from a man."

Marzia was also concerned that Afghan women do not believe they should stand up for themselves. "I know an example of a woman who was saying that the Holy Qur'an says she has to respect her husband after God." When Marzia asked who told her that, she said it was "'common knowledge in my village, and everyone says that I have to do that.' So if she doesn't know if it's true to worship her husband after God or not, the men usually say to the women [that they] . . . have to respect them . . . and the women don't have the education . . . [or] the economy" to oppose that opinion. Without economic empowerment, education, and gender sensitization—for both men and women—Marzia thought women would mostly be left out of social reconstruction.

Even in her unusual position, Marzia had encountered the very attitudes that she believed would prevent women from assuming true leadership in Afghan society. She gave one example from the early days after her graduation from law school. A man approached her at the courts where she was working and told her he could not find anyone to talk to about his concerns. "I said, 'I am here. Tell me, what is your issue?'" He replied, "'Who are you to be working in this court? For a woman, going to work in the courts is a crime.'" Even in her own family, her well-educated sister is not free to express herself. If she wanted to criticize anything in the society, "if her husband doesn't bid her she cannot, because she doesn't have the protection of her parents, the protection of her husband, the protection of her family."

Because of the nature of the court system, the family court offered little protection for women, either. Marzia reiterated that she and the other women who came with her to Ohio from Afghanistan were "rare. . . . We are not the examples of the average woman." But even they would have gotten a negative ruling about their travel abroad, had they asked a court's permission. "The culture says you can't travel without a man. If you go to the chief justice, he would say that such travel for more than three days is not allowed. You should have a man around who is a family member." And sometimes women such as the conference attendees are rejected by their families. "A man says, 'Oh, she is doing very strange things; she is using freedoms very much. She is wearing short clothes. She is wearing trousers to go to the office.'"

If there was any bright spot on the horizon for Marzia, it was the media. Like Jamila, she hoped that the multiplying television stations and newspapers would spotlight the women's organizations that support women's rights. "Slowly, slowly, it's expanding. Practice takes time. It's not one or two days to change all these things. It may happen in ten or twenty years." In the meantime, Afghanistan needs education for women; "then things will be solved."

Marzia was also encouraged by the many models of women who have exercised leadership in the Muslim world in general and in Afghanistan in particular. Indeed, most women at the conference considered the prophet Muhammad's first wife, Khadija—a businesswoman and close confidante of the Prophet, who worked after their marriage—an important role model for Muslim women. "So the idea that Islam doesn't let women go to education and to work or to be politicians can be completely drowned if we go to the history of Islam," Marzia explained. That history also includes women who fought alongside men "on the front lines for the jihad and for . . . fighting for the Islamic faith."

The women were also inspired by examples of women leaders in Afghan history. For example, the country's first king after the country's independence from Britain in 1919, Amanullah Khan, had a progressive wife who encouraged her husband, among other things, to support a law prohibiting polygamy. In part for that reason, the king was driven from Afghanistan in 1929 before the law could be enacted, and he and the queen both died in exile in Turkey. Still, such courage was inspiring.

Marzia was also pleased by the previous four years, which she considered the "strongest" for women's leadership in the history of Afghanistan. She pointed to individual women who had been delegates to various *jirgas* and other assemblies. She invoked the name of Meena Keshwar Kamal, the founder of the Revolutionary Association of Women for Afghan Women (RAWA), who was assassinated in 1987 at age thirty-one.[11] She touted women's political participation in recent elections. She found encouraging the small but growing number of women judges, since 1964, and of women engineers and doctors. She saw those as "clear signs that women can be part of political, social, and cultural history . . . nowadays." She boasted that Afghanistan had a woman candidate for the presidential election before the United States did.[12]

Marzia reminded us, correctly, that women were granted inheritance rights in Islam in the seventh century. She was somewhat less correct when she compared that advance to laws passed in England in 1884, as that date refers to the enactment of definitive married women's property rights rather than inheritance rights.[13] Still, she was correct that biblical rules of inheritance deprived women of any share in either their own families' or their husbands' estates (Num. 27:1–11)—a tradition that Christians followed in the case of wives for thirteen hundred years—and that property rights for Western married women were not really sorted out until the mid- to late nineteenth century.[14] In the United States those rights were not finalized in all states until 1913.[15]

The Qur'an is not Afghan women's biggest problem, Marzia repeated. "In today's Afghanistan, the problem is tradition. . . . culture." Marzia believed that changing that culture would require outside help. Not the kind of help that "disturbs women's rights in Islam," or tells "Afghan women what they should and shouldn't do," or tries to impose women's rights by fiat, or focuses on symbols (such as the *burqa*) rather than on substance (such as food shortages). She wanted the kind of help that supported Afghan women in their effort to "put pressure on the enforcement of the laws" and helped them justify their rights and greater social and political participation in terms that the culture can accept. She encouraged the Westerners in the audience to forget about the *burqa*. "I had my *burqa* during the Taliban, but I worked as much as now I am doing. . . . If you are a human being and you would like to help your country, it doesn't matter if your head is covered or not." It is important not to create so much cultural distraction in your work that your message cannot be heard. "We cannot go so suddenly with an agenda like . . . uncover your head" overnight. "Improvements will come slowly."

Outsiders should not reject Sharia law out of hand, according to Marzia, because "if we really enforced the Islamic Sharia law, we'd find out there are many good things that women can achieve on their basic rights" in Islam. Women became judges in Afghanistan on the grounds of Sharia law. They ran for president on those same grounds. Marzia was especially hopeful that "Islamic countries who are close to us" could offer models of laws and practices that are culturally sensitive in their support of women's rights. But she also admonished everyone within earshot to offer ideas that she and other leaders could bring to the table. "Your ideas, even one sentence, can be a very good sentence to apply . . . in our own laws and then bring some achievement."

By the same token, Afghans needed to accept change in their culture. First, the culture had to recognize its own inconsistency in embracing some changes, such as technology, and rejecting others, such as contemporary women's clothing. "If we are to be part of the international community, . . . we have to adopt each others' [ideas] . . .," Marzia said. "If there are good things, we have to accept them, and if there are bad things, we have to reject them." But Afghans can't just reject everything that has to do with women's advancement. They would do well to embrace the idea of love-based marriage, for example, and also clothing choices that do not necessarily confine women's bodies but "keep men and women in honor and a good way of living, to respect each other." Such choices are allowed in Islam. "We have to see Islam with an open eye and interpret it" in light of its larger purpose, "to make friendship and to [bring people] close to each other."

Second, Afghanistan had a lot of cultural repair work to do after the Taliban. Marzia mentioned the need to improve the quality of publications and intellectual work. She also talked about the gap in entertainment, which was completely banned under the Taliban. That gap was currently being filled by Indian music. "This is big business for India and Pakistan to come to Afghanistan and play" music. "The women are the main players of the music in the wedding ceremony. . . . This is something that has mixed with our culture, which is a very good thing. And it's improving day by day." With a smile, Marzia confessed that she really loved music. "If I heard a good song by a famous singer early in the morning at six o'clock, whether you believe me or not, I'd be happy all the day." The minister of culture decides who can sing on television, and Marzia thought things were opening up. "There are positive changes after the war and there are negative changes, but we are looking for the positive changes."

Looming over every question regarding women's potential to rebuild and reshape Afghan culture in a more peaceful direction was the problem of women's relationships with one another. Although there is a history in Afghanistan of women brokering peace between families or tribes and of holding their men to negotiated agreements, as Farida demonstrated, there is also a history of divisions and conflicts in the society that have divided women from one another into various factions, political parties, and tribal groups. Many women in the Parliament would not be able to overcome those divisions to work together to bring change for Afghanistan or for women in general.

From her more optimistic perspective, Jamila considered the present moment, in 2005, the best opportunity in years for raising women's consciousness about their role in bringing the society together and working together for women's rights. "We have women in the Parliament we can count on," she said, and women such as those at the conference should "take the initiative" to call on those sisters and get them to work together for change. "But unfortunately," she admitted, "in the Parliament women again will face the same problem," because most of them "are coming from political backgrounds and political-leader support, so everybody will try to have their own interests." Even among educated women, there was much rivalry and gossip. Jamila mentioned that a woman educated inside Afghanistan would be unlikely to accept her own education in Pakistan. "Then a woman who has got her education from Iran will not accept both of us. This is the situation. The idea of unity is not existing right now."

Jamila pointed out that her organization, the Noor Educational Center, was "working to build up the capacity of women parliamentarians and develop some connection and linkages between civil society and different ministries." They were working together with other advocacy organizations, which in turn had the support of international donors. It was important to support women in Parliament who were automatically considered weak members and who would be criticized for bringing up women's issues, especially by the warlords in Parliament who were trying to bolster their positions and keep themselves out of the International Court of Justice, where they could be tried for war crimes. "So if we are going to wait for the next five years, we will lose this opportunity." Jamila concluded, "If we are trying to support each other, hopefully the situation won't be that much worse, but it needs a lot of strength and work."

Reflections

Strength and *work*: those were the watchwords of the 2005 conference. But in the context of a country with virtually no infrastructure, a destroyed system of roads, little holding together its disparate regions and competing tribal interests, a weak and corrupt central government, and no organized, let alone cohesive, movement to produce social change, even among women, it was unclear how this impressive handful of women could muster the Herculean energy required to begin the process of change they saw as necessary. Even more daunting were the persistent obstacles they faced as women in pursuing their mission. As accomplished and successful as they were, many of these women had to fight or cajole their own family members just to get out of the house in the morning so they could wear themselves out each day pushing their particular boulder up a slippery hill. With continued bombings and firefights in their country, it was inspiring to me that these women and others like them risked their lives on a daily basis to improve conditions for their countrywomen. At the same time, the dire situation in their country offered them little alternative. Death was a constant threat for everyone; they simply chose active versus inactive risk.

Despite the desperate situation attendees recounted and the enormous tasks they set for themselves and the international community, the 2005 conference ended not in despair but in hope. Maybe with better knowledge of women's actual needs and aspirations and greater sensitivity to the historical and cultural factors shaping their perspectives, the international community could become more useful and effective. Maybe something could be done to link the expressed desires of international powers, including the United States, to improve the lives of Afghan women with efforts in that direction already under way in Afghanistan, some of which were directed by our visitors. Maybe the enormous energy of these leaders could produce change, even in the incremental steps that seemed most appropriate.

As Margaret and I returned the women to the international airline network for their trip home, we wondered what the coming years would reveal. Would such women survive? Would we see their names in U.S. newspapers? Would their projects be crushed, or would they flourish as Afghan men became enlightened to their value?

I determined that I would try to stay in touch with at least Marzia and Jamila because I thought that their energy, commitment, accomplishments, credentials, and particular pursuits held the most promise for change and had the best chance of success. Afghanistan would not survive in the long term, I reasoned, without the rule of law and the spread of education throughout the population. These women had won at least a modicum of official recognition for their work. Perhaps that would lead to more widespread acceptance and support for their ideas.

2

Two Strong Voices: The Making of Women Leaders in Afghanistan

The women at the OSU conference represented diverse and intriguing life experiences that had led to their unusual status among their countrywomen. Geographical location, ethnicity, economic status, and family influence were obviously very important to their achievements, but not all women in their situations strove for the kinds of positions they occupied. Individual talent and commitment were also factors, but in the context of Afghan culture, achievement depends on community and familial support. As I listened to the women's stories and descriptions of their work, I wanted to know more about the tangle of influences, beliefs, struggles, and contradictions that had shaped their lives. I wanted to know what kinds of preparation, what serendipity, what motivations, what aspects of family and community life had produced these female leaders.

As I listened for the women's perspectives on those questions, it was clear that the strand that most of the women leaders recognized and emphasized in that tangle was the liberating potential of Islam as a tool of women's freedom and agency. Indeed, every one of the women at the conference was inspired by that potential in her pursuit of her own achievements and of women's rights. They could all recite in detail stories of the Prophet's wives and his progressive attitudes toward and statements about women. They were especially eager to remind non-Muslims about the Prophet's first wife, Khadija, who was fifteen years the Prophet's senior and a successful businesswoman who continued to work after marriage. They also recited lists of the rights granted to women in the Qur'an, rights that were revolutionary for their time and ahead of those recognized in other religions. In Islam women and men have equal status before Allah, although they play complementary roles, they explained. Nothing in Islam curtails women's right to an education; the Qur'an provides a mechanism for married women's economic independence. For these leaders, Islam was a pillar in their own identities and hopes for their country.

But because contradictions abounded in their experience, the women also had to recognize how the liberatory potential of Islam conflicted with daily practice.

They thought that Islam was sometimes deliberately misinterpreted to suit the needs of the interpreters, few of whom are women. In the name of Sharia inheritance law, for example, some men shamefully enriched themselves at the expense of their sisters. In the name of the Prophet's relationship to his youngest wife, Aisha, girls as young as seven were basically sold to men in their fifties or sixties, who might consider their marriage payments a license for sexual companionship, regardless of the girl's immaturity.

In the name of Islam's prohibition against extramarital sex, some men imposed "temporary marriages" on desperate young women, whose lives were consequently ruined, and saved themselves from incurring expenses connected with long-term support. The polygamy that the Qur'an defines as rare and focused on rescuing widows instead facilitated some older men's access to nubile young women, often as second wives married without the first wife's consent, as the Qur'an requires. That blatantly un-Islamic practice was, in turn, justified by the fact of the Prophet's own polygamous family, which apparently overrode the details of his judicious attitudes toward and humane practices with women.

Despite such perversions, the leaders at our conference hoped to transform Islamic practice in Afghanistan through reform, especially through the education of women theologians. Equitable treatment of women is God's will, said these Afghan women, but it is thwarted by human frailty.

The women's stories also revealed the interconnection between two contradictory versions of Afghan culture. On the one hand, they decried the Afghanistan of the "forefathers," whose ideas about tradition and religion often took precedence over the actual contents of Islam's holy texts. This "bad" Afghanistan was rife with ignorant and uneducated mullahs, superstitious rural patriarchs, and conservative fathers, brothers, and cousins who controlled women in order to prove their virility and protect their own concepts of honor. This Afghanistan was responsible for women's lagging literacy, for forced child marriage, for women's limited right to divorce, for blowing up girls' schools and throwing acid in the faces of female students and teachers, for preferring that girls die rather than run out of a crumbling stone house or school without *hijab*. The abject, *burqa*-clad ciphers whose deaths by starvation, immolation (self- or otherwise), and childbirth went unlamented were a product of this Afghanistan, which holds Islam hostage to ignorance and fear of change.

This Afghanistan was the crucible of the "If you're not down, I can't be up" worldview that the women found so counterproductive to the future of the country, a future that requires more rather than less solidarity among the tribes, political parties, and sexes if Afghanistan is to flourish. I learned about that worldview as I discovered the downside of the Afghan spirit of generosity and hospitality that I had witnessed and relished at the Columbus airport when the women arrived. It seemed that the spirit of generosity coexisted with an intensely competitive perspective, in which kindness could be interpreted as a sign of weakness, especially in those considered society's "winners." Anyone with power or influence, especially a woman, who was suddenly seen as weak could lose status and support in an instant. Men's insistence on controlling women was, in part, a symptom of that competitiveness. Such control not only burdened and restricted women's everyday lives but also reflected an overall suspicion of efforts to raise the status of the downtrodden, who are often women. Moreover, generosity was typically reserved for male associates and strangers and did not necessarily characterize family relationships, especially men's treatment of their own mothers, sisters, and wives or women's treatment of their neighbors and daughters-in-law. Given chronic poverty, competitive Afghan generosity also had an evil twin—jealousy over the status gifts and favors could bestow—that could easily be provoked (Barfield 2010, 286).

This zero-sum worldview is best explained not as an immutable fact of Afghan life but as the result of centuries of war and foreign occupation and the caul-like poverty that clings to the populace. Public assaults on dignity and loyalty through imposed and unwelcome invasions were often avenged in the private sphere, where harm was typically justified by distorted ideas about tradition. Relentless poverty inevitably linked intangible values with material exchanges, so that everything—including or especially love—acquired monetary value.

The "bad" Afghanistan may seem especially egregious to outsiders, who wonder why the country's struggles over so many centuries had not increased men's appreciation for women's essential contributions to the well-being of families and communities that are the backbone of men's survival. But such outsiders should reflect on their own histories and recall the failure throughout the ages of most societies to promote gender equity as the means to fight adversity and promote social well-being. Few nations have based their economic and political future on men's increased support for, kindness to, and appreciation of women as people rather than as symbols or instruments in their own plans, fears, and pleasures.

The women at the conference also recognized another side to Afghanistan, however, which clearly inspired them and kept them going. They saw the "good" Afghanistan as a crucible of change, a place where the seeds of women's advancement were quietly sprouting in Afghanistan's cities and provinces. The good Afghanistan supported organizations such as Jamila's Noor Educational Center, which from its earliest days attracted enthusiastic students to its literacy and life-skills programs in provincial areas as well as in Kabul. By the same token, Marzia found support from ordinary Afghan women for promoting the rule of law and educating about women's rights in Sharia and civil law. Many were eager to learn about their rights, to protect their daughters from forced child marriages, and to achieve some kind of economic power.

Many women at the conference fueled their hopes for their country with the promise they could see in ordinary Afghan people to improve their condition and to fight the corruption, violence, and injustice that should not be accepted as fate. Many recognized the importance of girls and women to the future of their country. As I got to know Jamila and Marzia better, I learned how attached leaders like them are to that hopeful core, to the importance of women, and to the possibility that Afghans can become as generous among themselves as they are to outsiders.

International attention was another strand the women recognized in their tangle of leadership prospects. Not surprisingly, these leaders did not inherently resist either imported ideas of modernity or the presence of outsiders in their country, even in a military capacity. That presence seemed in 2005 the price of their hopes for increased security, political stability, and women's advancement. As Marzia said, they thought that modern ideas needed to be evaluated one by one before being either accepted or rejected. In particular, they did not want to see all ideas related to women's advancement automatically rejected as inconsistent with Afghan (or Islamic) authenticity. Their biggest fear was that the aid and attention then being lavished on Afghanistan would vanish in the (unlikely) event that the NATO coalition achieved its military objectives. Indeed, they were already lamenting the signs of distraction apparent in 2005, as the world's attention drifted to other disasters, notably Iraq.

Openness to helpful outside influences did not mean that the women supported permanent dependence for Afghanistan. Indeed, they cherished the idea of Afghanistan's independence, symbolized by the defeat of the British in 1919. Yet they were uncertain of President Karzai's ability to achieve let alone sustain a return to that status. Even women who had worked in Karzai's administration saw his shortcomings, particularly his "traditional mentality," which indicated his attachment to the nepotism and political manipulations that breed corruption. They wondered why the United States had backed the Northern Alliance against the Taliban in 2002, since that group had its own tarnished record, especially with regard to their treatment of women. Still, these leaders hoped the current government would somehow bring the factions of the country together and create a peaceful, coherent national identity and sense of consistent political loyalty.

The leaders' openness to Western influence, especially from Europe or the United States, created a conundrum for them, however. On the one hand, the women expressed the hope that emissaries from the West would provide ideas that they could use in promoting their democratic causes, from education for women to women's economic advancement to training female theologians. As discussed in chapter 1, Marzia even concluded her Columbus speech by asking the audience to send her their suggestions for advancing the cause of women in Afghanistan. On the other hand, these leaders recognized how damaging an association with the West could be to them as they promoted women's causes. Jamila emphasized in her 2005 interview that "every country has its own culture and own way of life." In Afghanistan, people "do not understand the sort of freedom as in European countries."

As an example, Jamila recounted a story about an Afghan woman who had participated in an international beauty contest the previous year. When her sexy picture appeared in the Afghan press, however, the NEC educational centers saw "a slowdown in attendance by women for about one week following that beauty contest." So, instead of helping other women by participating in the beauty contest, as she had hoped, her appearance had actually "blocked the way for other Afghan women." Jamila was wary of being that kind of leader and of watching her own efforts backfire.

The women's vision of a unified Afghanistan also included an improved civil society that would act as a bridge between citizens and their government and allow ordinary Afghans to participate in governance beyond their own village or province, provide a forum for discussion and debate at the national level, and permit citizens to hold their government accountable for its actions. These leaders believed that a national civil society was especially important for women, because traditionally their concerns had rarely left the village *shuras,* or councils of elders, whose decisions tended to rule their lives. But they saw the difficulties in promoting civil society as a democratic ideal and not a remnant of "godless" Soviet occupation. To make matters worse, activists promoting rights, especially women's rights, were often considered Communist sympathizers. Even without Soviet connotations, however, the concepts of rights and democracy seemed to many Afghans incompatible with Islamic social values.

This presented another difficult conundrum. Because the women leaders also rejected Soviet influence, they were careful to disassociate themselves and their plans and democratic programs from it. They tried to root their own democratic ideals in Islam. But it was sometimes difficult for them to articulate how their views of democracy differed from those of the Communists, thereby arming their conservative foes with the opportunity to associate their ideals and actions with the hated Soviet occupation.

Another strand in the women's conceptualization of their activism and progressive ideas was the relatively stable forty-year administration of King Mohammed Zahir Shah, for whom Marzia's father had worked and under whom the first modern Afghan Constitution had been ratified in 1964. These women spoke positively about the king's support for women's rights. The downside, of course, was the connection between the freedoms that women enjoyed during the king's regime, such as attending university and entering the workforce, and Afghanistan's developing alliance with the Soviet Union, via the king's cousin General Mohammed Daoud Khan.

With all of these complex and sometimes contradictory religious, political, and historical strands swirling in their heads, it was hard for the leaders to articulate to outsiders just what women's freedom and agency should look like in Afghanistan. They occasionally evoked models from other Muslim countries, especially Iran, which in 2005 had only just elected Mahmoud Ahmadinejad as president. They were clearly searching for manifestations of Islamic principles of gender equality and women's freedom.

From my outsider's perspective, the behavior, appearance, and demeanor of the women at the conference constituted a plausible if complex model of Afghan women's achievement and leadership as a mixture of religious and civic ideals and aspirations. The women were diverse in looks, dress, and self-presentation; they were (at least publicly) respectful of one another; they were struggling in their own ways to distinguish between the Afghanistan they loved and the one they rejected; they were dedicated, knowledgeable, and thoughtful; they were energetic; and they framed all aspects of their work in what they considered the right interpretations of Islam and Afghan traditions. Just being in their presence gave me respect for Afghan women and offered me hope for their continued resilience against all odds. At the same time, there was a shadow over their achievements as women, since during the conference it became clear that they had limited ways at home for coming together to collaborate on their projects and goals across diverse sectors of society. They admitted and lamented the fact that there were very few alliances among their organizations and no consistent forum for comparing ideas and cooperating to achieve greater efficiency or productivity. In a sense, each of them was an island struggling against the odds on her own.

The final and most obvious double strand affecting the women's achievement, which they both recognized and touted, was access to higher education and residence in an urban location, which in turn made educational access more possible. Conflicting with those dual advantages for them was the simultaneous reality that, in 2005, 70 percent of the Afghan population lived outside of Kabul, the largest and most developed urban area; 85 percent of women lived in rural areas; and 75 percent of Afghan girls were completely outside of the educational system. That contradiction loomed very large in the women's minds and led them to understand both their own privileged status and their distance and alienation from the very population they most wanted and needed to serve. They could and did travel around the country, but in many places their own opportunities and achievements made them seem like virtual foreigners in their homeland. That was a painful fact of life for people so dedicated to their country, and I could see that they did not yet know how to resolve it.

Different Stories

It was in the area of leadership development that Marzia's and Jamila's life stories emerged as evocative but diverse case studies. Both had spent their lives from early ages on working to effect changes in Afghan women's opportunities and to enhance women's understanding of their rights within Islam and Afghan traditions. Given their advantages and backgrounds, both could have had easier lives, but neither ever considered such a choice. Rather, they both volunteered for enormous challenges and sought meaning in attempting to meet them. Their hard-fought accomplishments and the hardships they had endured were written on their bodies and faces, so much so that when I first met them I had to remind myself that they were so young: Marzia was thirty-eight, and Jamila was just thirty. In a lineup, I would have added at least five years.

Jamila's story in particular exemplifies the early start and fast progress that characterized these leaders' experiences. In 2005 Jamila was directing an NGO she had started in her twenties—the Noor Educational Center, dedicated to women's education and capacity building—while she and her family were in exile in Pakistan during the mujahideen and Taliban periods. She was only fourteen when she arrived in Pakistan. Because her family was wealthy, she and her siblings did not have to live in the refugee camps. Exile actually facilitated Jamila's access to higher education, as it did for some other Afghan women. She completed high school and college in Pakistan, and she earned a master's degree in international relations from Peshawar University.

By the time I met her, Jamila was an accomplished educator and administrator. She was serving twenty-five hundred women in different projects in Kabul and other cities. "Maybe not very big," she said modestly, "maybe a small candle that I am lighting for their families." But that number astounded her listeners, even more so when she revealed all the obstacles she had faced.

Jamila also learned Arabic in Pakistan so she could read the Qur'an in its original language and argue with her male family members, who continually accused her of dishonoring them by working with men and going out so much on her own. Some of those men learned from her for the first time what the Qur'an actually says about women's rights. She was eventually able to outargue them and continue her work.

Marzia, who had served as a judge before the Taliban made that profession impossible for women, had organized and become president of the three-year-old Afghan Women Judges Association when I met her. Marzia wanted most of all to improve the capacities of Afghan women judges and advance the rule of civil law in Afghanistan. To that end, the AWJA had already helped fund two judges to attend European Parliament conferences, one in Italy and one in Turkey. In 2003 Marzia had been invited to attend the annual conference of the International Association of Women Judges (IAWJ) and the National Association of U.S. Women Judges in Washington, D.C. (I had to smile when I learned that Mrs. Bush had attended that meeting.) In the event, Justice Patricia Whalen from Vermont had asked Marzia what she needed most, and she had replied "capacity building." So, in 2004, the IAWJ and Justice Whalen supported a project that allowed four Afghan women judges to attend a judiciary college in Vermont and Washington, D.C., which was funded by the U.S. State Department. Marzia had found both experiences exhilarating. Judges from around the world established common cause as they honed their understanding of their judicial roles. Marzia also felt "healed" as the group celebrated their successes and commiserated about their marginalization, even among other women, around the world.

In addition to the undergraduate degree she had earned in law from Kabul University (KU) and her certification as a judge at age twenty-one, Marzia had recently finished a yearlong master's degree in law from George Washington University in Washington, D.C., at the time of the OSU conference. She was the first Afghan woman to get an American master's of law degree. She had also visited the United States in 2002 in the State Department's International Visitors Program, served as the national gender and justice officer for the United Nations Development Fund for Women (UNIFEM) Afghanistan, and worked as a project officer for UNICEF Juvenile Justice in Afghanistan.[1] In addition, she had served at the United Nations Assistance Mission Rule of Law Project, which established the Afghan Judiciary Commission. In 2002 Marzia had been a delegate to the Grand Assembly (Loya Jirga) in Kabul, served on the Women's Committee of the Afghan Constitution Commission Secretariat, and earned two medals from the Afghan Constitution Commission as well as from the Grand Assembly. (The year after we met, she represented the Afghan Civil Society to the London Donor Conference for Afghanistan.)

Marzia and her family had stayed in Afghanistan throughout the civil wars and the Taliban period. With her legal career on hold under the Taliban, Marzia ran a secret school in a nearby house for two to three hundred students. One day her worst fears were realized as the head of the Department for the Promotion of Virtue and Prevention of Vice arrived at the house where she was teaching. "Of course, it is shocking if you see someone is coming with the guns and with a whip wanting to take you to prison," she said. The first thing he asked was, "'Why are you teaching?' And I said, 'Who says . . . I shouldn't teach?' I don't know how I found the courage, because sometimes I think that if you work for your country and if you have good aim in your heart, then God will save you. And for me the protection of the society and my God kept me from going to prison. So then he asked me, 'Who are you? What are you doing?' I said, 'I am a judge.' Then he was silent."

Marzia's professional title had probably stopped the young Talib in his tracks, she conjectured, because it indicated that she knew more about the law than he did, and she could, therefore, argue with him. He also knew that his own power was limited to his weapons. "They are really ignorant people," Marzia explained, and they know it. "So he was quiet, and it was really terrible. It was 19 August 1999, but I'll never forget the moment that happened." The Talib walked away rather than go toe to toe with a superior woman.

Common Views

One thing that Marzia and Jamila had in common in 2005 was the fact that, for different reasons, neither had yet married, despite the very strong pressure on all Afghan women (and men) to marry young and produce many children. As a lawyer and judge, Marzia was a champion of delayed marriage for women. She had recently led a workshop in Kabul for two hundred participants, entitled Abandon Child Marriage, and she was working with the Afghan human rights commission to publicize the results of that conference, which had included a march on the city. Moreover, she and another OSU conference participant chose to work on the enforcement of laws against child marriage as their follow-up project after the OSU conference. Laws existed that required girls to be sixteen to marry, but they contained no enforcement mechanism to counter the customary but false belief that Islam supports consummating marriages with girls as young as seven.

Marzia understood how confining marriage could be in a culture (not a religion) that defines a married woman as the virtual property of her husband, subject to his approval for every action, every decision, every trip out of the house. If a woman's husband doesn't want her to work, she will not work. If he says she can't visit her parents or siblings, she will not visit them. If he decides she shouldn't travel, she will stay at home. Those restrictions can be enforced no matter how accomplished or independent the wife is, unless the husband (and his family) supports his wife's outside activities. Marzia reported that her own sister was as educated as she was, but the sister was (and is) stuck with a husband who does not protect her from his family. Without that protection, she is subject to their restrictions. To Marzia, such a conventional Afghan marriage was no life for an active female jurist with a penchant for international travel.

Luckily for her, Marzia's mother and father—himself a lawyer and a judge—supported Marzia in her work and did not pressure her or her sisters to marry. "People were coming in that time" to ask for her hand, "but I myself was not interested. Two of my other sisters married, but they didn't marry at the [mosque]." Sadly, her most beautiful sister, who really wanted to devote her life to her religion and education, was pressured into marriage at a young age. Because of her beauty, she was in high demand. So to avoid the risk of kidnapping or forced marriage with a family member, the "parents had to find a choice for her to marry with another one rather than to give her to an uneducated man." The Afghan custom of having to marry another man in order to decline a proposal from a family member, especially a first cousin, prevented that sister from getting educated "to the top level with other [sisters] who went to school."

Jamila's family considered her disability an impediment to a good marriage, despite their daughter's obvious gifts and physical beauty. She said in 2005 that she herself regarded her disability as a kind of blessing, because it allowed her to talk to her very conservative father—who had kept her from being treated for polio because it would require her to interact with male doctors—into education beyond the minimal schooling he would otherwise have allowed. As an adult, Jamila relished her freedom to conduct her life and to work without worrying about being turned over to a husband, which was a father's customary right to do at any moment.

A few years before we met, Jamila had entertained the idea of another kind of marriage. The mother of an educated, professional Afghan man who was living in the United States had approached her family to begin marriage negotiations for Jamila. According to Afghan tradition, a man's mother and sisters contact a prospective bride's family to express his interest. Although she did not want a conventional Afghan marriage, subject as it was to polygamy and men's interpretation of honor at the expense of their wives, she could imagine marrying such an enlightened man and living in a less restrictive, monogamous society as a productive worker and devoted wife. The relationship did not work out in the end, and for the time being Jamila preferred single life to the unegalitarian marriage she was likely to experience in Afghanistan.

Another thing that Jamila and Marzia had in common in 2005 was their belief that Afghan tribal traditions, not Islam, constituted the problem that Afghan women had to overcome. Marzia explained that basic rights for Afghans are taken from Islamic rights and adapted from the Egyptian and French legal systems. "And all those rights have been accepted for all citizens in [the Afghan] Constitution. It says no discrimination between men and women. It says that women should [have] compulsory education." Most Afghans, on the other hand, understand Islam based on what fathers, or brothers, or local mullahs say, even though they may know very little about the meaning of the Arabic text they can recite by heart. (Imams tend to be more learned than mullahs.) Literacy rates were so low (less than 50 percent among men, less than 20 percent among women) that even translations are inaccessible to most Afghans.[2] The result is that folk wisdom and cultural traditions, which usually support pre-Islamic male prerogatives and patriarchal power, take precedence over both holy texts and Sharia law and dominate common understanding of the religion.

Their shared belief about the importance of Islam to women's empowerment did not mean that Marzia and Jamila expressed their religious affinities in the same way. Though a committed Muslim, Marzia looked every inch a modern woman, whose lovely bone structure, brown eyes, and wide smile complemented her fashionable and flattering pants suits, styled and uncovered black hair, artfully applied makeup, and lightly polished nails. Her adherence to her religion's strictures seemed an internal matter. By contrast, Jamila's devotion was very visible. She was always covered from head to toe, not in a *burqa* or *chador* but in long, loose skirts and unshaped blouses. At the conference, her outfits were always topped with a large colorful head scarf, carefully pinned to cover her hair (which I have never seen), neck, shoulders, and chest. Her lovely face and large hazel eyes were free of cosmetics, and her blunt nails were unpolished. She carried a small prayer rug with her and found private places to pray throughout each day of the conference.

One thing the two women did not share was the same level of opposition to their independence and professional achievements from their families. Their determination, skills, intelligence, and abilities to persuade were received (and accepted) in very different ways by those families, although each had resorted to deception from time to time in order to follow her chosen path. The real key to both women's success was educational opportunity in the urban settings where it could best be found. That opportunity is not a given for any Afghan woman.

Becoming a Leader: Jamila

In Jamila's case, the primary naysayers about her educational and career aspirations were her male family members, who regarded her as a rebel and a threat to family honor for wanting a life outside the house. Originally from Ghazni, the family had secular but conservative roots, which Jamila illustrated by recounting the boast by some relatives (including some women) that no male outside of their families had ever seen their women's faces. The conservatism of Jamila's male family members was fed by their lack of education and their belief that women from a wealthy family, such as theirs, should be especially guarded in their behavior.

Every year Jamila had to persuade her father to allow her just "one more year" of schooling. "Just, Papa, this year, not more," she would plead. Because she would hold up her forefinger each time to reflect her modest request, her father finally cried in frustration, "I will cut off your finger. It's not going to be finished. Every year you're asking again for another year." But it worked.

Her ploy was motivated primarily by her love of learning, but Jamila also understood from an early age that her disability could eventually make her a burden on her family. She often overheard her female cousins and aunts plead with her mother to get treatment for her legs so that she could marry. But Jamila saw things differently. She became convinced that getting an education was a better way to ensure her future than becoming marriageable would be. If she was economically independent, she knew she would never be overly dependent on her family.

Even in her early years of schooling, Jamila encountered opposition from her male family members. Although her father had been persuaded to support her cause year by year, none of her siblings had pursued education, and her brothers felt shame that a daughter from their distinguished family attended school. If she had not been the seventh child, she said, she probably would not have been able to wear her father down.

Things got tougher for Jamila's educational aspirations after her family emigrated to Pakistan, as the Soviets pulled out of Afghanistan and the civil wars were raging. Her brothers, who had little to do, sat at home "cursing me all the time," even though she was only fourteen, because she wanted to go to school. Even without familial opposition, attending school in Pakistan would have been hard enough. For one thing, all classes were in English, and Jamila knew only Dari. For another, the family's Peshawar house was located close to the headquarters of a former mujahideen officer, Burhanuddin Rabbani, and it was surrounded by soldiers who made the streets very difficult to navigate, especially for a young girl alone.[3] Every day the soldiers would badger Jamila with questions about where she was going and why.

But on top of those obstacles, Jamila's brothers became ever more resistant to her pursuit of education as a violation of family honor. They instructed the family guards to make sure Jamila did not leave the house. As she explained, "They were saying to the guards of [the] house that 'if . . . she's going out, we will kill you; do not allow her to go out.' But still like I was compromising and I was asking them to allow me to go out, [saying] 'I will come back . . . earlier than my brothers are coming; I will be before them at home.' It was very interesting that my brother who was very harsh, he was having [a] white car. And believe me when I was going outside, every car seemed white car to me!" Still, she was not deterred. "I was feeling that getting an education was the only way that I can make myself happy," she said. Sometimes she even bribed the guards to keep her secret.

Luckily, Jamila developed a close relationship with her sisters-in-law, who agreed to protect her from her brothers by pretending that she had stopped going to school. In return, Jamila made sure she was as helpful as possible at home, considering her disability, particularly with her nieces and nephews. Helping out was consistent with Jamila's personality, but it also sweetened the deal with her sisters-in-law. So, while she learned English, completed high school, passed her college entrance exams, got admitted to the Jinnah College for Women in Peshawar, and completed her college degree, those sisters-in-law were making excuses for her scarcity around the house: "she's in the toilet"; "she's asleep"; "she's in the kitchen."

Surprisingly, the brothers were fooled all those years. (Perhaps women's power in the family does count for something.) When the secret finally came out that they had been deceived for so long and that Jamila not only had graduated from college but was still pursuing classes in English, computer technology, and business, the brothers "behaved badly," Jamila said. Only one brother kept still while his wife defended Jamila's desire for education. He was Hassim, her third brother, and he softened further when Jamila cried in front of him and said, "If I do not get education, what will I do? Because of my disability I am not able to cook lots of things and wash all the time. You know, sitting at home, what will I do?" Hassim agreed to talk with the other brothers, although he thought that Jamila should stop going to school and start teaching the family's children at home. She agreed to create a family school, but she also enrolled in a master's program in international relations, studied medicine and English, and continued her study of the Qur'an in Arabic.

Her graduate classes in foreign affairs and in Pakistan-Afghanistan history inspired Jamila to work for her country. Discovering "how Pakistan is interfering in Afghanistan's affairs and how Afghanistan is depending on Pakistani aid" motivated her especially. She joined the Afghan Women's Network, which had been started by some women she knew from her management classes. "So it was the start of my social activities that I was inspired by those women who were working in that network," she said.

She became a board member and worked tirelessly to assist Afghan women in the refugee camps in Peshawar. She personally helped to pack survival kits for families, and despite her physical limitations and the health problems that plagued other women in the organization, she and seven friends pooled their pocket money; collected donations from their families, friends, and neighbors and from people at the school they attended; and together purchased enough medicine, clothes, and food items to supply seven thousand Afghan families in the refugee camps. Others in the group had to handle the actual distribution of those supplies, but Jamila's participation led to even greater benefits for her countrywomen. She was encouraged to start her own organization—the Noor Educational Center. *Noor* means "light" in Dari, and Jamila was convinced that enlightenment through education was the best long-term solution for Afghanistan, especially for Afghan women. Without education, people could too easily be manipulated in the name of religion, she believed, or by some despot's political fantasy.

So, still in her twenties, Jamila began organizing and teaching vocational classes in embroidery for destitute women. She worked in conjunction with the Global Peace Mission of Malaysia, which took orders for the women's needlework. She also provided literacy education. As she watched her Afghan sisters die in the camps ("One day we had thirty-six women and children die"), her resolve to help only strengthened.

Jamila did make good on her promise to Hassim to conduct school at home, but she did not limit classes to her sisters-in-law and their children. She also started an evening class for her brothers on the interpretation of the Qur'an, which she was studying deeply herself. She explained to them, for example, that the holy Prophet's marriage to nine-year-old Aisha, after a two-year engagement, was not consummated until she matured and expressed her willingness to be in a sexual relationship with him. She also explained that her own activities were consistent with the Qur'an, since it says that the best human beings are those who serve humanity. There is also a hadith, or saying ascribed to the Prophet, which says, "A person who serves my family is closest to me." "Family" means God's universe, human beings, animals, all living things. And that's who Jamila was serving.

Jamila's teaching also touched on the Prophet's views about women and childbearing. She emphasized that the prophet Muhammad wanted his followers to be good human beings. So in a hadith when he said that "on doomsday I will feel proud of my *umma*, my followers, in their largeness and greatness," he did not mean that "women should bring a child every or even two a year if possible" so that Muslims would dominate the world. What he meant as a universal prophet—"not for a religion, not for a country"—was that those who followed his values should be worthy of his pride. Could he be proud "on a robber, on a kidnapper, on a killer? No, he will feel proud on a person who is an example, a moral example for the others. So that is the type we should feel proud on too."

She explained that when she interpreted this point to her brothers, "they were really quiet and they were not saying anything." So she pressed ahead and asked:

"Who can bring good human deeds to society? Of course, it's women, who are good mothers and can bring up good children. If you are going to tie up women inside the houses, you are not letting them get an education. They don't know about hygienic conditions. They don't know any good or bad outside. Sitting inside, fighting with each other, gossiping after each other, you know, cooking and eating. Such a mother can bring up a good human being that the holy Prophet should feel proud on them on doomsday?" And at the end there was a big clap for me, and everybody was silent. Nobody said anything after that. And one of the women came and said, "Really, no one has interpreted Islam in such a way. So we can use Islam as a tool, religion as a tool to change the mentality, to change the behavior. But we need women as scholars."

Of course, Jamila agreed. Without that, she thought, women just go to mullahs and blame each other if anything goes wrong.

Jamila understood that she had to tread carefully in teaching such lessons. She did not just tell the family that they were wrong; instead, she fabricated little stories to explore religious interpretations ("but I don't believe that God will punish"). She tried to judge their mood. If they were cranky or arguing, she backed off of her lessons. There was resistance from some of the brothers. One said, "What is this? You are introducing a new Islam for us! This is not Islam!" Her second brother who looks just like her, she said, and was "a problem creator" throughout Jamila's life, said, "Okay, if you want to remain a good Muslim, don't teach Islam. Don't read Qur'an. Whatever practices your forefathers are doing, do that!" But Jamila was undeterred. "I was slowly and gradually putting the topic on the table. I was arguing with them. This was the way through the strength of Islam I could achieve. Then my family slowly and gradually accepted that she is doing whatever she is doing at school."

When she returned to Kabul after the Taliban were ejected (however temporarily), Jamila pursued and even expanded her Noor Educational Center work, and her family grudgingly allowed her to continue.[4] Sporadically, however, male relatives from Ghazni would ask her father how he could permit Jamila to dishonor the family by traveling without a male family member, by meeting with men in her office, and by remaining an unmarried loose cannon pointed directly at the family's reputation.

Perhaps such questions were triggered in part by Jamila's responsibility for three of her nieces and nephews, whom she had adopted while still in Pakistan when her favorite sister-in-law died unexpectedly. When I inquired why their father was not raising them, Jamila replied that fathers do not necessarily take on responsibility for their own young children, although they will visit them frequently. Care by their grandmother was also not an option because she was ill. Because the departed sister-in-law had been "an angel" to Jamila—"very, very cooperative with me, she was like a mother, a friend . . . supporting me all the time"—she felt compelled to step into the breach, even though she was just entering her master's program when the sister-in-law died. So, as a new master's student, Jamila was looking after the children "as a mother" and entertaining guests at the customary weekly memorial ceremonies for their real mother.

Becoming a Leader: Marzia

Marzia's challenges in the path toward leadership positions were less related to family pressure than to politics. Indeed, her modestly well-off family encouraged her pursuits, while the changing political landscape kept getting in her way.

Marzia's father was from an Islamist background in Jalalabad in Nangarhar Province. He sought escape from his own family via his talents for public speaking, which his family actually encouraged when he was a boy. Indeed, at ages twelve and thirteen, he was speaking at the mosque. Such talents were eventually his ticket to Kabul University, where he became one of the first graduates from the Sharia law faculty. His speaking ability also placed him among the first qualified judges in Afghanistan, a position that brought him to the attention of the government of the last Afghan monarch, King Mohammed Zahir Shah, in the 1960s and early 1970s. He served the king's government as an itinerant judge and prosecutor and held other high-level jobs, including one at the Ministry of the Interior.

As a child, Marzia admired her father, and even though she was female, the feeling must have been mutual. Marzia's intellectual gifts helped convince her father to allow her and one other sister to attend school, even though her eldest three sisters had not done so. (Eventually, the three older sisters and two younger ones also completed their schooling.) The father clearly recognized Marzia's academic abilities, and his leniency was well rewarded. The two sisters were such good students that they completed twelve years of education in eight. Marzia was first in her class in her senior year of high school. (Although all of the schools she attended were for girls only, other schools allowed boys and girls to attend during a couple of years under Soviet rule.)

Marzia initially hoped to be a doctor, mostly because it was considered a good job, doctors were in short supply, and her grades were good enough. But in ninth grade, when students were required to choose between science studies and social studies, her father encouraged her to do the latter because the schools provided no laboratories to help her learn the scientific disciplines in any depth. That choice determined her future, as it helped her and her sister get admitted to the law faculty of KU. Their father encouraged but did not require the girls to choose law among the faculties to which they had been admitted. He told them not to worry about money; he would do anything, even sell property, to help them complete their educations. So, even though Marzia loved English literature and was admitted to that faculty as well, she chose the law and never looked back. Despite her father's generous offer, she worried about costs as an eleventh child was born to the family. She had even considered getting a job after high school so she could help support her siblings. But her father's support of her further education prevailed, and she graduated in 1985.

Marzia attended university when the Communists were in power and many people left Afghanistan, including many professors. Indeed, the law faculty was in open rebellion against the Soviets, who were pressuring them to adopt their version of the law. But Marzia stuck it out, sometimes hearing bomb explosions and watching rocket strikes from the campus, as the mujahideen began shooting from the hills around the city. Such experiences made Marzia recognize the dangers inherent in Afghanistan's volatile political situation as greater obstacles to her achievements than the familial pressures that limited so many of her Afghan sisters, like Jamila.

Marzia concedes that the Communists helped Afghan women to progress in their personal and professional lives. The Soviet-backed government never banned any kind of clothing for women. Men and women attended parties together. Women could drive and walk in the streets at night. Girls from the provinces began to attend university. Many women increased their professional capacities. Some served as judges, particularly in the juvenile court. Law students were still educated in Sharia law. But the downside was significant: anyone who wanted to achieve a position of power was required to join the Communist Party.

That kind of enforced political loyalty (or its pretense) made Marzia hate having the Soviets in Afghanistan, despite the gains for women that she appreciated and enjoyed. Like her father, she could not agree to Communist principles, even with her fingers crossed. The family did not support the mujahideen either, however. To them it was a choice between a government of invasion and one of violence.

Marzia and many other professional men and women, including Marzia's father, actually curtailed their careers in order to avoid joining the Soviet-backed regime. When she was offered the opportunity to study in India if she agreed to join the Communist Party, for example, Marzia refused. After she completed her judiciary training in 1987 at age twenty-one, as one of twenty-two women among the one hundred students in the class, she did not accept the regime's offer to become a judge, "because they asked us to go and just sign and be a member [of the party], but we didn't accept this." She and the other graduates realized that the Soviets "wanted . . . to influence judges slowly to make them" Communists, too.

Ironically, the Soviet occupation made some fathers, like Marzia's, wish they had produced only daughters instead of sons. That nearly traitorous desire, from an Afghan perspective, reflected the Soviet policy of drafting so many Afghan boys into the military. As a result, none of Marzia's brothers was able to attend university. One of her brothers had to serve in the army for six years.

Also ironically, the Soviet occupation drove so many of Marzia's relatives out of Afghanistan that her parents were under little pressure to marry off their daughters. Her mother's educated family would not have posed a problem, but her father's provincial, religious family would have. Marzia's home in Kabul further insulated her from extended family pressures toward marriage, and because her father ultimately believed that it was his daughters' choice when and whom to marry (although not if), she was able to pursue her career as best she could in ever-evolving Afghanistan.

With the withdrawal of the Soviet-backed government, Marzia became a government defense lawyer, as the civil wars in Afghanistan were raging. She defended many indigents and soldiers accused of giving their weapons to the mujahideen. In 1995 she received a life appointment as a judge. In 1996 the Taliban took power, and women's professional commitments had no more meaning, even in Kabul.

Although no women could serve as judges under the Taliban or hold any other professional position, Marzia still found work. She opened her private school. She taught for a French organization, and from 1999 to 2000 she worked for UN-Habitat, promoting immigrant women's rights.[5]

Marzia's resourcefulness during those years became a unifying theme in her life and career. She took pride in not allowing obstacles, no matter how large, to impede her determined dedication to remain economically independent herself and to serve women's causes through the law.

Reflections

The stories of these two women demonstrate to me that women's desire to develop their capacities and to serve others can emerge from a variety of life circumstances. Nothing in these women's self-presentations suggested that they were motivated primarily by greed or self-aggrandizement, although they were acutely aware of the competitive nature of their society, especially for ambitious women. Still, as they savored the personal achievement that accompanied their dedication to their work, they remained committed to a collective vision of Afghanistan's future. They also cared deeply about their families and wished to be viewed as good daughters and sisters. They had helped me to see how personhood and agency for women might sound in a different language.

At the same time, like the other women leaders at the conference, Marzia and Jamila took nothing for granted. They knew that all gains were tenuous and contested and that critics lurked around every corner, some of them armed with guns or vials of acid. None of the conference attendees knew whether they could ultimately help ordinary Afghan women increase their social and political participation, their literacy levels, their political and civil rights, or their economic welfare. They had no rule books and few contemporary models for achieving success in their particular endeavors. They did not know whether their own rising tide of opportunity would ultimately lift or sink the boats of women whose hardships and constraints the American invasion had not magically erased. As certain as they were that Islam could be used as a tool to empower women and promote gender equity in Afghanistan, they had no real proof that it would. As Marzia, Jamila, and the other women leaders left Columbus on another stormy day a week after their arrival, nothing about their future was certain.

3

Constructing Women's Rights in Afghanistan

One message of the 2005 "Afghan Women Leaders Speak" conference was that the so-called "medieval rule . . . under the Taliban's . . . repressive gender regime" was not the beginning of the struggle for women's rights in Afghanistan (Moghadam 2003, 227). Indeed, in understanding the women's contemporary perspectives, it was important to recognize that debates about women's roles, identities, relationships, and dress had been a source of contention throughout modern Afghan history, long before the Taliban emerged on the scene in the 1990s. It was also important to recognize that such debates—in Afghanistan and elsewhere—are seldom solely about what women can and cannot do. Rather, they are also indicators of the intersection of women's roles, identities, occupations, and behavior with cultural imaginaries, as well as with other social priorities, conflicts, and challenges. Such debates are not just an immutable characteristic of a static culture or a question of who does what and who is in charge. Rather, they are best understood as the product of local histories and international geopolitics.

A review of Afghan history reveals that the only thing definite about women's rights is that they have historically been anything but definite. What *rights* stands for and who enjoys them have varied from region to region and decade to decade. Some observers have reduced that variability to a common cliché: "Afghanistan is a backward, feudal, patriarchal nation that resists modernity. Since women's rights represent modernity, that's why they do not 'stick,' no matter how many times they are offered."

That cliché does capture part of the story. Conservative Afghans of both sexes, especially in rural areas, do invoke the idea of a static cultural tradition, including female and family honor and a stark view of Islam, when they oppose girls' attendance at school or women's public roles and unveiled presence outside of their homes. Resistance to social changes for women has also served the self-interest of diehard patriarchs, who justify indulging their sexual desires, exerting domestic power, and controlling family resources as a matter of traditional or Islamic prescription. Such attitudes have produced heart-stopping cases in which a woman pays with her life for crossing the lines of cultural tradition and family honor defined in those terms.

But the cliché does not capture the whole story. There is also a strain of sincere and deeply held belief in the separation of the sexes and in men's duty to protect, provide for, and guide women and children. In a war-ravaged country, such protection may appeal to women as well as men because a succession of weak central governments and self-interested warlords has done little to offer meaningful alternatives. Well-intentioned men may also use the Prophet's behavior to nonrelated women as a guide, meant with all respect. As we shall see in more detail in part II, those who adhere to such models do not necessarily intend to demean or restrict women.

Also defying the cliché is the fact that many aspects of Afghan tradition have molded and remolded themselves over centuries, around foreign invaders, civil wars, technology, and exile. Indeed, like all traditions, Afghanistan's cannot remain consistent and uncontested over time and on all matters. So while "Afghan traditional culture" remains a constant trope, what it refers to at a particular moment or location—even with regard to women—is a mixture of contemporary and historical politics; fear; family, ethnic, and regional identities; habitual practices; resentments; economic exigencies; pride; and local obligations, among other contingencies. That helps to explain why, under certain circumstances and at different times, both traditional rural and "modernized" urban people have accepted and resisted education for girls, women's employment or franchise, veiling, and other aspects of women's behavior, status, and rights. Most Afghans have also embraced other emblems of modernity, including electricity, radio, television, satellite phones, computers, the Internet, and air travel, when and if they could.

What Are Women's Rights in Afghanistan?

The basic definition of women's rights has also varied in Afghanistan according to region, social stratum, time, and educational levels, and it has rarely if ever been consistent across the country at any given moment. In the past few decades at least, many educated urban women (and some men) have understood the concept of women's rights according to two major referents. One is Islam, represented by the Holy Qur'an and hadith, understood and interpreted by educated people like Marzia and Jamila. Such Afghans typically recognize that the Qur'an and the Prophet's own life empower women economically and socially and mandate their education (Mills 2011, 68). They may also respect the reformist tradition in the Muslim world, dating back to the late nineteenth century, which has long advocated women's education. From such a perspective, Afghanistan is both a country with patriarchal roots deeper than Islam and a "modern, Islamic country with a mixture of European and Asian influences and diverse cultures" (Rostami-Povey 2007, 135, 134).

The second referent for this group is the international understanding of human rights and the rights to which all the world's women are presumably entitled. Activists such as Jamila and Marzia want their country and religious leaders to live up to the agreements and covenants their nation has signed and ratified, including the Convention on the Elimination of All Forms of Discrimination against Women, which it signed in 1980 and ratified in 2004 (Armstrong 2002, 135).[1] They welcome the reinforcement that international definitions provide for the very idea of women's rights.

At the same time, even this educated group tends to define women's empowerment as a function of a secure and vital family support base. Their goal is not to emancipate women from their families in order to pursue individual goals. Rather, it is to empower women to fulfill their responsibilities and roles, which sometimes means intervening if men are incompetent, unjust, or un-Islamic. Therefore, as Margaret Mills explains, the apparent "individualism of Western-style feminism seems to some degree an oxymoron, and as such, a deception" (2011, 68).

Less educated Afghan women tend both to recognize the importance of the family to their own well-being and empowerment and to see the patriarchal order as the source of kinship loyalties that sustain and strengthen them (Ahmed-Ghosh 2003, 9). Patriarchy can even be seen as a strategy in times of crisis, because although it disempowers women, it strengthens the kinship bonds that provide protection (Barakat and Wardell 2002, 918). This group is less likely to welcome definitions of rights that seem imported or to recognize that the Qur'an and hadith bestow rights on women. They are also unlikely to have what Marzia called "gender sensitivity," as there is no Dari word for *gender*, and most Afghan men's and women's economic and social lives, even their survival, are so interconnected that their distinct interests are hard to articulate, let alone disentangle (Heath 2011, 19; Ahmed-Ghosh 2006, 126). A focus on *gender*, then, which is often used as a synonym for *women*, sounds to many Afghans like an attempt to privilege women over men (Abirafeh 2005, 13).

Given Afghans' tendency to define themselves in terms of family, community, and clan, many Afghan women understand their rights in terms of food security, employment, health, and education, since those are crucial to collective survival (Abirafeh 2005, 14). But they may also recognize the injustice of certain cultural restrictions for women, such as jailing those who run away from violent husbands. Even without an education, they may also want an opportunity to shape their own destinies, but only in terms of their appropriate roles in society and "the positive side of [their] Afghan Islamic culture" (Rostami-Povey 2007, 65).

Given these variations, striking an appropriate note in addressing rights issues has been and will continue to be a tremendous challenge for activists such as the conference attendees. Even in the midst of their optimism, they defined numerous challenges and recognized the difficulty of translating for different audiences what they believed to be the vital rights women must enjoy if both they and the country should survive. And despite their own discouragements, they hoped to keep alive the spirit of reform in women's status and opportunities in general and gender roles, identities, and relationships in particular. They considered that spirit crucial, even if the exact meaning of "women's rights" in Afghanistan remains indeterminate.

Taking into account the diversity of Afghan women's experiences, perspectives, and social and geographic locations, I have come to define *women's rights* in Afghanistan as promoting women's fair access to social, medical, and material resources and to economic and educational opportunities, as well as to their ability "to claim political legitimacy and negotiate their rights in accordance to their social and cultural needs" (Ahmed-Ghosh 2006, 125). It seems clear that the concept of complementarity between men's and women's familial and social roles does not preclude women's economic and political contributions to the family and community (Ahmed-Ghosh 2003, 11).

Why Have They Varied?

As regimes and governments have come and gone in Afghanistan over the past century, so have women's status and rights. From King Amanullah in the 1920s to the Cold War manipulations of the USSR and the United States after World War II, Soviet influence and occupation in the 1980s, the mujahideen civil wars in the early 1990s, Taliban rule from the mid-1990s until 2001, and the U.S. and NATO occupation of Afghanistan since 2001, "contests between social forces [and] geopolitical entanglements [have] produced sharp swings of the pendulum between extremes" with regard to women's rights (Kandiyoti 2005, vi). That pendulum has swung because women's identities, sexuality, reproduction, occupations, dress, and roles have historically been used by Afghan leaders as well as by world powers—especially Britain, the USSR, and the United States in the past century—as bargaining chips in quests to control Afghan geopolitical alliances and strategic position.

The history of wars, invasions, coups, occupations, and power struggles over the past century reveals a recurrent pattern with regard to women's status and rights. At least as far back as King Amanullah's rule in the 1920s, I would say that pattern is roughly this: rights for women are imposed by a centralized power, whether indigenous, like the king, or foreign, like the Soviets. Those rights are controversial in themselves, but they are also tied to other centrally imposed reforms, such as land redistribution or revisions of tribal or regional prerogatives. Outsiders manipulate the intertwined rights-reforms situation to their own advantage. Rural Afghan leaders or warlords also incite resistance (often aided by a neighbor, like Pakistan, or a world power, like Britain or the United States). Resistance grows, not only to women's empowerment but often in its name. The regime is toppled. Resisters waiting in the wings exploit the chaos, and a new regime is instituted, usually by violent means. Then the new regime revises or reverses whatever rights women were given or denied in the last regime in order to solidify its power. The Taliban takeover illustrates the nadir of this pattern, as that regime demolished all access to rights and status Afghan women had ever achieved (or been given).

On the ground, the lives of most Afghan women may change very little through these upheavals, regardless of how they define their own rights. For one thing, they may have little access to official information and hear nothing about the latest edicts regarding their privileges and rights. For another, most Afghan women live far from urban centers and are subject in their daily lives to local and familial decisions about their behavior and status that remain outside of centralized rule. Nevertheless, this yo-yo approach to women's rights and their intersection with other political changes at the top can affect the symbolism of women's rights and privileges across the country, whether or not those rights have actually been enjoyed. Rural men may harden their opposition to their daughters' education, for example, if that opportunity is associated with a challenge to male authority and honor, the loss of local control, reduced security, or land-reform policies they do not like. The meaning of a girl's nonattendance at school can change within families or communities, even if her actual nonattendance stays the same.

The United States has been implicated repeatedly in this pattern, especially from 1945 to the present. Initially inspired by its own interests in the Cold War and by its commitment to hegemonic superpower status, the United States has often found itself in common cause with Islamic fundamentalists and other enemies of women's rights. In the process, U.S. policies have frequently demonized many of the values that enable those rights, including democracy itself (Fitzgerald and Gould 2009, 83). Thus, the United States has not historically been the ally of Afghan women's rights that Laura Bush implied in her radio address in 2001. In fact, Afghan women's rights have frequently been the collateral damage of U.S. policies.

Historical Perspectives on Afghan Women's Rights

Although reforms to improve the status of women did not begin with him, King Amanullah's reign is an important example of the persistent pattern with regard to Afghan women's rights.[2] Amanullah's rule began after the assassination of his father, Habibullah, in 1919. One of Amanullah's first acts was to negotiate an armistice with the British, thereby establishing Afghanistan as an independent state.

Amanullah was inspired by his progressive father, who had tried to limit burdensome marriage expenses and divorced all but three of his wives and allowed them to appear unveiled in public (Moghadam 2003, 237). Amanullah was also inspired by Afghan reformer Mahmud Beg Tarzi, editor of a modernist-nationalist newspaper, and by Turkish modernizer Kamal Atatürk (Moghadam 2003, 236; Ahmed-Ghosh 2003, 3–4). In the face of opposition from clerical and rural patriarchs, Amanullah abolished slavery, thereby freeing women from concubinage, and promoted women's full citizenship and education as part of his attempt to modernize Afghanistan's system of land distribution, trade, tax structure, health care, education, and infrastructure. Amanullah also encouraged women to abandon the veil and required Western dress in some parts of the country (Moghadam 2003, 237; Fitzgerald and Gould, 2009, 61). His reformist agenda culminated in a new constitution in 1923.

The king's reforms, including those for women, were widely considered "principled and in keeping with Islamic law" (Fitzgerald and Gould 2009, 61). His government argued that such reforms belonged under the rubric of *himayat-i niswan*, or the protection of women. He saw women's emancipation as the keystone of a new Afghanistan's future structure. The reforms predictably gained popularity with Afghanistan's urban merchant and middle classes. But in a pattern that would be repeated over and over, rural Afghans interpreted the king's reforms as an attempt to centralize power in Kabul at the expense of the mullahs and to abolish subsidies for tribal chieftains. Equally predictably, the reforms had limited application across the country. As infighting began, women's new status became the primary indicator of other hated reforms. Even the mullahs could not agree among themselves, as those who excoriated women's increased rights in the Amanullah regime were themselves declared un-Islamic by more orthodox mullahs, because of their failure to honor women's inheritance rights and their support for unjust marriage practices. The tribal revolt that ensued forced Amanullah to abandon his social reforms. Old tribal systems were reinstated; women were forced back under the veil; girls' schools were closed (Moghadam 2003, 239; Barfield 2011, 188).

In addition to the internal strife, the British deliberately undermined the king's regime. They suspected him of cozying up to Germany and Communist Russia, two of Britain's sworn enemies, and feared that his model of Asian progress might give ideas about independence to colonized Indians. British secret agent T. E. Lawrence (Lawrence of Arabia) was even deployed to roam "the countryside posing as a holy man and incite the tribes to rise against Amanullah" (Fitzgerald and Gould, 2009, 62–63, 64).

These international shenanigans in turn fed local antipathy to Amanullah and doomed both his constitution, which was abrogated in 1924, and his regime. After a victorious European tour, in which he was hailed as a modernizer, Amanullah came home to unrest. Queen Soraya's removal of her veil at a public ceremony ignited the spark of resistance, and Amanullah was forced to flee the country after a rebellion in 1928 (Fitzgerald and Gould 2009, 62).

The yo-yo pattern with regard to women's rights continued with Amanullah's eventual successor, Nadir Shah (a distant cousin of the king), who initially reversed Amanullah's alliances by making concessions both to religious conservatives, thereby undermining his program of women's rights, and to the British.

His renewal of the 1921 treaty with Britain seemed a step backward for some Afghans, since among other things it reinforced the controversial Durand line dividing Afghanistan and Pakistan by bifurcating Pashtun lands. Nadir Shah's government eventually ricocheted between progressive and regressive social and economic policies, but the progressive constitution he enacted in 1931 (which stayed in effect until 1964), while proposing economic reforms and a restoration of industry, "omitted any mention of women's rights" (Fitzgerald and Gould 2009, 14–65; Rostami-Povey 2007, 10).

Western powers touted Nadir Shah as a peacemaker and nation builder and approved of his cautious support for gender-based reforms (Ahmed-Ghosh 2003, 6). At home, however, sidelined Amanullah supporters, disgruntled Pashtuns, resisters to foreign manipulations (especially by London, Moscow, and Calcutta), and "disillusioned nationalists and impatient modernists" helped to spread rebellion against him. As a result, Nadir Shah was assassinated in 1933 (Fitzgerald and Gould 2009, 66, 64). He was replaced by his young son Zahir Shah, although his paternal uncles Mohammad Hashim Khan and Shah Mahmud Khan effectively ruled in his stead until 1963.

Women's economic participation in the country improved slightly during the 1940s and 1950s. In addition, a 1949 marriage law was enacted to help further reduce bride-price and the costs of ostentatious wedding ceremonies (Moghadam 2003, 240; Ahmed-Ghosh 2003, 6). However, women's rights took a backseat to the geopolitical concerns that dominated the country during World War II, as Afghanistan lurched between the support and influence of opposing foreign powers. At first pressure was exerted by Nazi Germany and Italy, who regarded Afghanistan as "an ideal base from which to harass Britain" (Fitzgerald and Gould 2009, 69–70). By 1943, however, Afghan antagonism toward Russia, an old occupier and enemy, sparked fear of a Communist victory and drove Kabul into alliances with Great Britain and the United States. Afghan leaders played on the U.S. alliance by requesting increased financial assistance to ensure Afghan loyalty in case of war between their American donor and the USSR (Fitzgerald and Gould 2009, 76, 79).

Women's rights were back on the official Afghan agenda as Zahir Shah assumed control of the government. Zahir is remembered to this day for providing education for women, supporting the voluntary removal of the veil to end sex segregation, and framing his secular constitution of 1964 (Rostami-Povey 2007, 10). But Zahir's leadership ultimately fell prey to the persistent pattern—internal political factions (he was not fond of the new Parliament), foreign superpowers, and a resurgent religious Right, led by mullahs who made women's rights a central symbol of discontent. The mullahs bemoaned Zahir's alleged spread of atheistic communism and touted "the need for shielding women from education and exposure to the world outside the harem" (Fitzgerald and Gould 2009, 119; Barfield 2010, 5). At the same time, Zahir Shah's long reign had done little for social development outside of Kabul. Many consider that he had a pitiable record and "failed to give the country any of the attributes of the modern centralized state" (Moghadam 2003, 235).

With a weak state, waning international assistance (especially from the United States after 1951), and increased poverty, exacerbated by the 1972 famine that killed one hundred thousand Afghans, Zahir Shah was overthrown in 1973 by his cousin Sardar Mohammed Daoud, who dissolved the monarchy; denounced the king's "pseudo-democracy," including women's rights; and made the issue of the Pashtun-dominated lands on the Afghan-Pakistani border—known as Pashtunistan—a priority (Fitzgerald and Gould 2009, 122).

Afghan women's rights moved into a new and controversial phase with Daoud's takeover of the government. Daoud did attempt further marriage reform and supported a 1977 civil law that established sixteen as the age of majority for girls and therefore as the lowest age at which they could be married, although it left intact husbands' right to unilateral divorce. Without sanctions for violators, however, "the law remained weak and ignored" (Moghadam 2003, 240).

Although the Soviets denied knowing anything about his coup, Daoud ultimately switched his allegiance to the USSR in return for the economic and military aid that was no longer forthcoming from the United States (Rostami-Povey 2007, 10–11; Fitzgerald and Gould 2009, 82, 90, 123). With that move, Afghanistan returned to U.S. attention, and Afghan women's rights became the centerpiece of the U.S.-USSR rivalry in the Cold War. In order to staunch growing Soviet influence in Central Asia, the United States allied itself with Afghanistan's most undemocratic elements. In so doing, the U.S. government not only overlooked signs that Daoud was trying to marginalize Soviet influence by founding his new National Revolutionary Party but also set in motion events that would destroy the country's fragile infrastructure (Fitzgerald and Gould 2009, 126) and reverse gains for women.

The Daoud regime ultimately fell to the Soviet-backed People's Democratic Party of Afghanistan in a bloody coup in 1978, as the Soviets stepped up their intervention in Afghanistan in order to promote leftist unity (Fitzgerald and Gould 2009, 125–32). The resulting Democratic Republic of Afghanistan, in direct defiance of perceived U.S. interests, brought a new surge of rights for many middle- and upper-class urban Afghan women, who mingled with men without head covering or *hijab*, attended university, and worked as scientists, doctors, and civil servants. But once again, the pattern repeated itself. The majority of Afghan women lived in poverty and enjoyed no such opportunities (Jalali 2006, 25). Moreover, the regime was suspected of relying on the predominantly male Afghan elite to formulate women's rights issues on essentially Western models, "which were culturally insensitive and unpopular with the majority of Afghan women" (Rostami-Povey 2007, 12).

Things worsened for the PDPA among rural Afghans in its waning months, as leaders issued stronger pronouncements on land reform, compulsory education for women, the abolition of bride-price, and the cancellation of rural debts, among other reforms (Ahmed-Ghosh 2003, 6). Even their Soviet backers thought they were moving too quickly, but the party regarded such reforms as their revolutionary duty. Meanwhile, even Afghans who had supported the party increasingly saw PDPA policies as "poorly conceived, structurally flawed, and badly implemented," as well as insensitive to social mores. Rural Afghans were becoming convinced that they should reject any non-Muslim government, and they started characterizing their resistance to the Soviets as jihad (Barfield 2010, 226–31, 42; quote on 230).

Afghan resistance to the PDPA resembled the widespread rejection of Amanullah's democratic experiment a half century before, but PDPA reforms were considered even more radical than the king's. Among other things, they attacked the economic foundations of rural Afghan life by trying to equalize land distribution, thereby undermining long-standing patterns of landownership (Barfield 2010, 233). Resistance to women's rights, which was a key symbol of those changes, was both hardened and Islamified in the process. Because of its Cold War mentality, the United States did nothing to intervene in that outcome. Indeed, some U.S. officials were so determined to turn Afghanistan into the USSR's Vietnam that they were happy to exaggerate the Soviet's backing of the PDPA, thereby further demonizing reform, despite evidence from the embassy in Kabul that the Soviets were not "'irrevocably committed to the PDPA'" (Fitzgerald and Gould 2009, 163–67).

Such U.S. attitudes contributed to the Soviet invasion of Afghanistan in 1979, following the disintegration of the PDPA. As a result, Afghan opposition to reforms such as women's rights, now considered Communist, only increased. Marzia's rejection of the opportunities for women that the Soviet occupation provided suggests how damaging the association of those rights with intolerable Communist political principles could be. Especially because women's rights had accompanied the almost complete disruption of the country's agriculture, the death and flight of millions of Afghans, the internal displacement of more than a million others, and the degraded status of Afghan refugees in Pakistan and Iran, Soviet occupation definitely gave women's rights a bad name (Barfield 2010, 234–35, 42–43).

American opposition to the Soviets in Afghanistan meant that the United States opposed the Soviet "campaign against illiteracy, the elimination of feudal control over women and marriage, the abolishment of usury for agricultural credits, and land reform" (Fitzgerald and Gould 2009, 167). Instead of promoting those harbingers of democracy for Afghanistan, the United States contradicted its own interests in modernizing and secularizing the Afghan state by empowering fundamentalist "freedom fighters" against the Soviets, including Osama bin Laden, knowing full well that it would undermine human rights and return women to purdah, subjugation, and social and economic exclusion. U.S. officials also knew that their anti-Soviet policies would further taint women's rights as Communist (Fitzgerald and Gould 2009, 219, 184, 165).

Such American self-interest, combined with rural opposition to Soviet reforms, helped to unleash carnage and destruction on Afghans that included "'extreme forms of gender-based violence under the mujahideen'" after the Soviets withdrew in 1989 (Kandiyoti quoted in Skaine 2008, 46). The mayhem continued for years, as "no faction was able to establish either political legitimacy or military hegemony," and no warlord was willing to compromise (Fitzgerald and Gould 2009, 56). For women, it was "the worst period of Afghanistan's entire history" (Ahmed-Ghosh 2006, 118). Some even longed for the Soviet puppet state. But worse was yet to come, as the mujahideen debacle fueled by U.S. support paved the way for the Taliban.

The Taliban was a cross-border movement, led by Afghan Pashtuns trained in Deobandi madrassas in Pakistan (Barfield 2010, 255). As Pashtuns, however, they had close ties with Afghan leaders. As their forces spread across the country with Pashtun support starting in 1994, the Taliban exploited Afghan discontent with warring warlords who no longer represented any interest but their own. In areas where chaos prevailed, Taliban ideology did not matter as much as their promise of stability. As they appropriated weapons from mujahideen stashes that could well have been provisioned by the United States, the Taliban offered Afghans a new jihad, dedicated to ridding the Afghan nation of foreigners (which they allegedly were not) and to bringing a more authentic version of Islam to the country, despite the Talibs' real ignorance of Sharia law and limited understanding of Arabic (Fitzgerald and Gould 2009, 256–57; Barfield 2010, 267, 262).

Although some world powers deplored Taliban policies, none was willing to intervene—possibly to prevent further damage to Afghanistan itself—not even to save Afghan women from ever more draconian treatment. Indeed, after helping to arm the Taliban, the United States actually supported the Taliban regime between 1994 and 1997 by supporting their allies, Pakistan and Saudi Arabia, and by negotiating with them for an oil pipeline project through Afghan territory. By supporting only girls' education during the mujahideen and Taliban periods, U.S. NGOs and the United Nations also unwittingly encouraged Afghan boys to seek education in madrassas—those "hothouses of indoctrination and fertile recruiting grounds for child soldiers." They did not recognize that Afghan boys were also deprived of schools because of mass destruction during the civil war (Rostami-Povey 2007, 25).

The U.S. government did not even criticize the Taliban's capture of Herat in 1995, although it meant that thousands of girls were thereby forbidden to attend school. Indeed, it was not until the pipeline deal was crumbling and Pakistan's position was deteriorating that Secretary of State Madeleine Albright publicly condemned the regime's treatment of women (Heath 2011, 3).

The United Nations also indirectly supported the Taliban in order to keep the flow of foreign aid going to Afghanistan (Barfield 2010, 264–65). To that end, UN officials even rebuked their own gender specialist, Nora Niland, for exposing the Taliban's violent tactics and slave trade in a report in 2000. Niland's report was not released until the Taliban was itself ousted from the country (Armstrong 2002, 140).

September 11, 2001, changed the calculus of U.S.-Taliban relations, but not primarily because the United States was determined to reinstate Afghan women's rights. Rather, the Bush administration wanted to avenge the al Qaeda attack on American territory, and Taliban leader Mullah Omar refused in the name of Afghan hospitality to expel its mastermind—the onetime ally of the United States Osama bin Laden (Barfield 2010, 269).

The Taliban regime fell within ten weeks of the war's beginning, hastened by Afghan resistance to the regime's history of arbitrary "justice" and violence, especially against women. The regime's huge network of spies and informers had terrorized and alienated much of the country (Rostami-Povey 2007, 35). Instead of welcoming Taliban rule as an opportunity to make religion a unifying force across ethnic, political, and regional barriers in their country, many Afghans resented the regime's imposition of a non-Afghan version of Islam that they considered inherently inferior. In addition, the Taliban had limited their leadership to Pashtuns, which built resentment in the North and West. They had also oppressed the Shia Hazaras and forcibly removed Tajiks from Taliban-held parts of the Shomali Plain. That they were increasingly reliant on foreigners—Pakistan and al Qaeda Arabs—demonstrated to many Afghans the Taliban's ultimate hypocrisy. Even the Pashtun stronghold of Kandahar ultimately refused them safe haven (Barfield 2010, 263, 269).

Though not the primary factor, despite U.S. claims, gender did play an unheralded and unusual role in the defeat of the Taliban. That is, many Afghan men opposed the regime's humiliating treatment of *men* in public, over beard length or other infractions. (They felt the same humiliation when they were dragged from their homes by NATO troops, according to Rostami-Povey [2007, 35, 37, 48]). For once, male honor actually benefited women.

President Karzai and Women's Rights

As the Afghan women leaders left Columbus in late 2005, they still hoped that President Hamid Karzai would somehow transcend his political roots and become an ally in the promotion of democracy and women's rights. Unfortunately, in the next few years, it became increasingly apparent that, instead, he would be an unreliable and quixotic administrator of the precepts of democracy. Structural constraints posed part of the problem. For example, he was unable to select the members of his cabinet without parliamentary approval (Jalali 2008, 32–33), with all the attendant obstacles that posed for women's rights. But many observers, eventually including Jamila and Marzia, thought that his behavior in office reflected his inability to stop looking over his shoulder at his enemies and his determination to survive in office and to hold on to power no matter what.

A prime example of those motivations was Karzai's determination early on that bringing former militia commanders and alleged war criminals to justice would "jeopardize the fragile political process." That determination violated his obligation to promote peace and reconciliation, as required by the United Nations Assistance Mission in Afghanistan and the Afghan Independent Human Rights Commission. Karzai also dismissed most criminal suspects as foreign agents. Unsurprisingly, Parliament was supportive of his decision. In 2007 that body granted general immunity to all suspects of past war crimes. Such immunity weakened the rule of law and benefited narcotics smugglers and corrupt government officials (Benish 2010, 46–47; Ibrahimi 2010, 43–44). To punish past rights violators, Karzai suggested that victims should bring charges against individuals instead of seeking collective accountability (Skaine 2008, 39–40).

Given women's limited access to any judicial process, that edict basically eliminated any accountability for women's rights abuses during the Taliban and mujahideen periods. In addition, Afghan women were never systematically integrated into peacemaking, demilitarization, demobilization, the reintegration of fighters, or plans for social reconstruction (Heath 2011, 4–5).

Predictably, Karzai's decision not to prosecute warlords and Taliban leaders, as called for by the Transitional Justice Plan in the Bonn Agreement, had devastating results for Afghan women, by keeping the enemies of women's rights in power (Skaine 2008, 39–40, paraphrasing Human Rights Watch in 2007). In addition, as Marzia predicted, the government failed to establish a functioning legal system. Without courts to enforce their rights, women could not exert them (Riphenburg 2010, 179). Moreover, Karzai's political calculations and, perhaps, his own views prevented him from appointing qualified women for ministerial and other governmental posts or from working with established women's organizations and women professionals. The women whom Karzai did appoint reported that he did not really consult or empower them.

Karzai is a wily politician, however. At various points in the years between 2005 and 2010, when I again probed the situation more deeply with Marzia and Jamila, he strategically demonstrated his support for women's rights when he thought it would help him, particularly around election time in 2009. For example, he supported the Elimination of Violence against Women (EVAW) law that was finally enacted in 2010. The law criminalized buying and selling women for marriage, *baad* or *badal* (the exchange of women to settle debts or feuds), child marriage, forced marriage, and forced isolation, as well as denying women the right to work, education, and health services. It also called on religious leaders, together with the Ministries of Hajj and Religious Affairs and Women's Affairs, to develop training and awareness-raising programs about women's rights for mullahs, imams, and religious teachers.[3] That law seemed to many women, including Marzia and Jamila, a dream come true.

As it turned out, however, the lack of enforcement mechanisms weakened the law so much that people suspected that Karzai's support for it was intended simply to put a benevolent face on permission to continue violent practices against women. For example, EVAW did not end *badal* or eliminate forced marriages or abuse. Indeed, only a tiny fraction of filed cases were actually prosecuted. A UN report in 2011 would be entitled *A Long Way to Go* to describe the law's slow implementation.[4]

Suspicion about Karzai's motives was reinforced by his virtually simultaneous support for the Shia Personal Status Law, which was quietly put into effect at the end of July 2009. Karzai had even signed an earlier version that legalized marital rape, probably in an effort to garner support from Shiites, who were oppressed by the Sunni-led Taliban government, and from the law's author, Sheik Muhammad Asif Mohseni, the country's most powerful Shiite cleric.[5]

The Personal Status Law meant that among Shia Muslims, who comprise 10 to 20 percent of the Afghan population, men now had the legal right to starve their wives if their sexual demands were not met. In addition, Shiite women had to obtain permission from their husbands to leave their houses, "except in extreme circumstances." Apparently, Karzai was counting on the probability that few women would learn about the law, so signing it was unlikely to affect their votes for him in the upcoming election. But those who did know about the law, whether Shiite or Sunni, worried that it would soon extend to all women.[6] That prospect became even more worrisome in March 2012, when Karzai approved the Afghan National Ulema Council's declaration about women (for more detail, see chapter 9).

Concern about Karzai's approval of religious law and his blatant neglect of the legal system helped to fuel a scathing 2012 report by the Afghanistan Human Rights and Democracy Organization. In it the group concluded that "'most of women's important achievements over the last decade are likely to be reversed'" (Levinson 2012).[7]

Women's Rights Activism

Despite such disappointing developments, women's rights activists continued their work in Afghanistan. The women at the OSU conference exemplified the tenacity such activists had maintained over many difficult years. Some of them, such as Jamila, were politicized and educated by their refugee experience. They developed their capacity to collaborate, compromise, and negotiate for their needs; developed greater self-confidence; and became increasingly aware of the importance of women's rights.[8]

Among that group was Fatana Gailani, who set up a school and hospital for women in Pakistan and hand-delivered her newspaper, *Afghan Women,* across the border to Afghanistan during the Taliban regime. There was also Sediqa Balkhi, after whom a hospital is now named, who led the Islamic Center for Political and Cultural Activities of Afghan Women under the Taliban from exile in Khorasan, in northeastern Iran. There she worked in cooperation with the UN High Commissioner for Refugees to get female heads of household involved with income-producing activities. When Balkhi returned to Afghanistan in 1991, she continued her work in secret in Mazar-e-Sharif, Herat, Kandahar, and Kabul (Rostami-Povey 2007, 31–32). She was later appointed to the Meshrano Jirga.

Orzala Ashraf Nemat was only twenty-two when she established Humanitarian Assistance for the Women and Children of Afghanistan as a refugee in Pakistan, and she also continued her work when she returned to Afghanistan (Brodsky 2011, 85). Suraya Paikan established the Afghan Women Lawyers and Professional Association in Mazar-e-Sharif. The group had four hundred active members in 1998, when she too was forced into exile by the Taliban and had to continue her work from Peshawar until 2001 (Rostami-Povey 2007, 34).

Other leaders included Soriya Pakzad of the Voice of Women Organization and Afifa Azim of the Afghan Women's Network. Their groups, like Jamila's and Marzia's, offered literacy, advocacy, social support, Qur'anic studies, job training, and shelter services to women for years across many regions of Afghanistan (Brodsky 2011, 85). Other NGOs included the Afghan Women's Resource Center, dedicated to improving women's right to security and access to education and employment. The AWRC also provided literacy and basic health training. Another group, PASRA, worked with widows and the needy to generate income opportunities, and still another, the Shuhada Organization, worked for the empowerment of Afghan women and children by operating home-based schools and mobile health clinics.[9]

Occasionally, groups tried to come together to influence the country's leaders, with mixed success. For example, a coalition of women, from Parliament, civil society, and the government (including Marzia), worked together to formulate the EVAW law. With less success, activists also joined forces in a demonstration in March 2009, asking to be involved in the peace process. Unfortunately, one member of that group, Sitara Achakzai, was assassinated a month later. Nevertheless, eighty-one more women won Provincial Council seats in 2009 than in 2005 (Nemat 2010, 176–77).

The Ministry of Women's Affairs also kept trying. In 2008, for example, Minister Husn Banu Ghazanfar designed two promising programs. The first was "Healthy Family, Happy Society," which encouraged religious leaders in various provinces to promote awareness of women's rights. The second, "Law and Women," was run by lawyers and prosecutors, who published posters and launched information campaigns (Skaine 2008, 135–37). Unfortunately, alongside such hopeful programs was the news that two provincial heads of women's affairs had been murdered since 2006: Safia Ama Jan was killed by the Taliban in Kandahar in 2006, and Hanifa Safi was killed by a car bomb in Laghman Province on July 14, 2012.

Next Steps

Reading and hearing the news over the years between my face-to-face meetings with Marzia and Jamila would both dash and raise my hopes for a good outcome for their projects and for their survival. Our e-mail correspondence, though spotty, at least assured me that they were alive. Every time I read about violence in Kabul, I contacted them to make sure they were okay. I sometimes would not hear back for weeks, which allowed me to imagine the worst. The prospect of my traveling to Afghanistan, which I had once entertained, became increasingly remote.

My hopes that President Obama could somehow reverse the disastrous policies of the Bush administration in Afghanistan were tempered by worsening fighting there and by the burgeoning economic crisis at home, as two years of sinking American housing prices and rising unemployment captured the administration's attention. Finally, in October 2009, my book having been published in August of that year, I decided to dedicate my ASU research fund to financing a meeting of the three of us in a mutually satisfactory location in this increasingly dangerous world. I had little power to help Afghan women in a material way, but I could continue to listen to two of the country's female leaders and bring their views to a poorly informed U.S. audience, of which I had once been a member. Given all the changes in the world in general and in Afghanistan in particular, I knew at the very least that I needed to update my data from 2005.

I began making initial contacts with Jamila and Marzia in November 2009 to propose a meeting, and by February 2010 we decided to gather in Istanbul that September to revisit some of the topics from the conference and to catch up with changes in their lives and views. This time I would be the one to deal with long flights, possible weather delays, and jet lag.

PART II

Reality

(2005–2010)

Prologue: Narrative History

Selecting Istanbul for my next face-to-face meeting with Jamila and Marzia in 2010 allowed me to move closer to the world in which the two women lived and offered them respite from their increasingly treacherous home terrain. They felt comfortable coming to a Muslim country that would be at least a little familiar and was then relatively peaceful. I was eager to immerse myself in a Muslim-dominated culture, which I had never done. Although I had been to the ruins at Troy, this would be my first visit to modern Turkey. I hoped that travel would be simpler for the two women this time, because there were direct flights from Kabul to Istanbul, and Turkish visas were easier for them to get than were visas to other nearby countries or the United States. But *easy travel* is another relative term. Each of the women had added a layer of complication to any travel plans she might make, as both had gotten married since 2005. Jamila had also borne two children. Thus, there were husbands to consider and, for Jamila, the needs of an infant and a three-year-old to take into account.

Neither of the women mentioned that the dates I selected for the interviews—September 3–6—fell in the last week of Ramadan and led up to Eid al-Fitr, the joyous celebration of the Holy Qur'an and of Ramadan's end. In my mind, Ramadan always occurred in the late fall, so I had not thought to check those dates. (I have since learned that the start date falls ten days earlier each year.) And neither Ramadan nor Eid was noted on any of my calendars.

Marzia and Jamila later confessed that they had discussed whether to tell me about the significance of my chosen dates and had decided not to, since they liked the idea of staying a few days beyond the interviews to celebrate Eid in a new place. Instead, Jamila informed me indirectly of the holiday schedule by asking in April if it would be okay if her husband and children joined her in Istanbul so they could celebrate part of Ramadan and all of Eid there together. She said that her husband would take care of the children while we met. In that indirect approach, I once again recognized the famous Afghan graciousness.

Arranging the Istanbul meeting was not as difficult as bringing five Afghan women to the United States had been, primarily because Turkey is more welcoming of Afghan visitors than the U.S. government. In 2005 every woman who came from Afghanistan to the Ohio State conference had had to demonstrate through written documentation that she would return to her own country when the meeting was over. It would be even harder today to gather a similar group. Turkey does not accept Afghan refugees either, but their officials must be easier to convince than U.S. officials that Afghans will actually go home. In any case, Jamila and Marzia easily obtained their Turkish visas, although not until after their airline tickets had to be purchased. The risk that the visas might be delayed or denied, along with the risk that the planes would not really fly or that one or both of the women would fall ill or be injured or detained (or worse), kept me wondering up until the last minute if the meeting would actually occur.

I arrived in Istanbul a day before we were scheduled to start the interviews so that I could recover from jet lag and make sure that the hotel rooms and other details were all in order. I discovered that the change in Jamila's plans to accommodate her family had somehow deleted the hotel reservation for Marzia, so I was scrambling for a room for her until the very moment I expected the two of them to walk through the hotel door on September 3. I knew their flight arrival times, and even accounting for the atrocious Istanbul traffic—which tended to snarl during rush hours right outside our hotel, across from the Marmara Sea—I figured they would arrive from their different flights by about six o'clock.

By eight, the time we had planned to meet for dinner in the hotel restaurant, I was beginning to fear that something untoward had happened. I asked the desk clerk to check their flights online, and she reported that they had both landed. I wondered what had made me think that this meeting was really possible across four continents, eleven time zones, and endless security threats. I had double-checked everything, even triple-checked it. Had they missed their planes or been detained in Kabul? Had an emergency kept them at home? Had there been an accident? How would I know if their taxis had crashed?

By then I was sitting in the hotel lobby watching the door, but somehow I missed seeing Marzia walk into the hotel until I spotted her at the reception desk—dark hair uncovered and wearing a bright blue blouse, an ankle-length black skirt, and her familiar pink lipstick. She was friendly and matter-of-fact, deploring and apologizing for the terrible traffic in which she had spent well more than an hour in transit from the airport.

While I was sorting out Marzia's room mix-up, Jamila appeared with husband and children in tow. She explained wearily that her flight on an Afghan carrier had been delayed for three hours (so much for escaping delays). I noted that she was dressed from head to toe in dark navy blue, punctuated only by a sunburst pin with light blue stones that was holding her head scarf in place. A pang of sadness also swept through me as I watched her maneuver the crutches she now required full-time and wondered if early care could have prevented their necessity.

Though tired from their trips and a little somber, neither of the women seemed very much aged, which I was pleased to see. Jamila's face still shone from her neatly pinned scarf. Marzia still wore the bright colors that flattered her, and her hair was still black and shiny. Once again, these women had survived travel adversity with grace and resilience.

Of course, it was too early for me to judge in that first glimpse just how much the preceding five years had altered the women's lives and attitudes. That they were resilient did not mean they had not experienced wrenching changes, hardships, discouragements, and pain. As our informal meetings and interviews proceeded, I realized that their demeanors were permanently sadder, even when they were more rested. I sensed the heavy burdens that rested uneasily on their shoulders. Jamila verified that her clothes were deliberately darker than they were in 2005, when every scarf was a swirl of color and pattern that coordinated with her skirts and blouses. Piece by piece, I learned about both the dramatic differences and the relentless constants that had shaped their lives since our last meeting.

Coming to Narrative

The women's request in Istanbul that I transform our past and upcoming interviews and other interactions and correspondence into a full-length book to bring their stories to the world presented a new challenge for the three of us, even as it seemed to me like the best way to honor the women's generosity in meeting with me and informing me about their lives and views.

As I thought about creating a written narrative from our oral exchanges, I reflected on the importance of Afghanistan's oral culture, which, given the country's roughly 25 percent literacy rate overall, remained the predominant way that contemporary Afghans exchanged "everyday information, community historical memory, and entertainment 'literature,'" according to Margaret Mills. Oral culture and radio broadcasts were especially important in Afghan women's lives, given that few of them attended public performances, congregated at the mosque, or interacted in civil society. Dependence on oral communication had made women vulnerable to Marxist propaganda and Islamic resistance to it, as both sides tried to rally women's loyalty by invoking female icons of Afghan history and other tropes familiar from the country's legends and tales. But their oral heritage also provided a point of entry for Afghan women's own tales of resistance, heroism, and commitment to national or Islamic values (Mills 2003, 478–79).

I hoped that my exchanges with these Afghan women leaders and the narrative I constructed based on them would honor that heritage. For me, it seemed a logical progression from the women's oral statements to writing that tried to capture their words and convey their meanings, inflections, and intentions as directly as possible, as a folklorist might present a story. That testimony would form the core of the book, while the historical and political contexts I could bring to bear would contextualize the women's experiences and perspectives for the Western audience they wanted to reach. For them, the oral interviews and other conversations constituted a comfortable way to proceed. When I asked if the two women had an interest in writing their own stories from the transcribed record, they declined. They are not writers, they said, but I also sensed their respect for the testimonial format. Should their situations or desires change, the transcriptions will always be available for them to use as they wish.

At the same time, I recognized the vexed history of subaltern narratives written by Western writers with different intentions than mine, what critics such as Gillian Whitlock and Sherene Razack consider the imperialist trick of making women's abjection in other parts of the world into more evidence that Western democratic and feminist values are all that will save them. Indeed, I had learned to reject that scenario, as well as to resist the objectification of Islam as "the obverse of Euro-American societies that self-identify as 'the West,' driving a constant creation and re-creation of imaginary boundaries between 'we' and 'others'" (Whitlock 2007, location 117).

I did not aspire to create the kind of "beneath the *burqa*" best seller that such critiques targeted, narratives in which veiled women are both exoticized and diminished. Though not attracted to such works myself, I knew what the critics meant. Those narratives were in the genre of the Oprah Winfrey and Eve Ensler event at Madison Square Garden in 2002, in which "Zoya" (a pseudonym) of RAWA was publicly unveiled by the actress while Ensler read from her poem "Under the Burqa" and a choir chanted a "melody full of grief" as Zoya's cloth symbol of Taliban fundamentalism fell to the stage. I could see how such scenarios fetishized the *burqa*, robbed the veiled woman of her role as an agent in her own history, and elevated Western women to the position of saviors. I could also see how they might help to justify a war that was supposedly dedicated to replicating that act for women all over Afghanistan (Whitlock 2007, location 753). Whitlock's analysis reveals that the best sellers had similar effects, while also making Western readers feel good about themselves as cosmopolitan in their "tastes, openness, sympathy, political commitment, and benevolent interest in cultural difference" (2007, location 787).

Despite my resistance to such narratives, I took seriously the problem of positioning myself as a universal subject and "other" women as what critics such as

Meyda Yeğenoğlu consider "non-sovereign objects of investigation," even though that was the phenomenon I intended to reverse. I knew that I was not innocent of my country's mistakes and offenses with regard to the Third World in general and Afghanistan in particular. Even though I hoped not to replicate such offenses but rather to communicate openly and to adopt the "moral humility" that Iris Marion Young prescribes, I worried that my own unconscious Orientalism might exhibit itself even as I designed my narrative in contradistinction to the male-centered, voyeuristic model at the core of that perspective (1997, 48). Therefore, I was happy to discover Reina Lewis's objection to the notion that Western women will "always and unavoidably [be] the stooges of Orientalism and imperialism." If non-Western women can escape imposed imperialist perceptions of themselves, Lewis asked, "Why cannot Western women also find a way outside of the confines of such totalizing dynamics?" (2002, 217). I hoped there was no reason they could not. I meant to find such a way.

The very foundation of our original project with Afghan women leaders gave me a good start. Margaret and I made the decision not to "reach across cultures in sight of the veil," as Whitlock puts it, in order not to reinforce the ethnocentrism implied by such symbols of "absolute difference." Nor did we design our project to probe only the "stunning sexual racism" of the Taliban. We did not want to replicate the "passive 'Third World' subject" or present "Western women as [models of] . . . secular, liberated, and individual agents" (2007, locations 670, 679, 702). Instead, we wanted to interact with the women as "active agents in history," without romanticizing them or their culture and without characterizing Afghanistan as an "impenetrable and unchanging primitive space outside modernity" (2007, locations 756, 1011).

As my relationship with Marzia and Jamila progressed in the following years, and the plan for the book evolved, I strove to continue those goals and compose a narrative from oral transmission that would allow the women to enter the public sphere of the West, as they wished to, and to make their case through "a cross-cultural translation of selves" and "discourses of history and memory," without serving any particular national interest. I wanted to share these specific voices of activists and professionals as they explored and created their own forms of Islamic identity and argued for more democratic forms of social organization and social justice than they currently saw in their country (Whitlock 2007, locations 943, 1104, 896). I intended for them to be understood in the context of Afghan history and contemporary politics and to represent Afghan feminist resistance (their term) that Westerners too rarely witness. I deliberately did not rely on a single voice but sought their different perspectives. Instead of letting their testimony represent isolated otherness for a foreign audience, I surrounded their words and ideas with context.

In some ways, constructing this narrative has been haunted by the opposite problem than the one that typically vexes the tale from beneath the *burqa*. That is, Marzia and Jamila are well beyond the *burqa*, both literally and figuratively. They are city women, and their educations and experiences have given them an internationalist perspective on women's roles, rights, and aspirations, which they are always balancing with their deep immersion in and love and respect for their "good" Afghan culture, their country's history, and their religion. Long before I met them, they had identified themselves with international organizations, albeit in different ways. They had also accepted the presence of internationals in Afghanistan, although they were insightful critics of internationals' ways of doing business. Balancing those aspects of their lives was among the biggest challenges they faced, and capturing their ways of negotiating that contested terrain strikes me as an important contribution of this book.

Without making any claims for perfection, I believe that the narrative that follows, like the one in part I of *Contested Terrain*, constitutes a good-faith effort of representation and analysis that fills some important gaps in Westerners' understanding of gender in Afghanistan.

Part II Organization

Part II consists of four chapters. The first, chapter 4, explores Marzia's and Jamila's assessments of the conditions for Afghan women in 2010. After a five-year hiatus in our meetings, I was curious to see what the women would consider progress for their countrywomen as well as their views of continuing needs.

Chapter 5 takes a deeper look at the two women's own professional activities in the intervening years. This chapter offers a somewhat soberer vision of the constraints and setbacks women activists were facing by 2010 as well as continued evidence of their persistence in the face of such challenges.

Chapters 6 and 7 look at the biggest change in both Marzia's and Jamila's personal lives—their marriages. Chapter 6 sets the stage for their individual experiences by exploring general characteristics of Afghan marriage traditions and expectations from the women's perspectives. Chapter 7 investigates the particulars of their decisions to marry, the circumstances of their marriages, and the impact of their new status on their professional activities.

4

The Basics of Change

When Marzia and Jamila arrived at my hotel room for our first interview the morning after their travel ordeal, they were smiling and eager to collaborate in my research project on women leaders of Afghanistan. True to his word, Jamila's husband, Fazal, was taking care of their three-year-old son and five-month-old daughter. And true to Afghan form, each of the women had gifts for me—Afghan almonds and sweets from Marzia and a white blouse, embroidered in pink thread, and jewelry from Jamila, who explained that the white stone-and-string necklace had come from Ghazni, her home province, where she said her organization was doing "very good work." Jamila also presented me with a green-striped, Karzai-style woven tunic, embroidered in white and red thread, for my husband, Tom, whom she had met in Columbus in 2005, when he became her unofficial chauffeur and escort into and out of cars and buildings that were difficult for her to navigate. I was glad that I had remembered to wear the lovely silver and amber drop earrings the conference women had given me in 2005. It was too warm for the two-sided woven wool jacquard shawl they had also brought me, or I would have been wearing that as well.

Our first minutes of conversation, when I was recording their consent to participate in the research, established that we were working together on a book project in order to spread the women's views "to the world." Then I asked Marzia and Jamila about their experience with the violence that I knew was starting to encroach on Kabul. They both responded that their survival was "more luck than our own efforts." Both told stories about their near misses with exploding cars and other dangers in their day-to-day lives. Jamila told about being caught in a shooting match on the road to the airport between two police cars heading toward each other, with her vehicle in the line of fire. Apparently, the car she was riding in resembled a stolen UN vehicle the police were looking for. She had to shout so the police would notice that a woman was in the front seat and was probably not a suicide bomber. Because of such incidents, Jamila said that she now resided primarily in her office, since travel to and from home had become so dangerous.

Marzia said that she missed by two minutes being killed in front of the Indian embassy, where a lot of people had died or suffered severe injuries. If her husband had not stopped to get his suit from the tailor shop, "we were [dead] for sure in that situation.... [When] it blew up, all the trees were in the sky and lots of red color and all these things. It was so sad that my husband... lost control of car, and the car went to the small lane; one tire was" caught in a ditch. Both women also reported the dangers of traffic jams in which an individual bomber could appear without notice and blow up dozens of cars, although such incidents were still rare.

Recognizing that they could not do much to keep themselves safe other than watch out and pray a lot, I realized with a sinking heart that my concern about them over the past several years had been completely justified. They were in danger at almost every moment of the day and night.

Assessments of Progress

I continued our interview that day by asking the two women how they would assess Afghan women's current situation in comparison with five years earlier. Fearing the dangerous situation might have halted activists' work in Kabul, I was both encouraged by their reports of progress for women's status and opportunities and unsurprised that almost every advance they described had a caveat, usually one that acknowledged that advances in rights, literacy, public activity, education, and health care were partial, unreliable, and often limited to women in Kabul or in other cities. It was here that the different professional foci of the two women became clearest. Marzia's dedication to the law and the legal profession necessarily kept her eyes primarily on the cities, where the rule of civil law was most likely to count (if not exactly prevail). Jamila's widely networked organization also worked primarily in cities and larger villages, but her emphasis on education and skills training for women had more applicability to nonurban settings. She was therefore in touch with many rural Afghans.

Marzia's list of advances in the legal profession included an increase in female defense lawyers. There were now close to 150, up from one in 2005, and that one had had to work at a private company in order to support her cases. Now it was different. "Some of the women even have their law firms outside their houses," Marzia reported. "So this is a good sign for the promotion of women in the legal sector." She was also proud of the new women's committee of the Afghan Bar Association, which was working to protect the rights of female defense lawyers. She was pleased that the Supreme Court had extended women's opportunities to serve as judges since 2005, a move that had increased the number of women judges and prosecutors. Marzia explained that those new prosecutors and judges were no longer restricted to cases involving women's issues or female clients, although they were generally relegated to family courts, which once sat only in Kabul but were now in four additional provinces, and to juvenile courts, which "are very important for girls accused of crimes," such as running away to avoid forced marriages.

Both women were also cautiously optimistic about the EVAW law prohibiting violence against women. It was then in draft form and approved only by Karzai, but its ultimate fate was still unclear. Marzia spoke first. She was pleased that the attorney general had established a new office dedicated to pursuing cases of violence against women in August 2010, just a week before our meeting. "It's great progress," she said, "but let's see what will happen." She praised the law's provision that raised the marriage age for girls from sixteen to eighteen and for boys from eighteen to twenty. She was less sure that the three-month jail term the law imposed on men who beat their wives would ever fly. "In a society that every minute men beat their wives, will it be accepted?" Marzia asked. "You know, it will be a challenge. Now all those leaders [who] are sitting in the Parliament, will they approve it? President Karzai approved it because it was just the time of his election and he wanted to also get support from women. And it was just between women and President Karzai, not in the public." (See chapter 3 for the law's final outcome.)

The campaign for the law's passage had been helped by women's growing resistance to abuses and injustices in their domestic lives. An increase in women's education was helping to raise their awareness and foment that rebellion, as was the return of Afghan women who had been exiled in Iran. "They're very well educated," Marzia said. "You like them . . . because Iran is a modern country and the women have more rights than Afghans, and [their example] could be also an education for [Afghan] girls to protect their rights and learn from them. They're very powerful; they are on TV; they're everywhere. . . . I like it; also from Pakistan some of the girls who came [back to Afghanistan] with higher education."

Marzia also reported that the media were finally beginning to play a role in promoting "freedom." She knew that there was a woman behind the scenes of Tolo TV, "a powerful TV [network]."[1] Tolo was "criticized much by those who are not accepting freedom. . . . [But] it has political support," Marzia continued, "because as much as [the government or conservative religious leaders] want to stop other TVs, they [know Tolo is] powerful, [so] they're careful. And the [TV stations are] critics also. They're very [good] critics of the government. They criticize Muslims." Jamila added that their critiques are often couched in irony and satire, and I thought immediately about Jon Stewart's *Daily Show* and the importance in the United States of comedy in advancing political perspectives.

Because of her recent childbirth experience, Jamila was familiar with improvements in health care for women, which included new clinics all over the country that treated drug addiction and delivered babies. The previous minister of health and education deserved credit for that development, she said. Not only was he actually qualified for his post—a rarity in Afghanistan—but he was also able to spend 78 percent of his large budget, which was second only to that of the Ministry of Defense.[2] That level was considered exemplary because other ministers had difficulty achieving even 50 percent expenditure of their allocated funds.

As a result of the Health and Education Ministry's success, Jamila continued, the current minister, a woman named Surya Dalil, could report a decline of 50 percent in maternal deaths, from one every thirteen minutes to one every twenty-five or thirty minutes. But Jamila reflected that "it's still a big loss to Afghanistan." Moreover, the improvement was probably limited to the cities, which the statistics did not reveal. "Maybe in some areas, there is no change," she continued. Indeed, the losses could have increased in some areas because security issues increasingly prevented women from visiting clinics. Marzia agreed and explained that security definitely did not extend to clinics in rural Afghanistan. "And the doctors do not go [to the provinces] from Kabul, the gynecologists, because there's no security for them also to work. So this could be improved in the cities, but I'm not sure if it's [possible] in the remote areas." The mere presence of clinics did not guarantee good care for another reason, too, as doctors in rural areas were poorly trained.

For Kabul residents, new international hospitals provided the best gynecological and maternal care. Marzia explained that "India has developed some hospitals, [as have the] French and Germans; . . . some specialists from these countries . . . are . . . working closely with . . . Afghan doctors."[3] Marzia was impressed by the U.S. military hospital, where her sister had done her residency. There Marzia witnessed Afghan x-ray technicians and others being trained by U.S. personnel.

Oddly, these hospitals were more likely to work with medical NGOs than directly with the Afghan government, so care was not being institutionalized throughout the country. This disconnect illustrates the shortsightedness of some international donors, who still tended to focus on high-profile, immediate projects rather than contribute to long-term, society-wide solutions. Rural women in every province were in special need of maternity hospitals, staffed by women doctors. "More midwives could be trained, women could get support for travel, and more support for the women doctors could be given," Marzia hoped. International donors needed to understand that women doctors needed "financial support and security support." Without adequate housing, protection at home and work, and a good salary, women doctors will not migrate away from the cities because their husbands will not follow them.

Jamila credited one of three international hospitals in Kabul, Cure International, with saving her baby daughter's life only a few months earlier. (She had also delivered her son there.) Because of fetal abnormalities, other hospitals were encouraging her to have an abortion, but with good prenatal care, she was able to bring the baby almost to term. Cure is supported by the United States and takes both public and private patients.[4] The latter receive more luxurious care, but all care is good, Jamila said.

The women then debated the role of politics in the success of Cure International. Marzia thought the head of the hospital was "one of the big mujahideen leaders, . . . who is also head of the Senate of Afghanistan? . . . His father is a famous religious leader. They could attract international support. . . . The people say he is very qualified, he's very respected by the doctors who come from U.S. It is also being run by Afghans, which is good news."[5] Jamila was not sure about that, but she said that even if it had politically powerful supporters, the hospital was still overloaded. One doctor and a few nurses and midwives were expected to handle four or five baby deliveries every hour, for example. "And many people are not getting access, and they are rejecting many cases because they do not have the capacity to deal with all the cases. So, besides the recommendations that Marzia made, if such hospitals are going to be extended to other parts of Afghanistan, the number of staff [should] be increased," Jamila offered. "Then that would be very good."

A progress report on women's education in Afghanistan followed the health-care discussion. Both women reported more opportunities for girls to pursue primary, secondary, and university educations as well as to enroll in professional schools. Graduates were increasing at all levels, they said, particularly in the big cities. And girls were beginning to have career aspirations. Marzia noted that she had discovered girls who wanted to be journalists, lawyers, judges, or engineers as she worked to increase legal awareness in the schools. Women who were already educated were beginning to own businesses and run organizations. "So this is a kind of change within themselves and also with their communities; noticeably, they can be example for other people, then for their families and for their communities."

Speaking of women as inspiring role models, Jamila reported that her most troublesome brother—the one who had paid guards to kill her if she went out to school—had developed a foundation by the name of Active Youth Foundation. "He's working with the orphans and children on the street, and they have very active women's wing inside their foundation, and they're working on some other social issues." Even better, Jamila saw that his "type of tight mentality has got changed" more broadly in the culture. Why? "Because some women put example, good example, in front of them that women can be a good politician, a good social activist, at the same time good mother and good sister and good wife to their family members. So this is a change." Even her own family, who "were not on the side of education of girls, . . . now they are trying and even now they are saying, 'You should go for higher education.'" Her own niece was pursuing higher education in Dubai. Jamila said, "You can see this type of change of mentality over all Afghanistan, even from very remote areas."

U.S. philanthropists were also making some difference by helping war widows get educated. (She was probably referring to the U.S. organization Beyond the 11th, which raises awareness about the plight of women in Afghanistan and provides educational and income-generating opportunities for Afghan widows.)[6] The widows' enrollment "increases the voices of women students in Afghanistan, at Kabul University, and at some other, private, universities," Marzia explained. She was excited that more and more faculties—law, engineering, economics, medicine—were opening up to women in both public and private institutions.

Among the private universities that had recently opened were the University of Dawat and Jihad, the Islamic University, and Abdullah Bin Masoud University, all of which had initially served Afghan refugees in Pakistan and then moved entirely or in part to Afghanistan in recent years.[7] Although the quality of some private universities had come into question, most people conceded that they had met a need for access, which was severely limited in state-run institutions. The private schools required families to pay, but more and more girls were registering every day. Marzia delighted in the schools' "good . . . education," characterized by "free kind of thoughts. . . . They give a lot of opportunity for expressing the children and expressing themselves. So once children have the ability, then they can be something."

The U.S. government had put a stamp on Afghan higher education through its support for the American University of Afghanistan (AUAF), which opened in 2006. The university resulted from a partnership between the Afghan government and the United States, and it was funded by a grant from the U.S. Agency for International Development. Although run by Americans, AUAF was committed to nonpolitical and nonsectarian education. (There were also ties between Kabul University and USAID.) It would graduate its first class, which Marzia thought included very well-qualified Afghan students, in the spring of 2011.[8]

Marzia reminded me that she had wondered in 2005 "if any university in the world would help Afghanistan [by taking] at least two, three students. Now we have hundreds and hundreds of students educated with master's degrees," she said, including several members of Kabul University's law faculty, who had earned master's degrees in the United States. "So now their professionality has increased."

There was still a concern that students would not come back to Afghanistan once they had a scholarship, but those who had returned were making valuable contributions. "In all Afghan legal society, we [now] have very [some] highly educated people, as the judges, as the prosecutors, and as a defense lawyer." But there was still a need for more. Marzia was interested in the possibility of attracting Fulbright scholars from the United States to work in law faculties in Afghanistan. She realized, however, that if anything like that were to happen, she would have to do the legwork. "They don't have this capacity to be connected by e-mails; it's not an easy way they work."

Women's improved economic status in Kabul had contributed to the boom in their higher-education enrollments, because better employment opportunities—often in international organizations—allowed them to pay their own university fees. The enrollment of women had "increased the voices of the women students in Afghanistan." But the news was not all good for those women. On an international scale, Afghan colleges and universities did not rate very highly. "Most of the universities lack the professional teachers and professional professors," Marzia explained, which kept the quality low. But still, they offered women the opportunity to complete their educations, so many of which had been interrupted by civil war and Taliban rule.

Women in many provinces were meanwhile improving their economic competitiveness by producing "better and [more] beautiful business items, like handicrafts and some jewels and fruits and some jam, jelly," Jamila reported. Afghan women had won "first division or maybe first prize" at a recent Asian exhibition, featuring women's work from countries such as Tajikistan, Uzbekistan, Iran, Pakistan, India, and Afghanistan. "They were well organized, and they were well finished [in] their products," she reported. In addition, "at Kabul and Mazar-i-Sharif, we have a women's market, a market which is running by women; all the shopkeepers are women, and all the items they are bringing and they are running like beside. Like they have a center for health and for beauty, whatever, inside that market, so these are the changes. And as Marzia said, the changes are coming mostly from the young generation, from the young girls. Like they have worked with some NGOs, with some organization, but they have learned that we can do better."

Jamila had seen that same effect from her own students. So "when I go to banks, when I go to NGOs, when I go to international organizations," she said, "in many of them I can find my students, that they were coming for basic classes, and they stand in very good positions today. They are women, mostly women [but also] male, and they are standing in front of me and saying, 'Teacher, how are you?.' . . . Then everybody is astonished. 'Yes, she is my teacher. She was my teacher.' . . . Even they are working in very good positions with very high salaries."

Sports participation was another improved area from the women's perspective. Marzia explained that female athletes "are traveling abroad, which is a common cultural issue that they didn't allow women to go and do [soccer] and these things, but now" they were also playing basketball and hockey. Jamila interrupted with more good news: "And they're bringing good prizes. . . . First-division prizes they are bringing." Although the athletes were not allowed to wear shorts, they were allowed to wear just "a small scarf, just a scarf or a hat. Just to cover the head, and then they are very good in international light." Marzia celebrated this success: "I love watching them because it is a cultural issue; people do not like the girls to go and do the physical exercise." In addition, a few gyms were popping up in Kabul, where "lots of the woman like me . . . lost their weight, and we encourage them to do the exercise," Marzia said.

Women's political participation had also increased. Indeed, twice as many women nominated themselves for the 2010 parliamentary election as did so in 2004. And many of them were "young, idealistic girls," including the winner of an *Afghan Star* competition on Tolo TV, which resembled the *American Idol* program in the United States. She was a singer, "and now she's running for Parliament." "Now you can see women are very modern, very fashionable, a lot of cosmetics; their pictures are all around," Marzia continued, with new enthusiasm in her voice. Is that what you really want to see? I asked. Marzia replied, "It means that they don't fear, you know?" They are not hiding themselves from public view. Marzia has seen their bold pictures—"big confidence, big posture"—on the BBC and on

American television. She was looking forward to the day when such courageous young women replaced the old men in Parliament who reside in "the dark age of women's development."

Doses of Reality

All of these advances sounded positive, and the women were clearly pleased about them. But it did not take long for them to admit that "women are discouraged a little, especially me, if I am talking about myself," as Marzia said. "Most of the promises [that] are given to the women of Afghanistan are not really [fulfilled] because women's issues are very political in Afghanistan, rather than to really work for the improvement of women's situation. Especially when you see that there are negotiations with the opposition, like if we are talking about the Taliban. This will cost a lot for the women's rights." Marzia felt particularly discouraged that the current government was already conceding to Taliban demands by excluding women from government positions.

It seemed too that "President Karzai sometimes plays a double role because he nominates [women] who are not really qualified, and he knows that they will not get parliamentary approval," Marzia said. He was not nominating leaders who would "take root." Jamila agreed, but she pointed out that Karzai was under pressure from different parties and tribal groups, who insisted that he nominate their picks regardless of their qualifications. "He's obliged to bring those people, to keep his position stronger maybe or to keep his allies allied to his benefit," she explained.

The Taliban just piled misery on top of such political maneuvering. They still constituted a huge obstacle to widespread improvement in education for Afghan women and girls. Taliban forces continued to oppose both education and paid employment for females of any age. As a result, at least sixty-four schools had closed in various parts of Afghanistan, including in areas within a few kilometers of Kabul, because "the Taliban threaten the girls not to go to the school, which is not good," Marzia said. Women were once again being forced to wear *burqas* "and cover their faces and . . . [they] have to work secretly. . . . At any minute, women on the way, women in the city, women walking, they are under the threat of security because of the different issues like maybe the insurgents' attack or some other problems. So the security is [a] main problem."

Schools that had survived were struggling for resources and equipment. Jamila talked about visiting a provincial school recently that was no more than a tent, whose floor had been ravaged by floods. So the children were sitting on oilcans, whose shape made them so unsteady on the muddy ground that the children wobbled from side to side as they perched on them. Some even fell off into the muck. "They have . . . interest in and love for education, but there are no resources for them. And they're trying to make something for them[selves]" by bringing whatever they can, like the oilcans, to support the school. "Even that can of oil was in a very bad shape, but still they were utilizing [it]. So this is very small example [of] how needy the community, the poor people of Afghanistan [are]." At the same time, however, "they are very sincere, . . . they are very hospitable, they are welcoming, they are appreciating. . . . Usually, they're not complaining." The women who run the schools are very good, Jamila says. "Lots of beauty is existing among them; lots of intelligence and courage exists inside Afghan women which needs to be empowered, which needs to flourish, which needs to become up. So this is the issue."

As this part of our conversation was winding down, Marzia confessed that she was wondering lately whether some of the women in rural areas might be happier than women like her and Jamila. "If you can see a woman with just having a few chickens, having a goat, they're very happy," Marzia continued. "Sometimes you can see even they're suffering, like for me this is a violence, but for them it is a normal life. . . . They don't complain . . . because they're not educated, they cannot recognize [the significance of the violence they endure]. They think, 'If I get a slap from my husband, it will hurt me; it will hurt me for a few hours, few days, months,' . . . For them it's a kind of normal thing. . . . While I am going in a village, you can see how they enjoy, they enjoy their children, they enjoy their horse, they enjoy their cows, they enjoy just their surroundings, they wear very good fashion clothes" when they dress up. "I'm happy that it's happening like this; otherwise, it would be very, very sorrowful for them."

I wondered whether Marzia's ruminations were a form of noblesse oblige or upper-class condescension. But then I caught the pain in Marzia's face and voice. Maybe, she conjectured, women like themselves, "who are working outside, suffering inside, trying too hard," are the unlucky ones. "We are a different people," Marzia said pensively, and of course that was true. But I also wondered if such wistful thoughts signaled true discouragement on Marzia's part.

International Interventions

Both women seemed quite worried about the fading interest of the international community in Afghan women, which they had predicted would happen after 2005. In 2010 they noted that few international organizations were placing women's rights at the top of their agendas. "Anytime I have gone abroad and have talked about [the] woman issue, this has been very interesting for the people abroad," Marzia explained. Not as interesting as it was in 2002, which "was really a harsh time. The situation [for Afghan women] has improved, I think, but then attention is also decreasing."

Interest from the U.S. government was difficult to read, Marzia explained. She had had high hopes, for example, when she met with Secretary of Homeland Security Janet Napolitano in August 2010 and raised the issue of women's rights with her. "If we have support from the government, then women's rights could be ensured," she explained to Napolitano. "Otherwise, as much as civil society shouts, and as much as we have progressed," women's improvement will not continue. Napolitano had apparently assured Marzia's group that she had discussed the matter with President Karzai and told him that the United States "is not interested in any negotiations with anyone even with the Taliban if the women's right will not be observed." But Marzia was not completely convinced. She wanted the United States to draw a line in the sand and say, "'If I am putting this money for you, this goes to military fund, this goes to this fund, this goes to this fund, this should go to women's rights fund.' And it should be transparent, and you should have the report, you know? We should see the progress; otherwise, 'we don't give you the fund'—that's easy." But that's not what she was hearing from Napolitano.

Adding to the difficulties of extracting such commitment was the fact that "now Karzai is much clever," according to Jamila. "Now he says, 'If you're going to give this money, you have to accept this condition. Otherwise, we don't want your money.' Yeah, he has become clever." She continued, "In the beginning, Karzai was very, very obedient boy, when you were saying anything he was, 'Yes, yes,' even without reading [what] he was signing. Now he has become clever and he is proposing ideas." Marzia suggested that one reason for his "becoming clever" was the growing competition between international donors. For example, Russia might say that they want to support Afghanistan, so "'if you don't receive support from other countries, we will support you.' This is another challenge that [the] international community is facing." There were several superpowers Karzai could rely on.

Still, Jamila insisted, the full blame for the lack of progress on women's rights could not be visited on the Afghan government alone. "The international community has also [been] a little bit quiet on the issue of women. Like the enthusiasm, the hotness that people had [in 2002] regarding women, like going to international community's meetings, you can see like, they have become like, 'Yeah, this is [an] Afghan issue. They need a solution. [If] we cannot involve [the] Taliban, there won't be peace.' . . . Now they're trying to change their verbal saying, whatever they had before. They are not that much strong and committed as . . . they were in 2002 and 2003."

In Marzia's view, one of the worst aspects of international attitudes toward Afghanistan was the prevailing neglect of the rule of law, without which there could be no rights for women. At a recent rule-of-law international conference Marzia had attended, many delegates argued that Afghanistan should abandon the idea of a national legal system because it is a traditional country in which 85 percent of cases go to local *shuras*. "Keep it that way," one man said. Marzia became irate at this reversal of cause and effect. "I was shouting, 'It is opposite of human and woman's right and children's right.' He said, 'No, because you have no option.'" In his mind, what already was must always be, right or wrong, when it came to women and tradition. Jamila reinforced Marzia's analysis when she noted that abstract questions of rights and justice always gave way to local prejudices and practices that "benefit a specific person or a specific group. . . . If we don't have rule of law, then it will be very difficult for women to exist," she concluded.

Jamila went on to give an example of the injustices women experience under current, localized legal practices. A few years ago, she had helped the woman who looks after her children seek a divorce on the grounds that her husband was abusive to her and her infant daughter. "So she complained to me [that] her mother was saying, 'No, this is bad, this is shame, you have to stay.' But I could help her in showing the ways that she could seek her divorce from her husband because if a person is that much [of a] bad person—he's druggie, all the time beating her, it is almost one year of their marriage, but all the time she is beaten by that person." So the woman tried to take her case to court, only to be confronted by her husband's lawyer, who told her she had to accept whatever her husband said or she would be sent to jail.

Jamila was shocked to hear what the husband's attorney said because she knew the lawyer was part of a social justice legal organization that rented a room in the building where she had her office. "I have heard many times from them that they are working for women's rights against violence against women. But the [lawyer], who's also a woman . . . has received money from the groom, or from the husband," and changed her tune. So Jamila confronted her: "'Look at your organization, your position. You're a woman. She is facing this many problems. Why are you imposing [this] on her?' And it was interesting what she told me, 'Look, this is Afghan culture. If she's getting divorced, who will be able to marry her again, and what will be her future after divorce? She will be in a very bad condition.' And it is like, whatever I want to say out of this story, it is that Afghanistan is [a] very culture-based community. And culture rules in every sphere of our life. . . . There are very few people that still have the commitment to [their principles]."

By failing to support the rule of law in Afghanistan, internationals were perpetuating such distorted views of women's legal rights status. Marzia considered internationals who accepted Afghanistan as a hopelessly traditional society to be enablers of not only a distorted legal system but also a distorted legal education system that teaches men and women separate versions of Sharia law and excludes women from learning certain things about Afghan civil law. They are also enablers of many local judges who do not document their decisions, which they make "on the bridges, in the villages, and then they're all uneducated." Internationals have failed to "bring judges more education [or] better, fair justice to the people." For that, "they won't give a million."

The United States has said it does not want to be that kind of partner, but Jamila thought that the American government had delivered more verbal than material support for women's rights. "Overall, I can see there is a gap between what they are saying and what they are practicing. So you know that this is a political game. Mostly, psychologically they are trying to influence the mentality, but practically they are doing what is in their own benefit. Personally, I was very hopeful that [then secretary of state] Hillary Clinton, as a woman, I was very hopeful by her coming to this important position that the life of Afghan women will be improved and there will be much, much more focus on the issue of Afghan women . . . but unfortunately, it was not up to our expectations. Verbal is not enough; . . . some concrete action is needed."

Even worse, the United States and other donor nations had recently taken to allocating 50 percent of their grants to governmental institutions and 50 percent to organizations of civil society and local and international NGOs. But "in this fifty-and-fifty [deal], . . . there was no single word about what will be the allocation of funds for women," Jamila explained. U.S. money went to various projects, "but when it comes to the issue of women . . . it's like very, very little amount, it does not cross $50,000 per year or per project, maybe project of six months or one year. . . . They are naming that project 'women['s] empowerment,' but empowerment is not going to be done in [a] short time and with less amount of money." In 2010 ten or twelve international organizations had offices inside the Ministry of Women's Affairs, "but we cannot see much improvement" in the work of that ministry, Jamila reported. Despite all international efforts, "[the women's ministry] could develop not one national strategic plan of action for women."

With weak international insistence on women's rights, the Afghan government had also weakened its commitment. Without gender units in all government ministries, what passed for a gender specialist in 2010 was someone who distributed flowers on March 8, the International Women's Day holiday. If you asked, "What is gender budgeting in each ministry, [what] the gender unit should do, unfortunately they do not understand . . . what that means. And women's positions in the ministry are [low], and they have limited accesses" to resources or to meaningful projects, Jamila explained. And across the country, "every thirty minutes one mother is dying. Every single minute . . . hundreds of women are beaten by their husbands, by their brothers. Every single minute in Afghanistan women are not allowed to go outside the house to go to a doctor or to visit mosque or whatever, to participate in social life, every single minute."

As a graphic example of what she meant, Jamila told about a ten-year-old girl in a rural province who looked like a "woman of forty or sixty years old. . . . She has become a wife, and she is wife of a person who has two, three other wives, and those wives are elder in age and condition, and how much violence they are doing on this poor child because she [does] not understand what to do or how to be. She is looking after the children of that old man; she's bringing water, she's cooking, she's cleaning, she's just like a servant. She's not able to go to school. . . . She's sexually abused by her husband; she's beaten by stepsons and daughters of the family." And she was not the only one.

These are situations that the international community has witnessed, but "nobody's talking on that, only they are happy to give grant for some women's local organization, just a few thousand, just give literacy classes for a few persons, just awareness this and that, then at the end there is nothing." What Afghanistan needed was "crucial and concrete planning in order to bring change in the life of Afghan women, to bring improvement in the life of Afghan women." Instead of acquiescing to the tradition of using Afghan women as political tools, international donors should hold the government accountable for the conditions women suffer and demand change. Nations should collaborate on that demand so that the government cannot play one donor against another.

Marzia pointed out that the international community did at one time support the establishment of a juvenile court, which had become very successful. However, the stop-gap programming of internationals had had the unintended consequence of increasing the number of cases brought before the court. With only partial knowledge that they have some rights, and without much enforcement of those rights at the local or national level, more and more girls were running away from home and "seeking support from the Ministry of Women's Affairs and other legal organizations. For example, the number of cases that we register in the organization that I am working in is increasing double size from 2008. It means . . . that the people know about protection systems somehow. However, it's weak." By the same token, "the number of suicides that the women burn themselves is also increasing, and this is another thing that the women challenge; at least they challenge life, and they want to express themselves by an action, which is wrong, and it is not good action, but at least they want to raise up this issue to the attention of their society and their community. But . . . I think [the] application of the laws in Afghanistan [has] a long way to go."

The international community had also supported the minister of women's affairs in her effort to enlist the help of religious leaders in stopping child marriage. A meeting of 320 mullahs was called in 2007, under the auspices of an international health initiative, in which donors argued that child marriage was a health concern. But the project had come to an abrupt end when one of the mullahs stood up and asked, "'Why [are] you internationals bringing all these issues to us? Why you are saying that, [when] the prophet Muhammad enforced marriage [with his wife Aisha] at the age of seven.' So this was a big argument that suddenly rose up," and the internationals capitulated to that false claim rather than confront it. "Once a big sentence comes from a religious leader," Marzia said, "you see how effective it will be rather than the other argument to that," which would include a different interpretation of the Prophet's marriage to Aisha.

With such tepid international support for women's agency or basic bodily rights, one religious leader felt emboldened to tell women at a "a big . . . international conference," held at the Ministry of Foreign Affairs, that "they should enjoy their husbands; they should make fashion. Why work, why [get an] education? Give them money to buy clothes and use lipsticks." Marzia reported that "the people from Malaysia, from many other countries" at the conference, argued with him, but "in a country like Afghanistan, his word will be very well praised."

Marzia's and Jamila's withering account of international efforts on behalf of Afghan women pointed to two destructive perspectives that donors tended to have. One was a pitiful lack of knowledge about the history of women's rights in Afghanistan or in Islam. That ignorance and its accompanying short-term focus led both governmental and nongovernmental organizations to work for change only in immediate, concrete, and material conditions, such as school buildings and health clinics, without tackling subtler cultural challenges.

The second destructive perspective followed from the first. That is, many international change agents and donors believed that cultural challenges are necessarily a matter of religion and, therefore, off-limits to outsiders. But donors' ignorance of the relationship between Islam and local customs empowered local leaders to the detriment of women.

Marzia and Jamila decried both perspectives. Although they remained deeply loyal to their country's history and cultural life, they had a healthy skepticism of allegedly sacrosanct traditional practices and a clear understanding of the distinction between such practices and Islamic precepts. They were also both steeped in their country's history, especially the ever-changing history of women's roles and status. That donor governments and organizations presumed to prescribe social change without the least understanding of the relevant background for their proposed projects was additional evidence to me of Western arrogance.

The two women's final critique of international organizations and donors provided an ironic finish to our conversation. They recognized that international programs actually perpetrated injustice for women by focusing exclusively on women and not educating boys and men about women's rights and human worth. If Afghan males are not asked to question their treatment of and attitudes toward women in light of Islamic history and law, the women said, then changes in that treatment are unlikely. For that reason, both women were including men and boys in their own work, as we shall see in chapter 5.

Reflections

I was not surprised by Marzia's and Jamila's mixed assessment of changes for Afghan women by 2010. In many ways, that was an unfortunate extension of their perspective from five years earlier. Nor was I surprised by their focus on their own urban worlds and work with international donors or organizations. But I was surprised when they said that they had not seen each other much since the Ohio State conference in 2005. Although their activities brought them into the international swirl of projects and foreign operatives, their interests and the demands of their careers actually kept them in different arenas. Among other things, that separation in their activities meant that they had not traded notes about any of their comments or opinions. I truly was getting separate perspectives from them, which made their broad agreement on many issues even more powerful.

Chapter 4: The Basics of Change

I was also beginning to understand the basic premises of the women's cultural critique. When they were pessimistic, I caught a glimpse of their concern that there was an intransigent underlying force that systematically keeps Afghan women out of power positions and denies them agency. Every advance was therefore beset by multiple forced retreats and hazards: "Oh, so you want to go to school? There's a new building for you, but you might get a face full of acid on the way to class." They sometimes feared that nothing—not even the Qur'an—could overcome that force. Indeed, they saw how frequently Islam was hijacked by Afghan men's interpretations of their own entitlements in the face of women's alleged inferiority. I wondered whether such power plays increased to the extent that men felt robbed by forces beyond their control of their own sense of power, dignity, and honor. In the current terrain, perhaps such feelings made many men think that programs for women were a zero-sum game for them: if women "win," then men must somehow be "losing." I was reminded again that the Taliban's views represented an extreme manifestation of that gender paranoia.

When the women were optimistic, I thought that they were seeing the ups and downs of developments for women as signs of gradual and incremental change. "What can you expect," they seemed to say, "when women have so long been used as political footballs?" It will take a long time to overcome the forces that make men suspicious of women and feel threatened by the elevation of women beyond their traditional status. Even many women have been socialized to hold disparaging views of themselves. Let us take heart from small changes.

The concepts of reason and justice seemed the two consistent standards the women applied in judging Afghan culture (a term they repeatedly used). If a practice, such as denying women education in a country that needs an educated populace to survive, did not make sense to a reasonable person, then that practice should not be preserved in the name of tradition. Just because a tradition concerned women did not make it immutable. By the same token, if something was patently unjust, such as incarcerating marriage-resistant girls who were within their Islamic and civil rights to refuse a forced marriage, then it too should go. A corollary to that second standard was knowledge of the true Islam. Both Afghans and foreigners must educate themselves to know the difference between religious doctrine and unacceptable instances of male dominance.

* * *

In chapter 5, the discussion becomes more personal, as it explores Jamila's and Marzia's continued professional efforts to advance Afghan women's rights and opportunities from 2005 to 2010. Those efforts also had their ups and downs. As that part of the story unfolded, we were all a little surprised that the women's different spheres overlapped in particular causes they had both embraced unbeknownst to the other—sexual harassment and Islamic education.

5

The Political Is Personal

As our conversations in Istanbul turned to Marzia's and Jamila's own professional lives, it was obvious that the same complexities and contradictions that characterized the process of change in Afghanistan over the previous five years in general had also characterized their individual work experiences. Welcome progress in their professional fortunes inevitably accompanied disappointments and reversals, more so than they apparently foresaw in 2005.

Jamila

As Jamila began to describe her recent work activities in 2010, she projected optimism. She reported proudly that the Noor Educational Center had become the Noor Educational and Capacity Development Organization (NECDO) and was active in six provinces, twice as many as in 2005. She and her advisory board had realized a few years before that they were actually doing more than provide education in the traditional sense. They were also engaged in capacity-building activities, advocacy training, and networking. "I wanted *human rights* in the title," Jamila said, but the board pointed out that the Afghan government does not listen to Afghans about human rights, so such an addition would be futile or possibly counterproductive. Even without that change, she was happy with her organization's new official profile.

Jamila told many stories about women whom NECDO had helped with skill development in a variety of fields, from fashion design to computer technology. People in the provinces were still coming to NECDO centers to get help with family problem solving, economic projects, and questions about rights and opportunities. Jamila was also happy to report that she had developed the organization's capacity to survive if she should move on or be removed. This precaution had put into practice the principle she wished other NGOs would adhere to—long-term thinking and staff development. At the same time, her planning was a bit ominous, because it revealed Jamila's recognition that her time in the public eye might be limited.

Jamila's other new "direct" activity—her term for her official roles—involved the Afghan Women's Islamic Network (AWIN), an NGO that she had established after 2005 and continued to lead. The purpose of the network was to get women who had Islamic educations to pool their knowledge with other similarly educated women in order to increase their own understanding of Islam and to support one another in teaching about their religion, minus the male bias. She hoped the network would bring female Islamic scholars out of the shadows. "I know many women; they're educated, but they're silent—they're hiding their face," mostly because they worry about defying male clerics.

AWIN had an international board of directors, including one of the women who was invited to the OSU conference but did not attend—Sajia Begham—as well as people from Canada and a few European countries.[1] With such a board, Jamila hoped to expand the network's activities outside of Afghanistan. She believed that female Islamic scholars were having more success in Pakistan and Iran than in Afghanistan, where they continued to "suffer under the shadow of the custom and culture which exist in Afghanistan."

Jamila was also engaged in extensive "indirect" or unofficial activities in 2010. She worked as a consultant on Islam, gender, and human rights behind the scenes in many Afghan organizations. She also worked with international organizations that had gender or human rights units but did not bring an Islamic perspective to those units. One of her clients was the Swedish Committee for Afghanistan (SCA), for whose international staff she had provided training in Islamic perspectives suitable for Afghanistan.[2] Jamila discussed her future plans to conduct a group training for gender and human rights advisers of thirteen other organizations, which for security reasons would have to be held in an embassy or in the organization's headquarters rather than in NECDO facilities.

As if all of this were not enough, Jamila's "indirect work" in 2010 also included her role as an elected member of the Afghan NGO Humanitarian Country Team (HCT), which decided on the distribution of government funds and donations in emergency situations. Jamila was the only Afghan member of the team; the rest were internationals. She had earned that honor by having the highest score among Afghans nominated to the position, based on a survey of national and international organizations. In her work with the HCT, Jamila helped to direct emergency funds to women, who typically suffer most in conflicts and natural disasters. For example, in the 2010 floods in Afghanistan, the HCT focused on getting clean water, shelter, and medical help to the ruined areas and decided how much money to spend, but Jamila had to persuade the group to pay attention to women's needs. She was pleased that the HCT respected her opinion and often took her advice.

Despite her well-deserved pride in this list of activities and accomplishments, Jamila was well aware of the difficulties that still stood in her way. For example, she had applied to be a lecturer at Kabul University a few years earlier, based on her master's degree from Pakistan, so that she could offer courses for women in management, finance, gender studies, and sexual harassment, as well as in computer science and fashion design. But that plan had foundered because of resistance from the university, possibly because of her well-known activism against sexual harassment. So, Jamila established her own Afghan Women's Professional Education Institute, which she officially registered with the Ministry of Education. She and others from NECDO taught professional development and sexual harassment courses through the institute.

Marzia

Marzia's account of the changes in her work life continued this darker perspective on change. She reported that she had resigned from her job with UNIFEM because it had become too policy oriented and involved more paperwork than action. Instead, she was working as a legal consultant on Afghan projects with the German Society for Technical Cooperation, or Deutsche Gesellschaft für Technische Zusammenarbeit, known as GTZ or GIZ. Most depressing for Marzia had been the demise of her beloved Afghan Women Judges Association, which disbanded in 2007 because the Supreme Court withdrew its recognition of the organization. Without much explanation, the Court suddenly forbade women judges to join the AWJA shortly after Marzia presented a proposal to support the travel of four Afghan women judges to the United States to attend judiciary courses in Washington, D.C., and Vermont, just as she had once done. Even though Marzia argued that the Court's action against the AWJA violated the constitution, she did not prevail, and the organization had to suspend its activities.

Marzia's mood lightened a bit when she explained that in 2008 she had started and for a time had directed another legal organization, the Afghanistan Progressive Law Organization, to fight injustices outside the purview of the Supreme Court. She had obtained support for APLO primarily from the GTZ. "It's a kind of legal aid, legal awareness for the women, all for women and all legal issues," she said. By 2010 she had become a part-time adviser and consultant for APLO. Marzia was also happy to report that she was an active volunteer for the recently established Afghan Bar Association's women's committee. But as she described these activities, it was clear she was stung by the loss of the Supreme Court's recognition of her work, not only on her own behalf and on behalf of women judges but also as a sign that a highly politicized judiciary was still the norm in Afghanistan.

Like Jamila, Marzia reported extensive "indirect" or informal activities. For example, she was serving on the board of directors of an Afghan bank involved in microfinance for women's projects. She also did occasional projects for the Ministry of Justice. One year she had even worked as a consultant on gender issues for the police department's women's unit. Such work reinforced her devotion to the rule of law and to legal issues despite the setbacks that she and law enforcement had experienced. "I am not in the justice sector formally anymore," she reported, "but the support that I am doing here and there, all mostly focusing for the Afghan women and professional development, like different lawyers, men and women, how could be developed and how could be skilled more. But all my work is for women, law and women."

Linked Themes: Sexual Harassment and Islamic Education

Although Marzia and Jamila had never worked together, our conversations revealed that they had both prioritized the same two issues, which they were pursuing from their separate perspectives. The first was the scourge of sexual harassment, to which Afghan women were (and continue to be) subject in all public settings but especially in "institutions of education." "We [at NECDO] consider that sexual harassment is one of the prominent elements that . . . deprives women [from] going to higher education," Jamila said, and Marzia agreed. That is true in part because victims are more likely to be blamed and more harshly punished, particularly by their families, than are perpetrators. The women's second priority was Islamic education. Both Marzia and Jamila believed that they could do nothing more important for Afghan women (and men) than train them in the Qur'an's perspectives on the treatment of women and in their rights under Islam and Sharia law.

Sexual Harassment

Marzia focused on addressing the issue of sexual harassment through "women and the law." She based her conviction that sexual harassment can be addressed through the law on several factors. First, Afghan society accepts that people accused of crimes should be prosecuted and, if convicted, punished. Second, sexual harassment has been identified as a crime through notes (but not a specific law) in the Afghan criminal code. Third, Afghanistan is a signatory to international conventions, such as the Convention on the Elimination of All Forms of Discrimination against Women, that identify sexual harassment as a punishable offense. (The United States has not yet ratified CEDAW.)[3] Still, Marzia reported, "it's a difficult job," because there is so much resistance by men who have power over women in the public sphere.

What Afghanistan needs, according to Marzia, is a "special law on sexual harassment" that will criminalize harassing behaviors. The current articles in the criminal code are not satisfactory. "In that time [when the articles were written] women were not working a lot" or going to school. But that has changed. The issue was especially difficult in higher education, because "it is very easy to abuse the girls" by promising a grade for sexual favors. Similar nefarious negotiations were also increasingly prevalent in government agencies, where many more women were working.

In teaching about the legal issues related to harassment through the Afghan Women's Network, Marzia had encountered several students who reported incidents of sexual harassment. Just before our Istanbul meeting, one of her students, who also attended law school, stood up and said, "Yes, I was facing that, and I dare to speak about it." Another student said that she had gotten "strong resistance" from her colleagues when she tried to teach about sexual harassment in a local university. She was accused of blaming people without evidence. And, of course, documentation is hard to produce in these circumstances.

Marzia had also worked with the Ministry of the Interior and other agencies to raise awareness of sexual harassment as a crime. She was hoping that the media could help Afghan women formulate the issue, understand the conditions that violate the rules, and learn how to construct a sound case so their complaints could be acted upon. But many obstacles remained, Marzia explained. "First, they should have the courage to talk out; otherwise, will they be ready to go in front of the court, because a courtroom needs proof? Will she be able [to provide it], in this society?" Women rightly perceive that "the system is not very supportive" and wonder in court, "'Why I should talk if you don't help me?'" Despite those obstacles, Marzia thought, "We need to start something, to begin with something," some legal mechanism to build support. "Nothing is difficult if we have a good plan and a good intention and good coworkers are together," Marzia said, with hope in her voice.

Jamila worked on the issue of sexual harassment as an educational challenge, primarily through teaching courses in her Afghan Women's Professional Education Institute. In addition, she had formed a network of advocates, loosely composed of individuals from NGOs and civil society and a few government and human rights commission workers, to fight sexual harassment cases, especially in the educational institutions of Afghanistan. Jamila pointed out, however, that sexual harassment also affected women riding buses, walking on the streets, and fulfilling their jobs in every sector of society, and advocacy for them was a much more difficult matter.

Jamila had also encountered stiff resistance to her work on sexual harassment. For one thing, she inferred from her rejection as an instructor at Kabul University that officials there were unwilling to instruct women in a problem that was so rampant among the KU faculty. Her attempt to get support for sexual harassment education at Kabul University from the Afghan human rights commission had also met resistance. Even though the commission was charged with examining cases of sexual harassment, its members were unwilling to confront the prestigious KU faculty. Instead, they just accused Jamila of "making a bomb," an intriguing metaphor under the circumstances, to which she replied, "For God's sake, why would I prefer to make a bomb? It is you who are afraid of this issue. If we are not dealing with it, who will do it?" But they did not budge.

Through NECDO, Jamila had done studies about the prevalence of sexual harassment in different social sectors, and she was working on a code of conduct to outline inappropriate behaviors, which she hoped to present to Parliament. "That code of conduct will be for all educational institutions, local and private, for teachers and for students, that how they should have the moral behavior, and if they're going to do any sort of discrimination how law will respond to that." Jamila thought that legalizing such a code should be a first step in addressing the widespread problem. Marzia thought, however, that Afghanistan needed a law first, and then a code of conduct.

The saddest part of the sexual harassment issue, according to both Marzia and Jamila, was the resulting retribution against women who brought complaints. Warlords would avenge women who revealed sexual offenses as well as their families, an outcome that understandably made people distrust the legal system. Even worse, Jamila revealed, "Families will kill their daughters to keep them from going to work or school," if they believe that sexual offenses are going on there.

Islamic Education

Both Marzia and Jamila had devoted much energy to promoting "true" Islamic education in Afghanistan. Marzia had spent years instructing women about their rights under Sharia law. Such education was necessary because "the first problem in Afghanistan is that we don't have Islamic scholars [who] understand the real meaning of [the] Holy Qur'an and interpret it as it is in the Holy Qur'an. Even if you talk to very high-level scholars [around the world] . . . they have different understanding of Islam. . . . If you go to Egypt, they are practicing something else, and if you go to Lebanon, you'll see the Muslims are practicing something else. However, Islam, I mean, is the same. Qur'an is the same for all Muslims, but interpretation is quite different." For example, the Taliban enforced the wearing of *burqas* as if that kind of covering were one of the Prophet's dictates, but the *burqa* is only one hundred years old, according to Marzia. She said it was first adopted to hide the identities of an emperor's concubines, many of whom were married women.[4] It is not mandated by the Qur'an.

Jamila had also spent years educating women about the Qur'an and worked to enhance women's power to understand and interpret Islam, particularly through her Afghan Women's Islamic Network. She believed firmly that Islam could do much to solve Afghanistan's problems, especially women's problems. In 2010 she explained that she wanted to extend the inspiration and comfort that she receives from understanding the "true" Islam to as many others as possible, just as she did for her family members years ago. "It doesn't seem to me it is the history of fourteen centuries back, but I feel that it is [a] very new revealed [truth] which is suitable for our problems," she said. She hoped that international donors and NGOs would pay attention to accurate interpretations of the Qur'an as they confronted Afghanistan's problems, so they, too, could understand that Islamic teachings can be used to empower women and to promote women's rights and their share in a better life. Jamila had recently been involved in projects that instructed powerful Afghan men about women's rights and the Qur'an.

Jamila understood why non-Afghans once resisted making Islam central to Afghan reconstruction, especially after the Taliban's false and dangerous interpretation of the religion. "Like the international community only could see the outward appearance and those who were wearing turban, who grow beard, and wearing white *shalwar kameez*. They were saying, 'Oh, just be aside from them.'" Indeed, some internationals once ignored Jamila herself because of her religious appearance. But more recently, "after eight or nine years of hard work," most internationals have recognized that their programs to fight drugs, to promote good health or education, and even to provide security must incorporate a culturally sensitive but accurate Islamic perspective. Ignoring imams and other religious leaders in designing such programs had bred distrust among Afghans, who typically turned to imams in every crisis.

The world needed to understand, Jamila said, that 90 percent of the Afghan population supports the role of Islamic philosophy in civil society. The problem, of course, was disseminating Islam's true philosophy in the face of poorly educated mullahs and rural patriarchs and the wide substitution of cultural tradition for the real words and intent of the Prophet. "Whatever comes by the name of Islam is accepted by the community, because basically people do not have real knowledge of Islam." And as she learned from her own brother, any resistance to what the imam or forefathers say can be branded un-Muslim.

Among other falsehoods that have distorted the true Islam in Afghanistan is the Taliban's prohibition against music, which both women found especially vexing. Nothing could be further from the Prophet's intent, Jamila explained. Indeed, "music is an expression of people's relationship to God." She and Marzia had attended a celebration of the end of Ramadan in Istanbul the previous night, and Jamila was reminded of the power of music as religious expression: "It was so beautiful, and it was touching heart." I recalled Marzia's comments in 2005 that a good song she heard at six in the morning could make her happy all day.

During our discussions, Jamila eagerly described two Islamic education projects she had conducted that suggested to her real possibilities for change. One project involved the training of imams, and the other involved the training of journalists. Jamila had targeted imams because they are more learned than mullahs, who get only madrassa educations, and "they are not having the knowledge of current affairs or the real new changes in the world community about the women's movement." She also thought NGOs had overlooked imams as allies in the struggle for women's rights. When you talk to NGOs about imams, Jamila said, "they will look towards you with bad eyes" and get suspicious about your motives.

On her own, then, Jamila had approached the minister of religious affairs and the American Society for Muslim Advancement (ASMA) and gotten their support to develop a training program for imams on women's basic rights from an Islamic perspective.[5] Those rights include a woman's absolute right to refuse a proposal of marriage and to receive a marriage portion (*mahr*) to cement the husband's investment in the marriage and to ensure that she has some economic independence, especially in case of divorce. Islam also gives a woman the right to negotiate her role in obtaining a divorce as part of the marriage agreement (women do not otherwise have a right to initiate divorce), to pursue an education, and to participate in society and in politics.

With advice from ASMA, Jamila had written a handbook presenting a modern interpretation of Islam "suitable for the environment of Afghanistan and acceptable for the community and imams." "After many meetings," Jamila had persuaded one hundred imams—initially from two provinces (Kabul and Jalalabad) and then from more than fifteen—to attend training sessions about women's rights in Islam at the NECDO center in Kabul. After the training was completed, she had exacted pledges from all one hundred to preach about women's rights in Friday prayers and to distribute her handbooks to worshippers. Then she had hired one hundred Kabul University students from different provinces, trained them in women's rights in Islam, and paid them (with "a pot of money" she raised) to "go to the mosque and sit in the mosque and listen to . . . what the imams are saying [and] . . . monitor the imams' prayers." They were charged with reporting their findings back to her.

> When they were coming with their reports and we were finding out where are the gifts, where are the positive points, [which] we were sharing with other imams in other meetings. And the next meeting, we were telling them that you should also follow these steps and . . . we were saying that these [other things] are shortcomings. The imams were surprised [about] who is there that [is] keeping record of every single word of us. Then we told them that we have these monitors that they are coming every week in Friday prayers. So it was very wonderful that we . . . utilized the energy of hundred youths in Kabul city with hundred imams. And hundred mosques were talking about women's rights.

One story Jamila heard from the monitors made her weep:

> It was the story of an old man. [The monitor] says when the speeches of imams were finished and all the *namaz* [prayers] [were done, and all worshippers] had gone out of the mosque, an old man was crying in the corner of the mosque, and he was not going out. So this monitor was observing why this man is not going out and why he is crying. Then this man came to the imam, [held] his shoulder, and shook the imam. He said, "Why you didn't tell us all this before? Because all these things that now you are saying are a sin I have committed with my daughters. I have sold my daughters. I have given unequal treatment to my daughters. I never asked their consent on their marriages. I put obstacles

in their way to not get education. If all of these are sin, why you didn't mention it before? Now I am an old man. How I can become saved?"

Of course, this man was not alone in his sin. Jamila explained:

> In Afghanistan, men are selling their daughters and sisters according to their own choice. Like if they're two, three families asking for the hand of a daughter, the father will ask, "How much you will pay?" The first family may say, "I will pay $50,000." The second family, "How much you will pay?" They will say, "I will pay $100,000." The other family, "How much you will pay?" They will say, "I will pay $150,000." So the father will decide according to the highest level of the money, without knowing if this family is good or bad, their daughter is happy or not. Like this decision of money is taken by father or brother or anybody, and girls are totally disconnected with the decision or with the money, and the money is going in the pocket of the father or the brother. Which is totally against Islamic mentality and teachings. Because Islam says that that money is for women [and she can utilize it in any way she likes].[6]

Jamila was also proud of another, more concrete, benefit from her training program for imams. There were twenty-five women's wings in the monitored mosques in 2010, whereas before there were only four or five mosques—and only in Kabul—where women could worship. She wanted next to train female social workers for the women's wings. She hoped that those social workers would "provide training for women who might be coming to the mosque on every Friday [and] also [increase] the awareness about their human rights, about gender equality and other issues. These women social workers will work as a connection between women and imams. If they have any question or any issue, then they will exchange the information. Because mostly all women cannot go to the men's side."

Jamila was delighted to

> hear by my own ear that women were saying, "Look at how many rights we have. We didn't know anything. We are just like animals. We didn't know anything about that...." So this is the way that we are working on [the] grassroots level to bring changes from an Islamic perspective in the community. As I said before, the problem is not lying with Islam; the problem is with our cultural custom that those tribal leader warlords, community leaders, for their own benefits interpreting the Islamic values according to their own choice. As the people are uneducated, they are accepting without understanding, and following it generation by generation.

Jamila also discussed her training courses for media employees, which she called "Gender and Journalism." At first people did not know what she was talking about when she used the word *gender*, but she explained that gender is a property of Islam as well as of every person. She explained that the Prophet did not say a man is superior to a woman. Only men who provide income to their family have superiority. If a woman brings in the income, then she is superior. "Capacity, morality, and leadership brought into the family are the ways one earns superiority." Of course, men were stunned by such information. One man confessed that he had spent his life believing that he was better than his mother. After the class, he realized he was wrong. Another said he had spent his marriage believing that his wife owed him everything. Now he realized he was asking his wife to do something superhuman.

Jamila further taught that the Prophet never said that the sexes should be separated in every aspect of life. After all, in the Hajj men and women are together. It is just a man's selfishness that makes him want a woman only for himself and cut off from everyone else, she said. This exclusivity gives prestige to the man. Some women go along with this idea by covering their faces even at home. Jamila wondered why a woman, like her own cousin, would take pride in covering her face even in front of her mother-in-law.

As Marzia developed her courses about Sharia law, she too was mindful of the widespread illiteracy in Afghanistan, both in general and with regard to Islamic law. "Most of the people do not know and do not have time [or ability] to research the laws and find out what is right and what is wrong" according to Islam, she said. Even mullahs frequently know nothing about what the holy texts say, despite their ability to recite them. Compounding this problem is the protection that mullahs get for *not* knowing what the texts say. Indeed, Marzia said, "these mullahs get more protection . . . than mullahs who are wise," because their views support patriarchal custom. What Afghanistan needs is "a system that protects women's rights and regards Islam in an academic way. We need a lot of scholars to really be trained and find out different issues about Islam and women. They should preach this all over Afghanistan, according to real interpretation." This does not happen "because of all those extremists in Afghanistan. Like if you go and argue women's rights to the Taliban, they say, 'No, you don't have any right to go to education; you don't have any right to go to work.' So how you can satisfy these people, you know?" They even interpret recent executions of girls and women in Afghanistan as properly Islamic.

Marzia found especially creepy the fact that the Taliban's influence was growing day by day. Radio programming provided one barometer of their advance: "While you are tuning radios at night," Marzia said, "all the songs [they] were playing during the Taliban you can hear it again on radios." These are "a kind of song without music," in which "the same speakers . . . who were in mujahideen period and who were in Taliban period, then they were talking on radio and TV, they are still" talking. "You can see that the situation is getting worse and worse, and they . . . are asking to achieve [the] rule of law in Afghanistan" by returning the Taliban to power, as if they were the only source of true security and order.

Of course, by "rule of law," Marzia meant something quite different from the brutal force of the Taliban. She saw Sharia as a legal system that "protects women's rights." Sharia law complements the Afghan Constitution, which "says that we have to apply the statutory laws, and if there is no statutory law, then we have to apply Sharia law. It's clear, so this is also our obligation regarding women and human rights, the treaties that we have done." Prioritizing Sharia law distorts questions of justice: "While the government cannot provide jobs for the people, . . . if they steal something should we cut [off] their hands? If we apply the Sharia law, can we cut [off] their hand while the government failed to protect them? There are reasons behind being a criminal," and the administration of law in Afghanistan must take that big picture into account. "How could we apply the pure Islam in Afghanistan right now?"

A recent case provided Marzia with a good example of the way Sharia law was being misused in the fractured Afghan justice system. The case involved a young couple who had run away together. They were lured back to their village with promises from their families that they could marry, which Sharia law would support. But the woman was stoned to death when they returned. "The man was released by money," according to Marzia. The whole village, including the couple's families, decided on their fates and carried out their plan without any inquiry or investigation. "Did we do a good justice?" Marzia asked, implying that the answer was a resounding no.

But Marzia was also discouraged about prospects for relying on civil law in Afghanistan. Because "justice is a question in Afghanistan now, the judiciary is a question," she explained. Even in court cases, few attorneys or prosecutors conduct investigations or call witnesses. Moreover, "You cannot really see the system work if the judge is corrupt; . . . how can we be sure he is making a good judgment?"

Perhaps more discouraging was the blind spot that even educated people seemed to develop about women's rights. For example, Marzia's relatives had trouble recognizing that women have rights under Sharia law. "When I'm arguing women's rights with [them] it's not acceptable. . . . Sometimes it's not acceptable because [they say], 'No, mullah says this, and Sharia says that.'" She shrugged. Imagine how much worse it would be to "talk to an ignorant man who has just seen war all the time with a gun. How could you argue with him?"

Marzia complicated Jamila's hopeful story about gender training for imams by reporting that "even these mullahs [or imams] who are interpreting Islam in a good way, they are facing obstacles. If you see sometimes the leader of some religious [site] they are killed . . . by [the] Taliban . . . because they go to the mosque and they somehow talk about rights." And if women's rights are mentioned, the mullah is accused of being a spy for the government. "This is the reason that the Afghan government is very careful, especially President Karzai, because it is a political issue. . . . Islam now is mixed in Afghanistan with political choices. Karzai is not really willing to bring changes to women's rights because he thinks that if we bring this to reform, then he will not get support from the religious leaders."

Marzia had also been personally challenged for speaking up about women's rights. She had recently attended a peace *jirga* in Afghanistan where she was told to sit down while men were present. She was standing up to volunteer for a committee leadership position, and "just suddenly a mullah rose up, and he said, 'No, while we [men] are here, you sit down.'" Marzia was shocked "because people are respecting [me] very much." When she protested, "Look, [women and men] have the same rights; we have to observe the constitution of Afghanistan," he said, "'No, we are the majority, and we are those who have to be at the head of the committees . . . because you're a woman, sit down.' . . . So you can see that if we are talking in very top level of decision making, if you cannot express yourself there, then how we can express ourselves on the lower levels? Because we don't have political will for women's rights to be supported."

Regardless of these obstacles, Marzia was dedicated to instructing women about their legal rights through several organizations she was affiliated with in Afghanistan. Such instruction was especially important, she said, because of the wide variety of interpretations women are hearing from their local mullahs, *shuras,* and families. One religious leader will say a woman has the right to education, but another will say that women do not have that right. Because of security issues and lack of facilities for women at mosques, few women can travel to hear different interpretations of Islam. That is why Marzia believed that her classes and those of other educators were so important. They were most women's only source of a consistent interpretation of Islam and their rights in the civil code.

The classes were not perfect, however. At one point, Marzia monitored a class about women's rights in a small neighborhood in Kabul. The teachers had invited an imam to come to the house where the class was being held and discuss "Islam in light of civil code." That encouraged Marzia, because she wanted people to know that women have rights at all levels of the law. At first she "heard that the imam was saying that women has this right, women has this right, women has this right." But "finally a woman asked, 'What do you think . . . about our . . . inheritance rights, for example? A man, a boy, a brother can have two portions and a woman can have [only] one. Why this is like that? Or also sometimes some of the people argue that the conscience of women, the wisdom of women, is not as much as [men's]. How do you interpret this, because this is a big argument of some people, that the women do not know, don't give them positions?'" Marzia continued:

> You know what this imam said? Interestingly he said, . . . "You're not as wise as me, because the Holy Qur'an says this. . . . Also Islam is not complete faith for you because you as a woman have seven days of menstruation period, and within these seven days, you're not doing prayers, [so] God [does] not allow

you to be a real Muslim. We are men that we have complete right of making one month for Ramadan, for example, but because you're a woman and have your period, then seven days you're deprived. So you lack also faith; you lack also Islam." [This] was [a] very shocking thing that I was listening [to], this experience, face-to-face, sitting with women.... I brought [up] this issue because unfortunately the interpretation of those scholars that they think they are very good and know Islam, it is not good.

Added to the lack of political will in the government, such lingering ignorance meant to Marzia that implementing women's rights in Afghanistan was still a distant dream.

Shared Visions

As Jamila's and Marzia's assessments of their own professional activities wound down, I asked if they saw any way around the obstacles to women rights and advancement they had attributed to their culture. The government was obviously an erratic partner. Their own efforts and those of other activists were impressive but also uncertain. Women's gains could be toppled by the change of regime after Karzai leaves office. The international community had a long way to go to help effect the long-term changes that would be necessary to turn things around for Afghan women. Could they identify any other supports they would like for their own work that might be productive?

Again, the women demonstrated a surprising level of agreement about two possible sources of such support: the enlightened use of media and the appropriate, constructive attention of the rest of the world. Jamila explained why she thought the media could be so important:

> It's very difficult in a culture-based community to bring change, but I think media can play very important role in making the community... understand the reality. TV and radio channels are active in all parts of Afghanistan. If [Afghans] are not watching TV, they are listening to radio, definitely. I have visited very far-[flung] areas which [are] almost in North Afghanistan, a border between Afghanistan and China, so people are very, very much connected to radios. I think if we develop some programs through radio and through television, on these issues, ... it will bring awareness on the community level.

Jamila knew from experience how effective a program on radio or television could be in dramatizing the horrific consequences of gender practices in Afghanistan. As one example, she recounted her experience in working with the youth committee in NECDO's center in Ghazni that created and performed a radio drama based on a true story. "And it had very, very good impact," Jamila said, especially on young men's attitudes about girls' limited opportunities.

The story concerned one of Jamila's students whose family did not want her to go to school. So, "she was wearing *burqa* that nobody can notice [who she was] and she was going to the house of neighbor from on top of the roof. (Ghazni has very connected houses, and they have ways from roof to roof.) So she was going to the house of neighbor, and she was going with daughters of neighbors to school. Her brother who was a jolly person, he was bringing some other friends to tease daughters of the neighborhood.... Every day he was following his sister on the street," not knowing that his sister was among the *burqa*-clad girls. Meanwhile, "the poor sister, she couldn't say anything because she knew that 'if I say a single word, he will recognize me; then my life will be in danger.'"

One day the brother "is bringing two other friends with motorbikes, and they are following these two or three girls, [and] one of these girls is his sister. So while crossing the street, this girl is in ... [a] rush to school, and these boys are following ... [and] while she's crossing the street, she is crushed by another car. And this guy who's her brother, he's afraid, and he's running away from the situation because ... this accident happened because of him. So, after a few hours when he comes back home, he sees that the people ... have come because his sister has died."

As the truth comes out that the sister was sneaking to school, "the father was beating her mother, 'Why you allow her to go to school? It's because of you—if she is killed, it's because of you. Why you didn't [tell] us?' But the brother was very shocked. And he was very, very upset at what he did. And he realized that 'this harassment that I was doing with somebody else, it was my own sister.' He was feeling the pain inside."

As a result of this dramatization, the NECDO youth committees made the elimination of violence against women in Ghazni their theme. "Like people were realizing that the education is a right of women and they should be allowed to go for education," Jamila explained. "I have heard from many families that when they heard this story through radio, they started allowing their daughters to go to school."

Marzia also thought that the media could be essential in creating changes in misogynistic attitudes and in expanding women's rights. She was sure that having the faces of female candidates running for Parliament splashed boldly on billboards and television encouraged other young women to go forth and claim their legal rights to social participation. At the same time, however, she had seen the media's antiprogressive potential. For example, some conservative groups had recently started television stations that ran programs warning women against asserting themselves, appearing in public, or defying the wishes of their fathers or husbands.

Jamila's and Marzia's other shared hope was that internationals would eventually figure out how to intervene effectively in Afghanistan. One reason they clung to that hope—despite the depressing evidence—was their greater distrust of the Afghan political process than of well-meaning internationals. Given the country's political history, especially the corruption rampant in elections, among officials, and in the judicial system, it was hard to contest that view. But given the record of the shortsighted, present-focused, and self-serving ineptitude of many international organizations and foreign governments, including the United States, I wondered whether international support could ever rise to the women's expectations. For that to happen, governments and agencies would have to design programs in consultation with the people they wanted to serve and with leaders like Marzia and Jamila who had expertise in serving their country. From the women's perspective, groups that had done so—such as the Swedish Committee for Afghanistan—had accomplished a great deal, albeit in a piecemeal fashion. It would be harder for such groups and governments to have the wisdom or courage to get to the roots of problems in a systematic way.

Reflections

I was a little saddened that, despite their agreement on so many aspects of both the problems for Afghan women and possible approaches to them, Marzia and Jamila did not choose to join forces and work together on issues such as sexual harassment or even improving relations between activist groups and radio and television stations. That they did not do so reflected, perhaps, the fragmentation of their society and the state of activists' relationships with one another, which both women had mentioned and would say more about. It also reflected their choice of a distinct entry point for addressing the complexities of gender in Afghanistan—education for Jamila and law for Marzia—from which they were unwilling or unable to deviate. Indeed, when I asked Marzia why she and Jamila did not work together on issues such as sexual harassment, when it seemed to me that their complementary approaches could be very effective, she replied that she could not really lose her focus on legal questions or else she might lose her effectiveness. Whether that was true or reflected the historical lack of solidarity among women in Afghanistan was hard for me to say.

I was also a little confused by the women's concept of Afghan culture and their repeated statements about the difficulties posed to women's rights by their "culture-based community." Although they were well schooled in Afghan history and well aware from their own experience of the changing parameters for and acceptance of women's behavior, dress, and access to education and employment, they often contrasted such history with deep-seated cultural traditions that resisted change. In some ways, that concept represented a paradox. They were agents of history, working incrementally to reconstruct Afghan women's opportunities and capacities and confronting two of the most recalcitrant political institutions in their country—the judiciary and the religious establishment. They also believed that conditions and values could be changed at the grassroots level, where, presumably, traditional culture was strongest. Yet they frequently identified the culture they were dedicated to changing as a bedrock of resistance.

I wondered how that characterization compared with the widely criticized Orientalist view by Westerners of endemic cultural currents that permanently kept some societies, especially in Asia and the Middle East, in a premodern state. Were Marzia and Jamila Orientalists themselves? In the end, I decided that they were not. In part, they were using the word *culture* as a recognizable term in conversations with Westerners without necessarily imbuing it with the apolitical, ahistorical meanings that contemporary critics infer. Indeed, they were often using the term as a synonym for *traditions,* many of which they believed were cobbled together from tribal practices and false beliefs about Islam in order to serve the interests of various groups, especially men.

I finally began to hear *culture* in their accounts as a challenge rather than an immutable force. Of course, they did not underestimate the power of resistance to change; there was too much evidence of its impact. But I never heard them just throw up their hands at the mention of *culture*, either. As their 2005 statements had indicated, what constituted culture at any given time in Afghanistan from their perspective was really a mosaic composed of "good" and "bad," obstacles and opportunities, support and resistance. On optimistic days, they could emphasize the good, the opportunities, and the support. On pessimistic days, or under some circumstances, they could see only the bad, the obstacles, and the resistance to new knowledge and change.

6

Afghan Marriage Practices

Marzia's and Jamila's marriages since our last interviews were a prime topic of our conversations in Istanbul. Their changed status was made quite visible in Jamila's case by the presence of her husband and children. I was curious about why I had gotten the news through the grapevine that both had gotten married in 2006 and why neither had mentioned her marriage to me in our e-mail exchanges before 2009. I wondered if that indicated their belief that marriage was so inevitable for Afghans that it barely deserved mention or if they were so affected by their new status as wives that they hardly knew where to begin in an e-mail message.

When I inquired in our Istanbul interviews about Afghan marriage practices in a general way, their openness to discussing the topic suggested it might have been both. Initially, Marzia said, "It's a common thing that everyone should marry. Ninety-nine percent of Afghan women marry." There may be "different cultures going on, different habits in different families," which would include hers, "but [the] absolute culture issue is that you have to get married, so this is the point. . . . Afghanistan is not like the United States that the people could enjoy freedom, stay unmarried for a long time." And what about her own case? Marriage "is something even if I want or not," it will happen; "it's a social kind of thing," she said.

What followed was a detailed discussion about the two women's particular perspectives on the way marriage worked in Afghanistan. During that discussion, it was clear that they were focusing on their own variations as urban Afghans and as educated professional women. At the same time, their discussion indicated that they recognized other variations on marriage practices depending on region, economic capacity, age, education, and individual family practices,

Different Habits, Singular Outcome

As the two women tried to explain how those variations in marriage requirements and practices worked in Afghanistan, Marzia emphasized the role of education in marital timing and choice: "For the [girls] who are getting more education and more education . . . marriage . . . brings a kind of problem. . . . The girl says [if] I don't finish my education, I don't marry. . . . This can be a good excuse for women's rights activists in Afghanistan because we want to put the age of marriage a bit more further from sixteen to eighteen or twenty." The older a woman gets, the better she is at arguing her way out of marriage, Marzia said—all the prospects are unsuitable, there are too few educated men in Afghanistan to choose from (many have left), or she wants more education. But Marzia considered marriage a reasonable option. "For the girls who are not going to the school, then what does it make sense if they should not marry?"

Education alone does not protect an Afghan woman from coercion around her marriage plans in all families, however. Jamila and Marzia told yet another chilling marriage story about "one of the big commanders," Haji Abdul Qadir, governor of Nangarhar Province during the mujahideen period from 1992 to 1996.[1] His educated daughter fell in love with her uncle's son, and they ran away to get married at the uncle's house. Marzia continued, "This news was spread to her father, and her father was in Saudi Arabia at that time." Then,

> he and his son, [who] were brother of the girl and father of the girl, they decided to kill the daughter. It is not because of the opposite family because she was running away from home to marry her [cousin]. You could bring her back home and say okay, "Don't marry," or something, but he said, "Okay, tell the daughter to come home, we will marry you in a very fashion[able] way. We'll have your wedding ceremony." But they brought her—this is a real story—they brought her and they put her in . . . a stable, a barn, all the cows, all the noise and stuff, they put her there [and her] brother shot her many times and killed her.

Then the brother "called her father [and said], 'I did this,' and [the] father said, 'Very well done.'" Clearly, this story demonstrates that an Afghan father's customary right to determine a girl's marriage partner can take precedence over her educational status, desires, or even her life.

The story also demonstrates that, even though marriage is as common for Afghans as the air they breathe, it is also serious business. It typically entails layers of ritual, custom, financial negotiations, and rules. It is also regarded as a near-religious requirement for both sexes, although it is in every way a different process and outcome for men and women. Because life changes much more dramatically for the woman after marriage, regardless of her social or economic level, most marriage resistance occurs on the woman's side. Women recognize that their greater social status as a wife will typically be gained at the cost of their personal freedom and of vastly increased responsibilities, while men's status and power both increase with marriage, and men's involvement in maintaining the household may be minimal. Marzia was especially aggrieved by women's increased responsibilities after marriage. "If the house is not very well organized," she noted, then family members will say, "Oh, what a bad woman you have." They will never say, "Why the men are not taking part?"

Not Islamic

Like many other Afghan practices, marriage customs in Afghanistan are typically defended in the name of Islam, but Marzia and Jamila noted that very little about the customs, rituals, and rules of Afghan marriage practices is actually Islamic. "Afghanistan takes [marriage as a] very, very important part of culture," explained Jamila. But because those in the culture believe their customs are Islamic, that belief "gives them the color of Islam as well."

Marzia and Jamila think that marriage in Afghanistan would be better if it were *more* Islamic. For example, the Qur'an indicates that marriages should be negotiated between the groom and his prospective bride, not by representatives, as they are in Afghanistan. Marzia thinks such direct proposals would cut down on arguments and negotiations about money. The Qur'an also specifies that women should receive a marriage portion, or *mahr*, consisting of cash or property, either given at the time of marriage or held in trust for the bride and paid later, especially upon divorce. Importantly, the Qur'an allows the woman to set the amount.

Both Jamila and Marzia see the *mahr* as an Islamic gesture toward married women's economic independence and a possible deterrent to impulsive divorce by the man who must produce the *mahr* in that event. Because Afghan marriage is not as Islamic as it should be, however, prospective husbands might lobby the bride not to ask for the *mahr*. Or the *mahr* might become a bride-price, or *walwar*, controlled by the bride's family and used to prepare the bride for marriage, meet the family's basic needs, or supplement the family's wealth (Smith 2011, 171). In some cases, especially with young girls, the price paid is a straightforward purchase, which is entirely against Islam (Kaufman 2003).[2]

If Afghan marriage practices were truly Islamic, they would also encourage unions between people of similar rank and background, in order to reduce conflict over status and wealth. To Marzia, this means that women should request a modest *mahr*: "If we ask for the bigger money, this is not faithful because it's asking some amount that is not acceptable and affordable for the men, so it is not good." But contrary to Islamic precepts, many Afghan families regard the initial offer as just a starting point, and sometimes the resulting high figure strains husbands' economic capacities and breeds resentment of the bride from the start, according to Marzia.

The practice of divorce in Afghanistan is also un-Islamic, in the women's view. They are proud that Islam was the first religion to allow divorce. "Islam said okay, if you cannot stay in the marriage contract together and if it is harsh for you, then get divorced," Marzia explained. Jamila told the story of the Prophet's marriage of his cousin Zainab bint Jahsh to a former slave whom he had freed, adopted, and raised as his own son. Zainab and the freed slave/adopted son at first lived a happy life. But eventually, Zainab told the Prophet, "'I don't want to stay with him any longer, I want a divorce.' And the divorce occurred because of her demand," Jamila said. Then the Prophet stunned everyone by marrying Zainab himself in order to demonstrate, among other things, "that women can ask divorce and she can remarry to whoever she wants."[3] Of course, the Islamic right to divorce was not entirely gender neutral. Men could obtain a divorce simply by stating, "I divorce you," three times, to the woman.[4] Women were given only the right to ask for a separation, unless their particular marriage contracts gave them the right to initiate a divorce.

Afghan law recognizes this history by allowing women to request a divorce if the husband has granted her that right in the marriage contract. Even more encouraging, according to Marzia, a new law specified that divorces should go to civil court for marriages that were registered with the state. But life for a divorced woman in Afghanistan was basically untenable. There were few ways for her to earn a living; her remarriage was rare (even as a second or third wife); and divorce was always a source of shame for the woman, according to both Jamila and Marzia.

Furthermore, Afghan society did not fully embrace a potential Islamic solution to the divorced-woman question—the second marriage as a way to protect divorcées and widows. Marzia explained, "While there is war and most of the women lose their husbands, [Islam asked] how we should protect them? . . . The second marriage . . . allows men to have a second wife at least to protect them because alimony is the job of the men to provide for the woman" in cultures with no publicly funded safety nets. The same challenge still existed in war-torn Afghanistan, but divorced and even widowed women were more likely to be shunned than protected. Virginal women younger than the first wife were the preferred partners for second marriages.

Overall, the divorced woman in Afghanistan "will be hated from the family," Marzia continued.

> There's no job for her; there's no protection for the children. What should she do? She has to sell herself on the street. You know? . . . We have to bring solution for that. Who will protect her? Okay, we are trying as women activists to release a woman from the very harsh situation, but what is our choice for how long we can protect them? How much money do we have? How many resources do we have in front of us? Who can help them? Of course, educated people, because they have a little economy, or those who have family support, [can get by], but most of those who get divorced, they're hated by . . . their own families first, because the brother will say, "Okay, you are divorcing; we can't keep you at home," and also the society, any minute, it will be a torture for her, and for her alone. Even the children, they will grow up—they will blame her. . . . This is the reality.

Divorced women were also liable to lose their children. "After seven years you brought her up," Marzia observes, "then the father will take her back from you. [Even if] you're married [again], the father suddenly could take [the child] from you. Would you like to accept that?"

A few shelters existed for such women, but even if they were allowed to operate (and some were being closed), "the shelter is not the solution for long life. Can we provide jobs for women? Do we give them some support for their [whole] life?... If you get divorced, then what is the protection from the government, what is the protection of the social workers, what is our commitment as women, how long we can keep this [up]?" People like Marzia and Jamila often advised women in truly abusive and degrading marriages to get divorced, "because a human being is a human being; you can't suffer." But when they hesitated to give such advice, even in bad cases, it was because they realized how dangerous divorce could be and how inadequate it was for ensuring the woman's future.

"If a woman goes to the court and applies for separation," Marzia said, "and then the husband and his family comes and appears in front of the court, then that is a kind of serious issue" in a society that emphasizes the importance and vulnerability of male honor. "I remember when I graduated from law faculty [and began my job as court administrator].... It was 1987, [and] at the Kabul court a woman wanted to get divorced from her husband. And her husband very cleverly put the pistol here in his shoes. And while there was a search, no one found that pistol. He came to the court—I was there—he shot his mother-in-law, shot his father-in-law, shot his wife, and then because this is a place that every police is there, he was captured. No woman could face such a thing."

Such cases motivated Marzia to push for increasing women's legal awareness. At one women's rights program she ran, for example, the curriculum included women's right to resist forced marriage and to obtain a divorce. But such training has its limitations, which one student quickly perceived: "I am learning my rights," she said. "I know that this is my rights, but I cannot practice it. If I get up and ask this right, who will support me?"

Marzia conceded that the student asked a good question, but she still held out hope that things would change.

> If we see the system is working well and protecting, like if we have a good family court, have a good unit of violence against women at prosecutor office, if we have [a women's protection] unit in police office[s], and if we have strong defense lawyers [who are] gender sensitive [in an overall strong legal system]... then a woman could be heard and a result could come of that at the end. Then this could make sense, that people will say, "Okay, if I do this, I get [justice]." Otherwise, if you are powerful in one party, if the husband is powerful, then you will never get your right, because there will be many chances for unfair justice because the case [can] be stopped at the police, can be stopped at the prosecutor, or it can [be] stop[ped] at the court, and they can pass the bribe and the bribe can [do its] work, and then the woman would lose.

What was really needed was a complete revamping of the whole system—the judiciary, law enforcement, relevant government institutions, even the informal sector—including full education on women's rights and Islam.

At international meetings and conferences, Marzia saw how much progress women had made in other societies "from family rights then to the community

[and] to the political level." Such "improvements that are happening now in [the] U.S. and Europe" made Marzia very happy and gave her hope for her own country. She pointed to another recently passed Afghan law that made a civil marriage contract available to engaged couples. It allowed the parties to specify conditions for divorce and for the taking of a second wife. Marzia figured that, even if a man rejected it, the contract made him recognize what a woman's rights are. "Who knows how many could be changed in Afghanistan?"

Jamila also had hope for women's marital rights in Afghanistan, but hers was based on an educational rather than a legal model. "I think . . . awareness raising is very important, through media, and through mosques; these are two important channels can bring change in the mentality." She also stressed the importance of models within Afghanistan rather than in foreign countries. She saw herself as such a model, as someone who lived in her marriage according to women's rights and supported them for others.

Jamila explained that Afghan marriage traditions and expectations were also un-Islamic because they were rooted in the idea that women embody shame, which is not a tenet of Islam. Being an Afghan (rather than a Muslim) woman meant living by prohibitions: "Usually men are saying to the women, 'You're a woman; don't talk. It's a shame for you to talk in front of people; don't argue. You're a woman; you have to keep silent. You're a woman; do not do this. You're a woman; it's bad for this or that.' Like for women, everything is bad; everything is shameful. But for men, we don't have these obstacles." Two men fighting on the street will reinforce the shamefulness of women and their role in destroying a man's honor. While arguing, the men will abuse "each other's mother and sister who are sitting at home . . . not aware that their brothers or other relatives are fighting with each other and they are cursing their mother and sister who are sitting at home. Like this is very complicated. And . . . men get furious in fighting because their honor is [implicated] in fighting."

Afghan men's attitudes toward polygamy also struck the two women as un-Islamic. They recognized that plural marriage was part of the fabric of many Muslim societies and that the Prophet was a polygamist with many wives, but they also believed that the Prophet's marriages were specific to him. They emphasized that he did not marry anyone else while his first wife, Khadija, was alive.[5] After Khadija's death, he married other women primarily to gather support from many tribes and to persuade them to convert to Islam. Some of his marriages also modeled progressive values, as in Jamila's version of the story of Zainab bint Jahsh. Others were designed to protect abandoned women. Marzia and Jamila further emphasized that the Prophet did not consummate marriage with prepubescent girls and that he sought the consent of his youngest wife, Aisha, before starting a sexual relationship with her after she reached puberty.

None of these perspectives seemed to guide plural marriage in Afghanistan, however, which persisted despite the Afghan Civil Code's prohibition against polygamy. Some officials dismissed objections to polygamy as Western-influenced and hypocritical, because Westerners do not admit to their own sexual exploitation problems: "'Your daughters are raped at the age of ten or nine or twelve or fourteen,' they say, 'but you're all coming to us to stop child marriage.'" As we have seen, there was widespread belief that the prophet Muhammad's marriage to Aisha gave Muslim men permission (even encouragement) to marry and have sexual relations with prepubescent girls. Even educated men who truly loved their first wives might be pressured to take a second wife if the first could not produce a child. Few husbands seemed to worry about the Qur'an's requirement that they treat all wives equally. Instead, some enjoyed their wives' quiet or fierce competition for their husband's attention, support, and love. The scarcity model made almost any man look good under such circumstances.

A Man's World

These un-Islamic qualities of Afghan marriage translate into a highly structured form of family life for most people. Afghans follow an extended, corporate family model, in which unions are more between families than between individuals, and individual needs and desires must be balanced against those of the extended family. That model, in addition to the patriarchal foundations of Afghan society and Afghanistan's chronic economic and security issues, means that marriage primarily serves dominant men's ideas of a family's best interests. Among other things, a son's marriage prospects are likely to take precedence over a daughter's needs or wishes, although sons often have no choice of marriage partner, either. Marzia reported that 60 percent of Afghan girls are married before they turn sixteen, and 60 to 80 percent of those and all other marriages are forced on one or both parties. She estimated that only 5 percent of Afghan marriages were love matches, which simply meant there had been consent. Exchanges of women between families to solve blood feuds, or *badal,* are also practiced widely in the culture. Because of its association with crimes and revenge, *badal* often leads to retaliation against the wife's natal family through brutal acts of violence against her (Smith 2011, 170).

Implicit in the entire structure of family life is the cultural preference for boys. "Why [do] people love boys?" Marzia asked. "Because in Afghanistan, mostly these are the boys that will support the family . . . so they consider boys as important players because they have their social status as an outsider, and women are sitting inside and they cannot bring incomes. . . . So this is why that they usually love their boys because they say, 'Okay, once they grow up, I can rely on them that they could keep us.'" Even though some girls were now earning enough income to help their fathers support the family, "in Afghanistan sometimes it is considered a shame if you ask for your daughter to support [you], or for your son-in-law. They prefer to ask from their son rather than to ask it from their son-in-law or from their daughters. So this is a cultural thing: they are proud of getting support from their sons rather than their daughters." Daughters are considered "something for the other family; [only] once we bring a daughter from the other family . . . [do] we have something. [That's why girls] receive love from their fathers-in-law rather than from their own family."

It follows from this gendered corporate perspective on family and marriage that men typically expect to be the unquestioned dominant partner in their relationships. Marzia emphasized that this is not quite so pronounced among educated men, but even educated men believed that they in some sense owned their wives and that everything a wife does reflects back on the husband. Thus, the belief in inherent female shame and threat to male honor infuses the marital relationship, despite Islam's efforts to imbue married women with personhood.[6] Marzia thought that Afghan men's sense of manhood depended on being able to control a wife. "Men would like to have their domination of women, so they want to keep their powers. Sometimes they say we have to have this power." Men think that women who resist do not realize that men's power is good for them as well as for society, as if everything would fly apart without male dominance.

Given that reality, Marzia suggested that smart women should not always push against custom. "Get permission [from your husband] if you are traveling," she advised women like herself. "Get permission if you are doing [anything unusual]; get permission. . . . This is their wish. They will give you permission, but they would like to be asked, 'Should I do that or should I not?' It's a kind of privilege that they want to have." And no matter what kind of work a woman does or how much education she has, "in a country like Afghanistan, we have to see our environment. Not to act as foreigner woman. I mean, we have to see who we are also. Cultural observation is also important for all of us because if we just ask [for] everything in one minute, then it will not happen. We can achieve slowly—like maybe in one year, I can have some rights and then next year and next year and next year, and then there will be improvement."

Plus Ça Change . . . ?

Even as she reiterated the patriarchal foundations of Afghan marriage mores, Marzia also reported some significant changes for some contemporary women. For example, she compared her mother's reproductive output—eleven births and ten living children—with that of her sisters. "Two of them are doctors. One has two children and the other has three. [Both] can bring more children because they're at the ages they can have." One of those doctor-sisters had a seven-year-old daughter, but she decided not to have more because "simply these are headaches because she's working also on duty at night."

Although Marzia wanted very much to have a child, she wondered why other women, especially poor women, kept having children in a country such as Afghanistan and conjectured that it was only because some women have nothing else in their lives. But she did not buy the usual argument that children are a resource for poor people. Rather, "it is a lot of responsibility, at least until the age of eighteen or twenty, before they go to work or before they go to marry; it's a lot of responsibility. [Parents] have to take care of them, and too [the children] are not taking care of the [parents] very much.... While the boys grow up, they have their own wife.... No guarantee if they could keep you and they will support you; so ... now it is changing." I wondered if that change would eventually have an impact on families' preference for sons.

Another change is the economic and professional status of at least some urban brides, according to Marzia. Husbands must respect the status of the women they marry, she explained, and Jamila did not disagree. If a bride was working when she became engaged, the husband "cannot say now 'no' to work for her because she was working before marriage" to him. He can object to a wife's working after marriage only if she did not work beforehand. "He could say, 'Okay, sit at home because you were sitting at home.' So the condition is different.... What was the status of the woman before marriage [remains] after marriage." That also applies to women attending school or college. "The husband cannot just say, 'I don't allow you to go,' because she was at the college, and she has to complete it." The courts would uphold this right, if the man challenged it, Marzia said.

Even if these changes were as widespread as the two women believed, however, they do little to diminish the strong emphasis on gender difference and male dominance in Afghan marriage practices. That difference even controls the partners' initial interest in one another. In general, an Afghan woman is not expected to be looking for a mate, regardless of her accomplishments or socio-economic level and despite the example of Khadija, the Prophet's first wife, who proposed marriage to him. "In Afghanistan the culture is that the men come to ask [for] the girl's hand," explained Marzia. "The boy's family [usually mothers and sisters] comes to your family, and they ask for your hand and then a kind of meetings, regular coming and going, and then after discussions, especially about who is the boy, what is he doing, what's his education—these are the important questions that the girl's side would [ask]. Also the boy's side, they will have the same questions." It is further expected that the proposal will be rebuffed several times before the woman's family shows any reciprocal interest. In the best case, "after [the couple] find each other pleasant, then they can marry," Marzia said.

That was certainly true in Marzia's case, but in many families, there is no direct contact between the parties involved, let alone an opportunity to find each other pleasant or discuss any terms the woman wants. The man may not have selected the woman himself, and most often the woman is never asked her opinion or preference.

Marzia claimed that it was the family's educational level that made the difference. "At least someone asks them, 'Do you want to marry with this, or what's your opinion if you want to marry?'" she said. Such women were also usually "at the age of twenty-two after they graduate from faculties or after they graduate from school.... For those who are not educated, it is not common to be asked," and the marriage age will be much younger, down to seven or nine in some rural areas, despite the legal age of sixteen for girls.

In addition, Marzia claimed that educated young women could exercise some power in their families, which was demonstrated by their greater right to accept or refuse a suitor. This power tended to grow if the woman worked as a professional. Such women get more independence "as they grow up, especially with their ages and status. . . . They are stronger, they would like and wish to have their own choices, and they reject [suitors] most of the time if they are not acceptable for them. And they play strong role also in the family because they allow their growing up, and while anything they say it could be something for the family, and it could bring decisions, changing the family status." In short, she implied, the fathers of professional women, like Marzia, were often educated themselves. They had invested in their daughters' education and benefited from the power and influence their daughters achieved. Thus, they tended to respect their decisions and choices. This possibility for at least some educated women made Jamila's situation all the more poignant. Though educated herself, she was subject to the controls and practices of male family members who neither had nor apparently valued education.

But even if education provided some women with options, as with most things Afghan, such options often came with a serious downside. For even the most respected professional woman, the consequences of never marrying constituted a huge downside. Marzia reported that many of the educated professional women of her generation who grew up between 1978 and 2001—"during the Communist regime and mujahideen and Taliban, we are talking about at least twenty or thirty years," when so many young men were killed "because of their political opinion or the war"—either did not marry, married way beneath their own educational levels, or became second wives because, in the end, there was no real way for any woman to live alone. Marzia continued, "They might have husbands who are not educated because like during the mujahideen, most of the mujahideen came to us for educated women. They said, 'We will marry you; we will pay a lot if you can be our second wife' or these things. Some of the women couldn't resist because there was no economic supports for them, no salary, or maybe the [woman's] family also didn't have any salary, so they compulsory got married." Marrying into an uneducated family with money in the 1990s typically meant the woman would not work. Even if "they were doctors, there was [probably] no job for them." And even if there were jobs and the Taliban was not in charge, most uneducated husbands would object to a wife's career, especially if the family was wealthy, like Jamila's family.

Women who resisted such marriages, "because if they are graduated from faculty they would marry to a husband who's educated, rather than to marry with uneducated man," might not fare much better. A typical recourse for such women is to live with a brother. But "brothers will get married, they will be with their children, they will not really think of you," Marzia explained. The unmarried professional woman might fit in well with her brother's household, and "if the brother's children are good, that's okay, but sometimes it comes that they will not be good, especially while you have your age. And while you have your own kind of status that you could have a special kind of character, people change their character time to time. So it will be not possible to be accepted.... People will ... say, 'Oh, what should we do [with] this old lady?' ... If you don't have a mother or father [or spouse] in a country like Afghanistan, others will not care very much about you." Even if families "do care, if you are not married, then it is disaster," Marzia concluded.

Women who do not marry and live in these ways usually regret it. In addition to the stress they experience with their own birth families as they age, Marzia said (perhaps thinking of her own narrowly escaped fate), "You will feel yourself an isolated person. You'll say, 'My goodness, why I didn't [marry] on time? Why I just graduated? Why I talked too much about this, that education is important. I have to get married with someone high level or, you know?' Then you will be sorry for that which is late." Aging unmarried women would feel jealous and deprived as they watched their surviving parents dote on their siblings' children. Or, worse, they might find themselves forced into marriage with a widower or given as a second wife to a man when "there are already children they have to take care of.... This is not good for them, you know, this challenged life."

Two Variations

Although Marzia's position as a single professional woman mirrored that of her unusual peer group, her story had a twist. In a culture that said, "Women cannot live alone by themselves [even] with their own economy," she had avoided marriage with her family's apparent approval until age thirty-eight. Instead of living with a brother, she had her own income and lived in her own house. She traveled internationally, and she had an active career in which she interacted with both foreigners and a variety of Afghans, including men. How did she do it? She took in one of her nephews and helped to raise and educate him. He had become an engineer. Thus, she was technically living in a family setting, and she had a male family member—a *mahram*—to accompany and "protect" her. Only after her 2005 trip to the United States did her family begin to discuss marriage for her. She said she always knew that the time would come when both she and her family would want her to find a husband. And when the time came, Marzia expected that her family would handle her marriage as they did everything else—rationally and calmly—and that they would respect her choices.

By contrast, Jamila's less educated family had not been sanguine about her educational and professional achievements as an excuse for her unmarried status.

Even when their "mentality was a little bit changed" with regard to her work—"not in time to say, 'Yes, good, well done,'" she said, "but at least they became silent"—her alleged assault on family honor through her "shameless" public work was a constant irritant to some of her male relatives and a threat to her own peace of mind. Although Jamila was embedded in her family when she returned from Pakistan to Kabul after 2002, remained a dutiful daughter, performed her role as an adoptive mother of her three nieces and nephews, and maintained a punishing schedule as she worked for NECDO and other organizations and causes, the marriage question for her was just a time bomb waiting to go off. She was unsure what role, if any, her choices would play.

The Afghan marriage obligation did finally come due for both Marzia and Jamila, albeit with very different levels of drama and suffering. Curiously, despite the difference in their ages, it happened at about the same time—in 2006. How odd (or serendipitous) that their different life trajectories would converge in parallel marriage stories in the same year.

Reflections

It is in the arena of Afghan marriage and family life that the old concept of "culture clash" may begin to reverberate in many Western brains. Because Western feminism has focused so much on "liberating" women from traditional ideas about unegalitarian marriage, male dominance in the family, domestic gender roles, and constrictions on women's careers because of family responsibilities, it may seem difficult to reconcile the patriarchal, corporate family model and its oligarchic control of wives, daughters, and daughters-in-law with the concept of women's rights and equal legal status. In that context, a story about a young girl who was tricked by her own father into returning home, thinking she would be married to her chosen groom, only to be murdered in cold blood by her brother with her father's approval, can seem unnatural or even satanic. The family value system that could support such an act may seem bewildering and incompatible with any concept of gender equity or even of women's personhood.

Keeping in mind that the "culture clash" motif often obscures the sins and shortcomings of Western cultures, however, it behooves Western observers to recognize what might be hidden in such a response. The prevalence of domestic and relationship violence and marital infidelity in Western nations is an example. Relationship violence is especially rampant in the United States and has been for decades. Indeed, the Centers for Disease Control and Prevention report that one in four American women will experience domestic violence in her lifetime.[7] An *Atlantic Monthly* article from 2013 reports that "one in three-to-four girls, and one in five-to-seven boys [in the United States] are sexually abused before they turn 18, an overwhelming incidence of which happens *within* the family."[8] We might well ask what lies behind such abuses and why a society that considers itself superior with regard to family form and women's social status tolerates them—even or especially by elected officials, coaches, and sports heroes—and manages to maintain the myth of an egalitarian and morally just society. When a conservative Afghan patriarch chastises the United States for the rapes of young girls by their uncles and fathers, perhaps there is truth in his observation that Americans' horror of child marriage is somewhat hypocritical.

It is also important to recognize the historical, economic, and political forces that have constructed all family forms and affectional ties, including our own. Today's middle-class nuclear family form in the United States evolved over time. Children were much less adored in the early nineteenth century than they are today. Most parents considered their progeny undeveloped adults in need of strict upbringings and firm adult guidance. To many Christians, children were "little fallen wretches, exposed to the wrath of God" by their very birth.[9] Because they often died young (with a 20 to 34 percent infant mortality rate before 1900, depending on race),[10] children sometimes remained unnamed until age five to temper parental commitment until survival was more likely. Surviving children might be put to work on farms, with scant schooling, or sent from home before puberty as apprentices or indentured servants. Slave and rural children worked very hard from early childhood on. The tendency to prefer boys for such labor actually benefited some white girls, because it made school attendance more likely for them than for their brothers.

The standards of parent-child relationships also evolved. For white middle-class U.S. families, those standards were shaped by increased prosperity in the late nineteenth and twentieth centuries, which allowed urban parents more leisure time to develop close, loving relationships with their smaller number of children. Motherhood became a full-time occupation and ideal for many middle-class white women toward the end of the nineteenth century, and with that new identity as "angel in the house," such women perfected their maternal emotions. African Americans and other minorities shared much less in this bounty and followed some different familial patterns, but those with smaller families and a middle-class income also increasingly valued and devoted time to their children. The ideal of a domestic identity, which had waned during World War II, resurged for white women following the war, despite their increasing labor-force participation. Both advertisers and the government touted the bounties of domestic life to female consumers, so that they would happily purchase the domestic appliances then replacing munitions in the country's factories.

The loving paternal role for white middle-class men owed much to their reduced working hours in white-collar jobs in the late nineteenth century. Modern fatherhood also evolved in the context of smaller family size, which was an urban phenomenon facilitated by nineteenth-century women's growing control over unwanted pregnancies, mostly by using their alleged delicacy to justify sexual abstinence. Parents also began to view children's futures as separate from their own, a trend that was hastened by the arrival of Social Security in the United States in the 1930s. That safety net freed children from becoming their parents' primary support in old age.

Such changes had a profound effect on the family form in the United States. Middle-class children could live ever farther from their parents without automatically abandoning them to a miserable dotage. The nuclear form that Euro-Americans inherited from their ancestors became even more self-contained and removed from extended families—so much so, some would argue, that it was the collective good that was sacrificed to the couple. In the twenty-first century, that pattern may be changing a little, with the fraying public safety net, the lack of affordable health care, and an economic recession that has reduced jobs for the younger generation and compromised the retirement savings of many senior citizens. Children unable to find jobs after high school or college have moved back in with their parents in greater numbers, and adult children have taken on more responsibility for aging parents.

Given the role of economics in Western parental love, many family values we associate with a Judeo-Christian heritage should really be attributed to the mutual love affair that developed in the United States between Protestant Christianity and capitalism (a key example of Western conflation of religion and secular culture that remains hidden). Monogamy facilitated the capitalist emphasis on individual and nuclear-family wealth by eliminating claims by multiple wives (or husbands?) and competing heirs. Daughters were never prevented from inheriting that wealth, but until the passage of Married Women's Property Acts in the United States, their husbands could control their inheritances.

By the same token, capitalism reinforced the patriarchy inherent in Judeo-Christian belief by valuing (and paying) male workers more than females and by excluding women from allegedly inappropriate (but high-paying) jobs. In return, Protestantism regarded the winners in capitalism as divinely blessed, leaving the poor and downtrodden to reap their rewards in heaven. Those who succeeded in the marketplace also had the luxury of regarding children as contributors to family wealth and reputation, not only through marriage but also by individual effort and creativity. This complex set of interacting forces is sometimes attributed to God with no more justification than a different set of forces is considered Allah's will in Afghanistan.

Afghanistan's corporate, extended, and patriarchal family form and its accompanying gender hierarchies and values reflect a different geopolitical heritage, as well as an impoverished and rural collective economic heritage. It was designed to guarantee "security, from birth to death, to each man and woman." The strength of that family form to this day reflects the absence of state services and infrastructure as well as the continued ability of honor codes to provide stability in chronically tumultuous political conditions. Those codes institutionalize pre-Islamic misogynistic and patriarchal tribal social organizations, in which women symbolize honor that must be kept inviolable (Mehmet and Mehmet 2004, 313). That honor code, in turn, is supposed to protect those women.

The corporate family system in Afghanistan sacrifices individuals to a certain extent to the collective will and collective good. It also routinely suppresses the relationship needs or preferences of adult homosexuals of either sex, according to Margaret Mills. Lesbians are basically invisible in the society, and male homosexuality is tacitly tolerated through male-male pedophilia, even though it is not condoned by Islam. Such "homosexual contact with male children is regarded as an inclination (or a recreation) secondary to required heterosexual family formation," Mills writes. And because few marriage partners are consulted about their wishes—marriage "is not regarded as an either-or preference or identity question"—homosexuals are among the many Afghans who might have chosen another match. "Young adult homosexual males are married off as family finances permit, not with any regard to their preferences."[11]

Afghan women's symbolic and actual roles position them historically as the lowest members on the family ladder for the reasons Marzia explained: their attachments to their birth families are defined as temporary, their work is regarded (and kept) as subsistence rather than exchange labor, and only boys are considered qualified to care for their aging parents. Therefore, girls who produce no income, albeit by family mandate, become financial drains on birth families struggling to survive. Their value increases through the bride-price, which a family might depend upon for basic needs, and in their husbands' families as they produce consumable products, such as carpets, and (male) children. It can also increase in some birth families, as Marzia has pointed out, with education, income, and age.

Whatever family forms the tides of history and geopolitics have created in the two worlds, it is also important to recognize that hypocrisies and abuses exist in both. It is also important to remember that practices evolve. They may be rationalized by so-called stable values, but those too are in flux.

In addition, most family and marriage practices involve trade-offs and compromises. If Western marriage constraints play a less significant role in Western women's social and economic participation than Afghan marriage practices play in Afghan women's lives today, that is only after centuries of struggle. The combination of marriage and public life for U.S. women still requires many trade-offs that may have changed over time but are far from resolved. Many women accept the compromises, which entail their own hypocrisies, because of economic or emotional considerations or career ambitions or goals. Afghan women engage in a different set of trade-offs. They accept those for many reasons, too, including their understanding of the value of the communal identities and support systems their families provide. That their family systems are riddled with hypocrisies is no surprise. Those are what women such as Marzia and Jamila have struggled to address, without necessarily eliminating the family form and arrangements of their society.

* * *

This general discussion of marriage and marriage practices in Afghanistan sets the stage for a more detailed look at the individual marriages of Jamila and Marzia. Chapter 7 explores both the women's decisions to marry and their lives as married, educated, professional women in urban Afghanistan.

7

Marriage Hits Home

It was clear from our conversations that marriage had changed Marzia's and Jamila's lives, bringing both joys and disappointments. Jamila's life was especially changed because she had produced two children in four years. Both women believed they had married worthy men and had used their knowledge of how marriage practices *should* work to affect how they *would* work in their own marriage arrangements. In their situations, it was also clear that region, economic capacity, education, and individual family practices affected their expectations of spouses and married life as well as their experiences as married professional Afghan women.

The Marriage Decision: Marzia

Marzia repeated in 2010 what I had understood her to say in 2005: "I was not very much interested to marry because I was thinking it's kind of more responsibility and more job for you, and you could lose your independence. In Afghanistan it is the real situation because once you get married you will lose a lot, especially your freedom is under question, you have to see if your husband allow you to go to work or not, if your husband allow you to go to relatives or not, also if your husband allow you to go to the doctor or not." She might have gotten more pressure to marry had she spent much time with her father's family, but she saw no reason to do that. "I think if you are strong and if your father . . . and your mother support you and your family, even one brother supports you, then that's enough."

Despite her history of resistance and the many negative models she had seen, however, Marzia believed that marriage should play a role in a woman's life, even if—or especially if—she was educated. "God created the people. I think one of the logics behind life is to marry and bring children and have more generations. . . . It's good to have children, at least one or two, [to be] a mom, the children you could take care of. Not too many, but two, three, it is good. I mean, it's good," she said.

But the marriage Marzia envisioned was not the typical Afghan arrangement: "Mostly in Afghanistan it happens that you will study eighteen years of education, then you will marry and just sit at home doing nothing, just raising the children. So this was a kind of impression that I had from the family life." What she had in mind for herself was a relationship free of violence and abuse and completely accepting of her right to continue working and traveling, "and because these are all not against Islam, so this is acceptable for everyone. They have logic."

Her challenge was to reconcile her positions at the moment in 2006 when her father suggested, "Okay, if people are coming to ask for your hand, you can see them, you can find out, you can sit with them, and then you can choose your future." She had made no particular plans about marriage, "because I had no idea how, who I would marry," and by then she had received several proposals, which she had rejected. Happily for her, she said, the family of her now husband, Ashequllah Orya Khail, came to ask for her hand. He was an "unknown man" to her, and "he is very young for me, he is ten years younger than me, more beautiful than me." But he was educated, he had a law degree, like Marzia, and he worked for the secretary of the Parliament. They visited together twice before they married so they could discuss "how he thinks of marriage life, especially regarding women's rights . . . if he would observe the women's right, he would allow me to work, because I was [already] working outside. But I found him interesting because he was saying, 'Everything allowed you in Sharia I would allow you to do it.'"

Recognizing that interpretations of Sharia law can vary dramatically, Marzia presented him with her conditions: "I'm an educated woman, . . . I am traveling, and I need also more education. I did my master's degree, and I will do more education if I find an opportunity. I am such a person, [a] woman activist, . . . and I'm open-minded. I need my freedom." And instead of running in the opposite direction, Ashequllah said, "'Okay, I have found [out] all about you, this because I learned about you and this is the reason I am marrying you. I would like to marry with someone who is a leader, or who is very hardworking and has a name. I want to marry you because you're somehow an exception among the others. So this is the reason that I want to marry you.'"

Marzia was pleased, and so was her father. Indeed, her father was so pleased that had she defied him and refused this proposal, she said, he would have been upset. He might even have used force to persuade her. When she told me this, I was surprised, because I had formed a very different impression of her father from her stories about him as a gentle and understanding guide in her life. Even his temperate suggestion that she should "sit with" suitors and "choose" her future sounded low-key. Marzia had shown so much pride in her father's integrity, especially his refusal to compromise his anti-Communist principles for wealth and his refusal to seek economic support from his cousins in America, even though they were rich and his family was struggling, that I considered him an eminently reasonable and respectful parent. But she understood that he, like other Afghan men, would ultimately require his daughters to do what he thought best for them.

A story she told about her father helped to explain his feelings. In 1998 Marzia was working as a translator for foreign health workers—a doctor from Portugal and a physician's assistant from France. She translated their English into Dari for their patients. At one point, the two women asked her to go with them to a remote area between the Punjab and Shahristan districts of Bamyan Province.[1] To be respectful, she asked her father if she could go, "and he said, 'No, no way.'" He was rightly worried about the Taliban confronting her at the multiple checkpoints along the route, where interrogation was especially likely because she would be traveling with foreigners. "They would kill me," she explained, "because they will not kill the internationals, because somehow they have some contract with them to do the humanitarian work. . . . They were the government, they wanted to keep internationals, not to kill them, . . . but they would not allow me," an unaccompanied Afghan woman, to go along.

Marzia was determined to go anyway because of the important work the doctors were doing, so she tried a few ploys to convince her father to change his mind. First, "I sent my sister's husband . . . to go and tell him," because "sometimes we cannot talk directly to the parents." She thought it was better for an intermediary to negotiate on her behalf. But that did not work: "He didn't agree, and my sister's husband came to me and said, 'No, your father doesn't allow you to go. Don't go.'" Then "I asked my brother if he could negotiate with him, and he said, 'God no.'" He knew it would be futile. Finally, she told her brother and sister that she was going anyway. She asked if she could take her sixteen-year-old nephew as her *mahram*, and her sister agreed (although the nephew did not ultimately go with her).

Having decided to defy her father's wishes, Marzia tried to explain herself by writing him a letter on the eve of her departure. She wrote that she understood why he did not want her to go: "'I know that you're worried about my safety, but I want to go and it's my wish to go. I want to work. . . . It's not just work for money. [I] have something, I mean, to give to the people. . . . This is why I . . . am going, but [I] apologize for not obeying you. I'm going because I think my country needs me to stand to go.'" At the same time, she was secretly hoping that he would not discover she was gone, because her initial commitment was for only fifteen days. Because her father typically came to visit her at her apartment on certain Fridays, she asked her brother, who was living with her, to "tell that I'm with my sister in other part of the city" if he happened to show up. She thought it was even more likely that he would not come at all while she was gone, since on average they saw each other once a month. She decided to hold on to the letter.

Unfortunately, fate was not on her side. First, conditions were worse than Marzia had envisioned: "The situation was really, really, really tough; you cannot imagine. . . . Even being as an Afghan and . . . reading [about such things] . . . I have never faced such a life." Indeed, she was in such a remote area that she could not leave even if she wanted to. Then the trip was extended an extra few weeks. Inevitably, after a month, her father discovered that she had not only put herself in danger but deceived him to boot. He was furious. He instructed her sister to write to Marzia to tell her, "'You're not my daughter, you're doing bad, you are disobeying. . . . What are you doing; why are you killing yourself? You're dishonoring all of our family because you know you are troublemaker. . . . I told you to not go.'" She received his letter only because people in her office were traveling to Bamyan. There was no regular mail service.

Upon reading her father's letter, "I burst to cry because it was so . . ." Her voice trailed off as she told the story. She had hoped that in the end, her father would recognize her ability to make a unique contribution in this difficult situation and be proud of her for risking her own life to save others and to build the country. Instead, he interpreted her work as a dishonor to the family, whose values Marzia thought she was upholding.

The French doctor's assistant she was with, Amelie, was surprised: "She was saying, 'Why you are crying, your father must be proud of you because you're doing such a good [thing]. . . . Look at me . . . I have left everything like my friends, everything, [my] luxurious life, but I'm here for [Afghans] and you're crying.'" But Marzia was devastated. She could not leave the mission, which was an arduous three-day journey from Kabul. She was also reminded of how dangerous the job really was. As she swallowed her disappointment, she turned to her faith, because in her mind everything she was doing was "all in support of God."

This story demonstrated to me the strength of an Afghan father's sense of control over his daughters, even daughters he respects and cherishes, and the difficulty that dutiful Afghan daughters have in defying a beloved family elder. But the story's ending also made me hope that whatever anger her father would have felt had Marzia refused her current marriage would have passed. When Marzia finally returned to Kabul from her extended provincial adventure, "He said, 'I'm really proud of you, my daughter.' He's such a character that I think in most . . . things I follow him." Deep down, Marzia believes, he admires her independence and self-sufficiency because he sees himself in her.

Although Marzia's marital history is unusual in Afghanistan, it is not entirely unique. Because she so values education, Marzia attributed much of her family's liberal attitude toward marriage to their respect for and pursuit of higher education. But according to a study by the Afghanistan Research and Evaluation Unit on Family Dynamics and Family Violence, conducted in 2006 and 2007, such variations from normal marriage patterns emerge more from individual variables in household structure and family dynamics than from "gross demographic factors such as education levels; economic position; place of residence, whether urban or rural; and ethnicity" (Smith 2011, 169). In other words, Marzia may have understated her personal power in her family by identifying an external characteristic that she considered less self-aggrandizing.

The Marriage Decision: Jamila

From everything I know about Jamila, she had also exerted immense personal power in her family since she was a girl. Her stories about her negotiations with her brothers with regard to women's rights in general and her own independence in particular provided ample evidence of that. Her power appeared to be growing in 2005, as her family, which is very sensitive to criticism, was hearing nothing but praise for the quality of Jamila's work: "Everybody was praising, appreciating: 'Look it, we thought Jamila's a disabled lady, she might be not able to do anything, and now she is helping lots of people.' Like everybody was coming to our family and they were appreciating my work." Even in Ghazni, her uncles and cousins were hearing positive things about her work, and the secluded aunts and cousins, who had once said that Jamila "is not a good woman working outside, we are good women we are inside," were finally saying, "We are proud of you, Jamila." One of those Ghazni ladies had told her, "I was praying to have five sons, I was praying to God to have five sons, but ... now I regret that. I wish I had five daughters, and all of my daughters I wish were like you."

Despite her resistance to inappropriate marriages for herself, Jamila's own attitude toward marriage was not entirely negative. She could envision the right marriage for herself, and, as an adoptive mother, she was already demonstrating her family values. Unlike some Afghans, she saw no contradiction between being an educated woman and being a wife and mother. She had said repeatedly to men in her center, "If your wife is educated, then, you will have a better family. She will understand how to look after hygiene issues. She will look after the health issues like, when she is educated she is more aware, she is well trained, and she will be acting very properly to have better generation for you."

But neither her power nor her success nor own wishes and attitudes were sufficient to overcome the feeling among her male extended family members that her work, including her trips to the United States, had gone too far and dishonored the family. They began pressing Jamila's parents to marry her off. "One of my cousins in Ghazni started teasing me a lot," she said. He accused her of becoming NGO-ized, of becoming snobbish. She countered their charges and explained that "anybody is coming we provide the service." But her explanations did not satisfy the critics. Two times some cousins came to her offices. "They sent people with guns and motorbikes inside our NGO in order to terrify the students and us."

In addition,

> one of my cousins then ... starts gossiping after me a lot [in] ... the community that "she is not of good character, she has gone abroad alone with foreigners, foreigners are coming to her office, and she has male employees sitting with her all alone in the office. What she is doing?" ... And from the other side he was making gossip after my father and brothers that they are not Afghans anymore, they do not have prestige and honor anymore because they are allowing their

daughter to sit with foreigners and go abroad. . . . They are shameless people and they are disgraced people.

Such gossip "put pressure on my father and brothers to again carry attention for me. And again they said, 'Where you are going? What you are doing? You should not do this.' Like that person create[d] that tension in my life."

After a few months of this unrelenting pressure,

> when the tension was very high, [the cousin] sent a proposal after me. . . . Although in front of people he was saying, "I want her hand, I want to marry her," at the back he was sending me [the] message, "I will teach you how I can stop you. Your shameless father and brother cannot stop you, but I will show you how I can stop you from doing all of this." So it was really difficult moments of my life, like I was really worried and even I shared with some of my friends [that] some cars were following me, different cars were following me, and some people were giving me warnings on the phone, like all type of pressure.

As a result of such gossip and threats,

> my family became very harsh again with me, and they said, "No, you have to stop." Then I had no choice [but] to leave my family. I had to leave them because it was really difficult to be in such a situation longer. But I had [few] alternatives. Sometimes I was thinking to leave Afghanistan, go abroad, because it was really difficult to face all the time—tension when you are outside working; tension when you're going; at home, you're facing tension. But from the other side then I was saying, "If I leave Afghanistan so all my work, all my efforts, like with all my struggles [will have been for nothing]. Now a large number of women are looking towards me, and I have become as an example to them, to look towards me that they can bring change in their life."

The struggle was taking a toll on Jamila.

> I remember in that time one day I was crying with myself, I was very much under pressure. The baby girl who was adopted and I was looking after her, she told me, "Jamila-jan, why you are crying?" I said, "Look at what the situation [is]. I am not doing something bad, but everybody is against me, like it's really terrible." You know what she told me? She told me, "You know why you are facing all these problems?" I said, "No." She said, "Because you're a woman. . . . [and] because you're a woman . . . you need to prove it that you're a strong woman. . . ." So it was a shift in my life, like I said . . . a small child can give me example and tell me what is the reality. She was in my house all the time. She knew what I am doing; and she knew. And sometime when I get pressured she says, "You know you have to prove yourself." And sometime I am calling her my teacher. She is a good teacher of mine.

Encouraged by her adopted daughter, Jamila recalled all of the hard work she had done for the community and all she had accomplished. She knew she "couldn't leave all of that for a stupid reason, which was baseless. And I thought if I leave Afghanistan, then maybe these women become disappointed, and their struggle for change will be stopped. This was my understanding, and I thought that it's better to face this problem as well and bring a way of change for their life. If everybody is escaping, then who will bring change in life? And really it needs lots of courage, lots of energy to do it."

Jamila finally realized that the best way to truly escape her family was to marry someone other than the cousin, whose proposal, according to custom, could not be rejected for any other reason. "It was the only option in such an environment," she said. Word must have spread about her predicament because at just that moment, the mother of a young, attractive religious scholar, an imam, appeared to ask for her hand. Jamila was very impressed with his credentials. For one thing, he "belongs in a very religious family," she explained. "He is belonging to at least four, five generations of Islamic scholars. . . . All his cousins and relatives are very Islamic, and this is something inherited to them. . . . Now the new generations are going a little bit away from Islamic teachings, like, they're going towards engineering or medical science, but in seven generations their family was Islamic scholars. And one of his uncles who was killed during Communist regime . . . was a prominent scholar."

Even better, his family was famous for their moderate Islamic views. A deceased uncle, Mawlawi Muhammad Ibrahim Hamim, "was the first moderate scholar in Afghanistan. . . . There are some books of him." He was known, among other things, for his ability to reconcile science and Islam. For example, he addressed some of his followers' doubts that people could send a rocket to the moon by defining *sultan,* a verb that is unique to the Qur'an, as an "arrow, something [that] goes very fast, having a triangle at the head, which is clearing clouds and moving very hard. And he justified through that."[2] Finally, the scholars in her suitor's family were known as gentle and compassionate men. "His father is also very knowledgeable person, very kind," Jamila said. She was pleased about the proposal and grateful for its propitious timing.

The couple became engaged. And then the other shoe dropped. Her new fiancé had told Jamila that he had been married before and that his wife had died, which was true. But Jamila said that he had not told her that he also had a living wife close to his own age with whom he had two young children. She learned of the existing marriage only after the engagement, which she determined was too difficult to break.[3] Given her own situation, Jamila felt she had little choice but to go through with the marriage and become a second wife.

Jamila understood what becoming a second wife might mean, as her new husband would have to divide his time and attention between two families. Other women she had known in that situation were often dissatisfied with the arrangement, especially if they felt affection for the husband but he was really in love with his first wife. Such women recognized that, no matter how much a man might try to treat each wife equally, it was very difficult to divide one's feelings of romantic love equally between two people. One second wife Jamila knew was heartbroken to realize that her husband lavished gifts on the first wife while she never received any. The woman had also despaired that anyone would ever really love her.

Jamila had come to respect her fiancé very much, and she wondered how such an honorable person could deceive her. When she asked him that question, he replied that he did it in order to fulfill his duty as a Muslim. He knew that she needed "rescuing" from a very difficult situation. He also knew that the institution of plural marriage in Islam was originally designed to help and support women and not to facilitate men's sexual dalliances. He had immense respect for Jamila and her work. Because he was learned in Islamic texts and values, he understood that women's basic rights are consistent with Islam, even within marriage, and that men have a responsibility to be kind to their wives and families. It was his intent to live by those values.

Jamila ultimately allowed herself to become a second wife in order to marry such a man—who respected her, both personally and professionally—and to do her duty to her parents and her traditions. Escaping matrimony with the uneducated, hostile cousin was certainly a plus, as was establishing a position in which she could age gracefully, continue her important work, and enjoy the pleasures of raising her own children.

Married Life: Marzia

"I'm happy," Marzia said. "I'm not sad for this married life." She and her husband felt affection for one another. She had her father's blessing. Her husband's family supported her, welcomed her, and believed that she was a good wife for their son. In all of these things, Marzia considered herself a lucky married Afghan woman.

But because she was attempting to establish a companionate and somewhat egalitarian marriage in the Afghan context, she said, "I still think that marriage life is a kind of confining liberty in Afghanistan." For that reason, in her own marriage, "still we have challenges in front of us." On one level, those challenges sounded very familiar, even to American ears: "The thought that I have in my mind is sometimes different than the thoughts he has; the demand I have is different than the demand he has; the expectation I have from him, he doesn't think of that. So this is a challenge . . . and it can be a normal challenge because no one can be of the same thought." Ashequllah was trying hard to live up to his prenuptial promises to be a different kind of husband in a different kind of marriage, but "he thinks also more about culture" than Marzia does, and sometimes "he doesn't want culturally to accept" her independence.

Part of the problem was his age. "He was brought up mostly during the Taliban and mujahideen periods . . . while they were talking 'no woman education, no woman education, this is the words of Holy Qur'an,'" Marzia explained. So even though he wanted to support women's rights, "a lot of changes [had] been awkward to him." In particular, he suffered at the beginning of their marriage worrying about "when he will be criticized by the community that why he allows his wife to go alone like one month outside of the country." He was particularly worried that "the neighbors will see who's coming, a woman come out from a car, a Land Rover car, from an international car, and then what will the neighbors say? They'll say, 'Okay, what a bad man [he is]. He allows his wife to go to work and get salary from international organizations,' which is not acceptable for the Afghan community."

Some of Ashequllah's objections focused on Marzia's security. "Sometimes he says that we have to be careful also, I mean for me, he says, 'Do not travel too much because it will create problems for your living. Surrounding us there are many Taliban around.'" He worried that her efforts for women's rights would not reap sufficient rewards to justify the risks she was taking. "His idea is like that you have to protect yourself also, not just only talk about women's rights." He predicted that she would not get the results she wanted, which "even the government doesn't support." Instead, he said, "your relations will be more bad with the Supreme Court because of that association that you are running." Marzia recognized that "he's correct somehow, because you see the situation. Women's rights is something that you will be pointing out rather than [getting those in power] to appreciate you." But, she said, "I don't care about this because once you have your [mind made up] about something and if you want to achieve something, then you can do as much as [you] can. But it might happen that I cannot move on because sometimes something will be more than your power, that you can do nothing."

Their disagreements had sometimes "become argument between us because if I am asking for my rights and then it is a challenge, and you have to struggle for that, and it's not [an] easy struggle. So you have to come up to a kind of argument between each other." But, Marzia said, "this five years of the marriage has brought a lot of changes to his mind." Recently, her husband had been mostly "satisfied. . . . He's . . . not really getting harsh on things. . . . Finally he accepts, I mean, he's not really pushing for things very hard." At the same time, Marzia said that he had the "normal Afghan [male] psychological and cultural understanding." So, he might cloak his real feelings about what is appropriate for a wife to do in admonitions about Marzia's security. For example, "he doesn't want to say to me, 'Don't go,' [so] he says, 'Be careful.'" By the same token, when Marzia traveled, "he's not saying . . . that 'you're not allowed,'" so he might say, "Too much traveling is not good." And instead of saying that wives should not be away from their husbands for too long, he says, "I'm alone, and I don't feel good while you're away." His way of approaching these topics endeared him to Marzia.

Perhaps more contentious was the issue of a wife's behavior as a reflection of her husband's honor. "Sometimes while I say something to my husband, he says,

'Okay, you are my wife, anything you are doing it comes to me.'" But Marzia did not accept that point. She said, "No, I'm daughter of someone, and I have a name, and anything [I do] comes to me. They say first 'Marzia,' [and then] daughter of that and wife of that." She represented herself, in other words, and if people objected to her activities, such as working for women's rights, then they should think "how bad girl she is," not how bad a man he was. She believed, "That's okay, you [my husband] are a part of me, [but] you're not every part of me. I am myself. I am my own, and anything comes to me, it comes to me. I'm a separate individual and have my independence."

This issue had arisen pointedly with respect to Marzia's retention of her maiden surname. "I haven't changed my second name yet to take my husband's family [name]," she explained. Sometimes Ashequllah saw that she signed a note as Marzia Basel, and he wanted her to change it to Marzia Orya Khail. He asked, "Why you are writing all the time Basel? You now belong to me." She said, "No, I belong to my father who is a good man.... He did a very honest job. The position that he had, he could have had a lot of bribe, and he could give us more luxurious life. But I enjoyed my life because he was very honest, and he just did what he could do by his hard work. He suffered, but he give us education,... he had the opportunity, as a judge, as prosecutor, he worked as a prosecutor most of the time rather than being a judge but also in his law firm he didn't do illegal things to give us [luxuries]... he was saying... be content." So Marzia told her husband, "I am enough mature now that you [cannot] change it." She prevailed on the name issue because "sometimes it depends how you could be strong enough to argue your rights."

As with the question of her surname, there were few precedents for many of the couple's arrangements, which caused Marzia some worry. For example, her husband chose to live in her house with her rather than occupy his family's property. That might have ramifications for the inheritances of Marzia's sisters, who Marzia says "are more in need rather than me." Should the house go to them rather than to her husband, if something happened to her? In addition, Marzia did not know how to feel about sharing finances. Should everything she earned be available to her husband and vice versa?

At some level, she accepted that "according to Islam, the money is his job, not my job.... He should facilitate all the life rather than me," although some Afghan men neglected to support their families. When Marzia considered that precept, she thought that what she earned should belong to her. Her own income was the best assurance of success for any children she might have and the best insurance for herself in her old age. "You know," she explained, "being a woman activist, sometimes I don't believe in men.... We women are very honest... with our families. Also we do respect our cultures and we do respect our families.... As much as [women] have incomes outside, they want to spend it on the welfare of the family.... The men usually think of their own business, rather than...

thinking of education for the children or other things inside the family." Women would not remarry without considering the welfare of their children, but men who lose a wife "can get married in one year, no more waiting [than] that."

On another level, when Marzia considered the fragility of her own and her country's future prospects and the reality that "in a minute in Afghanistan a bomb can come to your house, you will lose everything," she did not want to waste time fretting or arguing about money. "Finally I conclude that okay, of course, there's no division [of financial responsibility] between men and women in Afghanistan." What's mine is his, and what's his is mine.

Despite these worries, Marzia knew that her husband supported her work and her wish for independence, just as he said he did before their marriage. She said, "Sometimes my husband . . . says, 'I am really proud of you. You're suffering and you're working too hard. You protect [a] whole side of the family.'" Ashequllah even offered to help Marzia apply for a position with the Supreme Court through his connections at the Parliament. He agreed to share her résumé with the proper committee, and he attended the interview with her because he could speak with the interviewers in Pashto (Marzia speaks primarily Dari).

At a certain point during the interview, the committee told him "to tell me go out of the room and we will discuss this résumé," Marzia said. After several minutes, "he came out, [and] he was laughing and laughing. [I asked], 'Why you are laughing?' He said, 'Oh, I can't protect such a woman who has all women's rights activities in her résumé. [The Court thinks,] 'Tomorrow she will be a problem for us, even if she is at the Court, even if she is coming to the high position, because in any minute she will challenge women's rights, you know?'" Although she was disappointed, Marzia recognized the challenge her husband faced in trying to argue her case for the job. "We are kind of like a fire for the people, especially for the men that, if we know [about women's rights], and we teach one another, we will be a problem for them. Because their place will be tighter and tighter. So this is, this was very funny."

Beyond the couple's own relationship lay the challenges of the extended family. Even in the relatively affluent, urban environment of Marzia's and Jamila's marriages, life in extended families could be stressful. Both women had talked repeatedly about the infighting and gossip in many families "about who was eating what, who was wearing what . . . or the children doesn't have enough clothes, so there will be conflict of understanding." When wives were young, their lives were not under their control. If they married a family's eldest son, they would have to live with the parents, and the daughter-in-law might have the burden of the household and children on her shoulders, as the wife of the eldest. Peace came only when a woman's children were grown, Marzia explained. Then, at "age like fifty to fifty-four or like that, then they will . . . have a kind of separate life because now their children [are] grown up, their economy is also grown up, and they enjoy it, because in Afghanistan the . . . practical, not the legal age of retirement . . . is mostly after age of forty-five. . . . A few women would have . . . energy to work very well, but at the age of fifty they would like to stay home. In that time while they are staying at home, this will be more comfortable for them."

Before that, the working wife faced many challenges. In her household, "the women who are working outside, they take both responsibilit[ies]—inside [the] house responsibility and outside." Family expectations were high, and the woman shouldered all blame if the household was not well organized. By the same token, high-achieving women like Marzia "take life seriously, which affects our home also." She, for one, felt "furious about everything should be well organized, why it is not correct? Then it hits me, too much." "Men are not like that," she said. "They take life easy. . . . This is why I think that we feel much [more] responsibility than men feel around the house and around the caring of the children and everything." This is also why women feel it is "the responsibility of women to be . . . very, very well organized."

In addition, "if you are a good woman, then you have to take care of your mother all your life. We don't have houses for the old people to take care of them, so someone should take care of them for our long life." In many cases, "you have to take care of even your sister-in-laws, your brother-in-laws, your father-in-law, mother-in-law. Responsibility will go up while a woman is getting married. No matter if she is educated and going out [to work]."

For those relatives who did not live with you, you had a responsibility to be hospitable to them at a moment's notice, and expectations for that hospitality were high.

> You have to be very careful with all the relations that you have in order to have your reputation among the family, so usually women would like to not lose it. Because if you don't be [hospitable to guests] . . . then you will lose your reputation soon [with] the father-in-law's family or even with your family, because they don't care how much education or how much work do you have. They'll just say, "She doesn't, she can't take care of us." . . . Even if . . . you have a big meeting to go [to], a lot of responsibility outside, . . . you should take a day off and just say there are guests and [tell] your office that I cannot attend it. This comes with the culture, so you cannot sometimes say "no" because you have to, you have to respect it, otherwise it will not be good.

Marzia's immediate family understood her professional situation. They did not show up at her doorstep "without any calling me or without any appointing; they just call me and say, 'Are you at home, can we come?' . . . We got used to it; [it's now] my habit. It is not good otherwise." Her "sisters who are educated and are married and are working" knew that Marzia's work with internationals limited her free time more than their work did theirs. "Because I am working more strictly, working with international organizations . . . you have to be on time for everything," her sisters "usually call me and say if you are at home we could come. Should we come or not?" And if she were busy, "even no matter, if it's Friday, I just say, 'No, I have work, would you please come the other day, or I can call you back?'" With some other of her family members and friends, Marzia had also established a visiting protocol: "In my case I say, 'Don't come without Friday weekend, this is the time that you can come and I can work for you.'" She had also been very lucky with her in-laws. "My in-law's family, they're good. . . . If a guest comes from their family, I just give a call, and they just come and help them, help the guests with food and other things."

Despite all of this understanding and support, Marzia still agonized over the conflict between her responsibilities to her family—both natal and married—and her responsibilities to her work. Even if guests followed her admonitions about timing and notice, there was always the problem of what to do when the guests stayed longer than the time she had for them. "You would prefer to stay with them rather to go to the office because you know it is culturally something if you say to the guest, 'Good-bye, I am going to the office. You can sit at home alone.' No point for the guest to sit at home alone; they just leave the house instead."

She faced a particular problem because some of the time "the office" was in her home. If she did not have a meeting outside the house, she was in the awkward position of closing herself in her room in order to "go to work." "I mean, I, from the beginning of my marriage life, I had always been straightforward that I have a job, I have to do it," Marzia explained. "No one should come to my room; just lock the door and work. But it is difficult. Men get annoyed sometimes because you are too busy with your work and do not take care of them. They say, 'Oh, what is life meaning that you're always behind computer and just sitting and working? When do you have time for me . . . ?'"

"This is why that I think educated women suffer more than uneducated women," Marzia said, continuing a theme from earlier conversations. "The uneducated people they . . . are at home no matter if a guest comes, no matter how difficult work they do." And then reflecting the lament of many a working woman, she continued:

> But educated women, they have to work inside and outside, so it's a double kind of work. Men do not take care of the family and housework, most of them. Some of them are good, I mean, there are a few that they can help around the house. But most of them will not. So then your life will be hard because you have to be awake until twelve o'clock at night to just do the housework after you come back. Cook, clean, wash, and then on Fridays you will not have time to go [to the mosque]. You have to take care of the cleaning or these things. So this is too much, sometimes.

In the end, Marzia conceded that educated women in Afghanistan might have an advantage in extended families, especially in large households, where "as a daughter-in-law you have more responsibility, you should do everything." An educated woman was better equipped to negotiate her responsibilities. "Sometimes if you justify things," Marzia explained, "I mean it depends how much women are powerful, . . . you know? If you say, 'No I cannot do that,' then the people will get used to it. But if you say, 'Yes,' to everything, then they will be just used to saying, 'Do this for me,' so they usually will just expect you [to do] more things." But even as Marzia worked hard to justify her limitations with regard to family life, she was also working hard to meet what she considered to be her family responsibilities.

Married Life: Jamila

"Now, my husband is religious, but he is very open-minded," Jamila said. "Our marriage was more of [a] contract, not more of a normal marriage which we have and our families." From the beginning, her husband knew the marriage was conditional. Jamila was clear: "'These are my conditions, and if you accept it, that's okay. If you're not, then we cannot remain together.' So . . . he understand[s] that this is my commitment to my work and to my profession, I have to do, and he's support[ive] of that as well. . . . He never said to not go to this meeting or don't do this. I do not allow him to talk about that issue."

In keeping with her belief in the liberatory aspects of Islam, Jamila saw no contradiction between her husband's deep education in the religion and his kindness and consideration to her and his recognition of her rights. But both she and Marzia recognized how important a man's family and personal background can be to his attitudes in his marriage.

Early in her marriage, Jamila saw firsthand what that family background was in her husband's case. Although the family is conservative in many ways, she said, "I . . . noticed that all in their relatives they're very, very good with their wives. Like, very good." She recounted a story about her father-in-law's relationship with his own wife, her husband's mother, which was characterized by a loving form of teasing. In violation of the usual practice of gender-segregated eating, the father would say, "Oh, come sit beside me. I cannot eat. You have to feed me." Jamila explained that "he is all the time first of all, he's feeding his wife. He's giving first spoon by his own hand to his wife. Although she is shy and she is aged now her sons are grown up, [and says] 'Don't do this,' . . . he says, 'If you are not doing this to me . . . don't have this kindness to me, I will have this kindness for you.'" At first Jamila "didn't understand the phenomenon that my father-in-law was feeding my mother-in-law first of all, then I found that it . . . was practice of Holy Prophet. He was doing this to his wife."

The men in Jamila's husband's family had also consulted their daughters about their marriages. "My own father-in-law sits with his daughter and asks, 'This guy is coming for your hand. Do you like to marry him or not?' Then whatever groom's family is bringing, they are saying, 'That is totally your choice.' Then they can make a party like to invite some few people, like, they never argue whatever is common. And in my own parents' family, it was very, very big issue. Like I had seen that in my own family. Personally I suffered a lot. And the other [children] . . . but they're a very good example in their area." This reflected a difference between imams, like her husband's family, and mullahs. "Unfortunately . . . when you go to many other mullahs' family, you will not find this."

His family background definitely shaped the way her husband, Fazal, behaved with her and her children. He suffered ridicule for his solicitousness to her, especially by Jamila's family, but he was also changing some hearts and minds. Jamila explained:

> My . . . brother and [other] in-laws was laughing at my husband that he's so looking after [me], and he's helping me at home, and he's looking after children. So they were making like some fun or some gestures that [said], "Look at him, what he's doing." One day he, while we were serving dinner, he told [my] brother, "Okay, you consider yourself a man enough, an Afghan man." He said, "Yes, I am." "You're very prestigious man, and you believe in honor and dignity." He said, "Yes, I am." My husband asked him, "Okay, if you see a woman on the corner of the street, having two, three burdens with herself, carrying luggage, something, and she wants to cross the street, what you will do?" He said, "Definitely I will rush to help her." [Fazal] said, "Okay, if my own wife in my own house needs help to carry something to help her, this is not something of dignity? I feel proud to help my wife, my children, my family. If you feel proud to help a stranger woman on the street, I feel proud to help my wife inside my home." So it was really difficult, although I was about to cry in that situation because it really hurt me that they know that I'm not able to carry things because usually [when] I'm making a steak at home, and they are making gesture, and they are laughing, and they knew that my physical condition [is a burden for me]. But my husband argued in such a beautiful way that after that nobody said anything. And they were also trying—now when I go there or do something, everybody rush to help me or to even they are helping their wives to do something, to look after their children. Before it was a big shame in the family to help a woman.

I had the privilege of meeting Fazal in Istanbul and of watching firsthand his behavior with Jamila and their children. I had been skeptical that any Afghan man would really take over child care while Jamila was participating in our interviews, although she had assured me that he planned to do just that. But I was wrong. He watched the baby girl for the entire time we were talking together over four days, even though he was fasting for Ramadan from sunup to sundown for three of them. Their three-year-old son appeared only at certain mealtimes, when he was happy to be reunited with his mother. And when the boy got sick, Fazal took full responsibility for nursing him and for getting his medicine and meals while also caring for the baby. It was an impressive performance for any parent, male or female.

Jamila predicted that Fazal could suffer more ridicule for it, however.

> There is need of awareness and education of man. Like, look at right now he has come with me to support me in this meeting, and he's looking after children. He's a Pashtun man [from a] very conservative tribal community. If this story goes to Afghanistan, then they will [say], "Oh, he's a slave of his wife, he is looking after children." So it will be big shame for him in the community. But he's doing [what is practical]. Sometimes I think he is [a] more democratic person [than anyone I know], doing activities and helping me and other family members in this way. Sometime it's very beautiful.

Like Marzia, Jamila had not changed her surname to her husband's family name, which is Kakar. But unlike Marzia's husband, Fazal accepted and respected her decision from the outset. When his family was saying,

> "It seems you are not united with each other or maybe you're not in good relation with each other, why she's not taking your name beside her name," he told them in front of me that "she was Jamila Afghani before marrying me. I never did anything to develop her to become a person. She is already a developed person. And she's not going to change because of me. I know this. So whatever she wants, that is right. If she likes to put my name, that will be honor for me. If she doesn't want to put, that is okay with me."

Fazal's attitude is especially remarkable in its demonstration of his ability—in stark contrast with many Afghan men—to distinguish between his honor as a man and his wife's behavior and attitudes and to believe that her choices are inherently honorable. Jamila emphasized that his attitude resulted from his deep understanding of Islam, and she considered his dedication to practicing democratic Islamic values in "family life . . . [a] very positive point on this side." Marzia was quick to note that Islam is not enough, because misogynist Afghan culture is so strong. The fact that the "father and mother of him were friendly to each other, they were respecting each other, they were doing a normal life, not like a slave and lord . . . has given him a model of how to behave," she said. But it is also possible that Islam was the inspiration for the father, who, Jamila attested, "is also a very good person."

All of this is not to say that Jamila's husband was immune from the gender values of Afghan tradition. Jamila once tested the impact of traditional thinking on Fazal's views by asking him,

> "If I'm going to ask you [for a] divorce, what you will do?" Abruptly I ask this question to get his mentality, without any background or any situation. Just I wanted to check with it. He said, "I will kill you or myself." I said, "How you can say this? Islam does allow [divorce], laws does allow [divorce], and personally if a person is not happy to live together, then what is the result of living together? How you can say this?" Then he was trying to polish it, but naturally

whatever is taught by our culture, by our forefathers, that is very deep rooted. Just I wanted to check it, without any background I put the question to get what he says. [I told him], "I blame that you're a scholar preaching to others and how you can say this?"

But it was deeply rooted. As Marzia had illustrated in many examples, "if a person is going for divorce, [it is] not acceptable in the [Afghan] community, within the family."

Because her husband was with her only part of the time, and because of the enormous security issues a publicly known Afghan woman faced the minute she left her house, Jamila had been living in her office for several years. It was there that she raised her children, with the help of babysitters, as well as ran her various enterprises. Under those circumstances, her pre-school-age son had taken on some responsibility for his mother. "When I get upset," Jamila explained, "so he is very, very curious, 'Why my mother is upset?' And he's going and asking his father, 'Have you said something to my mother, why she is upset?' Like then he is going to the office member, to different workers, asking, '[Is] there anything wrong with my mother, what happened?'" Jamila also told me that her son waited outside the bathroom door whenever she went in there. He was listening for any noise that might indicate that she had dropped her crutches or was in some other way in trouble. If he heard such a noise, he would knock on the door politely and ask her if she was all right or if she needed any help. Jamila was very touched by and proud of this behavior because it indicated to her that her son "is feminist, at the moment he is feminist."

But there was also evidence that her son was struggling with the parameters of acceptable gender behavior in Afghan culture. On the one hand, Jamila noted that "he's very good playing with girls, not with boys." She believed that he gravitated toward girls because her "nature has transferred to him, I can see my own picture [in] him. Very emotional, very sensitive, curious to know new changes, development, and sometimes he's more than me, sensitive. And he respects women, loves women. If today I'm going to see Marzia with [her] makeup and colorful clothes, he will offer a marriage." She laughed as she recalled incidences of his enthusiasm for such feminine attractions. Even I got a taste of his affinity for women on the last day of our interviews, when the boy asked his mother to take a picture of him with me. I was pleased that he could feel some attachment, even though I had been unable to communicate with him in his language.

On the other hand, Jamila's son was understandably subject to the influence of traditional thinking. For example, Jamila explained that her

> in-laws' family taught him to say Jamila Afghani Kakar or Jamila Kakar, and one day he was saying to himself, "Jamila Kakar, Jamila Kakar." I said, "Why you are saying to yourself 'Jamila Kakar'? I'm Jamila Afghani." . . . He was saying, "Because you belong to my father." I said, "No, I do not belong to your father. I

am a person. Jamila Afghani is not an item to belong to someone." I said, "You do not belong to me. I will not tell you that you should select Afghani or Kakar; it should be your choice . . . what second name you will choose for yourself." Like, it was really difficult to convince him because . . . again and again, he was asking, "Then why they tell me that you're Jamila Afghani Kakar? Your name is Jamila Afghani."

Eventually, however, she was able to convince him. Now "when somebody ask[s] him, 'You belong to whom, you're son of?' he says, 'Afghani. Son of Afghani.'"

It was clear from Jamila's deep devotion to her children that they had compensated for some of the disappointment she might have felt as a second wife, even (or especially) to such a fine man as her husband. She took immense pleasure in her young son, who was so obviously blessed with his mother's bright intelligence and caring personality. It is also possible that being a second wife had bestowed more independence on Jamila than she would have enjoyed under other circumstances. Fazal had even agreed that she could study abroad for a Ph.D. in international relations. (In that event, she would bring her children and a female relative with her to look after them.) He seemed to understand that such a move would help her escape the security issues and other pressures put on her in Afghanistan, at least for a time, and better equip her to contribute to her country's future.

Reflections

Our meetings in Istanbul cast a new perspective for me on the marriage system of Afghanistan in comparison to the allegedly love-based marriage practices of the West. On its face, it might seem that marrying for love is an obviously superior motivation for hooking oneself up to another person for life. But the examples of Marzia's and Jamila's marriages provide an alternative perspective. It was too soon to tell whether the arranged marriage form they experienced will provide a lifetime of happiness for the two women, but at least as a starting point, having an opportunity to discuss what marriage means, how each spouse expects the other to behave, the obstacles that might hinder the couple's success, and other such factors appeared to produce some benefits.

Too few prospective brides and grooms in the West discuss those issues before the wedding occurs. Engagements might last for a few hours or a few years; there is no standard procedure for drawing out differing values or perspectives on married life. There are typically no marriage contracts or written agreements, except among the wealthy, although some religious traditions may attempt to provide those opportunities. The prevailing image of marriage in the West, especially in some parts of the United States, encourages being swept off one's feet, falling in love at first sight, and instinctively knowing that the beloved is the right one. Reasoned analysis and consultation with one's elders are seldom the preferred approaches to tying the proverbial knot.

That method (or myth) works for a few, but not for all. In fact, recent research suggests that the best way to ensure a low divorce rate in the United States is to promote higher education. In 2013 college-educated couples had about a 16 percent divorce rate in the first ten years of marriage, while couples with high school educations had nearly a 50 percent divorce rate for the same period. Education is also the best preventer of out-of-wedlock births. Ninety percent of American women with four-year college degrees wait to have children until after marriage, while "nearly all of the increase in childbearing outside of marriage in the last two decades is from births to cohabiting couples, most without college degrees" (Cherlin 2013, SR7). Of course, economic prospects typically correlate to educational level in the United States, which only adds evidence that a reasoned approach to marriage, considering both partner characteristics and economic opportunities, is more conducive to successful marriages and stable families in the United States. Perhaps elite Americans only *think* they oppose the practice of marriage arrangement and family decision-making about prospective spouses, while they actually engage in it to some extent themselves, as powerful families often intermarry and factors such as economic class, religion, geography, and educational levels drive their decisions about marriage partners.

Marzia's and Jamila's husbands were also interesting role models for almost any culture. Their support for their wives was exemplary, especially given the counterpressures they experienced from their peers and in Ashequllah's case from his educational background. I saw firsthand how Fazal approached his obligations to his wife and family by at least temporarily putting them ahead of his own needs in a public way. And from the perspective of U.S. and other cultures that privilege female youth, Ashequllah's attraction to an older woman was inspiring. According to Marzia, it is not that unusual in Afghanistan for some men to appreciate and marry older women.

Of course, it is also not unusual for an Afghan man to marry a much younger woman, especially as a second wife. The practice of polygyny (multiple wives but not multiple husbands) is perhaps more difficult for many Westerners to accept, but it is not just Western bias that creates opposition to the practice. Clearly, Jamila was opposed to the idea; indeed, in discussing it with her, I learned that she was as resistant to the idea of becoming a second wife as most Western women would be. Some objections were practical—conditions would be crowded; multiple homes are expensive, so economies would be pinched. Others were emotional—love could not be equally divided among wives; the competition among wives would create misery for them and inevitably feed the perhaps unworthy ego of the husband. But in the Afghan context, where marriage is a requirement and a necessity for most women's survival, support for polygyny can also be practical, as in the case of widows or divorced women or as an alternative to a worse marriage prospect for someone like Jamila. In such cases, polygyny can solve economic or familial problems, lessen the workload for any one woman, and give women some time off and distance from the pressures of marriage.

Perhaps the most important message from the contrasting marriage systems of East and West is the relationship of marriage practices to broader cultural needs, goals, and values. In both Afghanistan and the United States, such practices work with other social systems, for better or worse. So, analyzing and judging marriage forms must occur in the context of those systems. There are reasons beyond morality, for example, that monogamy works better in Western capitalist nations than would polygamy of any kind (polygyny or polyandry—multiple husbands—or both). In addition, there are some links between the two systems, such as "plural marriage" in the fundamentalist wing of the Church of Latter-day Saints in the United States. At the same time, it is important to recognize the variations among marriage practices and values that occur within societies because of religious belief, ethnic or racial identity, economic and educational status, regional location, and individual opinion, among other variables. Such variation is as true for Afghanistan as it is for the United States.

PART III

Uncertainty

(2010–2013)

Prologue: Ambiguous Futures

Sometimes the passage of time clarifies experience. Thus, it was only in hindsight that I recognized how significant Jamila's and Marzia's doubts and uncertainties in 2010 actually were. During our interviews in that year, I was more struck by the women's continued courage in the face of an increasingly dangerous climate for their activism. I marveled at their positive outlooks, focus on improvement, and investment in the future of their own causes and activities. I admired the way they had negotiated their marriages and continued their work despite familial objections and periodic lapses in their husbands' understanding.

Because we had talked in 2005 about the obstacles to advancing women's rights and opportunities, I had understood their concerns in 2010 as a continuation of a situation they had long endured and expected to change only slowly. I recognized that they identified perhaps more or more persistent intransigent factors in their country over the years, but I emphasized to myself their own persistent optimism as an important counterweight to those factors.

There were, indeed, some reasons for optimism in 2010. As Jamila reported, maternal death rates had fallen from approximately one in eleven to one in fifty, or fewer than five hundred deaths per one hundred thousand births.[1] Such dramatic change supported the idea that building institutions, such as the Department of Women and Reproductive Health established in 2003, could produce results (Banerjee 2008, 248). Unfortunately, the United States had done too little of that institution building.

A BBC poll in 2009 also contained reasons for hope. Results suggested that fewer than one in ten Afghans supported the Taliban in 2009.[2] The poll also showed strong support for women's rights, albeit in "an Afghan way." In addition, 90 percent of respondents did not believe the Taliban had reformed and blamed them for most of the violence in the country, although Afghan warlords, foreign Islamic fighters, the Karzai government, and Pakistan also got blamed for the country's problems. Not surprisingly, 80 percent liked the idea that occupying forces would soon depart. (Indeed, support for the U.S. occupation had reversed from 2005, with 70 percent supporting it in 2005 and only 30 percent in 2009.) But even those respondents worried about losing U.S. and NATO assistance in reducing violence after 2014.[3]

The two women's optimism was also supported by other news. Women had constituted 60 percent of students in teacher-training institutions in 2007, and they were beginning to work in schools. Women were also working in the media, but contrary to Marzia's hope, they served mostly as cleaners and cooks. More important, perhaps, women constituted 24 percent of Community Development Council members—a sign of their increased civic participation (Skaine 2008, 98–99). Women had also demonstrated that, given the chance, they were willing to put themselves forward politically, despite the risks. Although female voter participation was lower in 2010 than it had been in 2004, more than four hundred female candidates ran for office in the parliamentary election that year and won more seats (sixty-nine) than in the earlier election. At 28 percent, women exceeded their specified 25 percent parliamentary quota (Nemat 2010, 176).[4]

Perhaps because of such positive news, when at the end of our interviews I asked about barriers to their visions of Afghan women's improved status, I took in stride Jamila's and Marzia's feelings of frustration. Only later, in light of the developments discussed in part III, did I recognize how certain facial expressions and tones of voice, sentences that trailed off in bewilderment rather than reached crisp conclusions, and occasional revelations of truly gargantuan impediments constituted the women's growing despair. I finally realized that I should have seen Marzia's comment in Istanbul as a bellwether for both women's descending emotional spiral: "I as an Afghan who is educated, while I see the woman's situation I cry, you know? For my own nation."

Those tears could have been triggered by any number of events and developments in Afghanistan in 2010 that paralleled the positive news. For example, the overall picture for women's education was actually mixed. Despite more enrollments, twenty schools associated with women had been bombed or burned, and approximately 126 students and teachers had been killed, an increase over similar statistics in 2009.[5] Although 2.5 million girls attended public schools in Afghanistan in 2010, up from 5,000 during the Taliban regime, and many local communities were again sponsoring underground schools, 2 million girls did not attend school at all, and some U.S.-built schools never opened. Indeed, few rural girls at all attended school in the southern and south-central parts of the country, mostly because facilities were too distant (no one asked the locals where to build the schools) and security was poor. Moreover, only twenty-five high schools were functioning nationwide, and the thirty functioning universities were in various stages of organization, repair, and quality. Countless children and adults still attended classes in home schools, tents, and cargo containers.[6]

The state of the country's mental health in general and women's mental health in particular was also grim. As a result of the 2009 BBC poll, in which men and women participated equally, pollster Michael Clarke summarized mental health findings by saying that the Afghan people were "patient, stoical, politically realistic and depressed."[7] The BBC poll did not measure differences in depression by gender, but Nahid Aziz, who did so in the next year, concluded that women were more depressed than men. The combination of traumatic war experiences, including the anxiety and emotional disturbances caused by sexual violence, was exacerbated further by the denial of women's rights in the post-Taliban period. Indeed, continuing gender segregation in and of itself contributed to women's poor mental health, Aziz said, because it encouraged women to dislike themselves. As measured during the Taliban period in different studies (1998–2000), from 70 to 97 percent of Afghan women in Taliban-controlled areas were clinically depressed by Western criteria, 42 percent met the criteria for post-traumatic stress disorder, and 65 to 77 percent had considered suicide (Brodsky 2011, 75–76; Aziz 2011, 234–38).[8] Like everything else, those effects did not disappear when the Taliban regime was toppled.

Men's responses to their own emotional trauma, economic and political stress, and anxiety about their proper masculine roles and identities also threatened women's mental and physical health, Aziz concluded. Continued forced and child marriages and domestic violence by husbands, as well as increasing abuses by in-laws and cowives, had contributed to more self-immolations by disempowered women, who used suicide as a way to be heard. Added to these tragedies was women's increased drug abuse, which also reflected the female population's fatigue and grief, caused by heavy workloads, psychosocial stressors, mistreatment, marital dissatisfaction, family trauma, and loss of family members (Aziz 2011, 238–39).

The prospects for treating these problems seemed dim. As Marzia and Jamila had repeatedly said, seeing any doctor was unlikely for most Afghan women. For one thing, access to health facilities was limited, and 40 percent of those facilities had no female staff with whom women could consult. There were also few therapists in Afghanistan. Even fewer families would recognize a woman's behavioral symptoms, such as irritability, attention deficit, insomnia, or nightmares, or her physical symptoms, such as low energy, back pain, muscle weakness, or heart problems, as signs of her clinical depression, especially in a society that lets so many of women's life-threatening physical ailments go untreated. Indeed, although the life expectancy for both men and women was forty-four in 2010, women aged fifteen to forty-nine were three times more likely to die than men (Aziz 2011, 234–36).

Women's low literacy rate—15.8 percent versus 31 percent for men by some measures—was another obstacle to a deep understanding of mental health, as well as to recognizing their rights or developing marketable skills (Skaine 2008, 98–99).

In addition, women's overall social and economic status remained problematic. Fifty-seven percent of girls married before age sixteen, 70 to 80 percent of them in forced marriages. A million widows in Afghanistan had limited options to promote their own survival, let alone rights. Women's general economic status also remained well below that of men, with a gross domestic product of $402 for women and $1,182 for men in 2007, and a pay scale only one-third that of men's (Nemat 2010, 174). By 2007, 38.2 percent of women were economically active, but women's employment still tended to be locked into low income–generating activities, mainly in agriculture and handicrafts. Creating new enterprises that generated higher-wage employment depended on increasing security (Kandiyoti 2005, 32; Skaine 2008, 98–99).

There were also many contradictory trends influencing women's status in Afghanistan. On the worrying side, a growing number of Afghans had begun seeing themselves as the *umma* being attacked by the West and defining themselves as part of an international jihad. Even in its heyday, the Taliban, which increasingly encouraged this view, did not define their project in that international way. But this perspective developed gradually, starting in 2003, as the allied forces continued supporting Karzai's increasingly corrupt government (Clark 2010, 51–52). The growing openness to the jihadist rhetoric reempowered the most violent actors in Afghanistan and threatened women's rights efforts that appeared to emanate from Western values. Such rhetoric also threatened programs such as Marzia's and Jamila's that rooted women's rights in Islam.

At the very least, this mosaic of positive and negative developments reflected an unreliable climate in 2010 for women's ultimate flourishing and improved social status and rights, even in the Afghan way. It also reflected the uncoordinated pastiche of programs and policies promoted by Western governments and NGOs, about which Marzia and Jamila were so critical, and the missteps and false assumptions of international policy makers and planners. Finally, it suggested how unfortunate it was that such planners did not do more after 2001 to build on the work of local women activists.

Before bringing this manuscript to a close, I had several more conversations with Jamila and Marzia. Those included a face-to-face meeting with Marzia in Tempe in the spring of 2011, several Skype interviews with Marzia in the following year, and phone calls with both Marzia and Jamila in 2012 and 2013. Margaret Mills also visited Afghanistan in 2013 and shared her observations with me.

The meeting with Marzia in Tempe came about through one of the Luce Foundation–funded seminars I participated in through ASU's Center for the Study of Religion and Conflict. In 2010–11, the title of the seminar was "Religion and International Affairs: Through the Prism of Rights and Gender." The Luce Foundation grant included funding for visiting speakers, such as Daniel Philpott, Elizabeth Shakman Hurd, Rachel Cichowski, and Isobel Coleman, and a short residency by a visiting expert. Because Marzia's qualifications were perfect for such a residency, I nominated her for the position, and she spent mid-March to mid-April 2011 in Tempe. In addition to attending her lectures and participating in seminar meetings with her, I also interviewed her several times and recorded our conversations.

It was during that visit that I truly understood how emotionally overwhelmed Marzia was by her own stories about the obstacles Afghan women faced and the opposition to change in her country's gender practices and relations. On the day after she gave her overview address about the current situation for Afghan women to a mixed audience of ASU students and faculty and several Afghan Americans from the community, she told me that she had returned to her room that night and "cried for one hour." She said that it was getting harder and harder for her to describe what was happening in Afghanistan. It pained her to admit that the only moderately free Afghan women were those living in Kabul, that Afghan women would never have rights if the Taliban were allowed to share power in the government, that the media she had relied on in her vision of change had not fulfilled their promise to promote expanded roles for women, that the legal system was still inadequate and essentially unwilling to address women's needs, and that the impending withdrawal of international forces could create worse conditions in Afghanistan than those that brought the mujahideen to power in 1992.

Even in the midst of such despair, however, Marzia still clung to any signs of hope for the future. For example, after she had lunch with retired Supreme Court justice Sandra Day O'Connor in Phoenix in April 2011, she was almost ebullient with a future vision for her country: "I think if security comes in Afghanistan, progress will come in one minute . . .," she said. "If you think of [improvements in] education, the new generation are the good sources for change."

Marzia's visit to Tempe would prove momentous on a variety of levels, which the chapters in part III will reveal. At about the same time, I started working with Jamila to support her applications to Ph.D. programs under various auspices, by advising her about taking the Graduate Record Examination (GRE) that is required for most U.S. graduate schools. Margaret and I both tried to help when some glitch prevented her from receiving the test scores back from India. We also consulted with Jamila on a few fellowship programs that became available. Meanwhile, her situation in Kabul was causing increased stress and health problems, despite or perhaps because of her organization's success.

My increasing participation in the women's lives added a new layer to our relationships and brought their daily struggles much closer to my own world. I recognized that I was no longer just an observer or a narrator and interpreter. I had become a minor agent in their lives whose actions could affect their futures. I also reevaluated the women's strong internationalist perspective, which I understood less as an expression of internalized imperialist values than as a cry for help, a plea for a lifeline from the upheavals they faced and the reversals they feared from the inadequacies of their society and government. The international collaborations they wanted were not the ones they already had, however. Rather, they imagined that internationals could help educate, organize, and motivate indigenous Afghan talent to work on the country's—and especially women's—behalf.

Given the mass devastation they had experienced, I understood why Afghan women leaders might welcome international involvement in their country more and on different grounds than most male leaders did. Rather than judging them, or assuming that all international involvement must be imperialist in mission and effect, I accepted their hopes for productive collaboration beyond Afghan borders and took seriously their critiques of existing international programs and policies. Like them, I wanted to consider novel possibilities for such collaboration that respected their wishes on their own terms.

Organization of Part III

Part III includes three chapters and an afterword that navigate the changing circumstances in Afghanistan and in Marzia's and Jamila's lives from 2010 through 2014 and bring the narrative arc of *Contested Terrain* to a close. The first, chapter 8, assesses the significance of the obstacles the two women identified in 2010 and 2011, which included criticisms of Afghan women leaders and the fear that their limitations would keep ordinary women's prospects from flowering in the desert of their own delayed opportunities.

Chapter 9 recounts the dramatic changes in the two women's lives that started in 2011 and were ongoing as of 2014. The story is more dramatic for Marzia, but it is equally complex and, ultimately, disturbing for Jamila.

Finally, building on the women's own perspectives on the uncertain future that lies ahead for their country and its women, chapter 10 explores the views of that future by various experts on Afghan history and politics. Building on my own evolution as a participant in the lives of these two women, the chapter also considers what other kinds of participation in Afghan women's aspirations for their rights and improved opportunities might be appropriate from the perspective of transnational feminism.

The book's afterword brings readers up-to-date on the women's circumstances and activities through mid-2014, when the manuscript was completed. Though the final word for that time, the afterword is not the final word on the story this book has begun.

8

Addressing Afghanistan's Problems

When we met and spoke together in 2010 and 2011, Marzia and Jamila had given much thought to the strategies their country should adopt in order to address the problems it faces. In our conversations, the women offered some pointed suggestions about moving Afghanistan forward on a number of fronts. In their usual manner, their discussion combined hopes and fears, but it was increasingly clear that obstacles were casting a longer shadow over possibilities for change than they had in 2005. I was impressed that the two women wanted to discuss strategies for change in the midst of their discouragement, but even as I clung to their positive insights, the pain in their voices as they discussed enduring obstacles was unmistakable.

Persistent Hopes

Of primary importance in the women's minds in 2010 was the positive role that international donors and governments could play in promoting women's rights in Afghanistan. They continued to believe that outsiders' "hands-off" approach toward the country's cultural and religious practices mostly reflected the fears of the Karzai government. For example, Marzia said that the Ministry of Justice would not put women's rights at the top of their agenda because they believed, "If we want to touch it, then we will not get political will [either] from international community [or] from the extremists in Afghanistan." This is a "critical time," she said, and the international community must see how its reluctance to address religious extremists or so-called cultural issues such as women's rights was robbing Afghanistan of its future. Jamila and Marzia wanted a newly sensitized international community to become more rather than less demanding and more culturally than militarily focused.

For almost any program an international donor or NGO might be sponsoring, the two women could suggest a better, more long-lasting approach. For example, the U.S. State Department's Justice Secular Support Program in Afghanistan, which was working in a piecemeal fashion, really needed a "full-time adviser [to] work on all capacity-building issues like in the Supreme Court and the president and stuff." And instead of sending more Afghans to international universities to study—a desire Marzia had simultaneously supported and lamented as a brain drain—some international-level educational experiences should be brought to Afghanistan. That was particularly important, since so many Afghan students studying abroad were declining to return home. The Fulbright program was one possible source of such experiences. Marzia saw the potential for training defense lawyers in Afghanistan through exchanges with U.S. law school faculty. She thought it could start in Kabul and expand to other provinces.

The women also thought that internationalization should be a two-way street. They wanted to consider their own problems, such as sexual harassment, within an international framework that could enhance their understanding and expand their options for addressing them. Marzia saw the benefits of building international legal coalitions on the subject of sexual harassment. She said, "I might receive lots of support from others, how they deal with the issue. . . . Or maybe there are some things . . . we should [become] clear [about] ourselves, once we . . . understand the topic first. . . . We have to learn [from] many international conventions [as well as] Afghan laws, how we could be protected." She also envisioned coalitions across borders. Jamila was pleased that Iranian and Pakistani scholars were already coming to Afghanistan "defending their women's rights issues from [an] Islamic perspective."

Jamila further touted the success of an international conference in Kabul where delegations from around the world networked about women's issues. Many international NGOs attended, "and we had a woman there in that conference to talk on behalf of civil society. She talked about women's rights issues," and she said how difficult it was now to get the "attention of the world community [now] that Afghan women are [not] a hot issue to take in their agendas." Jamila was delighted to see how many women from all around Afghanistan were there, but "whether [I] ideologically like that person or not, that is another issue." She was elated to be part of the conference, even though it occurred too close to the delivery of her daughter for her to attend very many sessions. "It's not important that everywhere should be Jamila," she said, "or every discussion should be Jamila. . . . It is good sign of improvement that women are coming. And hopefully by passage of time and further capacity building, [negative competition among women] will be diminished."

Jamila also emphasized the changes that could and should occur through local efforts, such as those of NECDO. She had seen with her own eyes how literacy training could transform Afghan women's desperate situation. It could even change a girl from an economic liability to an economic contributor in her birth family. Jamila said, "One of the reasons that people are selling their daughters in marriage [at an] early age . . . is money. Because they consider, . . . 'If I earn some money on her, then that money will be given to brother or to father. They will establish a business or maybe some type of a work they will do, and they will have some lively income.'" But girls' literacy changes the calculations: improved literacy is "one of the elements which reduced child marriage in remote areas." Families understood that "because when their daughters were getting education, directly they were becoming teachers . . . and they were getting good type of salary, and they had good type of income, and they had families." Especially "governmental families . . . were preferring that [their] daughters, instead of getting married, complete their education and become a teacher or a social worker." Mothers in those areas "have ignored men" who think otherwise.

Jamila continued to hope that Afghan imams and religious scholars, like her own husband, would help deepen Afghans' understanding of women's rights within Islam and inform people of the varying interpretations of the texts (*ijma*) and religion. Strict, conservative interpretations, such as Wahabi and Ash'ari, did not "consider that changes in life is natural and with the passage of time there will be different situation. You have to take basic foundation from Qur'an, but you have to take decision upon the need of your time." There were already well-known and "highly educated, highly professional people who know about Islam. . . . I can [name] for example, Imam Abd [Abdul Rauf, who is anti-Taliban and] a very professional person. . . . [Also] Dr. Mohammed Ayaz Niazi—is very well known, he's leading one of the biggest mosques [in Kabul] and also . . . Maulvi Hanif [a *peshimam* or prayer leader in Peshawar] is [a] very well-known person."[1] All of these men were working to broaden acceptable Islamic opinions and behaviors. What such scholars were not doing, but still needed to do, was expand women's exposure to moderate Islamic teaching at the mosques, Jamila said. Most mosques did not yet have rooms where women could pray, even though women were legally entitled to attend the mosque. In addition, few women drove cars, although that was also not forbidden. The culture must let women know their rights.

Jamila also advocated greater networking among Afghan NGOs, especially those focused on women's causes. "There's a need of . . . strong networking among women organizations. Like as I said, after many years I met Marzia. We don't have the time, we are very busy with our organization issues, with personal issues, even we cannot get time to be part of a better, larger, networking."

As she had in 2005, Jamila stressed the need for women's organizations to arrange for their own succession in a businesslike way. She knew that her organization would last beyond her leadership,

> because the last two years I spent in capacity building of my organization. . . . We use internationalist Internet software for dealing [with] our finance system. We have internationalist standard administrative system, . . . and everybody knows what to do, how to do, so the system is built up inside my organization.

If I am there or not, everybody knows what to do. If they are not doing, they will have these punishments or maybe side effects to their career or to their jobs or to their salaries. Everybody is set up, every system is set up, so the system needs to be built up, and there is need of capacity building inside professional level, organizational level; there is need of awareness among community level.

She repeated that the reluctance she perceived within other organizations to make way for successors stemmed from the way daughters are ill-treated in their families, so "they have ... deficiencies [in] their characteristics, and they are trying to impose that on the other stage of their lives, to others. So it is like a chain going on."

Marzia also envisioned changes to the currently uncollaborative professional environment of the women's activist community. The first order of business, in her mind, was to heighten the gender sensitivity of women professionals. "Professional women ... should be a part of the decision making at their own organizations, like women as prosecutors ... [should consider] how they could play an important role as a prosecutor ... [and ask] 'How many women professionals are supported as the prosecutors, as a judge, as a defense lawyer in this department?' ... [Also] we have gender law, I mean, there's a department of elimination of violence against women at the prosecutor office, but how many percentages of women prosecutors support this?"

Once awareness increased in such matters, Marzia hoped to establish a better "relationship between the Ministry of Women's Affairs and ... the professional groups in Afghanistan." At the same time, she wanted Karzai held to his promise that "each ministry should establish their gender department." Finally, Marzia said that "the women should come together." She explained, "As a board member of the Ministry of Women's Affairs, I was proposing to have such a strong ... collection." Despite the reluctance she then perceived, she believed that professional women should be willing to talk about any issue—"even [if] it's a law regarding mother's mortality, or if there's a law regarding environment"—whether it is related to their expertise or not. "You can have a talk and you can express yourself," she said.

It was clear from Marzia's and Jamila's approaches to their own professionalization and work commitments that they were not revolutionaries. Marzia said, "We shouldn't go too strong on women's issues currently because we don't have the situation ready for us. So a kind of gradual movement for women's rights is needed rather than to have a strong voice that no one will listen [to], and instead you will destroy yourself rather than to improve the situation." Equally important, "We should work together with men. Otherwise, it is not possible to just be on our own and be separated from men to have our women's rights. So we should work with men that they should believe on women's rights." Unless men and women reached an understanding of women's rights together, men would continue to undermine the achievements such as those to which Jamila and Marzia had devoted their lives. Marzia realized, for example, that if she were then a sitting judge, "if my other colleagues as a judge do not believe on women's right or my own right as a judge . . . they [can] say, 'Okay, go home,' and they take bribe on behalf of woman." In short, corruption would trump fairness if men did not agree.

Persistent Barriers

As realistic and reformist as the women's solutions for their country's problems seemed, they also recognized a fairly daunting list of barriers to the progress they envisioned. Those barriers included the fierce competition among women that continued to inhibit professional women's achievements; intransigent tribal and political factionalism, exacerbated by foreign influence; women's continued commoditization and dependence on unreliable, even cruel, men; violence against women, especially within marriage; the broken system for divorce; Afghanistan's dependence on yet simultaneous victimization by international forces; and a weak, corrupt, and unresponsive government.

Competition among Women

The barrier that Marzia and Jamila felt most deeply was the ongoing competition among women activists working to achieve the same goals. Of course, this problem is by no means unique to Afghanistan, just as it is not unique to women. Nor is competition always bad. Healthy competition can enhance work on social issues as well as business enterprises and academic research. Nevertheless, female-based competition had a particular flavor in Afghanistan that discouraged the two women, even as they recognized their own role in it. "Unfortunately still we are facing discrimination from each other, like, to be honest," said Jamila, "I'm meeting Marzia after very long time. We are living in Afghanistan working for the cause of women. Like it's very rare that we sit together and meet each other, even share our problems, being women."

The causes for what they considered negative competition among women were the same in 2010 as they were in 2005. That is, competition persisted because of Afghanistan's patriarchal and hierarchical family system, which commoditizes women as expendable "merchandise" in their birth families and as investments and resources in their husbands' families. Because of the respect for age in the family system and the sequestering of women within domestic spaces, mothers-in-law still had significant power over their daughters-in-law, especially a daughter-in-law married to the family's eldest son. Confined together, typically in tight spaces, women in extended-family households competed and gossiped, often pitting sisters against their brothers' wives, mothers against their sons' wives, and cowives against each other. It was still the case that the less women had to do outside of their homes, the more infighting they were likely to engage in. That situation made family life difficult for many women, but even worse, the gendered family system continued to poison relationships among women in every segment of society.

Such negative competition coexisted with the occasional cooperation that Jamila and Marzia noted among activists who worked individually and together to advance the cause of Afghan women. "Fortunately, we have a few women . . . [who] are . . . playing their important role for reconstruction. [For example], the acting minister at the moment, Surya Dalil, heading the Ministry of Health . . . we can see her [on the] news every night or maybe every second night . . . that she has traveled to some areas and she has established clinics." I counted Jamila and Marzia among that reconstructive group.

In addition, some women's rights organizations were functioning well. The Afghan Women's Network, for example, was still "emerging actively. They are leading women's issues," as Marzia said, with "a separate branch for women to deal with [the] violence issue, which has very crucial role," Jamila continued. Although they had not so far brought any cases to the authorities, "it was because of efforts of women" that the EVAW law was introduced at all. "Different women's groups were working on this issue of elimination of violence, and . . . [the] government was under pressure to build up such a unit."

And then the "buts" began. Jamila said, "Although [AWN was] doing very good job for the cause of women," internal problems often reduced the organization's effectiveness. Jamila knew about these problems as a former "active found[ing] member" of the AWN board who had been edged out. She said that over time, "new people came and . . . our role became lower there." AWN became "focused on a few specific organizations and a few specific individuals." Other groups are also "not welcoming to others, or different mentality or different peoples from different communities," she said.

The traditional gossip culture compounded the disconnection and isolation women activists felt. "Gossiping among women is increasing . . . instead of decreas[ing]," Jamila said. "When you go to a meeting . . . they start, 'You know about Fahima? She has done this, she has done that.' [They just] start gossiping." Jamila confessed that this tendency "makes me very disturbed." Marzia nodded and said, "Negative competition." Jamila agreed. "Negative competition among women . . . Whenever active leaders are coming up, people start gossiping after them. [They try] to ruin her image. It seems like a person has to [climb] stairs to reach to a building, and they're trying to pull out that stair from her legs [so] she should fall down."

Intense competition among organizations for donors was one reason for this kind of undercutting behavior. Jamila explained that a typical grant applicant might say to herself, "I should be a good boy in front of a donor. . . . I should say very bad words about Marzia . . . to ruin her image, and the donor should pay attention to me, not to her or to her organization. . . ." Lack of capacity among women was another. "Women organizations, they are afraid, because they do not stand on professionalism, on international standards. They're just there trying to take something and get something and utilize something." Marzia added, even more cynically, "And make some money."

Examples from Jamila's experience helped to illustrate the extremes to which this gossiping and undercutting could go. "When I came to the conference in Ohio when I went back from USA to Afghanistan, first of all nobody was believing that, they were saying, 'You went to USA and you came back?' I said 'Yes, what's wrong with that?' They said 'Okay,' [but] they were making different type of gesture," which indicated that they did not believe her. "Then one day, [I said], 'I insist, you should tell me, what is the reason, why you are doing this type of reaction?'" she continued.

> They said, "We [have] heard that you are a member of some terrorist group, maybe al Qaeda or some religious group. Your name has become on the blacklist of America, and America is after you to cut you up and to put you in Guantánamo." I said, "For what?" It was astonishing news for me! I said, "Okay, what type of blacklist is [in] America that only they are showing [it] to a few women organizations in Afghanistan? I mean, like, how weak they are when I put my passport in front of them, and they gave me [a] visa and they gave me entry, and I came back from their country and they said nothing to me . . . like if I'm wearing hijab or veil or wearing my chador or scarf, it shouldn't be a sign that I'm extremist."

Luckily, this particular accusation was made in a group that included some of the other women who had been to the United States with Jamila. "They were saying, 'No, no, Jamila was with us. We went and we came back, like it was.'"

When personal attacks like that did not stick, some of the activist community in Kabul began questioning the integrity of Jamila's NECDO organization. They accused it of "eating money." So, Jamila said, "I put all my audit reports in front of donors. . . . A professional consultant company is coming and doing audit, so their viewpoints are more proper than a person who's coming from the street having no proof and talking. And one thing else, [when] I got married to my husband, who's more of religious mentality, . . . it was another reason for them that 'Jamila belongs to fundamentalist group. She looks like this and that,' but you know that there is no change in me."

Jamila also criticized professional women for turning on one another when they were trying to break new ground. Even though she believed that men and women running for Parliament should have qualifications (she did not personally support "a singer, maybe a fortune teller or a barber [or a] beautician," who runs for the Parliament), she did not like the fact that "the first negative words for a woman you can hear [are] from a woman in Afghanistan . . . it is wrong competition." She noticed that men did not do that to one another: "I have seen many warlords, many other people [become] candidate[s] themselves. They are male; nobody's talking. . . . Men are supporting each other."

When Jamila heard people gossiping about another woman, she asked them, "[Do] you personally know her?" In one case, a man of her acquaintance who was criticizing a woman said,

> "No, I don't know her. My relative of relative, one of my relative, he said this." I said, "How logically it is acceptable if you personally do not know a person, if you don't have a solid proof in your hand, you're gossiping after a person? From an Islamic point of view this is very [wrong]. There is big quotation of Qur'an that says, 'Never, never say a word onto which you are not sure because tomorrow you may get sorrow that [you] have said such a bad thing. And you may put some blame on a person, wrong blame on a person who's not involved in that issue.'" . . . And I said, "When you don't know a person, just you're like 'Somebody said this, somebody said that,' so how you can rely on that?"

Although Jamila had developed some strategies to counter the gossip culture among her friends and professional acquaintances, she was hurt and discouraged by the personal attacks. She said:

> Personally I am facing lots of problems, because when I started working people were saying, "Oh, she is young woman, she do not understand, only she understand English, that's why she is highlighting herself." . . . When I start to talk about Islam from Islamic perspective, they were saying, "Oh, she is fundamentalist, that's why she is talking from Islamic perspective." When I was talking about political situation, they were saying, "Oh, she wants to get the position, that's why." But all these were part of my education. . . . [Later] . . . lots of people were not happy when men are praising me that Jamila is doing very good. . . . Then [they would say], "Oh, she has beauty, she is beautiful, that's why she's attracting men."

When she came back from the United States, people had said that she must have been using her wiles with the Americans who supported her projects. "It means that you prove every stage, every gossip, every blame, you have to prove [yourself]."

As a result of this negative competition and gossip, Jamila felt quite isolated. "Sisterhood among sisters is the main idea. . . . [If] I faced money problem in my personal life, I cannot share it with Afghan sisters." Even though her own work was devoted to solving other people's problems, "when you come to [a] personal issue, then you're burdened with your emotions, feelings. You feel that somebody else should come and help you in that situation." But when she asked one of her friends to help her with such a personal issue,

> she laughed [and] said, "Jamila, I have a shelter. Just go and kill a person, come to my shelter, I will protect you." I said, "For God's sake, I don't need this type of protection." . . . There is no sister in Afghanistan that I can share . . . my

personal problem, and they can support me. Rather, they start gossiping after you. Your weak points become more weak, and [you risk] your position in the society. That's why you keep silent. Instead of supporting you and the idea of sisterhood, I have [not seen] all women [come] together and support each other.

Marzia had also been subjected to personal criticism in a very public way. Perhaps the worst example occurred after a trip to the United States in 2002, sponsored by the State Department, during which Marzia met and was photographed bareheaded while standing with President Bush and other high-level officials. After the trip, she was greeted at home with headlines condemning her uncovered head. Even though the deputy chief justice said that women have a choice about what they wear, Marzia believed that the Afghan Supreme Court High Council used the incident to dismiss her from her position, perhaps recognizing that the Afghan government would not challenge the Court on a women's rights issue. Afterward, Marzia was "angry, hurt, and depressed about the criticism," and she feared for her safety.[2] No women activists came to her defense. "Having no option left," she said, "I decided to be silent and . . . work for the international community where I was offered a good job with UN Child Fund Program, UNICEF Afghanistan."

Despite her devastating experience, Marzia's criticism of the negative competition among Afghan women activists and professionals was somewhat more structural than Jamila's. Marzia emphasized the cultural influences that undermine women's support for one another: "Women, we are not united with one common goal and gender sensitive because . . . we grow up by ourselves and we are working by ourselves. Without knowing . . . what the civil society and woman groups should do, how we should come together, how we should lobby, and how we should support each other. This is something that we have to teach each other. In a country like Afghanistan, always we have war and we have never been active in women's rights, so how we could blame people?"

At the same time, she also lamented the lack of cooperation, the lack of professional capacity, "and also lack of gender sensitivity and selfishness." For example, "if there is a legal organization [and] there are many other legal organizations, we do not coordinate. If there is a medical organization or educational organization, we do not know what to do. We don't learn from each other. Even we are not sitting at one table. . . . So the first thing is that we should be organized . . . , learn ourselves what we are and what we could do. That could be acceptable for the Afghan society because the work for the Afghan woman is not even acceptable for our society." Equally disheartening, "the women professionals are marginalized. And they're forgotten within these movements," according to Marzia. "If you go to the AWN, they don't have . . . physicians, for example, they don't have engineers, . . . they don't have lawyers on their board, like, they don't have pharmacists, they don't have professional category of the society."

Some of that exclusion could be chalked up to professional jealousy. "Even at the top level, if we have minister, if you go and sit with her and if you have more knowledge than her, then she will never ask you to come to that meeting [again]. Because [she fears that] you will [first] be on the list, and the next day you will be her assistant, and then you will be the minister." I asked her how this could change, and she answered, "Capacity building and professionalism, I think, which comes with passage of time. And going through experiences and facing many problems."

By the same token, because of their isolation and extremely small numbers, individual women activists in Afghanistan were protective of their status and training, Marzia said. "Because, if we have a single knowledge, then we are very proud, you know? It is not much, and we need more, but we are very proud. And we boast that we know [what we] don't know. . . . So this is a bad culture."

Perhaps for that reason, organizations jealously guarded their own turf. Marzia acknowledged that even her own women's committee of the bar association would resist focusing on a topic, such as sexual harassment, that was already being addressed by other groups. She thought that the bar committee could play a vital and unique role, by helping victims learn "how to find facts and how to make documents and how to present these documents and how to encourage women to talk the facts, this is also important," but she also thought it unlikely. Still, she mused, "This could be an issue that I could bring it to the Afghan Bar Association women's committee."

Jamila reinforced Marzia's observations about the self-protective aspect of the situation among women activists and professionals. "Like if somebody says, 'I got word about Jamila or about Marzia,' the other person [doesn't] like that. She wants . . . praise before Jamila and Marzia." Marzia agreed, "We don't want to . . . see others' promotions." She laughed as she continued, "I think sometimes they are right, because they have been deprived. . . . It's not like United States that everyone is [already] a professor, and everyone has a master's degree, everyone is researcher. Here in Afghanistan they are very limited. And everyone would like to be in the same position. It is a kind of negative competition . . . because of . . . the scarcity."

When I asked Jamila if she included collaboration skills in the capacity training she did for women in NECDO, so that they could begin to see their common interests, she replied, "Exactly. We do aim of all our activities . . . on the issue of working for women and bringing women up to level." She knew that without "capacity," people would worry, "If we bring [women] in higher position . . . they will be busy . . . fighting with each other, with other women, so what is the benefit of bringing those women on the good positions?" Her goal was to help women gain sufficient skills so they would have enough confidence in themselves and not try to bring other women down by gossip and backbiting.

Jamila and Marzia had some disagreement about another topic related to activist women's competition, however. Marzia associated the existing desire for personal recognition, understandable as it might be under the circumstances, with women activists' weak connection with the needs and interests of ordinary

Afghan women. "There are many, many women who are expecting us [to be] leaders. We usually are not among them to ask them, 'What is need of you?' . . . We are not talking on behalf of those women who . . . have been deprived of their rights and they don't know what is their right. . . . They [might] say that 'Okay, we think it's all right for the men [to] do that. Why are you telling me this?' . . . So this is why we are not achieving things." Instead of working at the grassroots, Marzia offered, "We are mostly focusing at the top levels, which is wrong. I think for the Afghan woman we should [connect with] the lower levels. . . . This is the big problem. Or maybe security will be one reason that we are not, but mostly selfishness also a very huge topic among professionals."

This concern was at the root of her critique of the Revolutionary Association of the Women of Afghanistan. Although Marzia had invoked the founder, Meena, as a model of activism in 2005, five years later she did not think that RAWA really represented Afghan women. (Though the group was founded in 1977, Marzia thought RAWA dated only from the 1990s. Perhaps her understanding indicated the group's invisibility within Afghanistan, even though it does operate in the country, albeit clandestinely.)

Marzia's criticism of RAWA focused on two problems. First, she thought its exclusivity and foreign headquarters in Pakistan were no longer useful. Such tactics appeared to separate the group from ordinary Afghans who "don't read about their movement and the activities that they're doing. It will not be a credit for them, for their future." Marzia understood that RAWA's public criticism of warlords might be one of the reasons that many members lived outside of the country. As "you know," she said, "the Parliament consists of those warlords." But she admitted that RAWA did some good work. "They are right in some points, some positions that they take, they're right," she said. As things stood, however, RAWA was "not accepted by other groups that they are working inside Afghanistan." Thus, their perspectives "will not affect directly to the people." It would be better if RAWA were "part of the Afghan women's movement," Marzia concluded, by which she meant a team player along with organizations like hers and Jamila's, rather than a self-contained, umbrella-style organization.

Second, Marzia thought that the "shouting" that often characterized RAWA's approach was not the solution for Afghanistan. "Like, they go too far," she said.[3] Instead, "we should also think of what are the ways that we could bring peace and reconciliation in Afghanistan." For example, RAWA never pointed out what was right with the government or what changes in Afghanistan were positive, things that people based in the country would appreciate. "Like when they are criticizing the government, they . . . criticize everyone . . . they say everyone is corrupt or everyone at the government is opposite of education for the Afghan girls or like that. . . . But I think they should justify also positive . . . things."

Although Jamila agreed that Marzia's view about activists' disconnection with ordinary Afghan women applied to some groups, she stressed that her organization had a different emphasis. "We [at NECDO] *are* [working] on grassroots level," she said, speaking also for some other Afghan NGOs. But even so, she added, "Different organizations work in different areas of Afghanistan, and everybody tries to support ten, twenty, hundred, one hundred, [one thousand] women on the community level. But as Marzia just said, we who are doing these activities we are not collected and united among ourselves. In order to make a proper triangle, to reach to a proper level, . . . we [cannot be] disconnected with each other." Organizations should address women's needs on multiple levels through collaboration and cooperation.

From their comments about organizations such as AWN and RAWA, it was clear that Marzia and Jamila did not think that umbrella groups were the ultimate key to advancing Afghan women's rights. They wanted collective efforts to work, and they were always touting collaboration, but they believed that such groups suffered because Afghans do not trust organizations with all-encompassing titles and missions. "It had very bad name during the Communist regime," Marzia explained. "Youth association, . . . women's association, like any association that you are talking [about], still the people would think of the Communist regime associations."

What was needed, according to Marzia, was an organized "network within all the sectors, you know? One is report writing; one is working to improve the situation." Lobbying was also important, but "we don't have [a] system actually." Sometimes Marzia felt overwhelmed by the odds against success. She summarized the problems: first, "the number of educated people are very less, and, second, the competition is very negative, and, third, we really do not know what is gender and what [it is] to be sensitive in a common understanding."

The Karzai Government and Parliament

Jamila and Marzia gave President Karzai's government some credit for Afghan women's advancement. They were encouraged by his support for the violence-against-women legislation. Marzia also thought Karzai respected women, although that attitude had backfired because it made him unwilling to "speak harshly" (that is, truthfully) with women as he did to his male executive partners. She hoped that his deference to women might ultimately serve as a kind of opening. If "woman should go first, for example, if you are in official things, . . . these are some kind of formalities that women could use [to] bring" their issues to men "at the top level." But she did not see that happening yet.

But the women's praise for Karzai was highly circumscribed. They criticized the absence from his government of women with sanctioned power. They also criticized the president's failure to really empower the women who did serve with him. One example was physician and human rights advocate Sima Samar, who, as we saw in the prologue to part I, was briefly deputy president and then minister of women's affairs in the Karzai interim government in 2001 and early 2002. Apparently, Karzai did not consult with her very often or give her any power, and she was not included in his permanent government, which was established in June 2002.[4] Since then, most women had been appointed as "acting" ministers or deputies because of the complexities of Karzai's relationship with the Parliament and the Taliban, neither of which wanted to see women truly empowered. The controversial parliamentary election of 2010 only exacerbated the situation, as it caught Karzai between the rock of loyalty and the hard place of corruption.[5] As a result, women in government were kept powerless by circumstances, if not by intent.

The lack of women in the government was not the biggest problem Marzia and Jamila identified with the Karzai administration, however. Of even greater concern was the government's failure to connect with women activists and professionals. The problem was two-way, according to Marzia. On the one hand, many women professionals were not interested in attending a governmental meeting about women's rights or issues that were not directly concerned with their area of expertise. On the other, even the Ministry of Women's Affairs had "no connection with women professionals." Furthermore, there was a lack of "common understanding" of gender issues between the few women who were in the government, such as the minister for women's affairs and the acting minister of health. For example, Marzia doubted that those ministers meant the same thing when they talked about women's health issues. In addition, she said, they "are not good with each other; negative competition is going between them." Moreover, as we have seen, they felt threatened by women whose credentials matched or exceeded their own.

Marzia was even more critical of the Parliament, where only a few female members had any voice at all and where the warlords who dominated that institution never really supported women's participation in the first place, despite the constitutional mandate to include them. That "is a big challenge between government and the Parliament," she said. The Supreme Court and the legal system had also been extremely disappointing to Marzia. She knew firsthand "how much [the] chief justice will be happy with having a women judge's association or how the chief prosecutor will be happy with having a [women] lawyer's [or] prosecutor's association," which is to say, not at all.

Not only had the Court disbanded Marzia's Afghan Women Judges Association, but it had also failed to provide training for female judges. Moreover, the Court had demonstrated self-defeating xenophobia by resisting the kind of internationally sponsored capacity building that Marzia saw as so essential to strengthening the judiciary in Afghanistan. For example, the Court had refused to participate in training workshops given by the Italian- and U.S.-sponsored Independent National Legal Training Center (INLTC). Those workshops were designed to help graduates of Afghan law faculties integrate their knowledge of civil and Sharia law and advance their understanding of the "practical aspects of legal and judicial practices" before they started their first official jobs.[6] "The Supreme Court said, 'We are independent, we want to keep this our own, and we want to keep the appointment ours,'" explained Marzia. They wanted no "meddling" from outsiders.

Perhaps the biggest governance problem for the nation from the two women's perspective was Karzai's desire to stay in power for both of his terms no matter what it took. (Even when his second term is up, they thought he would try to hold on to power, a prediction that appeared to be coming true in early 2014.) That tenacity had a lot of consequences, including his stated intention to include the Taliban in his government. Karzai's "flexibility" on this point reflected his willingness to sacrifice women, Jamila and Marzia said. It also indicated his perception that international donors wanted such inclusion. Equally unsettling, the public recognized that the "application of the law is weakening day by day, and this brings President Karzai's power under question," Marzia said. The media were full of questions about "law and good governance" and corruption. Obviously, corruption undermined the government's legitimacy, "because no law applies to corruption within the government and also private sectors," Marzia explained.

Overall, she continued, "illegality is very common nowadays." What used to be a ten-dollar bribe to the customs office "while you bring clothes from abroad or other things . . . now they take you to thirty dollars." Petty corruption also infused the courts. For example, the Supreme Court refused to go along with a new effort to verify the educational levels of civil employees. They would not do it because they knew that "these staff people [who might be relatives of the justices] should be out of the employment of the Supreme Court." Apparently, there was no agency with the power to make the Court comply.

All of these examples must have struck Jamila and Marzia as déjà vu all over again. They had both lived through governments that had engendered chaos, broken or ignored promises, undermined public trust, and sacrificed the collective good—especially women's collective good—for dubious benefit. Afghanistan's long history of such governmental disappointments must have made the two women and many other Afghans wonder whether all efforts to create good governance in their country were destined to come to this. Even more disturbing to Jamila and Marzia, attempts to assert civil law were still easily squelched by religious leaders. They had repeatedly seen how a cleric could silence a room and end a debate by citing a few words from the Qur'an or a hadith, however distorted or decontextualized his interpretation might be.

Security and the Returning Taliban

"If security returns to Afghanistan . . .," Marzia had said after her lunch with Justice O'Connor in 2011, and I thought, "That's a big *if*." In story after story, both women had been telling me for years that security was the biggest problem for Afghan women. Marzia said in 2011 that it was getting worse. Women "cannot go out.

... maybe after seven or eight at night. Rarely they can go for a party, and they are also worried if they are returning from [the office] to the house what could happen. So you can see that things are not according to choice and according to welfare of the Afghans. This is another kind of reason this war, which is continuing, ... is trying the nation. I just ... It makes you crazy."

Of course, no one could blame Marzia for dreaming of peace and imagining what Afghanistan would be like with fewer guns, bombs, thieves, and armed insurgents. And hope and dream she did, despite all the violence she had witnessed in her life. Sometimes she evoked the promise of an earlier time: "Fifty years back was much better than today. Because at least we had security fifty years back; people could travel around Afghanistan all the night."

Marzia emphasized that Afghans were not acclimating to the violence. Rather, "no one can get used [to] guns and ... fighting," she said. Now, when "there is a blast ... you can see people are running to that site, and they are watching, you know? This is not like everyone is protecting themselves, but they are rushing for support, how to get the bodies to the hospital. So this is a kind of thing that you can see." Some might say it's God's will, but in that case, "Okay, if it's God [or] it's our destiny, take us all [or] give us life. . . . Mentally it [has] traumatized all of us. [Everyone] ... can imagine the result and feel the situation. It [is] ... harder ... because we were hoping day by day that the situation will improve, that we will have good news actually, not just fighting, killing: 'This one was killed from opposite side or from government side.' . . . We don't know [when] this war ends. This is something that we don't know."

The two women's stories of perpetual public violence were horrific. Jamila reported in 2010 that "just a few days ago [terrorists] killed . . . thirty-five people from private companies of security. . . . [O]ddly, they cut [off] their hands [and] feet. Pictures were on TV . . . the bodies were just sliced up." This was something she could not understand: "For me I can't kill a small ant that [is] walking in the way. If I was allowed, I wouldn't kill even sheep and [other] animals to eat their meat. . . . How it is possible for a human being to get a gun and then cut all the bodies and destroy it and take out the eyes? I mean, how simple it is for a human being? What happens, actually psychological[ly speaking]? . . . No one is created a criminal . . . but this is the situation [that] criminalize[s] people." Jamila thought that terrorists such as those in the Taliban "were brought up as a killer, you know? . . . They grow up, those who never had a book, never friendship or friend environment, all the time fighting. Now they are already hard people; they can destroy easily."

The two women blamed the Taliban for most of the public violence. Marzia reported that "they kill[ed] a young . . . woman [accused] of spying for internationals in Ghazni. It's not an isolated incident." She also reported that "members of the Ministry for Women's Affairs get night letters telling them not to come [to the ministry]." These threats were personal and hard to prove, so little was done about them in contrast to public shows of concern at sites of mass violence. "Even if you have a gun behind your door and you just call and shout that I am at risk, . . . no one [w]ould come to you to protect you because they'll say, 'What should we do for you?'"

Jamila added to the growing heap of horror stories by reporting that the sister of one of her students had been killed on the pretext that she had some relationship with government officials, although the girl's biggest offense was visiting an agency to deliver some documents. "She was shot, and she was killed," Jamila said. "And then all the family member[s] were on that threat that 'We are going to kill all of you, all of your family members.' Then they escaped, and they came to Kabul with very miserable condition that they don't have money, they don't have [a] place." The Taliban do not know what they are doing, Marzia emphasized. "Like a very young boy, like at the age of eight or nine, is just exploding himself. . . . Does he know what is the real goal of being a Muslim, for example, and the [purpose] of Islam?" The women also had contempt for those who gave the Taliban succor. Someone is "feeding them," Marzia said. Without that, they would die.

Even Jamila's brother had recently been detained by the Taliban. Because he was carrying papers written in English, they thought he was a spy. "They trapped my brother for long days, and then they demanded $20,000 USD," Jamila explained. "From a common person how you can ask [for so much money]?" She thought the Talibs were simply criminals serving their own purposes. She also thought they were deeply embedded in the society. "I have heard from my own students, from my own colleagues. They are saying [that] during the day, they are government employees; at night they are Taliban. At night they are holding gun after the same person [the] government is supporting. At night they are going and say[ing], 'We are Taliban, you are Afghan,' and this and that. This is very ambiguous situation in Afghanistan."

Jamila and Marzia decried the Taliban's willingness to sacrifice the good of Afghanistan in their quest for power. Jamila said that the "creation of good Talib is a new phenomenon to reduce the tension of bad Talib over all the world." But she considered that a ploy that would not "be supporting Afghanistan political situation." She suspected that some in the "international community . . . are supporting Taliban by providing them weapons and money." She had also heard that weapons headed for U.S. or NATO military forces were being siphoned off by the Taliban. "Thirty percent of them are missing on the way," she said.

Jamila worried in particular that the internationals who were saying "the Taliban should . . . come in and they should have part in the current government and structure of Afghanistan" were being duped. "Although they name those Taliban who agrees on constitution of Afghanistan, those Taliban who are fed up with fighting, . . . how you clarify who's good Taliban and who's bad Taliban? We don't have that mechanism, that capacity." She heard "Mr. Obama and others

[say] that we are supporting Karzai for bringing those Taliban who are accepting constitution, the good Taliban. . . . [They claim,] 'This Talib will be different,' to keep interest of international community, to keep a little bit interest of those Taliban. But I think it's a creation of new face and new structure of Taliban and political scenario that is [all for show]. I think those bad Talibs always remain in their places, at the background." "We don't want such a peace that women will be targets of the Taliban," Marzia said. "Peace at that price is not worth it."

The two women agreed with heavy hearts in 2010 that the Taliban was stronger than ever—"more support, more financial support, more powerful like"—mostly because of the international recognition they were getting. Among other things, they had made many election sites unsafe. "So you can see the security situation," Marzia said. "It means that the Taliban makes the life tighter and tighter. They are coming closer, closer. . . . It is destroying . . . whole families, especially for a man [who] leaves ten children [and a] widow woman, and then all the family's destroyed. So this is not a good news anyhow," as the vast majority of Afghan women were still dependent on men for their survival. The Taliban were clever at undermining the government, "so the people will be displeased with the government and they [will] take the side of the Taliban," Marzia said. And if they get into power, "The first target will be human rights workers and women's rights advocates."

Marzia herself had already received death threats from them, delivered to her door. At the same time, both women held out hope that Afghans were too smart to welcome the rule of the Taliban for a second time. Most people "want to produce, they want to work, they want to bring things from abroad, they're working for international organizations," Marzia said, perhaps projecting her own views a bit too widely. "So [they know] if Taliban comes, this opportunity will be gone . . . then people are wise enough that they wouldn't allow." In addition, Afghans had learned from their compatriots who had lived in Iran and Pakistan. Jamila said, "They have new learning, and they . . . have experience that women can work and their daughters can be better than their sons."

Moreover, Marzia said that Afghan "women [despite their lack of unity] are more organized than [in] 1992 and before that, because now even women have rise[n] to international organizations through their friends, through their relatives . . . and we can get more support, and they are more wiser. In that time, we were ignorant . . . but now the situation has changed. I mean, everyone would like to not repeat history, and there are many, many messages to President Karzai from women's organizations. Just if you could go to Internet, you could find this writing in English. There was a declaration issued by women, many organizations they signed it . . . [telling him] not [to] make this mistake to sign any agreement [at the] cost of women's ability and bring Taliban to that." As she also said, however, it is unclear that Karzai would really fulfill any promises to women, even though he was "promising time to time . . . while he's visiting women's organizations . . .

that women's rights and human rights are things I will observe with all situation that I have." But had he? Would he?

In addition to the resistance the women hoped the Taliban would face, Marzia and Jamila were also quite skeptical that the group could really "provide [the] jobs or education, let alone social protection," they promised. Many people joined the Taliban because "they pay a good salary." They can pay their soldiers more than the government can. So, "if you were jobless and if you have a child and your wife says, 'Bring me food,' what would you prefer? To die or to bring money?" Jamila asked. "And then they just go the military, and one night [they] just die and then all the family is weeping. . . . It's sad, I mean." The Taliban looked good only to the extent that other options looked bad, the women said. Despite the West's determination to bring a military solution, the best way to fight them was to strengthen those alternatives—better security, stronger civil society, and greater opportunities for ordinary Afghan men and women.

Poverty and Security

As bad as it was for Afghanistan, however, the Taliban was not the only enemy of increased security for the country. Another was the people's relentless poverty. "Poor families . . . have to send their children to make money rather than to study. . . . These children I see, these are the criminals for the future of Afghanistan," Marzia said.

> Because I have a luxurious car, I'm going up the street, and [a child starts] cleaning my car; how hard it will be for him . . . just begging for one dollar, while I will say, "No, close my door." And then [he] will call many times, "Can you bring me a loaf of bread?" So it is difficult. Because [this] generation will be a kind of, you know, they will be sensitive. They would like to have these things. How then [to keep doing] lawful things [when] illegally they can have them? And they can be used very fast by the narcotics [thugs] because they could be dealers with them . . . because they are children and they are not receiving much punishment [if they deal drugs].

Such children also made good recruits for the Taliban, Marzia continued, "like they're using the children to just go and commit suicide, just for God, you know. . . . 'Kill yourself and kill others, it's holy, it's holy. It's holy jihad.'" Although Marzia was convinced that the Taliban were originally from Pakistan, "now they merged. . . . They are in the community now." And they were spreading their lawlessness throughout the population.

Afghanistan does not have to be a poor country, Marzia pointed out, because their land is rich in minerals. And she was right. Afghanistan's steep mountains contain huge veins of iron, copper, cobalt, gold, and critical industrial metals such as niobium and lithium, which are used respectively in manufacturing superconducting steel and laptop batteries and smartphones. (Indeed, the Pentagon reported in 2010 that Afghanistan's lithium deposits could be larger than Bolivia's, currently the largest known deposits. "Afghanistan could become the 'Saudi Arabia of lithium,'" it said.)[7] In addition, Afghan land harbors oil and gas. For centuries, clandestine mining and drilling operations have basically stolen those resources from the Afghan people.

Marzia continued, "But because the leaders are foolish, the central government is weak, and no coherent policy about mining has ever been drawn," outsiders, such as the Chinese, have been given contracts to mine minerals, and the gas has been siphoned off to Tajikistan and Uzbekistan. Small-time mining operations flourished "in these ancient wild places," and some people were getting rich. Lapis lazuli, for example, was being mined with primitive axes and sold for personal gain. In addition, a long-standing plan to siphon off Afghan gas to Pakistan was still in operation, Marzia noted.

Because of that particular piracy, most Afghans had no central heating in their homes, only small charcoal braziers tucked under their tables to keep them warm. Such devices barely made a dent in Afghan winters, when nighttime temperatures even in Kabul average only 18 degrees Fahrenheit, and temperatures in mountainous areas routinely dip well below zero. "This is only in one room people just come together" in the winter, Marzia said. "Even if you are five or ten people, they come all sit in one room to eat, and during the sleeping" they put heaters in their rooms in order to "at least [warm] the environment." "Believe me," Marzia said, "I have salaries and dollar[s], [but] I cannot keep twenty-four hours my room warm," let alone "heat all the house." No one can afford to heat a whole house. Even a wood fire going all the time in one room "would cost me hundreds of dollar[s] just one month."

In addition to creating a fire hazard, generating foul smoke and ash pollution in the cities, and reducing productivity in winter months, depriving Afghans of the basic necessities for survival "opens a way of corruption, that one is eating the other's born blood to keep himself alive," Marzia said. In addition, the high price and scarcity of fuel rob children of education. For the poor, "if you provide water, then there's no food. If you provide food, there is no fire. If there is no fire or wood, then there is nothing else. The small amount of money that will be left at the end, they don't give it to the education because they're hungry, and they won't do it." This vicious cycle meant that more people were vulnerable to exploitation and extremism, which in turn threatened security.

Marzia had some respite from the cold that most other Afghans did not have, since the GTZ office where she sometimes worked had a "good system, because there [is] a lot of money there. They heat all the building, and you feel more comfortable," she said. She also let her memories keep her warm. "While I was a child," Marzia remarked, "I remember that we could heat our corridors; we could heat our rooms. I mean even with two . . . fireplaces at least. . . . It was not too big, but we had something."

The solution was not to heat Afghanistan one room at a time, Marzia said. Rather, the country needed a system. "If you're rich, you have very good life. I mean, you have very good cars . . . you can heat many rooms, and you can have all that. . . . [But] all the people are not like that. This is a minority of the people that have such a life. [That's] because the system is lacking." Ironically, the only residential district that had a twenty-four-hour-a-day heating system was one built during the Soviet occupation.

The International Presence

Whenever I heard the U.S. news media report the views of "ordinary Afghans" about the presence of international donors and forces in their country in 2010 and 2011, I noticed that they never asked women, including women leaders who might be accessible to reporters. Instead, they quoted the men they had easier access to, who tended to express negative opinions, especially about the presence of foreign troops, which threatened their sense of national sovereignty, identity, independence, and possibly their manhood.

Such worries were of less concern to Marzia and Jamila, even nine years into the U.S. war, as they had been for the women who attended the Ohio State conference in 2005. Then the women seemed uniformly hopeful that the presence of internationals, even troops, in their country, especially from the West, would promote women's rights as well as peace and security. By 2010 Marzia and Jamila clung even more tightly to that hope, despite their harsh critiques. As already discussed, they continued to hope that international involvement would increase security and build their country's professionalism and social and political capacities, as with the efforts of the INLTC to professionalize the Afghan judiciary and legal community. They were discouraged when such opportunities were missed.

The women were especially concerned that the withdrawal of U.S. and NATO forces would decrease security in the region. For one thing, if it happened before 2014, they thought the Karzai government would collapse, which would be worse than having it in power. (By 2013 it became clear that Karzai's second term was truly his last, as the constitution requires, so planned troop withdrawal would coincide with an election and a new president.) In addition, the women believed that security problems would increase for the rest of the world because Afghanistan would become an open training ground for the terrorists who had found a home in their country. (For this they could have blamed the U.S.-sponsored war, although they did not.) The women further believed that the Afghan people were so traumatized by generations of war that they could not function without external support. Marzia estimated that 80 percent of the population was that traumatized. Moreover, a large proportion of Afghan men had become addicted to drugs, they said, which also endangered the nation. "Afghanistan needs a lot of support," Marzia said. "We have a long way to go to enjoy women's rights and human rights."

As much as they dreaded the withdrawal of international troops, however, the two women also decried meddlesome interference by foreign governments in Afghan affairs. Interestingly, the nations the two women identified as the real culprits for Afghanistan did not fall on one side or the other of a Muslim versus non-Muslim or East versus West divide. They said that India, Pakistan, China, and Iran threatened Afghanistan's future most immediately, primarily because they saw Afghanistan as an attractive market. They did not want Afghanistan producing or exporting its own products or commodities. Jamila said that all Afghan markets featured "Indian materials, Pakistani materials, Chinese materials, and Iranian materials. If it is food item, if it is clothes item, whatever. Like Afghanistan is a market for all of them. If Afghanistan is cultivating their own vegetables and developing their own factories and they're producing, then who will buy the material from Pakistan and other countries? . . . Afghanistan is poor, because . . . our wheat belongs to Pakistan, our oil belongs to Pakistan and Iran; like, these are for their own benefit, for their own strength."

At the same time, the two women were still critical of the uncoordinated and short-term programs of U.S. and European NGOs and of international support for the "informal justice system" of *shuras* and *jirgas* (which, Marzia said, were still "disappearing after every decision, they are not documented"). Marzia believed that many internationals "intentionally keep us in tradition, do not want us to be developed and to challenge things according to the constitution of Afghanistan."

Jamila and Marzia also attributed the increase of tribal and political factionalism to misguided historical international intervention in Afghan affairs. Having never lived outside of Afghanistan, Marzia said in 2010, "Now at forty-three I can see that these words *Tajik, Pashtun* have never been words among us. While I was a law school student, I had best friends from Hazara, I had best friends from Tajiks, I had best friend from Pashtun, they're all sitting together—I mean, the government was for all of us." But since the rise of the mujahideen in the 1990s, thanks to international financing, "the Hazara couldn't walk on Pashtun area, the Pashtun couldn't walk on" Hazara areas. The international sponsors of the mujahideen, including the United States, intended to promote "every nationality, every tribe, every ethnic group . . . like the constitution of Afghanistan states," Marzia conceded, "but Afghanistan is not at that stage to make up one group and make down the other group. . . . I think for the common understanding and the fate of Afghanistan, we are all Afghans, and people are thinking of that." In addition, ever since 1919, when Afghanistan got its independence from Great Britain, "some part of Pakistan is belonging to Afghanistan." She believed that "it should be returned back," but she also understood why people "need also sometimes to have their independency and they request for it. . . . So this is a hard question—which is out of Afghanistan, but within Afghanistan." In the end, however, she said, "I'm sure that people don't want to be separated and have a small, small government, separate from the Afghan [nation]. . . . For this time, I think we need a strong government."

The women's comments helped me to see how the problem of factionalism had been exacerbated by Western sensibilities about multiculturalism, which in some ways prompts people of all backgrounds to reify their racial or ethnic identities when they might otherwise be more interested in assimilation and social unity. I could also see how attention to women's issues could exacerbate gender tensions in a situation where men believe that they are thereby unappreciated, ignored, or dismissed. But as Marzia also said, this is a perplexing problem. When different groups have unequal status and access to resources and opportunities, how do you improve their situation without alienating others? Afghanistan offers a cautionary tale about the promotion of social justice. If such efforts are reduced to elevating a particular group or groups, pushback from others may be inevitable. Ways must be found to make social justice a winning situation for everyone in the society.

Reflections

Chapter 10 will offer some grounds for assessing Marzia's and Jamila's ideas about ways to address Afghanistan's problems and about remaining obstacles to women's progress, the conditions of Afghan women's lives, and possible solutions for the country's future by discussing the ideas of other Afghanistan observers, activists, and scholars. But before I close chapter 8, I want to explore the foundations of some of the two women's perspectives, including the Islamic precepts that support many of their positions.

First, it is important to realize that part of the women's enduring hope for their country stemmed in 2010 and 2011 from their realization that they and other activists like them had contributed to their country's progress on women's issues. Partly through their efforts, Afghan women could better negotiate their marriage contracts, more women and girls could get educations and learn about their rights, and more women could work and achieve some economic power. In addition, by 2010 the legal age of marriage for girls had risen and a law prohibiting violence against women had been approved (and would finally pass). Even some rural families were beginning to recognize the value of educating a daughter for the family's economic well-being. Some Afghan women could choose what they wore outside their houses, and even some men, like the two women's own husbands, understood the benefits to themselves, their families, and society of increased education and recognized rights for women.

Marzia and Jamila were also hopeful because they believed that Islam was ultimately on their side. They understood that the subordinate or even abject conditions of Afghan women's lives were not their Islamic destiny and the idea that female submission and obedience to men during their lives on earth was not required for them to enter paradise. Such ideas only reflected men's interpretation of God's word and were un-Qur'anic. As Amina Wadud explains, the Qur'an defines men and women as equal in Allah's eyes (as they were equal at Creation) and considers their social roles, though complementary because of reproduction, equally valuable (1999, 35, 73).

Furthermore, Afghan gender ideology undermines the Qur'an's message about equally valuable gender roles, because, according to Jamila, there are not equivalent controls on male and female appearance, behavior, and actions in Afghan life. Indeed, there are few prohibitions for men, and those that exist are fairly flexible. For example, apart from the Taliban period, men's dress and beards have never been routinely policed by families or public authorities. Men pursue their sexual desires with impunity, because many (wrongly) believe that is their religious right. An Afghan man can divorce by repeating a simple phrase, as the Qur'an allows, but the shame and hardship of divorce devolve primarily to the woman he renounces. And while the Qur'an enjoins men to support their families so women can fulfill their responsibility for bearing children (*qiwamah*), Afghan men do not always perform that function, as Marzia observed (Wadud 1999, 73). When that happens, Afghan law offers little help, although it too requires husbands to provide food and shelter for their wives and children. A wife's only recourse in the absence of financial support is divorce—a self-defeating alternative—rather than any form of court-enforced solution to her situation.[8] And because an Afghan man has the right to forbid his wife to work, even when jobs are available, or to control whatever income she might have, many women are left to figure out for themselves how to maintain their homes and feed their children. None of this is Qur'anic.

Of course, the concept of honor that dominates Afghan lives is not Qur'anic either. That honor code can result in women's deaths or imprisonment for real or suspected infidelity or for premarital sex, seeking a divorce, being raped, refusing to enter into an arranged marriage, fleeing an abusive marriage, eloping or even talking with an unauthorized man, and engaging in any kind of disobedience, such as defying dress codes. Sadly, honor killings have been on the rise in Afghanistan, although accurate numbers are elusive because so many killings go unreported. But there are concrete clues. For example, in June 2009, Amnesty International reported a record twenty-four cases of honor killings in Afghanistan by that midpoint in the year. By July 2012, Afghanistan's Independent Human Rights Commission recorded forty-two such killings (out of fifty-two murders of women and girls) just between March and June.[9] The United Nations Population Fund estimates that as many as five thousand women worldwide may die for male or family honor every year.[10]

All of these practices and trends must be understood in the context of a fractured country devastated by war. Increased controls over women's behavior in recent years are, on one level, a reaction—albeit a counterproductive one—to increased insecurity across the land. Stricter marriage mores, for example, coupled with the continued stigma of divorce, keep women more dependent on men, regardless of their treatment by them, in the name of protection. But as the lives of those men become more tenuous, women actually face greater dangers. If their husbands die, women's forced dependency drags both them and their children down. Marzia has said that a man's death typically means the death of a whole family. She noted that the shocking level of male deaths from the country's protracted wars and growing lawlessness had pushed 120,000 children onto the streets and forced many small children to work instead of attend school.

Such complex interconnections of particular issues with much larger political, social, and personal calculations and fears make strategizing for significant change in Afghan women's rights, economic opportunities, and civic participation very difficult. Do you promote incremental change from many directions—law, education, industry—on the theory that directly targeting underlying ideologies that keep women from progressing will only foster backlash and retaliation? Or do you directly address the deeper beliefs about gender distinction and women's inferiority and educate about the "true" Islam? In other words, not, "You should let your daughter go to school so she will be a teacher and make money for the family," but rather, "You should start treating your daughter as Islam really endorses, like a person whose life is valuable for its own sake and matters as much as her brother's." Or is there a way to do both: to get the girls in school in the short term and to promote their long-term intrinsic value as human beings at the same time? Jamila and Marzia were trying to do both and to make women, newly educated in their rights, allies in the quest for change. As we parted in 2010, they were still committed to that approach, even though it was unclear what those efforts would ultimately produce.

9

Fast-Forward

Because this narrative is a living document, whose ending will necessarily be arbitrary, it includes the sometimes dramatic shifts in plans and circumstances that can rewrite contemporary history in a moment. So it was that shifting events in late spring 2011 and early 2012 produced some different outcomes than Marzia, Jamila, and I had expected during our talks in the year before. For Marzia, the changes were more dramatic than her marriage. For Jamila, new circumstances confirmed both her fears about and her hopes for pursuing new options in her life's work.

Marzia, 2011–2012

The news from both women came to me via e-mail. Marzia's message arrived on May 31, a month and a half after she had left Tempe. It began:

> I do not remember if I had told you or not that one of my office employee[s] who was a lawyer was kidnapped in 2006 in one of the provinces of Afghanistan by the Taliban. He was released but later on the Taliban were searching for me. I was out of the country in Australia that time. I delayed my return back home for almost two months. By the time I came back to Afghanistan, I changed the office location temporar[il]y. But later on the situation was ok, I got married and was not staying all the time at that location which was my office and house before. [T]herefore I forgot about what had happened, but in late 2010 I got a night letter from Taliban threa[ten]ing me to stop working for international organizations and do not work for human and women rights issues because they considered these things opposite to Islam.

The lawyer Marzia mentioned was kidnapped because he was preparing to represent a woman from a distant province who wanted a divorce. While the woman was visiting the lawyer in the provincial office of the Kabul-based legal aid service Marzia worked for, the husband, "who was a local gun man, entered to our office and . . . had a serious argument with the APLO defense lawyers for why he is representing his wife." The confrontation was interrupted at the time because other clients intervened. Marzia advised the threatened lawyer to return to Kabul, and for her "this was the end of the case." The provincial office was closed for a few weeks. Marzia received the Taliban night letter, but she was not very worried because "Kabul is at least 9 hours by bus to that province." She never even reported the threat to the police because, she said, "I think the police are also a part of the insurgents."

But the threat to Marzia was not over. Her message continued: "Closer to my time coming to US [in April 2011] and later while I was in the US, *other* letters [appeared] just at the door of my house, which was . . . from the Taliban mentioning that they will kill me if they find me. I might have mentioned to you all these because I have talked to you many times about the facts of my life, or might not because I always believe working inside the country is much better even if it will be a risk for me."

Marzia had mentioned to me that the Taliban's contempt for Afghans who work with foreigners posed a danger for her. Still, I was stunned by her full disclosure of the story. Suddenly, her sadness while she was in Arizona made more sense. Her message reinforced what I had noticed: ". . . While I came to Arizona I was not feeling well, I could not concentrate with my assignment at the ASU." I had accepted her explanation at the time that she was depressed whenever she recounted the dire situation of Afghan women. When she mentioned that there were sometimes death threats, I took that as routine, as she seemed to. I had not understood that she believed her life would be in imminent danger if she returned to Afghanistan.

Her May e-mail revealed the depth of her fear and sadness:

> The night I was in your home, sitting at the balcony, . . . the only thing I was thinking some thing very vague and a dark future waiting for me. I wanted to be alone sitting at your apartment balcony and cry. I have been so sens[i]tive now. [S]orry for ending my story [like] this. I have [no] way to go back, but . . . I do not know who I will go on [to]. I love my country and my country['s] women who have no voice to write to someone and no one listen to them. They die silently.

Marzia's message also clarified that she had made a surprising decision: "I fe[e]l strongly that by my return to Afghanistan they will find me and will kill me. [A]fter the incident of the UN staff whom were killed in one of our provinces, and the poor people who had come to collect their salaries from the bank and were executed one by one gives me this idea that it would come to me. I do not know how many times [I] read the news about these two incidents and [was] remind[ed about] my own situation." The upshot of the message was simple: "Any how I am at the situation that I need to receive protection here at the U.S." In short, she would seek asylum. She requested a letter of support from me and from Linell Cady, the director of the Center for the Study of Religion and Conflict at

ASU, who was her official host for her Arizona visit. Both of us wrote our letters and sent them to Marzia's lawyer within a few days.

Waiting in Exile

In subsequent conversations with Marzia, I got more of the story. Marzia had left Arizona and gone to Washington, D.C., as planned. But instead of returning to Afghanistan after the expected two-week visit with her old friends from her George Washington University Law School days, she implemented a plan she had been contemplating for months. She relied on a friend she had met in 2004 through the International Women Judges Association in Washington, Elizabeth (Liz) Brundige, now associate director of the Avon Global Center and an adjunct professor in law at Cornell Law School. With the help of Professor Cynthia Bowman at Cornell, Liz arranged for Marzia to become a visiting scholar in international law at Cornell University Law School until mid-December.[1] Liz also found an immigration lawyer for Marzia. Thus, by May, Marzia knew she was moving to Ithaca for the summer and fall. She invited me to come visit and stay in the spare room in the apartment the law school had provided for her.

Marzia worried that I might judge her harshly or be disappointed by her decision, but I was actually relieved and proud of Marzia for taking care of herself in this way and getting her needs met. I understood that a person in her position must develop such skills in order to survive. I assumed that she did not reveal her new plans to me or to anyone during her stay in Tempe because she did not want to involve or implicate us in her decision or appear to exploit the hospitality and support she received at ASU. She confirmed that was the case in a later conversation. She explained that she had been unsure whether it would be safe or smart—for either of us—for me to know about her plans.

I also recognized that the situation in Afghanistan must be truly awful if a woman who had stuck it out in that country throughout the Soviet, mujahideen, and Taliban periods, who feared for her life many times as rockets zoomed over her head (she once counted fifteen hundred in one day), as the morality police patrolled the streets, and as misogynistic Talibs stalked Afghan women even into their homes, had finally reached her personal tipping point. (I only later learned that her father and husband were also encouraging her not to return.) I concluded that her fears must be justified, that she truly could not reenter Afghanistan and resume her former life.

At the same time, I was worried. I wondered if she could ever go back, as I imagined the kind of criticism her "defection" might generate among other women's rights leaders in her country. Given the history of women's relationships that Marzia and Jamila had recounted, I could almost hear the grumblings about abandoning the cause and the "cut eyes" that would sting Marzia if she should ever return. Some of that response would be fueled by jealousy and some by understandable dismay that the women's cause in Afghanistan may, indeed, be lost. I asked Marzia if she had told Jamila about her decision, and she said that she had.

The Next Big Decision

I was never able to travel to Ithaca to visit Marzia at Cornell because of summer research plans that were all in place, as well as an unplanned family crisis that occupied all my vacation time. So, with Marzia's permission, I began arranging to conduct a video interview in September to discuss her decision to seek asylum in the United States and her future plans.

From the beginning, our negotiations about that call made me suspicious. We first decided to do a Skype call in September, but as the date neared, Marzia stopped responding to my e-mails. I would suggest some times, and she would let them go by without letting me know if they were convenient. The messages I did receive were cryptic. After a week or so, she wrote that we had to do the Skype call right away, the next day, because she did not know what her schedule would be like the following week. My graduate assistant and I were ready and waiting for the call at the appointed time, but it never came. We tried calling Marzia, but she was not online. We waited for an hour, but no call came. Marzia wrote in a later e-mail that she could not make the appointment after all. So we set another time for the next day.

I was delighted when that second call happened right on schedule, but I immediately noticed that the room Marzia was sitting in, which I expected to be her apartment in Ithaca, did not look like a residence. I also heard voices in the background. So, I asked her where she was. She answered, "This is strange. I wanted to just share my recent decision that I did." "Yes?" I asked. She replied, "I just crossed the border this afternoon, and now I am in Canada."

There had been some hints in our earlier e-mail exchanges that this might happen. I knew that Marzia had relatives in Toronto—an elderly aunt and her family, as well as a sister-in-law, a sister of her husband's. The aunt was growing concerned about Marzia's being lonely while she was living on her own in Ithaca, without any family members in the United States. So the aunt had met Marzia in Buffalo on the morning of our first scheduled September phone call and persuaded her to cross the border right away. Marzia returned briefly to Ithaca to collect her belongings and hurried back to Buffalo to make preparations to cross the Freedom Bridge to Toronto.

The aunt was right about Marzia's state of mind. On one level, while awaiting her asylum hearing in Ithaca, Marzia had basked in the wonderful support she was getting from her friends and had thought herself among the luckiest asylum seekers in the United States. She considered her major contact at Cornell, Liz Brundige, "one of the best persons in the world." Liz had helped with the details of her stay in Ithaca, like shopping and getting Internet service and a credit card. Thanks to Cynthia Bowman, Marzia had much-needed financial support from her fellowship. She loved the apartment where she was staying. She found Ithaca a beautiful and interesting place, which I knew from my undergraduate days at Cornell. Nevertheless, the situation was difficult. She felt entirely dependent on others, a feeling she disliked, because "in my life, I grew up very independent. I was the one giving support to others, but it was very sad when I was knocking on the door of professors and telling them, 'Would you please loan me your card, your Visa card, because I need a twenty-five-dollar credit.'"

Although Marzia was uncertain about what would happen to her in Canada—and she confessed that she had just been crying before our call—she knew that she did not want to return to the United States. "It is hard to stay in a kind of life that every day you get up and have to write a note that says, 'Can you please do this for me?.' . . . You don't know the system, you're not familiar with the system, [so] you . . . have to rely [for] everything on others. It was a kind of thing that I don't wish to return to. . . . It might be my foolishness because these are the friends that are for this purpose. . . . This was the love they gave me, and they grant to do this for me. My friends were telling me . . . 'You do for others and now they are doing for you, so no problem.' And they were so lovely and so patient . . ."

Still, Marzia was very aware that "people are really busy with their own work." The feeling that she was being a burden on the people who supported her was exacerbated by her depression. "I was alone and being out of the country. There was no one from Afghanistan in Ithaca." She loved the classes she attended—"I enjoyed the international [law classes], the best professors in the world"—but outside of those, she was isolated.

Moreover, even in Marzia's relatively privileged position, there were no long-term solutions for her. "I was thinking that if I finished visiting [at Cornell] on December 15, then . . . what will I do? . . . How could I get a job? [Even] with my knowledge and my capacity, being a lawyer, . . . what kind of job will be waiting for me? . . . When I was reading the news, they were saying that fifteen million [Americans] are jobless. It was shocking. If they are already qualified, if they can't get a job, how can I get a job? Even if it's just a small job. Maybe it was these thoughts that were eating me too much inside."

To make matters worse, Marzia was learning that there is little support outside of personal networks for newcomers to the United States. "If you are an immigrant . . . there should be some support, especially support for the people who are confused," which would include almost anyone suddenly thrust into Marzia's situation. "You know, there is no health care. . . . I couldn't even open a bank account because I didn't have IDs." The bank in Ithaca did not at first believe that Marzia was affiliated with the law school and treated her rudely. Without IDs for things like that, "I was quite indebt[ed] to the law school teachers. I was telling them, 'Can you buy for me an online credit card, or can you buy a ticket pass for me to go from here to there?' Because everything now is technology, you have to pay through Visa. I couldn't even have access for that. So if I [became] sick . . . if you don't have health care, you never know how it will happen because besides if there was no law school, then what would happen with me? Because if you don't have any relatives, then what will happen?" That last sentence may have been the key to Marzia's decision making. In Canada she had an aunt, cousins, and in-laws. There she would have family to count on and to show her the ropes.

Furthermore, Marzia was discouraged about the prospects for asylum in the United States. Her own hearings had been repeatedly delayed by a few weeks each time. But she knew of another immigrant who had left Afghanistan because of sexual violence, and her interview was delayed repeatedly by six months at a pop. That woman had already waited more than a year. Marzia did not want to be in her position.

> It's like how does the law see the United States' immigrants' lives, especially those who are refugees. They cannot return back home. It's sad . . . if you see [people] waiting for just having an interview for six months. . . . I got a notice that they meet me on 5th October, but [even] if I get all these papers worked . . . then I [might still have] six months, you know? . . . It will be hard for me. . . . If you don't have any support, you don't have any money or you don't have any house or if you don't have any relatives or you don't have any friends . . . or opportunities like I had or the people that I knew, then what would happen?

Being introduced to people in the United States as an immigrant had made her "brokenhearted," because that status seemed to replace everything else about her. Every story she heard about an immigrant or every case she studied in her law classes seemed directed at her situation. One drawn-out citizenship case made her think, "This is me, you know?" She also worried that being Muslim would be an obstacle. "There are many good people, and they don't think about these things. They just spend all their time on their work," she observed, "but you can feel that."

Marzia could not help imagining the worst about the U.S. immigration and asylum process. "Maybe this was my own worries," she said. She knew "my case was different because . . . I had more opportunities, I had . . . all of you with me and . . . all your different prayers and support, because I had the letters, I had the recommendations, I had the calls, all these things." But she remained unconvinced that her asylum request would be granted. "Policies could be changed. The situation could be changed. . . . You never know if the immigration person is a good person or not. . . . [or] if they are going to put me in front of the judge and say, 'Okay now you should go and argue.' It could take two years, and I wouldn't have social security, and I would have to bug everyone, 'Can you do this? Can you do that?' And then [to] have no job . . . I don't know, being very independent, I was very anxious to get work."

In the end, Marzia realized that she could not really blame others for her anxieties. "I could blame the system or I could name someone, [but really] I have to blame myself, you know? If we are traumatized, if we have a lot of problems in the country, then sometimes it comes that you cannot be there anymore." The United States was becoming Marzia's new Afghanistan.

Marzia had visited Buffalo once before, earlier in the summer, to meet with her aunt from Toronto. It was she who told Marzia about a shelter for anyone in the United States planning to emigrate to Canada. "I met interesting people and I found very good friends there. Catholic sisters who were in administration and they took me to their home because they were feeling that the crowded situation with all the different culture[s], they were saying that 'you have to be in a quiet place.'" Just a few days before our first scheduled phone call, Marzia had returned to Buffalo to visit her aunt again. Marzia's heightened anxiety since their last visit alarmed her aunt. She began pressuring Marzia to come to Canada. "She was saying that when you are here, there are all your relatives," according to Marzia, who was also responding to the aunt's frail health and advancing age.

With a call to the shelter and the friendly nuns, the pieces began falling into place. The sisters worked some magic so that Marzia was able to gain entry to the shelter in only one day instead of the weeks that other prospective émigrés were waiting. "It was like [every]one was pushing me to go," she says. "My aunt said that you should just come urgently." Leaving the United States began to seem her fate.

The next challenge was collecting her belongings and arranging her departure from Ithaca. She did not even take time to get her money from the bank where she had finally gotten an account. Her aunt said, "Don't worry about that. The bank will be there. We are here; we can give you some support. Then later you can decide." The worst part was that she did not have time to discuss her departure with "the group that was supporting me. It is just tough. It is like . . . something is eating my inside. I can't understand why I respond to the life that is given to me. Because from the beginning, Liz was the one who was helping me through all this with the law school." By this time, though, Marzia had decided that the situation was really out of her hands.

Crossing the border proved both easier and more difficult than Marzia had feared. The best part was the help she received from one of the volunteer Catholic sisters from the Buffalo shelter who came to the border and spent three hours helping her negotiate with the officials. The sister had long experience working with Canadian immigration as she helped people cross the Peace Bridge. "She was giving me a kind of hope," Marzia said. "She was saying, 'Don't worry.'" But Marzia's seventy-three-year-old aunt became a bit flustered, and at one point the officers said she could not be Marzia's aunt because she was unable to supply some information they requested. Marzia explained, "She meant 'yes'" in replying to one question, "but she said 'I don't know.'"

Luckily, Marzia herself "gave a good interview," and she was grateful to see what the Canadian government was offering her—free health insurance, residency at a shelter, a promise of almost six hundred dollars a month until she got a job, and eligibility for employment within two months. "Unfortunately, you have to go through the procedures, which are always the government's responsibility," she said, but unlike in the United States, "there are systems for immigrants, and they are entered, and they are registered." Marzia decided right away that Canada was a more supportive country than the United States, but with her new status only a few hours old, she was also withholding final judgment. "I will see what will happen now," Marzia mused. "I need to get adjusted, like I mentioned I could work much easier here than in the U.S. Of course I want my husband to come here, but I don't know . . . It's just like I saw the immigration officer and he was very lovely. He, while I was talking with him, he respect me very much. I think . . . before talking to my aunt, he was feeling that I really should be able to stay in Canada."

Marzia had not quite realized how final a decision she was making until after it was done, however. "I noticed that my head was not working," she said. A U.S. immigration official told her that she had had "a lot of opportunity [to remain in the United States] and [even an] appointment date for the interview." They asked why she had "'just reject[ed] all the love that we give to you. You are not a person that we can give you more of an opportunity to be back in the United States.'" Then she realized that "if the [Canadian] immigration rejected me then I couldn't return to the U.S. . . . You can't go back. And then I [also] know that I should not go back to Afghanistan."

Feeling like a woman without a country, Marzia knew that the encouragement she was receiving from her husband and father to stay away from Afghanistan constituted a strong message about the danger she was in. If her father, who "believes in the country and work[s] for the country," told her to seek asylum elsewhere, then her life in Afghanistan must really be over. "Because he is . . . close to the judges in the Supreme Court in Afghanistan and he goes all the time," her father knew that those in the legal system "hate if you are Americanized. If you have your education in the U.S. or you don't cover your head," you are in trouble. And "this is my history. It will always be behind [me]." Such thoughts brought tears for Marzia. "Being an immigrant is like begging, begging from someone. It's really, it's not good. I don't feel important. . . . Being homeless is one thing that you should never experience," she advised. "God thinks that this is the time I should enjoy a new life, with new people. It is not easy, I told you. It's not easy." But this is what she would do.

Despite making a new start, feeling secure remained difficult for Marzia. She was concerned, for example, about talking in her own language on the telephone. "Everyone thinks we are terrorists," she laughed. "We are not, but once you are speaking in your language, . . . the detective or police will be wise enough to listen while we are talking, even if we are talking about life." She considered getting involved with human rights issues in Canada—"because here there are also human rights"—and sharing her knowledge about her country. She hoped that such activism would help her find work and professional opportunities. But then she had second thoughts: "You know, once I meet with the world on TV, on the news, I don't like it because . . . I will risk my life."

The murder in September 2011 of former Afghan president Burhanuddin Rabbani at the hands of a Taliban representative who masqueraded as a peace negotiator but hid a bomb in his turban was a cautionary tale for Marzia. Although she was no fan of Rabbani because of his violent warlord past, she recalled that two weeks before his death, he had made a "strong opposition speech against the Taliban. He was saying that they were taking young boys from their missions to use them for sudden attacks and it was not good. . . . When I hear[d] that, I was thinking . . . this is a warning for him, for his life. He made himself in danger." She thought it would be the same for her: "He was a president. If he couldn't save his life, then how could I do that?"

Her fear of media exposure was also being fueled by the increasing willingness of world leaders, including those in the United States, and the Karzai government to bring the Taliban back into power positions. If that happened, she knew that United Nations and other international NGOs would be threatened, and her association with such organizations would haunt her indefinitely. The warning letters she received "were harming me," she said, making her believe that any public attention could easily mean the end of her life.

Once her decision was made, though, Marzia began having second thoughts. She worried especially about her abrupt exit from Ithaca. "Recently I have been feeling very sad," she said. "I left a note, before just a few minutes to Liz," her Cornell mentor. She considered writing more, but worried about what to say. "I don't know how many hours she spent to have me there, to give me a prosperous life. But now I'm here." At the same time, she believed Liz would care only about her happiness. "This is her wish," Marzia said.[2]

Marzia also remained very grateful for the support she had received from her U.S. contacts, including George Washington Law School dean Susan Karmanian; Judge Marian Horn, a professor at GW; Joan Winship, executive director of the International Judges Association; and Rosanne O'Hara, her host during her GW days. "These are the people that [give] me . . . hope for the future. . . . I feel that I am under these kindnesses that they have given to me. . . . This was unlimited . . . kindness and generosity that I have got from U.S."

She was especially grateful for the letters of support she received for her asylum-seeking bid.

> I told you that those letters . . . keep me alive. . . . Once I was very sad, and . . . late at night, I got all your letters. You sent me the letter I needed, Paula Dobriansky [undersecretary of state for democracy and global affairs, 2001–9] sent me the letter I needed, Professor Bowman, from Cornell, [sent the letter] I needed.[3]

Then I was forced to cry. I was really crying because the way that you had written about me that I should get support from the U.S., I was really sensitive and I wrote to my lawyer. It was late at night, like 11:00 at night, and it was my first letter I wrote to my [kind, hardworking] lawyer [Jenny Stapleton] ... this was the time that I was supposed to have an interview very soon. I wrote to her that I don't know what will happen in my future ... how officers will look on [these letters], but for me it's a gift ... Whether they will accept it or not, for me the way that you had written. ... And she wrote me back, the same moment ... saying that I am not alone, "I am also with you."

Marzia wondered if she could have endured the six months of her "transitional period" without "the love that I had, the e-mails."

Marzia also remembered fondly and longingly her experience with the educational system in the United States, both from her George Washington days and from her experiences at Cornell and ASU. "I always admire studies in this country," she said, "... the way students and teachers were reading ... how the teachers are knowledged ... the structures that are evident. I don't think that other countr[ies'] scholars are like the U.S. scholars." She was amazed that she saw students still engaged in conversation about her lectures even during breaks. "This is the kind of thing someone should learn from education," she said. "It could be ... a great example of education. ... anytime I see it, I enjoy it very much. I always say that that was the best gift from God that was given to me."

Despite the emotional strain she was under, Marzia was trying hard to focus on the future. Even as she sought solace and support from family members and familiar faces, she did not want to inconvenience them for very long. "Anywhere you go, you will be disruptive because now they don't have a bigger room." She also resisted becoming part of the Afghan expat community because she was imagining a brand-new start. "I prefer to not even stay in Toronto in the future if I can because here, especially in this small community that I am in now, it's all like back in Pakistan. ... I mean it's like if you want to have a change, you have to change your mind, you have to change your talk, you have to change your education, the level, you have to be the same level that the others are," by which she meant mainstream Canadians. "You should at least try," she concluded. She was discouraged by what seemed the unchanging nature of "Eastern culture," where women "sit around and talk and talk and talk." Rather, she wanted "to go to a big academic environment" and have "more academic friends rather than Afghan friends." She was not abandoning her family, whom she would "be very happy to go and see because they are here. My aunt on Fridays, on weekends." But she also reiterated, "You know we say that 'let's become white now,'" by which she meant "let's assimilate."

Her parting assessment during that first call showed how fraught her decision to leave Afghanistan was. "I hope that this will be the final destination," she said. "So I have to sit on my legs." But she knew there would be a cost. Not only had she left behind her best possibility for employment, in Afghanistan, but she was also worried about her health: "I don't know how long I will live, how long I will be alive because my life will be cut in half, as being an immigrant person. . . . I feel like a lost woman." At the same time, she relished the possibility of devoting time to her own interests. "I think I do need to relax and work on my own agenda," she said, "other than think about the other things."

Afghanistan Still on Her Mind

Even in the midst of Marzia's confusion and anxiety, I doubted that she could really stop thinking about "other things." Indeed, as much as she grieved for herself, she also grieved for her country. "I keep thinking every day, any minute, actively checking the BBC website for what is happening. This is my heart back there but I can do nothing. I don't know how it will be, the future for Afghanistan."

She recalled that "five million of the population are dead already because there is sickness and no jobs and poverty." She mourned for her home city of Kabul, which was "all smoke, from the cars but also from all these things that are happening." She wished that international decision makers could spend even one day in the shoes of people in her country, for "if you don't feel, if you don't suffer, you don't feel others." She said that Afghans have the right to live in peace. "This is something that I wish internationals should think of ending the war." She knew that "9/11 . . . did a lot of strong damage to [American] lives and we can't forget it." But that "was a one-day issue," while "in Afghanistan we have lost millions and millions and millions."

She was highly critical of what passes for leadership in Afghanistan. "They didn't take care of the country, so now we are the home for terrorists." For that reason, she believed "peace is in the trust of the international(s), not in the trust of the people. Because [the Afghan] people are very weak. They don't have the power to decide on the future of Afghanistan. This is [why] the international community should come together and help us. We should stand up beside each other." She thought the U.S. government was too indecisive. She worried that the departure of U.S. troops would leave "giant damage" in Afghanistan. She could not see how they could keep "a tank in half way" while "trying to leave." She thought that departure would "lose the hope for the whole nation. We will feel like we are so helpless. . . ."

Like a recurring nightmare, she kept remembering her life under the Taliban. "How could I forget those days when I was covering my head, and I was warned for having one hundred or two hundred dollar salary . . . working for the international community." She continued:

> True, the job was not easy to take because it was a risk for my life, but I was begging . . . to get a very low job [so that] I could have a salary, not because I was poor and I didn't have food, because everyone could feed me, my father

was good. But it was because I wanted it. It was my wish. It was all my education that I could give to others. It was my aim that I should work to help. But you know I was under the veil and I was knocking, "Can you, can you, can you hire me?" I can't forget that. One day I came out from the bus and the bus took my veil. . . . my veil was stuck in the bus and it left . . . I was supposed to die and go under the wheel because of that veil.

Two Months Later

I felt privileged that I had talked to Marzia on the first day of her residency in Canada. At that time, she was still breathless from making her decision and agitated about the difficulties and uncertainties that lay before her. When we spoke two months later, on November 14, 2011, she was much calmer. She was feeling more independent than she had in the United States. She was not yet able to drive, but she hoped to get a license after her immigration interview in six months to a year. She had opened a bank account with ease. She had her own lawyer and doctor. She was feeling so comfortable, in fact, that except for the immigration processes, she was wondering why the United States and Canada were considered different countries. "It is all the same language," she said. "The whole system is very close. I don't know. . . . These are two countries, but I don't see any difference."

The promises of the Canadian immigration system made Marzia "hopeful for the future." The United States was great, she said, but not as penetrable as Canada. She had a good lawyer, who thought that her case would be fairly straightforward. The lawyer intended to use the same facts from her case for U.S. asylum, although rather than asylum, she was seeking refugee status in Canada. She had rented an apartment in the same building where her aunt and a cousin lived. "I don't know sometimes, it might be a kind of temporary happiness for me, that I should be more close with the culture," she said, but she quickly added that "my point will be . . . to reintegrate myself into Canadian society. I will because that one is more important." She planned to take advanced English courses and driving lessons and to continue her professional education as soon as she could. She hoped that her U.S. contacts, the fellowship she received at Cornell (where she happily reported that her relationships were still strong), and her stint as a visiting expert at ASU would be recognized as credentials in Canada. Once she became a permanent Canadian resident, she could go to visit her husband in India or Pakistan (it seemed unlikely that he could visit her in Canada). Getting to that point would take more than a year, she said, and things were still uncertain. Nevertheless, although she did not "know how this plan could work . . . it is a plan."

Marzia was receiving the promised monthly welfare check from the government, although at $592 per month, it did not come close to paying the $950 rent for her unit. (Exactly how she would pay her full expenses was unclear, but she did still have access to her own money.) Although paid work was not yet available, she could do volunteer work, preferably in an agency or organization (of which there are several in Canada) working on Afghan women's rights in some way, which might lead to paid employment in the future. Expressing less concern about the dangers of going public, she said, "I have to be more close with human rights organizations, women rights organizations. I think that my commitment back to my country is to find out how Canadian projects work for Afghanistan and then be connected with some international organizations that are working in Canada. But it is a future plan. I don't know how it will work." After achieving permanent residency, getting a work permit, and pursuing continuing legal education for what she wanted to do, she thought she might qualify for a good job.

By the time of our November call, Marzia recognized that the wheels of immigration turned as or more slowly in Canada than they did in the United States (which she then regarded as the more organized country), but she appreciated that they turned more reliably. The management of her apartment building displayed a similarly slow pace of responsiveness. Still, she found Canada a beautiful and more obviously multicultural country than the United States. She marveled at the size of and opportunities in Toronto. And she appreciated the Canadian government's attention to immigrants. While her case was in limbo, for example, a caseworker was assigned to advise her during the immigration process (as well as to monitor her as a welfare case).

Two months into her new status and location, Marzia was less critical of the expat Afghan community. Although her long-range plan was still assimilation into Canadian society, she appreciated being near her family and other Central Asian refugees, although she was feeling some tension between the demands of her sister-in-law and those of her aunt's family. (Propriety demanded that she be closer to her blood relatives than to her in-laws.) She found the proximity to her aunt comforting, and she was glad she could assist her as her health deteriorated. For the moment, she liked being able to participate easily in Muslim holiday celebrations.

Although far from home, Marzia was on the lookout for opportunities to help other Afghan women. She was deliberately trying to be a role model for the sequestered, veiled women in her apartment building, for example, which was mostly populated by Indian and Pakistani immigrants, as well as by Afghans. "Once you open the door, you face that culture," Marzia said. So she decided, "Maybe I could be an example for them to change." With that prospect in mind, she visited with some families from Kandahar, the "place of the Taliban," without covering her head. "I talked with them and said that I am educated and [explained] what are the benefits of education. I talked about why they shouldn't have [so many] children. . . . Sometimes I think this is a need to be among them, to bring a positive change. They should know that those who are not covering their heads, they are also human beings and they are very good . . . and talented and moral."

Even after her eight-month absence from Afghanistan, Marzia was staying well-informed about the situation there. She knew about the Loya Jirga called by

President Karzai to strategize about Afghanistan's relationship with the United States in 2011 and about the Taliban's threats to disrupt it, for example. She communicated by Skype regularly only with her husband and one sister back in Afghanistan because of the price of Internet connections, but she kept in touch by e-mail with a few female judges and former NGO colleagues. She also received newsletters from several organizations, including the Afghan Women's Network. She was pleased that colleagues had volunteered to take over the leadership of her Afghanistan Progressive Law Organization. She wanted to keep that going, to "keep the good reputation that it had, though it was newly established." And she worried. Being away is in some ways worse than being on the ground, she said, because "if you are inside the hell, its okay, you will feel the flame and burn. But if you are outside, you will feel it worse, because you don't know what is happening."

Marzia was cautious about revealing her application for refugee status in Canada to her friends and colleagues in Afghanistan, implying to some that she was just continuing her education abroad. This reticence resulted from the concerns I surmised in our first conversation. "There is a resistance from going from abroad to going to Afghanistan," Marzia said. "Because . . . if I get an education here and then in five years go back and help more my country in that position, not in the government but even in the [Afghanistan Progressive Law] organization, there is a kind of jealousy that is going on. . . . They don't feel good because they will say that 'we were here in Afghanistan and we should have these jobs, not you.' They are competing negatively. . . . They sometimes say, 'You went and had [a] luxurious life there, and you saved yourself. Then why are you back here?'" She knew how this worked in part because she had shared some of those feelings about expats when she suffered through the wars in the 1980s and '90s.

At some point, she planned to write to everyone and explain, but for the moment she was keeping a low profile. At the same time, however, she worried that people would forget her, even if she stayed in touch by e-mail. Even more disturbing, she worried that her husband would never get to join her and would be forced to find another wife, despite his protestations to the contrary. "So I feel bad. I have to think how I should express my situation in Afghanistan. But it is the reality. I left. It is not a joke."

Developments in Afghanistan mostly discouraged her. Even her usually upbeat father was beginning to think there might be no hope for the country. He said that Afghanistan would be an unsafe place for people like Marzia for years to come. Marzia reiterated her belief that Pakistan supported the Taliban because, like other powers in the region, Pakistan did not want Afghanistan to have any stability. It was better for those powers, including Iran, India, and China, if Afghans fought among themselves. The Taliban represented that influence, but they were so convinced of their own power that they had refused to negotiate with anyone. (Of course, Marzia was also opposed to negotiating with them.) They regarded themselves as the ultimate superpower.

Despite these real worries, Marzia continued to imagine a better future for her country. For instance, she hoped that Afghanistan might develop a pure parliamentary system of government to replace the mixture of forms that the Karzai government represented (president and Parliament). Afghans needed a way to hold their leaders accountable, she said, and the presidency (which the Bush administration imposed on the country) looked too much like a super-warlord position in which women were invisible and the purpose was to reward one's friends and disenfranchise one's enemies. Karzai also did reckless things, according to Marzia, such as signing a strategic contract with India. "Pakistan thinks this is a warning for Pakistan," which would feel threatened by the suggestion that Afghanistan had its own economy and borders. Pakistan had enjoyed the historically fluid "Pashtunistan" regional border with Afghanistan—although that ambiguous territory had allowed the Pakistan-based Taliban to infiltrate Afghanistan—and could retaliate. Iran and China would also be alarmed, because they wanted Afghanistan as an exclusive market. "The government is in a bit of instability from the inside because the support that [Karzai] had in the past, he doesn't have it now," Marzia explained. In contrast to most news reports in the United States, Marzia believed that the U.S. interest in using Afghanistan as a strategic partner could create more stability and be good for the country.

In her optimistic moments, Marzia also hoped that she could do more from Canada for her country than she could from within its borders. She was impressed that "anywhere the Canadian government works for Afghan government, they include a woman issue." She hoped to continue her work on behalf of Afghan women's legal issues, especially working with Afghan women judges and lawyers to increase their capacity as jurists.

> I don't know how fundraising will be in this country, but maybe if I found an honest organization that are really thinking about Afghanistan women organizations, I would be very happy [to] work for them. Make money and then send it back to the Afghan women. I can do this here. I don't know how it will work, but it's a kind of dream for me if I think that I can, if I can do some speeches, visit some woman society and get the issues on the table, be ready to talk to women who are helping Afghanistan donors and some people who are funding the Afghan women or the women around the world. But I have to find them. My knowledge is zero yet.

She had so far been in touch with two organizations to volunteer her services—even to do office work—but she had not heard back from them. She did not know what to think about that, but she knew "it's a waste of life" for someone like her to be sitting at home.

From her new outsider position, Marzia advised the women of her country never to give up their struggle for rights, even though they were still rarely included in decisions (none were invited to Karzai's recent Loya Jirga, for example), and those in any position of power were still too intimidated to offer criticisms or go against the tide of male leadership. Still, she was encouraged by talk of nominating a woman to the high council of the Supreme Court in Afghanistan. "I'm not sure if the women judges . . . can get the one position on the high council, but I heard that there [is] some progress going on. I heard that the International Association of Women Judges [was] there back in Afghanistan. They want to establish again Afghan Women Judges Association."

Yet, as she had been over the years, Marzia remained almost as critical of women's efforts as of the government's failures: women's rights groups were not necessarily helping themselves or the country; they were too dispersed; their projects were too small. Instead, they needed to focus on larger goals, such as increasing opportunities for education throughout the country, not just working for change in a single village or province. Marzia advised women's groups to insist on a role in civil society, which had virtually excluded women. Professional women's groups and rights groups should join forces and work for all women. Educated women should join forces with educated men, who may not recognize their existence. In 2002, for example, Marzia had to remind the minister of justice that women judges existed in Afghanistan.

Beneath such optimism and wishful planning, however, was a constant current of doubt and worry that threatened to overwhelm Marzia's worldview. Making her momentous decision to start life anew came with self-recrimination and regrets, as well as with deeper bouts of depression. In November 2011, Marzia wondered why she had not concentrated more on her personal life. "Because . . . life is also very important and I think I have lost too much, especially with the traumatized situation. . . . Sometimes people should also think about their life. . . . I don't know how stupid I was," she said. "Since 2002 I have been traveling too much abroad." She also wondered if she had wasted her energy on a lost cause. "It is good to help the country, but if there is no solution and the solution is not up to you, then you cannot build a country."

By September 2012, Marzia still had not had her immigration hearing in Canada. In an e-mail on May 16, she had written, "The hardship of immigration life has disgusted me besides, having no jobs and no activities makes things more complicated. Until I . . . have my hearing I cannot enroll at any academic places. . . . Though I have [begun] volunteer work in a library, tutoring the children, which makes me to leave home at least." She was wondering whether emigration was more difficult than remaining in Afghanistan. She was by then thinking, "It might had been good if I had died back at home rather than to face such long hardship in my life."

Jamila, 2011–2012

The second surprise in June 2011—a more pleasant one—came in an e-mail from Jamila. The message started with information about her progress on submitting her GRE scores to the Fulbright fellowship program through which she hoped to gain admission to a U.S. university in order to study for a Ph.D. in international relations. She and I had been communicating about her dream of continuing her education in that way. At first she had not mentioned her wish to her husband, Fazal, fearing that he might not allow her to come. But sometime before the Istanbul meeting, she had told him, and he had consented to the idea. Fazal was hoping that he and I could talk in Istanbul about what conditions would be like for Jamila, should she enter the international relations program at ASU. But their son's sickness and Fazal's preoccupation with caring for him and the baby prevented that conversation from taking place.

So, when Jamila wrote me on June 18 to report on a delay in transmitting her scores because of "mismanagement" by Educational Testing Service (ETS) India, which was responsible for conveying her test scores, I was concerned but not alarmed. I was sorry to hear that she had had to pay an additional $221 on June 6 but had still not heard if the scores were reported. Then, in the final paragraph of the e-mail, she slipped in her surprise: "Another point I would like to share is that I am going to visit USA in August 2011 for receiving an award of 'Peace Maker' in New Jersey. I hope we can make some time to visit from ASU as well."

The more I learned about the award, the more impressed I became. The Tanenbaum Peacemakers in Action Prize, awarded by the New York–based Tanenbaum Center for Interreligious Understanding, is very prestigious. To be eligible for the prize, nominees must do peace work that is fueled by religious beliefs and located in areas of armed conflict. They must have risked their lives or freedom in pursuit of conflict resolution; be on the ground in the conflict situation, preferably in their own communities; and be relatively unknown. Who could be more perfect for such a prize than Jamila? Winners receive $15,000 in cash to continue their work, recognition for their contributions, and entrée into a network of peacemakers as they continue their activities. There were ten nominees for the 2011 award and two winners, Jamila and Bishop Ntambo Ntanda of the Democratic Republic of the Congo. Because of the award, Jamila and the bishop were invited to attend the 2012 peacemakers' retreat in Abuja, Nigeria.[4]

Jamila was nominated for the award by WISE, the Women's Islamic Initiative in Spirituality and Equality. I knew firsthand from Daisy Khan of the American Society for Muslim Advancement that WISE had recognized Jamila's initiatives in Afghanistan, especially her work with imams to preach in the mosque about women's rights. According to the WISE website, the organization invited Jamila to join the WISE network and to participate in WISE's second annual conference in Kuala Lumpur, Malaysia, in July 2009. They claimed that Jamila's idea for her work with imams was inspired at that conference by a case study about an imam-training program in the Philippines (although she never mentioned that to me).[5]

Jamila never sent me more information about her trip or about our potential meeting there (I did not know the exact dates of her travel). But I learned from web sources that she went to Drew University in New Jersey in August for the annual Peacemakers in Action Working Retreat, where the award is given. (The retreats are held in different cities around the world, including New York, Sarajevo, and Amman in recent years.) In response to a message I sent her on August 11, 2011, Jamila confirmed that she had been in New Jersey for the award ceremony, but she added yet another, less happy, surprise: "Unfortunately [I] broke my leg, and . . . had to return to Kabul for treatment and rest." By mid-September she was able to report that the leg was healing well and that she was feeling much better.

Another surprise in Jamila's life was actually revealed to me by Marzia. During one of our calls, Marzia said she had heard that Jamila had given birth to another baby. I was able to confirm that with Jamila by e-mail. When I talked with her again in January 2012, the baby—a daughter, named Fatima—was seven months old. Although Jamila was clear that she did not want another baby, and she did not have time to pay much attention to her, she said that she recognized Fatima as a gift from God, "because she is smiling all the time and she is very quiet, not crying, not giving me hard times. She is a good baby." Jamila also added that she was still taking pleasure in caring for her children, although her worries about their future were increasing day by day.

The Darker Side

For much of my acquaintance with Marzia's and Jamila's professional and personal lives, I had been acutely aware of their differences. Although both worked tirelessly to promote the rights, education, and economic independence of Afghan women, one had lived through the hell of war for most of her life, and the other had lived in exile for her formative years; one was wealthy, and the other was more middle class; one was overtly religious, and the other was more secular in her looks and occupation (though also deeply religious); one focused on civil law and rights, and the other used religious doctrine to promote women's causes. And although both had earned distinction on the international stage, I believed that their different commitments would lead them in different directions.

When Marzia ultimately found life untenable in Afghanistan, it seemed their differences would only multiply. As Marzia pursued permanent residency in Canada and figured out how to continue her work for Afghan women from abroad, I envisioned Jamila sticking it out in Afghanistan, raising her children in seclusion and isolation while she continued her work from within the country, through her ever-growing organization, NECDO. Even if she left the country for an education, I thought, she would always go back.

In January 2012, I discovered that my focus on their different life trajectories had been somewhat misguided. A conversation with Jamila in that month revealed that the two women's stories might not diverge so much after all. Ever since receiving her Tanenbaum award, Jamila had been getting death threats from the Taliban. Even while her friends and coworkers and the imams she worked with were praising her achievement and enjoying her recognition, the Taliban had been targeting her and her organization with harassment and intimidation. "From the Taliban perspective, we are a very big concern," Jamila said.

"Some of the people in the Taliban are dropping acid on the faces of those who they think are [involved with social change] . . . especially women activists," she explained. Things were especially tense in Ghazni, Jamila's family province, although she had no more contact with relatives there. The threats and warnings Jamila received were so bad that she no longer allowed her then five-year-old son to attend school. Some of the threats mentioned her husband's family, which the Taliban considered too liberal. "They are always blaming me for teaching a new Islam, which their forefathers never experienced," she said. But of course what Jamila taught was a version of Islam that madrassa educations did not include. The police offered no protection, because "usually during the day they are different at dealing with people than they are at night," when they, too, do the work of the Taliban.

Soldiering On

Fortunately, Jamila's work was continuing because she had a "grown-up organization with experts and staff in different provinces. So the activities are not to stop. . . . They are doing the activities without any hitches." Rather than starting new projects, Jamila dedicated the Tanenbaum award money to continuing those ongoing activities, "especially in the area of peace creating and human rights and women's rights training." Her organization was by then active in seven provinces. But she herself "[could not] do any other things, like going out into the community with other people." Indeed, she could barely leave her home-office at all. "This is the price that we have given for women's rights but we cannot stop," she said. Jamila had always known this might happen, which was why she had emphasized training her own successors and building the capacity of her organization from the very beginning, so that it could continue without her.

Jamila's work with imams had gone particularly well. In many of the provinces where NECDO worked, women were attending mosque for the first time. Even some conservative communities had become receptive to "continuous communication and continuous exchange of information, especially about the Qur'an," Jamila said. Her training helped them to understand "the reality on the ground because usually Imams in the community are more resistant because they are afraid of change." They had finally understood that women's rights are "nothing new from an Islamic perspective . . . the life of the Prophet [is also] an example for them in many cases." But the Taliban was relentless. Some of the imams Jamila worked with had also been threatened. "One of the Imams working in Jalalabad who made a section in the mosque for women, he received a warning last week," Jamila reported.

Thus, despite the wonderful news about her program's success, there was discouragement in Jamila's voice. When pressed, she admitted that the climate for women's rights was deteriorating. It was much worse than it was a year ago, she said. Like Marzia, she was extremely discouraged that "the international community wants to include [the Taliban] in the peace and reconstruction process." She wondered if they had abandoned women's rights entirely. She still distrusted all reports of Taliban reform.

Jamila was soldiering on, but her life was "really difficult to manage." She took pleasure in her children, even though she had not really wanted her third baby. But God knew best by blessing her with this "new life," a smiling, quiet, happy baby. She found all of them, even the troublesome two-year-old, a welcome distraction. "When I am very busy with them, to feed them, to clean them, to work with them, it is a pleasant time and makes me forget about the tension." But at the same time, the children inevitably taxed her strength and threatened her health. Although her broken leg had healed, it was still painful. And, of course, she was still disabled from childhood polio.

Despite, or perhaps because of, these extraordinary challenges, Jamila continued to dream about going abroad for a Ph.D. in international relations. But the challenges were becoming quite daunting. For example, in the spring of 2012, she applied for a new scholarship program at Durham University in the United Kingdom, sponsored by the Open Society Foundation, which targets "female Afghan students who have demonstrated both academic excellence and the potential to become leaders, decision-makers and opinion formers in their country." The scholarship supported doctoral work in several fields (including international relations).[6] It had sounded perfect for Jamila, but she was not admitted, probably because she is not planning to teach at the university level.

In June she became interested in a Fulbright fellowship for study in the United States. That turned out to be unsuitable for her because it disqualified applicants with trailing dependents. "You know in the current situation I could not leave my children in the uncertain circumstances in Afghanistan," she explained. Even more discouraging, ten months after she had taken the tests, Jamila was still unable to obtain her GRE scores from the Educational Testing Service branch office in India. Without those scores, despite her payment of more than seven hundred dollars on the test and a follow-up with ETS India by Margaret Mills, she would be unable to apply to most U.S. graduate schools. When Jamila was discussing all this on the phone, she said with a laugh, "My life is not working so well right now." I guessed that she appreciated her own understatement.

New Challenges

As if Jamila, Marzia, and other champions of rights for Afghan women needed more obstacles, the Afghan National Shura of Ulema added to their woes in March 2012 by issuing new guidelines about women's rights from an Islamic perspective.[7] After articulating women's rights under Sharia law, such as an adult woman's right to choose her husband, the council also articulated some regressive precepts for women's rights. Perhaps the most challenging was their interpretation of verses 1 and 34 of Surah an-Nisa' of the Qur'an to mean that "men are fundamental and women are secondary" and that "lineage is derived solely from the man." The council also reinforced the rules of polygyny, thereby condoning it, and admonished women to wear strict *hijab,* to avoid mingling with men even in education and work, and always to travel with a *mahram*.[8]

In July 2012, Jamila told me that she was outraged that Karzai had approved these guidelines, which include prohibitions against a woman's leaving the house without her husband's permission, traveling without a *mahram,* and mingling with strange men in schools, markets, and offices, as well as support for polygyny, especially with regard to widows. Wife beating was prohibited in the guidelines only if there was no "Sharia-compliant reason." The clerics also judged the Afghan Constitution, which guarantees equal rights for men and women, as "flawed from a religious perspective."[9] Even though the guidelines were not legally binding, Jamila feared that they had undermined all the progress women had made. Her worry reflected others' judgments that the guidelines set the stage for "Talibanization."

In explaining his support for the declaration, Karzai said that he believed the Ulema Council's guidelines would strengthen the status of women's rights by reminding men of their obligations to women under Islamic law (Levinson 2012). Maybe . . . but Jamila had a different take. She expressed surprise at the "international community['s] silence on very important issues such as polygamy, travel without *mahram,* going out of house without husband permission, which has limited our scope of work and put efforts of last two decades under question." About polygamy, Jamila noted the council's probable concern about war widows and disabled women, who were likely candidates to be second, third, or fourth wives. That said, she clearly disapproved of reinforcing the concept that all women must be "reachable" as objects of men's sense of responsibility or desire.

Despite this setback, Jamila had a plan. "As using Islam as tool of domination in Afghanistan is common, and there is no women group to justify their rights from Islamic perspective, . . . we [must] work on establish[ing] a network of human rights from [an] Islamic perspective for Afghan women, where Afghan women [have] to take [a] stand on such . . . important occasions, and this network has members of civil society, individuals, educational institutions, scholars Imams to work together." Indeed, she was already "working with NECDO, and our work with Imams for EVAW (Elimination of Violence Against Women) and peace education is going very well, and it is extended to 9 provinces and for the first time Volunteer Network of Afghan Imams has [been] established." I could again hear a smile in her voice as I read her conclusion: "I know once again I step in another challenging task."

I was heartened to know that her sense of humor was still intact and that her spirit, though bent, was not broken. But I also knew that she was serious about getting out of Afghanistan and inhabiting another world, at least for a while. "I'm just really tired," she said in January. "I may need some time for myself. Otherwise I will collapse." So after years of total and tireless dedication to working from within her country, Jamila was now envisioning a productive exile, not only to pursue more education but also to save her sanity and her life. "It is the only remaining wish for myself," she said. Because she planned to bring her children with her—If "not as soon as I start my education. . . . maybe after some times when I am settling or find a job to support their expenses"—I suspected that she would be in no hurry to get back. The realities of Afghanistan, poisoned as they were by a history of deceit, corruption, misogyny, and violence, seemed to be driving Jamila's and Marzia's fates closer together.

Reflections

In an e-mail she sent to me in July 2012, Margaret Mills described the difficulties that her department at Ohio State—Near Eastern Languages and Cultures—had encountered in trying to obtain student visas for foreign students from the Middle East and Central Asia. "It's not just the Fulbright rule," she wrote, "but the difficulty of anyone from combat zones trying for a student visa who wants to bring their family—for men it's about impossible, for women we at NELC have found it pretty difficult too—but worth trying, obviously, if support can be found." The biggest worry, apparently, is the risk that the students admitted to study in the United States will not want to return to the ruined countries they have left behind. Margaret admitted that the risk existed, as illustrated by a single female graduate student from Iran, whose admission to the United States had taken two years to negotiate and who then "jumped her visa" by dropping out of school and disappearing.

Margaret's message, along with Jamila's problems with the Fulbright fellowship policies, shed new light on Laura Bush's argument in her 2001 radio address that the United States had an obligation to Afghan women. After all I have learned about the role of the West in general and the United States in particular in creating the mess Afghanistan is in, I certainly agree that the United States has an obligation to Afghanistan and to Afghan women. But I do not believe that armed combat, political manipulation, and enormous cash bribes paid by the CIA are the best ways to fulfill that obligation. In fact, a wide spectrum of politicians and analysts agrees that such interventions have backfired, as Marzia's and Jamila's analyses and chapter 3 demonstrate. But I believe there are other, more productive, ways for the U.S. government to conceptualize its obligations to Afghans.

I would propose that one of them should be to make educational opportunities available to people whose lives have been devastated by more than a decade of war that was begun by the allied invasion of 2001. Among those people would be leaders such as Jamila, who wants more education so that she can help mend her country and promote Afghan women's health, rights, religious understanding, and economic capacities, even from abroad. Indeed, Jamila's track record is better than that of many if not most governmental and nongovernmental agencies in Afghanistan, and she deserves official U.S. support.

Especially in light of the recent betrayals of democratic principles in general and Afghan women in particular by the U.S.-backed administration of Hamid Karzai, I would ask U.S. policy makers to weigh the risks of people "jumping visas" against the obligation our country has to help Afghanistan build a future. I would ask them to examine the evidence, such as this book, that empowering Afghan women leaders is an important strategy. I would ask them to remember the international principles of human rights as well as findings by the United Nations and other agencies that "'societies that discriminate on the basis of gender pay a significant price in greater poverty, slower economic growth, weaker governance, and a lower quality of life'" and that "education, health, productivity, credit and governance work better when women are involved."[10]

I would further ask U.S. leaders to reread UN Resolution 1325, passed in December 2000, which promises to protect women in war and conflict situations and to ensure their centrality in conflict prevention, peacekeeping, and peacemaking. I would ask what the United States has done to enforce UNR 1325 in Afghanistan. More important, I would ask what the United States has done, with all of its drones, missiles, and combat deaths on all sides, to keep Afghan women from being sucked back into a lawless, Taliban-style abyss in which they would be destined once again to lose their humanity.

Providing high-quality higher education is one of the things the United States does very well. In fact, American institutions of higher learning have long been the envy of the world, and foreigners' experience with U.S. higher education has often helped to (re)build bridges between nations. I hope that U.S. immigration policy can be brought into line with the country's moral obligation to Afghanistan, especially to its women, so that U.S. educators can share a truly meaningful American gift with people who want and need it the most.

10

Future Prospects

Because I have so long viewed Afghanistan's future through the lens of gender issues and women's rights, I have been surprised to learn how few contemporary historians, economists, political scientists, journalists, or other analysts, who discuss transforming Afghanistan into a successful, independent, and rights-respecting nation, assess the role of empowering women and restructuring gender relations to such a future. Indeed, it appears that only feminist scholars and activists take seriously what many pundits note but then ignore: gender discrimination undermines Afghanistan's survival as a state (Armstrong 2002, 184; Ahmed-Ghosh 2006, 125). Even the U.S. military has quietly concluded that "attention to the different needs, interests, and experiences of men and women" enhances their nation-building activities and that gender equality is a "force multiplier in operations planning and execution strategies" (Dharmapuri 2011, 56).

This massive oversight flies in the face of the grim conditions, missed opportunities, attacks on women's rights activists (some of whom, like Marzia, have fled for their lives), and strong signals that the familiar yo-yo pattern with regard to women's rights (discussed in chapter 3) will recur. That outcome is especially likely given the imminent withdrawal of allied troops, Karzai's apparent determination to become an adviser to his successor, and the likely hazards of the 2014 presidential election.

Despite such grim evidence and prospects, it appears that there is no official strategy from the Afghan government, donor nations, or mainstream academic or political analysts for rebuilding gender relationships and allowing Afghan women from various regions, ethnicities, economic circumstances, and family structures to define their own goals and concepts of agency. And the way forward for urban activists who remain in the country, like Jamila, is equally unclear. Existing interventions by international donor nations are inadequate to the task, and there is little reason to trust that any Afghan president likely to replace Karzai will make gender relations a priority. Simply including women in the governmental structures and NGO projects that Afghans will inherit when allied military forces withdraw would not solve the country's deeply embedded gender problems.

So what would? Some feminist analysts blame the international community for what they consider perhaps the most troublesome challenge and recommend that internationals reduce their involvement in Afghanistan. They argue that the imposition of neoliberal governance practices, which comes along with many programs, has created a conundrum for activists like Marzia and Jamila in places such as Afghanistan. Such practices increase those activists' mobility and cosmopolitanism, on the one hand, and depoliticize their struggles for social justice, on the other. So instead of directly addressing corruption and inequality in Afghanistan, foreign governments and NGOs tend to minimize conflicts as signs of individual or group customs and lifestyles and to substitute market outcomes for deeper political achievements. Chandra Mohanty, for example, argues that the transformations necessary to achieve women's rights and social advancement in Afghanistan require "specifying women's struggles and identities in the context of" the negative forces of globalization (2013, 971–73, 985), instead of assuming those forces are inevitable. She and others claim that foreigners should privilege grassroots activism beyond Afghanistan's cities, thereby granting all women "agency in the construction of their new reality" and the reconstruction of their nation (Rostami-Povey 2007, 77).

Marzia and Jamila would likely agree with those assessments to a point, as do I. But the two women put more stock in the positive potential of international agencies and donor governments than such critics do. They distrust Afghanistan's indigenous governing institutions and social structures because they offer no strong, uncorrupt local alternatives to the international presence in their country. The two women hope to keep international organizations and donors interested in local situations in Afghanistan that focus on rights, such as health and education (Merry 2006, 227), as well as in its larger national challenges, and thereby to develop rather than resist that international interest.

Besides, the two women might also point out, the lines some analysts draw between local and global are already blurred in Afghanistan. Throughout its history, Afghanistan has been shaped by globalized political, economic, and cultural forces. Since 2001, "the invasion and occupation of Afghanistan and the international project of Afghanistan's national reconstitution illustrate the complicated working of global power, capital, citizenship, and justice" (Jalalzai and Jefferess 2011, 1–2). That translates into a problem separating "grassroots" from "top down" and "insider" from "outsider" with regard to advancing women's rights and opportunities. For example, many apparently local women activists, even in small villages, are already internationalized in their associations and perspectives. Some resettled exiles have been educated abroad and retain allies just over the border. A few of those exiles already employ international (UN) terminology to describe the meaning of local problems or events (Merry 2006, 213–15).

Sorting through such competing perspectives and approaches to envisioning and working to increase gender awareness and women's rights, opportunities, and civil participation in Afghanistan is the task of this chapter. It interprets contemporary analyses of Afghanistan's future by mainstream political observers, historians, economists, and other "experts" through the perspectives of women's rights advocates, feminist theorists, and gender scholars, myself and others. The chapter takes into account, first, the continued presence of international donor governments and aid agencies in Afghanistan for the foreseeable future, despite the scheduled allied troop withdrawal. It then considers what various approaches to Afghanistan's future central government might mean for the country's women—urban and rural—and for their social status and access to resources and opportunities. Chapter 10 further analyzes the implications for women's rights of negotiating with the Taliban and of conceptualizing Afghanistan as a coherent nation-state. The chapter's final section explores possible new ground for transnational collaboration between Western and Afghan feminist activists and theorists in light of the checkered history and structural power inequities that have hampered mutual understanding and plagued collaborations in the past.

Genderizing the International Community

Just because Marzia and Jamila have depended on and welcomed international involvement in and support for women's struggles in Afghanistan does not mean they are uncritical of current programs and strategies, as discussed throughout *Contested Terrain*. Based on their critiques, it seems clear that a major priority for improving the quality of internationals' involvement in their country is enhancing their "gender sensitivity" and understanding of Afghanistan's gender systems. Extrapolating from the women's many suggestions for improving those interventions, I offer three changes that could make international support more useful in improving Afghan women's status and rights.

The first step is increasing agencies' and foreign governments' understanding of *gender* as a political concept rather than simply a catalog of different reproductive functions and social and familial roles. Gender differences and related traits, responsibilities, and privileges in various cultural settings are not simply extensions of and variations on nature's plan for reproduction; rather, they are the results of human beings' ideas about power—who should have it and why. Moreover, *gender* is not just a synonym for *women*. Rather, the term connotes the ways in which both men's and women's lives are defined by gender ideologies—ideas about the social and ethical meanings of physiological differences; about concepts of worth, honor, and propriety; and about who has what access to which resources and opportunities.

Thus, gender-related programs have implications for all social relationships and material realities in Afghan society to varying degrees. International agencies and governments should understand how Afghan gender ideologies function for different women in various settings and circumstances, but they should also recognize the structural ways in which gender hierarchies are reproduced by external forces, including by globalized capitalism and by foreigners' efforts to help Afghan women (Merry 2006, 231).

With gender politics in mind, internationals should further embrace the idea that gender equity and women's improved social and economic status are central to Afghanistan's political, social, and economic past, present, and future. They are not soft "cultural" or religious issues to be avoided because of local sensitivities or left to religious extremists; rather, they are structural issues that are deeply embedded in the country's material conditions and ultimate survival. Therefore, internationals should focus on women's issues in the context of broader social and economic issues and goals, recognizing that negotiations about gender in Afghanistan entail conflicting social and economic priorities, multiple contingencies and compromises, cost-benefit analyses, and constant reconsiderations. As a result, when contexts and interpretations change over time, women's rights and social participation might be more negotiable in some settings than they seem (Zahedi 2011, 299–302).

The second change in international intervention that seems warranted for the future is related to the first. That is, the international community should include Afghan men as women's partners in addressing gender relations and rights (Abirafeh 2005, 4). Some Afghan men already support women's causes, although they are often tarred by internationals with the same brush as those who do not. There should also be better understanding of men's objections to women's rights and social participation. Many have been taught that education for women is un-Islamic and makes them promiscuous, for example. Men may object to women's employment because it competes with their own identities as providers. Such objections can be addressed by education and governmental action, if the government is so inclined, and by broad-based programming that involves men's interests.

International organizations and governments should simultaneously work to address some men's jealousy of targeted attention to women's status. Explaining why women's advancement benefits men is a way to counterbalance that reaction, possibly by taking to heart Margaret Fuller's prescient nineteenth-century observation: "By subjugating women, men subjugate a part of themselves and thereby obstruct their own personal, as well as humankind's general, aspiration to God. . . . Societies that stifle women's freedoms make men sick and miserable" (Harrison 2013, 37–38). Once men become aware of their own need for women's rights, that awareness can lead to men's engagement in women's causes (Zahedi 2011, 302).

The path toward such engagement might include projects that help Afghan men recognize how their own lives are affected and constrained by gender conventions and expectations with regard to masculinity and male identity, which may be invisible as accepted norms. Values such as *namus* (achieving honor by protecting women, land, and possessions) and *gheirat* (displaying manliness as a source of honor), among other masculine requirements of various ethnic groups, can dictate actions that many men find onerous. In addition, Afghan men can be helped to recognize how those values have generated a regime of sexual scrutiny that oppresses women; inflects family, economic, and community life; and stifles men's important relationships with women and girls. Increasing men's awareness of those costs to themselves, their families, and Afghan society is one of the purposes of NECDO's imam project. Participants in that project are beginning to assess the negative effects of their own male entitlements.

Afghan men could also be helped to see the differences among themselves with regard to beliefs about gender. For example, although men in some provinces believe that allowing their wives to work or participate in NGOs or government programs makes them no better than pimps who prostitute women, others not only accept but welcome such employment (Azarbaijani-Moghaddam 2010, 184, 186, 185). The same is true for girls' school attendance. Reflecting on reasons for those differences might spark fruitful conversations in Afghanistan about the true basis for the restrictions and deprivations imposed on women.

To reach the ultimate goal of international support, which is to enable women to articulate their needs and preferences and to set goals for themselves and achieve them, Afghan activists suggest that women should be empowered to make decisions and to access and exert control over resources. They do not necessarily have to exert direct power over men (Zahedi 2011, 297).

A strategy related to working with men from an Afghan perspective is first meeting women's practical needs, such as child care, living conditions, access to food and water, and employment, and then addressing strategic gender interests in culturally specific ways, such as changes in power relations between men and women that could enhance familial well-being (Zahedi 2011, 302). By the same token, instead of focusing on the *burqa* or *chaddari* or other aspects of public presentation, foreigners should notice that Afghan women have never been compensated for their losses by any government or organization or made more secure. Nor have they been empowered to participate in their country's reconstruction (Rostami-Povey 2007, 75). These larger needs must be addressed, and international organizations and governments, many of which are implicated in those losses, should assume at least part of that responsibility.

One idea internationals traditionally favor that may have to go is the concept of gender mainstreaming, which requires the analysis of all policies to determine their impact on gender. Aside from mainstreaming's lack of measurable criteria for success and of reliable monitoring mechanisms, it is not very useful in societies that have not yet embraced the concept of gender. An exclusive focus on gender can also obscure other forms of discrimination (Zahedi 2011, 295–96).

The third change internationals should consider is recognizing Afghan-run NGOs and women's networks as their best allies in promoting women's rights and improving their lives. Such groups, including Jamila's NECDO and many others, have done the most to address poverty, ill health, illiteracy, and women's desperation over many years and in many provinces (Rostami-Povey 2007, 53). They have also supported minorities; promoted disarmament; fostered democracy, religion, and freedom of expression; allied with moderate men; kept Afghan families alive in times of war; supported clinics and economic development; and put themselves at risk in order to serve their communities (Kandiyoti 2005, 21–25). Instead of designing their own projects from scratch, internationals could improve their odds of success by supporting such organizations and networks and learning from them. In addition, international donors could directly address the problem of competition within and among those organizations and their leaders, promote collaboration around issues, and link organizational funding to such collaboration instead of inciting competition among them for resources. Such efforts would help reduce the infighting among women activists and grassroots organizations that Jamila and Marzia have observed.

Had the U.S. government financed and supported grassroots organizations and activists "rather than dispatching their own representatives to Kabul" in imperialist self-righteousness, according to Nicholas Kristoff and Sheryl WuDunn, it "would have accomplished much more" after the initial fall of the Taliban (2010, 162–65). Jennifer Heath names many successful but struggling Afghan NGOs that should have been supported by and affiliated with international aid organizations but never were, including Afghan Empowerment for a Better Tomorrow, Afghans4Tomorrow, Women for Afghan Women, Future Generations, and Trust in Education (2011, 39n70). She considers how much more effective those organizations could have been with international support.

A Strong Central Government or Regional Powers?

Although few analysts who consider this question think about it in terms of women's status or rights, it seems clear that the relationship between Afghanistan's central government, whatever it turns out to be, and the villages and rural areas far from Kabul, Herat, and Kandahar will be crucial to Afghan women's flourishing in the coming years. Because a constant state of democracy has not been established to promote gender justice across the country, a Plan B for Afghan governance is in order.

Prospects for next steps that will benefit the most women lie as much in what pundits omit as in what they include. For example, Thomas Barfield recommends the "Swiss-cheese approach" in which the central government focuses the influence of its laws and administrative apparatus on the most populated and economically prosperous parts of the country, leaving poorer people in the mountainous regions, steppes, and deserts to fend for themselves, "as long as they [do] not challenge state authority." If they do, mechanisms would be put in place to counter such challenges. This strategy contrasts with the "American-cheese" approach, which seeks to blanket the nation with central authority. Barfield believes that successful centralized regimes in Afghanistan's past used the former approach. Given that history, he wonders why Karzai has seemed more determined than the United States and NATO to implement the American-cheese model (2010, 338, 339).

Anatol Lieven also supports the Swiss-cheese approach to enhancing women's rights and status. The best the United States can do, he says, is "to preserve the cities at least as areas where women can continue to enjoy more rights and greater social participation in the hope that a new culture will gradually spread from them to the countryside" (2012, 32).

As pragmatic as their perspectives may sound, Lieven and Barfield ignore factors that undermine the claim that women will flourish in a Swiss-cheese–governed Afghanistan. One is the urgency of the women's rights situation for the 85 percent of Afghan women who do not live in cities. Without their rights, says Sima Samar, such Afghan women will probably not survive. Statistics about their lack of nutrition and medical care, their low rates of literacy, and their risks in childbearing make that clear (2011, 182–83).

Another factor missing from the Swiss-cheese analysis is the interconnection of women's status and rights with larger questions of power and control. Because gender issues are always already intertwined with conflicts about land, honor, resources, and authority, especially at the local level, approaches that reinforce the power of those who now manipulate women's rights as they vie for regional or tribal influence and advantage in the Swiss-cheese "holes" will also reinforce those manipulations. Without women in leadership roles at the regional level, no one will fight for their rights (Samar 2011, 182–83).

The Swiss-cheese approach also misses important aspects of Afghan public opinion. Minority ethnic leaders have long favored a strong central state, according to Sarah Lister and Hamish Nixon, because they want to curb existing regional power brokers and reduce the danger of criminal influence over structures of local government. Ordinary Afghans have also favored a strong central government because they want to undermine "the power of local commanders, at whose hands they have suffered for so many years" (2006, 207). So any approach to government that solidifies existing ethnic and regional divisions, at least some of which result from the misguided efforts of foreign powers (including the British, the United States, and NATO), both ignores such opinion and encourages regional corruption and ethnic power plays that so often misuse women's status and rights as pawns in their conflicts.

These deficiencies in the Swiss-cheese approach do not necessarily argue for the American-cheese approach, however. The vexed history of Afghan central governments suggests how difficult it would be to form a government that could produce nationwide compliance to a uniform set of laws and practices, especially about gender. As Marzia has indicated, perhaps a pure parliamentary system would come closer with its less polarizing view of political parties and more integrated balance of regional and national power. According to Merry, a good balance between centralized standards and local control creates the best chance for advancing women's rights. Merry claims that "human rights ideas are more easily adopted if they are packaged in familiar terms and do not disturb established hierarchies, but they are more transformative if they challenge existing assumptions about power relationships." A local-central balance maintains that helpful tension (2006, 222).

Pursuing human rights through a local-center balance actually strengthens states, Merry explains, despite historic worries that internationally focused human rights would weaken them (2006, 223). The opportunity to take advantage of that possibility with regard to women's rights was squandered during the early years of backlash against the ousted Taliban. Then, a deliberate focus on gender equity and women's empowerment "in the Afghan way" could have provided an effective rationale for consolidating central power and rethinking the relationship between the central government and subnational governmental institutions.

Even though that window has closed, many analysts agree that any real challenge to existing assumptions about Afghan women's status, rights, and social participation must come initially from a reconstituted central government, backed by a rigorous and uncorrupt judicial system that enforces civil laws such as EVAW.[1] That combination, should it ever occur, might help to educate women throughout the country about their rights and to extricate women's rights issues from familial and community conflicts, including safety fears and personal feuds. At the same time, however, regional and community decision makers, most of whom are men, must see the benefits to themselves of loosening controls and bringing women into the mainstream of educational and economic activities.

These are daunting challenges, to which the current state of Afghan politics seems unlikely to rise. So some analysts look to more incremental approaches. One idea—increasing women's representation on local councils and *shuras*—seems like a good place to start, and as it happens, some progress has already been made toward that goal. Women have already achieved greater representation on the Provincial Reconstruction Teams and Provincial Development Committees that were instituted by the 2006 Interim Afghanistan National Development Strategy. Although the work of the PDCs has been impeded by ambiguity about their "relative responsibilities, resources, and relationships" and by the absence of mechanisms for coordination among them or with Kabul, women's meaningful participation in those councils could make a genuine difference in future years. Improving that coordination seems a worthy project for international donors (Lister and Nixon 2006, 211, 217, 221).[2]

Negotiating with the Enemy

A realistic assessment of what might help to advance women's rights and social participation in Afghanistan must acknowledge the elephant in the negotiating room—the patriarchs, warlords, drug dealers, Taliban sympathizers, and assorted opportunists who currently benefit from the country's entrenched gender-unbalanced social and political system. They are the ones who oppose any power other than themselves in their families, communities, and tribes. They ask "who could better decide than they who and when their daughters should marry," or why Afghans should support any concept, such as "better lives and protections for women," that has the support of the United States or the European Union (Rubin 2013).

As Marzia and Jamila have repeatedly said, that opposition does not simply hover around the margins of Afghan society. Rather, it resides within the government, including some members of Parliament and the current minister of economy, Abdul Hadi Arghandiwal, who also leads the conservative Hizb-i-Islami faction that reasserted its influence in 2013. Even the motives of some women parliamentarians, such as Fawzia Koofi, have been suspect, in her case because of her association with the Northern Alliance. Koofi proposed amending the EVAW law prior to the 2014 presidential election in order to include provisions against sexual harassment and to require men to pay child support if they leave their wives or marry new ones. Many wondered whether Koofi really wanted to improve the law or to undermine it by opening it up to new debate in the conservative Parliament (Rubin 2013).

The debate initiated by Koofi's proposal was halted in fifteen minutes, which was fortunate because revisions "would [likely] have eliminated the minimum marriage age for girls, abolished shelters, and ended criminal penalties for rape and domestic violence," according to Human Rights Watch. Even an extended debate would have undermined the current, albeit sporadic, use of the law, which the Afghan Women's Network said in 2013 had been cited by family courts throughout the country in resolving 60 percent of violence cases. The best news at the time was that the brief debate left the law unchanged. Still, Heather Barr of Human Rights Watch thought that "the fallout . . . could make conservatives more motivated to organize and call for a repeal of the law in its entirety."[3]

Despite such laws, of course, mullahs all over Afghanistan consistently ignore constitutional and legal supports for women's rights and defend the prevailing gender imbalance in the name of Islam. They often base their rulings on the constitutional article that says, "No law can contradict the beliefs and provisions of Islam" (Rotberg 2006, 5). Dealing with such forces will not be easy, although a strengthened and reformed central government, reinforced by a rights focus, could make a difference.

On the way to that or any desired outcome for the country, a decision must be made about whether or how to negotiate with the Taliban. The "whether" is less robust as of this writing. Official U.S. views on the "whether" have been somewhat mixed. Then secretary of state Hillary Clinton said in 2010 that "any reconciliation process . . . must require that anyone who wishes to rejoin society and the political system must lay down their weapons . . . and be committed to the constitution and laws of Afghanistan, which guarantee the rights of women." But a senior Western diplomat in Kabul, speaking anonymously to *Time* in the same year, said, "'We are not going to be sending troops and spending money forever. There will have to be a compromise, and sacrifices will have to be made'" (quoted in Baker 2010, 2). He did not specify who or what would have to be sacrificed.

Perhaps the question would not be before the world community if the Taliban and other insurgents had been included in the Bonn Conference. Such inclusion did not occur for various reasons, including Western concern that it would amount to appeasement. Instead, the lack of restrictions on the qualifications for office seekers made possible the participation of former belligerents in the new government, which is probably a worse outcome than formal inclusion in Bonn would have been (Semple 2009, 24–25).

Prospects for integrating today's Taliban as Clinton envisioned have been marred by past efforts that have failed. For example, a Peace and Reconciliation program to reintegrate low-level Taliban fighters stalled in 2011, not only because the $250 million committed by international donors never fully materialized and Afghan officials could not agree on how to manage the project but also because the flow of fighters wanting to reintegrate had slowed from nine thousand in 2005 to only one hundred by the autumn of 2010—another missed opportunity (Heath 2011, 4–5, paraphrasing Nordland 2010). Among other problems, the allied forces did not recognize that reconciliation is a collective and not an individual process, since participation in an insurgency involves networks of individuals who share beliefs, values, fraternal bonds, and economic interests, primarily through patronage links. Indeed, those who did reconcile in the early post-2001 period did so primarily because officials in the government agreed to become their patrons (Semple 2009, 69–70).

Women activists such as Jamila and Marzia have additional reasons for opposing reconciliation or even negotiation with the Taliban. They believe that revisiting the Afghan Constitution to women's detriment would necessarily be one of the sacrifices required. They also understand that the Taliban's view of women's rights as a Western concept that contravenes Islamic teaching could prevail, even though it is both incorrect and ignorant. Parliamentarian Sabrina Saqib predicted years ago that the article mandating the parliamentary quota for women "would be the first to go." She was proven right in 2014, as the erosion of that percentage began in February of that year (Nordland 2014). One harbinger of that outcome was the Islamist economy minister Arghandiwal's earlier assertion that the quota for women "'makes them lazy.'" "'What we want for Afghanistan is Islamic rights, not Western rights,'" he said (quoted in Baker 2010, 3).

Other reasons for the women's opposition to negotiations include the Taliban's persistent violent attacks on women and girls, as well as their night letters that many women activists, including Marzia, have received in recent years. The letters often bear the insignia of the Taliban's former Islamic Emirate of Afghanistan. These missives represent the tactics of the "new Taliban," which Mullah Omar has allegedly ordered to cease burning down schools and cutting off ears, lips, and tongues (Rubin 2010, A1). Instead, Talibs are supposed to deliver their intimidations in writing. Although the letters vary by the particular group initiating them, they all warn against associating with the United States and the current Afghan government (Johnson 2007).

The letters' grizzly language suggests that Omar's orders have not really reduced the specter of Taliban violence. "We warn you to leave your job as a teacher as soon as possible otherwise we will cut the heads off your children and shall set fire to your daughter," reads one. "We will kill you in such a harsh way that no woman has so far been killed in that manner," says another. Such letters, obtained by Human Rights Watch, did not stop the Taliban from throwing acid in girls' faces and burning down schools (Baker 2010, 1–2).

Finally, the idea of negotiating with something called the Taliban overlooks the lack of a political organization with which to do serious negotiations, as well as the disparate and self-interested factions now included under the Taliban umbrella. Even more disturbing, without a consistent definition of Sharia law, any change the Taliban might make in the political climate of the country could mean a radical reinterpretation of women's rights (Baker 2010, 3).

The best approach to dealing with the Taliban is what Marzia and others call "good governance." That means involving women around the country in serious and unhurried talks with insurgents to work out a long-term solution. It also means resisting calls by Western powers for a quick deal that would bring a temporary lull in the violence—enough to permit the international coalition a face-saving withdrawal—but not much more than that (Baker 2010, 4).

Reinforcing that approach, Michael Semple calls for "serious strategic planning and management, a clear assignment of roles and resources, a well-defined program for monitoring progress, and a willingness to adjust course as necessary." There must also be parameters for accommodation and room for insurgents to express their concerns. The government should empower a "senior focal point" to initiate collective action and administer appropriate security, administrative, and economic measures. Semple does not address women's rights specifically, but his prescription reinforces what others define as necessary to improve women's status: a strengthened central government subject to civil laws, international agreements, and constitutional provisions that support women's rights. In addition, by urging negotiators to recognize the importance of the regional administrative structure to the reconciliation of former combatants, Semple supports the central-local balance between forces and influence that Merry outlines as vital to a rights-focused government (2009, 92–93).

Unified or Tribalized?

The idea of nationhood for Afghanistan, on which the expansion of women's rights and social participation seems to depend, is misguided to some longtime

Chapter 10: Future Prospects

Afghan hands, as well as to Western critics of nationalism and its self-interested tendencies. Many who claim that Afghans do not really want a unified nation look to history. They argue that the name "Afghanistan" actually means "Pashtun" and that the nation exists only because colonial powers created it as a buffer state. Such analysts consider visions of national unity to be political manipulation turned utopian dream. They contend that Afghan nationhood emanates less from political will and social experience than from the 1964 and 1977 constitutions (Centlivres and Centlivres-Demont 2010, 37–38). Even the country's topography argues against unity, they say, as does the power of recently politicized ethnic groups (Azoy 2010, 15).

But according to recent polls and to patriots such as Marzia and Jamila, many Afghans do find something compelling about keeping the nation intact. They have felt sustained by that goal throughout years of wars and displacement. Many who left during the mujahideen and Taliban periods, including Jamila, were eager to return and serve their communities. Many Afghans believe that their customs and their form of Islam distinguish them positively from their neighbors. They have derived their Afghan identities from institutions such as the Kabul Museum, starting in 1930, and the National Archive, established in 1973. Access to radio, starting in 1940, has also given some Afghans a sense of national identity, despite very weak reinforcement in the nation's mostly religious school curriculum (Dupree 2002, 977).

Afghans' desire for national unity is reflected in polls that show support for selecting a strong central government through democratic means, as long as the framework for it is Islamic (Larson 2010, 94). Most poll respondents in 2009 even considered the Karzai government legitimate, despite its inability to deliver justice or economic growth, its corruption, its lack of inclusiveness, and its failure to keep the insurgency from destabilizing the country (Sinha 2010, 122). One can only imagine how legitimate Afghans would find a central government that did deliver justice, stability, and economic growth without corruption.

It also seems that many urban Afghans, at least, do not automatically reject all things foreign or Western. As Marzia advised years ago, they recognize the good things, such as technology, education, and development, that can be imported from abroad, as well as the bad things, such as alcohol, fashion, raucous popular culture, and pornography, that they want to exclude from their society (Rostami-Povey 2007, 73). They may also recognize that rights accompanied by responsibility and obligations are not Western inventions but rather belong within an Islamic social context.

Perhaps women activists have developed a more positive vision of a strong and unified Afghanistan than some of their countrymen because nationhood does seem the best path to sustained support for women's rights. They need to believe that Afghanistan can both honor its traditions and evolve into a modern state, encouraged, perhaps, by most Afghans' rejection of the Taliban's "puritanical Islamic mold" in 2001 (Dupree 2002, 977). Activists have also recognized that international donors support nationhood, and those who desire more productive international involvement in their country, including Jamila and Marzia, have also welcomed at least some international models for change. For them, even feminist critiques of nationalism and Western intervention sound very much like the xenophobic assertions of Taliban spokesmen and mullahs who resist a centralized government and strong state. For them, rejection of a national identity for Afghanistan sounds like a rationalization for opposing any standards for Afghan women's educational, economic, and personal rights.

Models for Working on Women's Issues across Cultures

As important as the changes and priorities discussed above are to Afghan women's future, they do not directly address how and on what terms Afghan women activists might work across geopolitical boundaries and borders to advance the cause of gender justice. Even the idea of such transnational collaborations may be tainted. As we have seen, transnational feminist approaches to women's status and rights around the globe have been weakened by internal charges of imperialism and derided by feminists themselves. For example, Meyda Yeğenoğlu has observed that Western women trying to support "other" women's rights are inevitably stooges for imperialism (cited in Lewis 2002, 217). Chandra Mohanty has suggested that Western efforts to "help" across borders or even to describe non-Western populations betray assumptions that they are unworldly and inevitably oppressed by their families, cultures, religion, and clothing (2003, 42). Gayatri Spivak has warned that transnational feminist efforts could reinforce the project of imperialism that resists seeing the Other as a self (2010).

Transnational collaborations also bear the taint of globalization, which is a notoriously tricky and fickle bedfellow for feminism and the advancement of women's rights. Often global influences designed to advance women's rights and expand their opportunities and status have created more resistance than improvements. Moreover, global powers' growing national interests have historically exploited women's status and rights for their own economic or political advantage, as in *maquiladoras* in Mexico. Any advances that do occur can be easily reversed. It is not unlikely, for example, that in order to advance American interests in Afghan sovereignty and stability, the U.S. government will once again abandon gender issues and women's rights as it exits the country (Jalalzai and Jefferess 2011, 2–5; Bergner 2011, 113). Indeed, it may already have done so.

Even the most effective transnational feminist programs to redress "the history of exclusion and oppression endured by Afghan women" have also been tainted by globalization because of the shortsighted or otherwise inadequate efforts of the international aid projects or agencies to which they seem (or actually are) connected. Indeed, the transnational "feminist apparatus" of NGOs and some foreign governmental agencies in Afghanistan must now assess the way their goals of engagement with Afghan women have been compromised by their own history of witting or unwitting association with the forces of global capitalism and the pursuit of foreign powers' "multiple and contradictory agendas in the country." It is important to understand that many ordinary Afghan women have been left in the lurch by such programs, as Deniz Kandiyoti says, with no source of protection or justice apart from the very communities and households that are often the source of their problems. In addition, the ubiquitous presence of international aid agencies has rekindled some communities' efforts to protect Afghan women from the "foreign gaze," "thereby not only hindering women's participation in aid projects, but further restricting their access to public space" (Chishti and Farhoumand-Sims 2011, 127–28).

Maliha Chishti and Cheshmak Farhoumand-Sims recount numerous ways that international efforts even by well-intentioned feminist NGOs can go and have gone awry. For example, misguided international aid projects have exacerbated demarcations in Afghanistan between religious and secular, urban and rural, formal and informal, to the detriment of whole communities. Internationalists have often misjudged grassroots-reform efforts as amateur and lacking in sophistication, despite their positive track records. Those misjudgments have, in turn, intensified competition and raised suspicions between urban- and rural-based networks of Afghan women organizers and undermined attempts to build "a politics of solidarity across the diversity of women's locations and experiences" (2011, 129–30). Surely, this failure has contributed to the competition Marzia and Jamila have deplored among women's rights activists with whom they work.

Efforts to support and promote international agreements, such as CEDAW, have also been undermined by the attitudes and behavior of Western forces. How can CEDAW be advanced by a Western-installed government that has welcomed warlords, failed to provide real security, and neglected to coordinate its own efforts to improve gender policy in Afghanistan? Why would international feminist projects not be suspect as tools of Western propaganda designed to "modernize and secularize Afghanistan's cultural and religious traditions" and to destabilize women's existing social status? And what good is something like CEDAW, anyway, if abuse in the home cannot be prevented or effectively criminalized (Chishti and Farhoumand-Sims 2011, 135–36)? Although such missteps and disconnects could be seen as evidence that the international community does not have a unified exploitative agenda, such a case may strike the women waiting for safety and opportunity as a weak argument.

Even more egregious, returning to Mohanty, are the effects of "neoliberal governmentalities" on the feminist apparatus of the NGO world. Such governmentalities "construct a public domain denuded of power and histories of oppression, where market rationalities redefine democracy and collective responsibility is collapsed into individual characteristics." Feminist activists, like other internationals, must recognize that gender justice is inevitably tied to power relations and larger issues of social transformation (Mohanty 2013, 971–72).

At first glance, Marzia, Jamila, and the other activists discussed in *Contested Terrain* might seem to deserve the same opprobrium as the foreigners who have funded them and their organizations. But I think the situation is more complex than that. Indeed, it may even be paradoxical, because such activists in what Antonio Donini calls the "Kabul Bubble" have also been victims of the scattershot, uncoordinated foreign aid apparatus, just like the rural women who have been overlooked or underserved by its operations (Chishti and Farhoumand-Sims 2011, 129). That is why they have been among its harshest critics. At the same time, urban activists have suffered enormously from the Taliban backlash against foreign intervention because of their association with it, as Marzia's exile demonstrates.

Marzia's and Jamila's situations are also paradoxical because they could have helped to coordinate and funnel international money and efforts toward the most pressing problems that they and their clients and students identified. Because the aid community has been largely unable or unwilling to coordinate with local efforts without undermining them, these leaders instead have suffered fallout from internationals' ineffectiveness. Given the factionalism and distrust that now confuse the picture for rights activism, some Afghan women have concluded that Western values and fundamentalist Islam are equally limited ideological views that threaten to circumscribe women's experiences, agency, autonomy, choices, and freedom (Chishti and Farhoumand-Sims 2011, 141).

Toward Transnational Collaboration

In light of these daunting complexities, ironies, and mistakes, it is difficult even to contemplate how those of us in the West who have affection for and attachment to the promotion of Afghan women's rights, opportunities, and survival might define a respectful, productive ground from which to exchange ideas or discuss actions to promote those goals.

As I understand the challenge, cross-cultural, collaborative initiatives on behalf of Afghan women should build on what Chishti and Farhoumand-Sims call "principled solidarity based on collaborative efforts and genuine dialogue" to define mutually acceptable goals that "promote the overall well-being of Afghan women, . . . build on existing capacities," and incorporate "all Afghan women—conservative and moderate, urban and rural, literate and illiterate"—in questions of women's rights, agency, and roles (2011, 141, 125). Such collaborations should help local women develop their own agendas, articulate their own claims, and design their own strategies for confronting existing power structures (Guenther 2011). Perhaps most important, such efforts should facilitate "local supporters of democracy and women's rights, [which] is the most effective way to ensure those rights," according to Jalalzai and Jefferess (2011, 21). Developing strategies for realizing gender justice in an Islamic framework and actually implementing strategies are both pervasive needs yet to be addressed by the international feminist community (Chishti and Farhoumand-Sims 2011, 137–38).

Contested Terrain has offered several suggestions that could guide a reformed international presence: coordinating efforts among feminist activists and other donors and NGOs, promoting women's participation in local political groups, developing models for programs that empower Afghan women for the long term, working with men, and embedding gender issues in projects that address larger community concerns, such as clean water and health care. General suggestions offered to improve international engagement in Afghanistan apply to feminist collaborations as well, with a special emphasis on eliminating perspectives on women's rights that reflect imperialist standpoints, understanding *gender* as a political concept applying to both sexes, learning to listen, accepting varied definitions of agency, and studying Afghan as well as Western imperial history. Indeed, all the caveats discussed throughout this book should inform collaborative feminist initiatives.

In working on gender issues and women's concerns, activists must also keep in mind the country's inadequate infrastructure for supporting Afghan women's advancement. The Afghan Constitution may grant women formal rights and equality (unlike the U.S. Constitution), but there are few if any mechanisms in place for enforcing either. Indeed, there are many competing institutions that simultaneously erode rights-giving laws such as EVAW, as well as the potentially competing constitutional clause requiring all civil laws to conform to Sharia law, which is subject to multiple interpretations. In addition, the courts have limited function and are often corrupt, there is no educational system to support women's school attendance, and many Afghan women are subject to child or forced marriage, relationship violence, unattended childbirth, and becoming barter to settle disputes (*badal*). As Marzia has said, "The role of women is very low."

Existing or future official NGOs and gender-based programs within international aid organizations with the funds to develop programming in Afghanistan have their work cut out for them in designing appropriate projects to meet this long list of challenges. As someone who is not affiliated with that feminist NGO apparatus, however, I would like to consider what kind of feminist engagement with Afghan women might be appropriate for Western scholars such as Margaret Mills and myself or others who would like to advance Afghan women's causes and needs and to accept some responsibility for the shambles the West has helped to create in Afghanistan. In thinking about possibilities, I envision working with women such as Marzia, Jamila, and others to help create "more spaces for the exchange of ideas, critical reflection, and mutual learning" (Chishti and Farhoumand-Sims 2011, 140).

Although there may be many reasons for foreigners not to intervene or even to contemplate such idea exchange and collaboration, as we have seen, there are also many reasons for mutual engagement, critical reflection, informed concern, ethical redress, and compassion. For me, there are also personal ties and affections that connect real faces with the phrase *Afghan women*. I hope that the vexed histories and competing heritages between Western and Eastern women need not be taken to their logical extreme and allowed to prevent any cross-cultural collaborations, supports, or coinvestigations, thereby paralyzing Westerners into a state of inaction. It would be a shame to throw the baby of Afghan women's needs and aspirations out with the bathwater of anti-imperialist aversion.

In that spirit, I would like to conclude *Contested Terrain* by offering three interconnected ideas that could help establish some new grounds for collaborative conversations and strategizing between Western and Afghan women's rights supporters and activists. These ideas are not linked to particular projects. Indeed, they are intended to move the conversation beyond the catalog of programs and projects that have so far dominated the international feminist presence in Afghanistan and toward a more comprehensive rethinking of gender justice in that country.

The first new ground for such collaboration that I would suggest actually involves embracing some realities of globalization, beyond the toxic effects of global capitalism and corrosive cultural products, the globalized privatization of the commons, and the proliferation of "security-driven penal state practices" around the world (Mohanty 2013, 970). It is clear that such forces have made Afghanistan "a paradigmatic example of a globalized national space" that has suffered in the extreme from repeated "neocolonial reconstruction[s] of [its] politics and culture" (Jalalzai and Jefferess 2011, 9, 14).

What I have in mind, however, are different aspects of globalization, including greater possibilities for communication and information exchange that have already become instrumental in promoting transnational feminist identification and theorizing across the globe (Chakrabarty 2013). It would be foolish to overlook the role the Internet already plays in bringing attention to women's status even in remote areas and in promoting international conversations about women's rights and activism. The power of this tool is evident in the efforts of some governments to restrict access to it. And while its reliance on electric power and literacy may prevent most poor and rural women in Afghanistan and other impoverished regions from participating in it directly, the Internet might help to inform and empower them via a ripple effect. Cyberspace also allows users to mask their identities as they pursue unsanctioned alliances and lines of thought. It is not risk-free, of course, but it is safer than walking the streets for many women. And with cell phones and other devices, it might affect more women than the Swiss-cheese approach to women's rights.

Transnational efforts to promote women's rights and welfare over the past seventy-odd years are another aspect of globalization that feminists should recognize. Despite accusations of Western bias and backlash against documents such as the International Declaration of Human Rights and CEDAW (discussed above and in chapter 5), some international frameworks can be credited with putting women's rights onto some local radar screens, prompting various countries to recognize rights for women within their borders and exposing the hypocrisies of a particular nation's self-image and policies.

I suggest that future transnational feminist idea exchanges and collaborations adopt a pragmatic approach to international agreements and treaties such as CEDAW and openly discuss how or whether to utilize them in local circumstances. Foreign feminists might facilitate that discussion by revealing patterns of acceptance and resistance across cultures. For example, comparisons across recent democracy movements have exposed a common tendency to welcome women to the revolution but to send them back home after the victory (Saktanber 2006, 27). This offers an example of the disregard of UN Resolution 1325 that can help inform the neglect of that resolution experienced by Afghan women. Without such comparisons, local women might consider their own experience unique to them.

My discussion with Jamila and Marzia about Sally Merry's work on gender violence, as it relates to social violence against women across cultures, provides an example of the kind of fruitful comparative conversation I am imagining. Although Merry's work did not include antiviolence movements in Afghanistan, it did offer an opportunity for the two women to compare notes across borders and to develop more capacious arguments and strategies to counter local oppositional voices. Moreover, Merry's descriptions of successful activist campaigns contain models that could help fractured Afghan activist groups unify their efforts (2006, 220–21, 202).

In addition, Merry's study highlighted the significance of Marzia's and Jamila's own work. They could see themselves in her observation that most activists took one of two approaches: the social service approach (Jamila) or the human rights–advocacy approach (Marzia). The former offered support services to victims of violence and retrained offenders. They created shelters, convened support groups, and provided legal aid. The latter, led by lawyers and political elites, worked to change national laws and institutions and to define women's human rights. They also formed rights commissions, promoted rights education, and responded to violations at the national level (2006, 138). Merry's analysis further suggested how documenting the two women's successful efforts, such as Jamila's imam program and Marzia's neighborhood-based training classes on women's rights in Islamic and civil law, could contribute to the global feminist conversation about strategies for advancing women's rights.

The second new ground for Western-Afghan feminist collaboration that I would suggest focuses specifically on the U.S.-Afghan interconnection. It emerges from my thought that the negative litany about Western imperialism emphasized by feminist theorists such as Yeğenoğlu, Mohanty, Spivak, Razack, and others provides only a partial historical context for linking (or unlinking) women across geopolitical boundaries. There are also other relevant histories that should help frame idea exchange and collaboration. For example, while some U.S. women were exoticizing the veiled women of the East and judging the West superior, others were probing the hypocrisies of U.S. democracy and demanding rights, specifically the right to vote. Although that movement suffered from its own racist and classist hypocrisies, it still provided some powerful arguments about women's rights. When I asked Marzia and Jamila if they were interested in learning about the women's suffrage movement in the United States, especially its development of religious arguments to support women's civic participation, they said yes.

So I mentioned Sarah Grimké's use of the Protestant belief in the authority of all believers to ground rights claims for women in the 1830s. I quoted Grimké's demand that religious men "take their feet from off our necks and permit us to stand upright on that ground which God designed us to occupy" (1837, 12). I discussed the writings of Julia Foote, the first ordained deacon in the African Methodist Episcopal Zionist Church, who claimed in the 1870s that men were the ones who needed to prove their worthiness to preach the Gospel, since women's moral sensibilities positioned them closer than men to Christian ideals. I pointed out that some African American Christian women argued for gender equity by interpreting the coming of Jesus as the antidote to original sin and God's curse in Eden, thereby making the sexes equal again and proclaiming that "there is neither male nor female in Jesus Christ" (Guy-Sheftall 1995, 51–53). I explained how this transformation was necessary because the Judeo-Christian tradition, unlike the Islamic tradition, emphasizes the Creation story of Genesis 2, in which woman is formed as man's "helpmeet."

We also discussed a possible parallel between Muslim women's invocation of the independent women of their tradition, such as Khadija, as role models and Western suffragists' invocation of biblical women, such as Deborah, Judith, and Esther, to demonstrate that women's political roles have religious roots. In addition, they saw a link between the two religious cultures in the tendency to dismiss women's claim that their subordination is not God's will as either un-Christian or un-Islamic (Kirkley 1990, 510, 512–13).

The 1960s and 1970s provide another relevant historical period for comparison, because those years mark the inception of what some call the "second wave" of the U.S. women's movement, which included an active feminist theological component, as well as the development of Islamic feminism, parts of which Jamila and Marzia embrace.[4] In those years, the pillars of that movement, such as Amina Wadud and Fatima Mernissi, began exploring Islam's foundational texts as well as their historical contexts to understand their gender implications. Mernissi found evidence, for example, that the monotheism of Islam disempowered seventh-century women by emphasizing male dominance and patriliny, in contrast to pre-Islamic practices of polyandry and matriliny. Indeed, she said, some Arabian women cheered the Prophet's death because of his negative impact on their rights (Barlow and Akbarzadeh 2006, 1484–89).

In those same decades, feminist theologians in the United States, such as Mary Daly, Rosemary Radford Reuther, Elisabeth Fiorenza, Judith Plaskow, Delores S. Williams, Phyllis Trible, and many others, were demonstrating how scripture had often been misinterpreted and poorly translated to men's social, cultural, and political advantage. They also acknowledged biblical evidence of women's inequality: Women were the property of men (Exod. 20:17; Deut. 5:21); they did not control their own bodies. Women were supposed to be virgins at marriage to protect the honor of their fathers and husbands, but men were not. Violations resulted in death by stoning (Deut. 22:13–21). Women had no right to divorce (Deut. 24:1–4) and, most often, no right to own property. Women could not be priests because they were unclean (Lev. 15). Even a woman's monetary value was less than a man's (Lev. 27:1–7) (Trible 1982).

Aligning these historical movements reveals other surprising convergences. For example, Islamic feminists' ideas about *itjihad* resembled the insistence by Protestant and most Jewish U.S. feminists at the time that the individual believer has ultimate religious authority and, therefore, the right to determine God's intentions, including for women. They argued that clergy have no more ecclesiastical authority than any other believer, just as *itjihad* resisted privileging one interpreter over others. Manuel Castells described *itjihad* as "a hermeneutical opening for Islamic feminists" in challenging men's traditional idea that they are superior because they support women financially (cooke 2001, 62–63). Both movements therefore substituted community consensus deriving from individual interpretations for unchanging, top-down religious rule.

Parallels can also be found in the responses of Islamic and Western feminists to their discoveries of misogynist religious texts. Both groups have used them as grounds for a new *hermeneutic,* or method of interpretation. Western feminist hermeneutists promoted empathic relationships with abused biblical women and matched the texts' antiwoman perspectives with the critique of patriarchy that also exists in scripture. They found images of God as female (Psalm 22:9–10) and references to God as a birth giver (Deut. 32:18). They retranslated verbs and nouns from the Hebrew and Greek. Their new translations recharacterized familiar women. For example, some interpreted the description of Eve as *'ezer kenegdo* in Hebrew to mean a *superior or equal helper,* not an *assistant.* Scholars further accentuated the biblical women who protested or countered patriarchal culture. They emphasized progressive relationships among biblical women, including between the Egyptian Pharaoh's daughter who rescued Moses and his female relatives. In short, they promoted "a biblical theology of womanhood" (Trible 1982). Similarly, Islamic scholars such as Amina Wadud developed a new hermeneutic, as discussed in chapters 6 and 8 and elsewhere in *Contested Terrain*. Jamila's investigation and interpretation of Islamic sacred texts with her family provide another example.

Recognizing such historical parallels does not equate to a Eurocentric bias, as some critics might charge. Rather, in the best case, it reveals the forces that shape women's lives and inspire social change around the world at particular times. Such comparisons also raise exactly the kinds of questions that could promote effective idea exchange and strategizing across geopolitical boundaries. For example, why did these theologically based feminist movements develop at roughly the same time? How were conditions both different and the same in various world regions? What, if anything, did the movements learn from each other then? What might they learn now? What do the movements reveal about the conditions that promote both compliance with and resistance to religious reassessments at different times? What impact did the two movements have on mainstream religious devotion? What kinds of backlash did they provoke?

Another historical phenomenon that could be probed to mutual benefit is the effect of the Cold War on women's roles and opportunities in the United States and in Afghanistan. The historical discussions in *Contested Terrain* illustrate that American priorities during the Cold War had a negative impact on Afghan women's rights and social participation. But suppose we probed and compared the effects of Cold War politics on women's rights in the United States during the same period?

The many differences in women's experiences in the two countries would perhaps be most obvious, but there might also be links between the effects of Cold War thinking on gender attitudes in both. For example, did post–World War II efforts to impose limited hyperfeminine roles on U.S. women intersect with the gendered calculations of U.S. foreign policy with regard to Afghanistan? Was the thinking that dismissed Afghan women's rights as collateral damage to U.S. geopolitical interests implicated in what Betty Friedan (1963) identified in the United States as the "the problem that had no name," which essentially removed a generation of educated, middle-class white women from the labor force? And did the U.S. government's determination to oust Soviet troops from Afghanistan in the 1980s, which ignored Afghan women's rights and prospects, have any connection with the backlash against feminism in the United States under the Reagan administration during the same period (captured by Susan Faludi [1991] in her popular book by that name)? Probing such interrelationships and parallels could be instructive on both sides of the historical and cultural divide.

Using such historical parallels and other comparisons effectively requires understanding the difference between *metaphor* and *analogy*. Whereas *metaphor* entails speaking about one thing as if it were another ("My love is a red, red rose"), *analogy* looks for likenesses in certain respects or circumstances between things that may otherwise be very different. Legitimate historical analogies are not meant to establish sameness or to explain one phenomenon as the cause of another. Rather, they are designed to reveal relationships that might be obscured by an emphasis only on distance and difference and to resituate previous assumptions and conclusions in light of comparative information. Of particular importance to overcoming the power differentials between the groups, individuals, and geopolitical locations being compared, analogies allow disparate events and phenomena to occupy equal positions as they are explored. Analogies can invite discussions about what is relevant about the comparison and what is not; they are instructive about both similarity and difference. They can also set new agendas and provide thought exercises outside the confines of conventional historical categories.

The third new ground I would suggest for creating a space for idea exchange and feminist collaboration is a deep understanding of what U.S. feminists call *intersectionality*. Originally popularized by feminist critical race legal scholar Kimberlé Crenshaw in 1989, the term represents the difficulty of capturing the full experience of U.S. women of color "by looking at the race or gender dimensions of those experiences separately" (1997, 179). In other words, ideas about racial difference and hierarchy, as well as the material conditions determining the life experiences of nonwhite U.S. women, develop in conjunction with ideas and material conditions related to gender.[5] Therefore, policies that address racial discrimination alone miss the way women of color experience their gender identities, and policies that address gender discrimination alone miss the way women of color experience their racial identities.

While Crenshaw's definition might imply that intersectional identities are unique and unfathomable to outsiders, it actually suggests the opposite. Intersectionality theory supports the idea that all individual identities, including those of U.S. women of color, should be understood "as coalitions—as internally heterogeneous, complex unities constituted by their internal differences and dissonances and by internal as well as external relations of power," as Anna Carastathis explains. At the same time, it implies that "groups are already internally heterogeneous" (Carastathis 2013, 942) and that "every person is a crowd" (Chun, Lipsitz, and Shin 2013, 923).

For the purposes of this discussion, then, neither the Western women critiqued as "stooges of imperialism" nor the Eastern women cast as their victims should be seen as monolithic groups fully defined and circumscribed by those labels. Instead, members of both groups should be seen as amalgams of their historical context, religious identities, family relationships, and regional locations, as well as of their own independent thinking and familial and educational experiences, among other variables. Approaching collaboration on the basis of this coalitional and sometimes internally conflicted concept of identity, in which pieces of each potential collaborator's identity can perhaps relate to pieces of the others,' promotes "relationships of accountability and compassion across lines of difference and dominance, internal as well as external to 'group' identities," and allows us "to pursue a liberatory politics of interconnection" (Carastathis 2013, 943, 942; Chun, Lipsitz, and Shin 2013, 923).

Honoring the existence of intersectional identities requires discovering subtler means of coalition building. Coalitions no longer involve being invited in by people presumed to be like oneself. Rather, they entail forming alliances outside of our comfort zones, abandoning assumptions of similarity and safety, and expecting instead difference, confrontation, and risk (Carastathis 2013, 945). As the shield of assumed shared identity falls away, Iris Marion Young advises negotiating the newly unexplored territory by discovering the interests that emerge from shared proximity or entrapment (or both) within the "structural relations" of a particular social milieu. Young calls this process constructing *serial coalitions*, based on a common material cause, such as water insufficiency, or a shared hope to alter a particular circumstance such as girls' access to schooling.[6] Because entrapment in structural relations can be a global phenomenon, as illustrated by the examples above, it can be experienced in disparate sites.

Using the techniques of analogy and historical comparison, similarities and differences of experience and values can be identified around "entrapments" such as sexual harassment and gender-based violence. Instead of collaborating on the basis of shared identity (Asian American, Latina, Pashtun), participants agree to collaborate not on their psychological or ideological subjectivities but on the analogous realities of their status (MacKinnon 2013, 1028). They may consciously disregard or table issues outside of those parameters. (People who have missed a bus, for example, might recognize their common situation and pool their money to hire a taxi.) Once individuals recognize their own and others' intersectional identities and statuses, such seriality can become a meaningful device for creating flexible coalitions beyond identity labels.

Intersectionality and seriality offer possible responses to Reina Lewis's question posed in part II's prologue. If colonized women can find a way around the effects of Orientalism and imperialism, Lewis asked, "Why cannot Western women also find a way outside of the confines of such totalizing dynamics?" (2002, 217). Intersectionality theory and seriality offer such a way. Added to the benefits of selected analogies, the possibilities offered by globalized approaches to communication and information sharing, and the expansion of comparative historical analysis, a deeper understanding of intersectionality helps us to reimagine the contested terrain between the world's women.

Of course, these ideas are only a beginning. They are potential tools, not guarantees. The process of mutual learning and reconceptualizing must continue. The search for actual or virtual spaces where such coalitions can be built must persist. Nothing can be assumed. Other forces besides well-meaning collaborators will continue to affect and possibly derail efforts and outcomes. The danger of conflating Western donor agendas and cultural norms with Afghan women's needs and aspirations remains (Bergner 2011). The social change required to promote gender justice in Afghanistan is enormous. Individuals and groups must continuously hone their tactics, recalibrate their goals, provide constructive critique and mutual support for one another, and take risks. Nothing may work, or something might. *Inshallah.*

AFTERWORD

The Clock Is Ticking, 2014

At the time this book went to press, Afghanistan itself, as well as all the issues connected with women's rights and advancement, seemed to be hanging over a precipice awaiting the effects of allied troop withdrawal as well as the Afghan presidential election in 2014. Would any of the opportunities for the expansion of women's rights and opportunities that some experts foresaw be maximized? Would the insurrectional violence creeping toward the centers of power simply overtake the country like a spreading bloodstain? Would a centralized government be possible? Would the emotional and physical wounds suffered over decades finally overwhelm the populace? Would the practice of Islam be redirected toward women's rights, aided by Jamila's training program for imams? Or would Talibanist restrictions return? If the latter, would Afghan women resist a fundamentalist regime? Had their new capacities equipped them to shape the destinies of their sex?

Even in 2014, the answers to such questions are not fully known. Nor is the future of this book's main protagonists at all clear. As this book reaches its conclusion, I can only continue to report on Marzia's and Jamila's status and well-being.

Marzia

The New Year's message I received from Marzia in 2013 alluded to her "critical situation." I later learned that she had been suffering from severe depression, which had kept her from communicating with many of her friends, including me. Later in January, she asked me to update the support letter I had written in 2011, which I did and sent both to her and to her lawyer. In early February, she wrote to say that she had passed her interview and was "eligible to stay in Canada and apply for a Permanent Resident Card." That was good news indeed, and I could see that her mood was lightening.

After that communication from her ceased for months, despite my frequent e-mails and phone messages. I finally heard from her in the summer of 2013. In a phone call in August, I learned that she had returned to Afghanistan in April to visit her sick father but was then back in Canada, working at the Afghan Women's Organization and moving into another apartment. She was managing her depression and planning to take legal training so she could work in the law. She still had to wait to get permanent residency. Although she knew things were going well for her, she still felt displaced. After all, she said, "Home is home."

Jamila

By the spring of 2013, Jamila was reporting in our telephone communications that the security situation was getting worse in Afghanistan and that she was still without a clear option for studying abroad. But despite her continuing fear and frustration, and the fatigue in her voice, she wanted to emphasize how important it was for her to continue with her work. "If we don't work today," she said, "we won't have a good country for our children." She recognized that "not all of NECDO's activities are welcomed by all groups," but she thought, "thank God," that a majority of Afghans were "understanding and seeing a change in our community by our activities." That was encouraging her "to keep going on." NECDO's project with imams had been especially successful. It had expanded to fifteen provinces, with more than a thousand imams. She recalled starting the program with only twenty-five, but some of the early group had convinced additional imams, and gradually others came on board. Jamila was holding monthly gatherings for participating imams, where they discussed how and how often they had mentioned women's issues in their prayer sessions.

Jamila was also happy to report that most of the imams were themselves allowing their daughters to go to school, whereas 50 percent of them had not done so before receiving NECDO training. Because "imams are very influential, their decision was having an effect on their villages." The training program was mostly "trying to encourage them to see women's rights as part of Islam," but it also included information about human rights, CEDAW, and the EVAW law.

She reminded me about the old man she had talked about in 2010, the one who was crying in the corner of the mosque in Nangarhar Province after he learned that his treatment of women, including his wife and daughters, had been a sin. Jamila learned that the man had become an "advocate for women's rights." He had five sons, and he was encouraging them to send their daughters to school. "Girls in [his] village were also going to school."

Jamila herself was focusing more and more attention on the upcoming presidential elections. This would be a real opportunity for a new beginning for the country, since Karzai announced he would not try to extend his constitutionally limited terms, and a clean sweep of the lingering warlord presence in the administration might be possible (because the president directly appoints so many in the government). Only a few women had yet declared their candidacies, including Fawzia Koofi, but Jamila was confident more would put forth their names. (Because of fear of reprisal by the lame-duck Karzai, few male candidates had announced either.)

NECDO had organized some roundtables to discuss the issues and conducted leadership training for more than forty-eight women from different political parties. "We are very conscious . . . that we should not mess this up," she said. "We should utilize the opportunity" to make a difference for Afghanistan's future. Jamila was planning to hold training sessions with imams about the election's importance and the importance of women's participation in it. "Hopefully, by end of year, we can do this all over Afghanistan," she said. She had no financial support for this effort, and she was facing a lot of criticism. "But I understand that this is a crucial moment for our future, which depends on the outcome of the election. A good leader will make [the risks] worth it. Otherwise, women will lose."

Her most fervent hope was that women activists "would become united and form a platform of action and realize [the] importance of upcoming election and importance of saving the country." The women of Afghanistan were more capable than in previous years. "They are more linked with the international community; they have a voice; they can use their power," she said. "Slowly and gradually some unity is coming," as organizations are more aware of the need for common action than before. Under changed leadership, even the AWN was "more positive toward [the] unification of women's organizations." Although many activists were fleeing the country (such as Marzia), "everyone won't be able to leave, so we are trying to be united."

At the same time, Jamila recognized that the challenges the women's activist community faced would only increase after 2014. I got a chilling taste of what might lie ahead, in addition to increased retaliation against activists by newly empowered Taliban forces after U.S. troop withdrawal, in a story Margaret Mills conveyed from Afghanistan by e-mail in April 2013. Jamila's husband, Fazal, drove Margaret to Jamila's house for dinner one evening during her visit to Afghanistan and told her that he had recently attended a conference in Jakarta as a representative of civil society organizations in Afghanistan. The purpose of the conference was "peace and confidence building," he said. He was surprised that Afghan government representatives there "asserted that there was no civil society in Afghanistan; everything that gets done is done by the government." When Fazal quoted statistics in his talk to prove them wrong, "they were not pleased."

Margaret asked, "Why would they want to assert that there is no civil society? Governments need civil society. They can't operate without it." Fazal replied, "Yes, but they see civil society organizations as competition for themselves." Margaret found that "a very telling and totally true observation—it says volumes about the problems with achieving any kind of effective governance or electoral process here."

On the personal level, Jamila was not faring well. She still barely went out in public. Fazal was monitoring the imam project for her. "My life is so limited," she said, and she was experiencing "lots of pressure from all sides." She could get no exercise; she had developed carpel tunnel syndrome in her hands from computer use and manipulating her crutches. The children needed a lot of attention. Her son was in a school that no one liked, but it was the closest to where they lived and, therefore, the safest for him to attend. Her husband or an uncle walked him to school. Jamila's mother was also quite sick, and Jamila had given up her own household help to care for the mother at her brother's house. That meant Jamila was doing all her own housework and child care herself, despite her physical limitations.

Jamila reported being shocked by how old she looked in a picture she recently saw of herself. She said that she also suffered from depression. She mentioned that her blood pressure and cholesterol readings were so high that the doctors were amazed. Margaret confirmed quite shocking readings on both measures. Margaret also mentioned that Jamila was having headaches and had suffered a hemorrhage in one eye, which the doctor dismissed as "God's blessing [because] it was in your eye and not in your brain." I guessed that was Afghan faith-based health care.

Although Jamila reported that she had not had a direct death threat since the previous October, except by phone, she also thought that women activists were in increasing danger. The police were still so corrupt that she would never report any threats to them, she said. "If they become aware that I am important, they will make more trouble for me." The police had already asked for protection money when NECDO recently moved offices. She told them that theirs was an educational organization with little cash on hand. Mostly what they had was stationery. Her own salary was only one thousand dollars per month. So they left her alone. Maybe that was the best she could hope for under the circumstances.

The one bright spot in her future was an impending trip to New York in late June, where she would meet with the Tanenbaum award winners and give the talk she had had to postpone in 2012. She asked if I might come and meet with her, but that did not prove possible. The sessions of the conference were closed to the public, and participants were so highly scheduled that there was literally no time to fit in an outside meeting. I so regretted I couldn't see her, but I looked forward to a next time.

Final Words

As Marzia continued to adjust to her new life outside of Afghanistan in 2014, the news from Jamila indicated that life inside the country was getting worse. Corrosive corruption, continued killings and attacks, and the unstable and unreliable government, operating increasingly outside the rule of law, had exacerbated conditions for women in general and for women's rights activists in particular. Her own health continued to deteriorate, with a heart problem added to her list of medical conditions, and her mother's health was fading.

Still, she managed to find hope in love and work. Her children were "growing well"; her "daughters are the up [and] coming leaders," thanks to blessings from God. Her "organization has been very active for promoting women political participation in trainings, awareness raising and women voting outreach in 8 provinces. . . . We work with Imams successfully for promotion of Peace & EVAW." NECDO's Afghan Library Project "trains hundreds of teachers and children in 18 provinces for increase of literacy rate with children story books." She was still "struggling to find a way for my Ph.D." But she wanted me to know, "With all challenges I am struggling to move ahead for the Goal in my life to light candles in order to reduce the darkness from my society. How much I will be successful I am not sure, but maybe next generation can see the fruits." Let us hope.

NOTES

Introduction

1. The other conference attendees were Aziza Ahmadyar, foreign relations officer for the Ministry of Information, Culture, and Tourism; Farida Azizi, manager of the D.C.-based Afghanistan Program for Vital Voices Global Partnership; Marzia Meena, gender consultant for the Asian Development Bank; Lisa Sorush, a medical student and educator; and Masuda Sultan, program director of New York–based Women for Afghan Women.

2. For critiques of the Feminist Majority's Afghan campaign, see Khan 2001 and Ann Russo 2006.

3. U.S. women struggled for more than fifty years before achieving rights to control their wages and the franchise. It took another fourteen years, until 1934, for U.S. women to achieve full citizenship. See Kitch 2009, 178. Even today, U.S. women have no constitutionally guaranteed right to legal equality with men.

4. This list of organizations comes from Hafizullah Emadi's *Repression, Resistance, and Women in Afghanistan* (Westport: Praeger, 2002), cited in Gallagher 2004.

5. Margaret Mills's gender-focused publications at the time we met included "Gender and Ethnography: A Report from the Twelfth International ISFNR Conference" (1998), "Folklore" (1999), "Seven Steps Ahead of the Devil: A Misogynist Proverb in Context" (2000), and "The Gender of the Trick: Female Tricksters and Male Narrators" (2001).

6. Azarbaijani-Moghaddam and Antonio Donini are among those who might consider that collaboration with English-speaking women living in the "Kabul Bubble" necessarily reinforces Western values and feminist visions. But that assumption is too simple, since such collaborations can be contextualized within the "complexities of religion, culture, and history" and avoid oversimplification and assumptions of connections (Chishti and Farhoumand-Sims 2011, 124–25).

7. The conference is more fully described in Kitch and Mills 2004, 2006.

8. I received IRB training and permission for the project in July 2010. I got approval both to conduct the Istanbul interviews and to grandfather in the transcripts from the 2005 conference. Even as I changed my ideas about the project that would result from our meetings, I used the IRB-approved questions to guide our conversations. I received verbal agreement from the two women (digitally recorded and in writing) to record their words and to quote from both the earlier and the current transcripts in writing the book. If either or both of them asked me not to use specific information as we went along, I have honored that request. I promised to let them read and approve the manuscript before it was published, and they have now done so. I also renewed my IRB approval for academic years 2011–13 and then took a refresher course in July 2013, which extended IRB authority until 2016.

9. In my view, theory and activism are intertwined, since new strategies or programs to improve women's status require *rethinking* or *retheorizing* the premises on which meaningful change might occur. Effective activists must establish principles on which to select actions, consider consequences, evaluate possible outcomes, and establish programs. Without such theoretical judgments, activism may be random, ineffective, and even counterproductive. For more on this topic, see Kitch 2002.

10. For more detail, see Brown 1992.

11. I have used the terms *West* and *Western* throughout the manuscript instead of newer forms—*Global North, First World,* and so on—because those are the terms Marzia and Jamila use to describe the United States, United Kingdom, and continental Europe as a cultural and political entity. I also use the term *rights* because that is the term they use to describe what they are working toward for Afghan women. For a discussion of what that term may mean in Afghanistan, see chapter 3.

12. In constructing the women's narratives, I quote directly from the transcribed recordings of the 2005 conference sessions and interviews and from our 2010, 2011, 2012, 2013, and 2014 in-person, e-mail, and telephone conversations (most of which were recorded with the women's permission). In quoted material, I occasionally add a word or a few letters in brackets for clarification. If I take phrases from different locations in the interviews or condense a particular speech, ellipses (. . .) make clear that content is missing. I have not changed any words without indicating in these ways that I have done so. At their request, I have disguised some details of their lives and views, but all attributed remarks are as true and accurate as I could make them.

Part I: Hope

1. Sixty to 70 percent of Afghans are Pashtun, for whom the code of *pashtunwali,* which places social interaction above Islamic tenets (except for female modesty) and restricts female interaction with the outside world, is a dominant determiner of daily life (Burki 2011, 48). But Afghanistan also includes Tajiks (10–25 percent), Hazaras (10–15 percent), Uzbeks (8 percent), and other minority groups, such as Kirghiz, Qazilbash, Balouchis, and the Farsiwan (10–13 percent). Eighty-four percent of the population is Sunni Muslim, and 15 percent is Shia, leaving only 1 percent of "others" (Ahmed-Ghosh 2006, 112; Jamila Afghani, oral testimony, November 2005).

2. These figures, which are slightly different from those cited in Barfield 2010 (see chapter 3), are approximations. Everyone is simply estimating.

3. Although the Taliban agreed in 1996 that female government employees could continue to draw salaries without actually performing their work, by 1999 the UN secretary-general on the situation of women and girls in Afghanistan reported the "widespread dismissal of female civil servants in a move to cut government spending" (http://daccess-dds-ny.un.org/doc/UNDOC/GEN/G00/143/56/PDF/G0014356.pdf?OpenElement United Nations Economic and Social Council Commission on Human Rights, *Report of the Secretary-General on the Situation of Women and Girls in Afghanistan,* July 21, 2000 [E/C.4/Sub.2/2000/18]). Both the United Nations and the NGO assistance community helped to keep some women employed (a total of 5,874 by mid-2000). In addition, the international assistance community employed 1,020 doctors and health workers, 2,066 traditional birth attendants, and 900 bakery staff in Mazar-e-Sharif and Jalalabad in the same period (Barakat and Wardell 2002, 914–17, 923).

4. According to an e-mail from Palwasha Hassan on September 14, 2013, she also served in that role from 2002 to 2004.

5. See Jalali 2008 for a succinct analysis of this situation.

6. The two prominent Afghan "Simas" are sometimes confused. Sima Wali, one of three female delegates at the Bonn meeting in December 2001, is a human rights activist who is now president and chief executive officer of Refugee Women in Development (RefWID), Inc. Dr. Sima Samar, the first minister of women's affairs for the Interim Administration of Afghanistan, is also a human and women's rights activist who has focused on health issues as well as education. She has also served as the chairwoman of the Independent Afghanistan Human Rights Commission, which she founded.

7. Statistics about women in parliaments worldwide are available at http://www.ipu.org/wmn-e/classif.htm.

8. M. Jamil Hanifi complicates this description of Karzai's heritage. He does not accept that any so-called Pashtun leaders of Afghanistan have ever been completely Pashtun, since none has exhibited Pashtunness in language, behavior, and patriliny. He also denies that Karzai is actually a Dorrani Pashtun and disputes Thomas Barfield's claim that the Popalzai clan of the Dorrani tribe enticed Karzai to return to Afghanistan and lead them against the Taliban. He depicts Karzai as a total creation of the "American-engineered 'Bonn Conference' to head the Kabul government" (2011, 260). In personal correspondence, Hanifi explained that Karzai is a place-name, not a name that expresses a Popalzai identity. He said that Karzai's family "reinvented themselves as connected to Ahmad Khan Dorrani." During that process, they had first to insinuate themselves into the Popalzai clan. Hanifi finds no historical support for claiming "Karzai" as a segment of the Dorrani tribe (e-mail, July 17, 2012).

9. It is also unclear that the private U.S.-funded project the Kabul Beauty School really helped Afghan women to become both the subject and the agent of their own care as an assertion of political identity after their degradation during the Taliban. See Nguyen 2011.

Chapter 1: Working for Women in "Postconflict" Afghanistan

1. The three women in President Karzai's cabinet in 2005 were Dr. Masuda Jalal, minister of women's affairs (a serious presidential candidate in the 2004 election); Sediqa Balkhi, minister of martyrs and disabled (one of three women at the 2001 Bonn Conference, which outlined the post-Taliban government in Afghanistan); and Amina Afzali, minister of youth affairs (participant in the 2001 Afghan Women's Summit for Democracy in Brussels). See http://www.vday.org/node/992.

2. Aziza became the director for foreign relations in the newly named Ministry of Culture and Youth.

3. Although this figure is approximately correct, estimates of literacy in Afghanistan vary depending on their source. According to the CIA website, as of January 2011, 28.1 percent of the total Afghan population over age fifteen could read and write, with males at 43.1 percent and females at an alarmingly low 12.6 percent. In the same year, UNICEF, citing the Ministry of Education, put adult literacy at 39 percent and adult female literacy at 13 percent (http://www.unicef.org/infobycountry/files/ACO_Education_Factsheet_-_November_2011_.pdf). UNICEF had reported higher statistics for both sexes in 2007. Then they calculated that 49 percent of males and 18 percent of females were literate (http://www.unicef.org/infobycountry/afghanistan_statistics.html). By 2013 the United Nations used "government figures" (given to the Convention on the Elimination of All Forms of Discrimination Against Women [CEDAW]

Committee) to report a 26 percent literacy rate for all Afghan adults and a 12 percent literacy rate for women (http://www.unwomen.org/en/news/stories/2013/7/afghani-women-strive-to-get-an-education).

4. Women for Afghan Women is "a grassroots civil society organization dedicated to securing and protecting the rights of disenfranchised Afghan women and girls, in Afghanistan and New York, particularly their rights to develop their individual potential, to self-determination, and to be represented in all areas of life: political, social, cultural and economic. We advocate for women's rights and challenge the norms that underpin gender-based violence wherever opportunities arise to influence attitudes and bring about change." For more information, see http://www.womenforafghanwomen.org/history.php?ID=/history.html.

5. Women constituted only 18.3 percent of the U.S. Congress in 2013, the 113th Congress. That percentage is significantly below Afghanistan (at 27.3 percent in 2006 and 28 percent in 2010) and even Rwanda (the world's highest at 48.8 percent, in 2006). See http://www.nationmaster.com/graph/gov_pro_of_sea_hel_by_wom_in_nat_par-seats-held-women-national-parliament.

6. The then chief justice, Fazil Hadi Shinwari, had no education and ran the Supreme Court for four years. In 2006 he was rejected and removed from office by the newly established lower house of Parliament, the Wolesi Jirga. See http://www.afghan-web.com/politics/government.html#judicial.

7. Article 22 states, "The citizens of Afghanistan—whether man or woman—have equal rights and duties before the law" (http://www.afghan-web.com/politics/current_constitution.html).

8. The nonprofit organization Rubia International is named for a red dye from a plant by that name used in Afghanistan. The name associates the organization with the color of life. RI is dedicated to literacy training and paid employment for mostly rural Afghan women. Its activities continue today.

9. Vital Voices Global Partnership identifies, trains, and empowers emerging women leaders and social entrepreneurs around the globe in an effort to create a better world for all. They work on issues such as human trafficking and other forms of violence against women and girls. Their goal is to enable women to become change agents in their governments, advocates for social justice, and supporters of democracy and the rule of law. They educate women in management, business development, marketing, and communications skills to expand their enterprises, help to provide for their families, and create jobs in their communities (http://www.vitalvoices.org/about-us/about).

10. Textbooks were also distributed by the United States through the University of Nebraska–Omaha's Center for Afghanistan Studies. Even during the Soviet era, UNO received USAID funding to publish and distribute K–12 textbooks to 130,000 Afghan refugees in Pakistan. After Soviet withdrawal, the number of printed texts jumped to 14 million, but the Taliban takeover curtailed distribution. USAID-funded textbook printing resumed in 2002 and 2003, "with another 15 million copies reaching Afghan teachers and students" (http://world.unomaha.edu/cas/mission.php).

11. RAWA was established in Kabul, Afghanistan, in 1977 as an independent political and social organization of Afghan women fighting for human rights and for social justice in Afghanistan. The founders were female Afghan intellectuals under the leadership of Meena, who was assassinated in Quetta, Pakistan, in 1987 by Afghan agents of the KGB in connivance with a fundamentalist band of Gulbeddin Hekmatyar supporters. RAWA's objective was to involve an increasing number of Afghan women in education and in social and political activities aimed at enhancing women's human rights and establishing

an Afghan government based on democratic and secular values. For more information, see http://www.rawa.org/s.html. RAWA is not without its critics, especially those that associate their kind of political activism with Soviet rule.

12. In making that claim before Hillary Rodham Clinton became the most serious female presidential candidate in U.S. history in 2008, Marzia was only partially correct. She was forgetting about Victoria Woodhull (1872, 1892), Belva Lockwood (1884, 1888), Margaret Chase Smith (1964), and Shirley Chisholm (1972), among other women who threw their hats into the presidential ring.

13. Although British law never prevented English women from inheriting property, custom did. Laws of primogeniture favored eldest sons until 1925. Both unmarried and married women had different property rights from men through much of the nineteenth century, and married women did not begin to have property rights at all until Parliament passed the Divorce and Matrimonial Causes Act in 1857. Those rights were extended in the Married Women's Property Act of 1882, which required the courts to regard husbands and wives as separate legal entities. See http://www.umd.umich.edu/casl/hum/eng/classes/434/geweb/PROPERTY.htm.

14. http://www.islamicity.com/mosque/w_islam/inhrt.htm.

15. Texas was the last U.S. state to pass a Married Women's Property Act, in 1913.

Chapter 2: Two Strong Voices

1. For more information on UNIFEM, see http://www.unwomen.org/.

2. https://www.cia.gov/library/publications/the-world-factbook/geos/af.html.

3. Rabbani moved to Peshawar after the coup that ousted Daoud Khan in 1978 and Soviet troops invaded Afghanistan in 1979. He became one of the mujahideen leaders of the so-called Peshawar Seven, who used Pakistani, Saudi, U.S., and Chinese support and weaponry to fuel a full-scale insurgency, which did not take power until after 1992. He was the first Tajik president of Afghanistan since the eighteenth-century founding of the state. Rabbani was assassinated by a suicide bomber posing as a Taliban envoy in 2011. For more detail, see http://www.e-ariana.com/ariana/eariana.nsf/allArticles/E60F62B1020381E28725791800567FBD?OpenDocument.

4. One of NEC's initial NGO funders was CW4WA (Canadian Women for Women in Afghanistan), which gave their first grant of $10,000 in 2004. By 2008 CW4WAfghan had given Jamila's organization $168,205 (Armstrong 2008, 61–62).

5. UN-Habitat supports many causes in a variety of locations, including the environment, land and housing, urban development, and disaster management. One of their themes is "social inclusion," which helps vulnerable groups in society such as the urban poor and women and young people. They have a strong focus on gender equality.

Chapter 3: Constructing Women's Rights in Afghanistan

1. Other agreements include the Children's Convention (signed in 1994, with the proviso that compliance depends on agreement with Sharia law), the International Covenant on Civil and Political Rights, and the International Covenant on Economic, Social, and Cultural Rights (both signed in 1983 without reservation) (Armstrong 2002, 135).

2. For more detail about nineteenth-century reformers, such as Mahmud Tarzi and King Abdur Rahman Khan, a "ruthless ruler" who nevertheless abolished slavery and a customary law that wives were bound to their husbands' families, see Moghadam 2003, 236.

3. http://www.un.org/apps/news/story.asp?NewsID=37003.
4. http://www.un.org/apps/news/story.asp?NewsID=40491&Cr=violence&Cr1=women.
5. http://thelede.blogs.nytimes.com/2009/08/17/afghan-husbands-win-right-to-starve-wives/.
6. http://www.cbc.ca/crossroads-afghanistan/story/2009/08/17/afghanistan-family-law-wives-husbands.html.
7. The erosion of women's rights in Afghanistan was well under way as of early 2014, including a move in Parliament to repeal a requirement that one-quarter of the seats on provincial councils be reserved for women. See Nordland 2014.
8. Hassan 2010, 170–71; for Hassan's résumé, see p. 170.
9. For additional activists, see Skaine 2008 and Rostami-Povey 2007.

Chapter 4: The Basics of Change

1. Although Marzia thought the woman behind the scenes at Tolo was the station owner's daughter, she was actually his sister Wajma, who helped to run and manage the station along with her brothers Saad, Zaid, and Jahid Mohseni. Saad was the public face of the company. He had been denounced as "un-Islamic" by fundamentalists for allowing women to appear alongside men on his radio and television networks, for showing Indian soap operas featuring unveiled women, and for allowing women to compete with men on one of Tolo TV's hit shows, *Afghan Star*. See http://feraljundi.com/2010/08/08/media-news-the-rupert-murdoch-of-afghanistan-saad-mohseni-and-the-moby-group/.
2. According to Afghanistan's 1388 (2009) national budget, the security sector was the government's highest priority. But the health sector had more Millennium Development Goals than any other sector.
3. India ran the leading children's hospital in Afghanistan in 2010, Indira Gandhi Children's Hospital. They also ran several other medical centers. See http://www.dnaindia.com/india/report_india-won-t-scale-down-missions-in-afghanistan-shiv-shankar-menon_1356137. The DK German Medical Diagnostic Center opened in Kabul in 2004 (http://www.medical-kabul.com/index2.html). The French Medical Institute for the Child opened in Kabul in 2006 (http://www.afghanmania.com/en/news/0,news,4844,00.html).
4. http://cure.org/staff/?cat_id=2. The 2011 executive director was Joe Davis-Fleming.
5. Jamila did not correct Marzia, but there is little to back up her conjecture that Sbeghatulla Mujadeddi, then president of the Meshrano Jirga (Senate) of Afghanistan, had any direct connection with Cure International, although he did come from a prestigious and religious family. Nevertheless, he may have been a strong supporter. Among his legislative accomplishments was leading the *jirga* that approved the new Afghan Constitution. See http://www.afghan-bios.info/tinc?key=2vB1wwzV&session_currentpage=data&session_mode=guest&formname=afghan_bios&session_sortby=field_3&userid=1262924167;572160;52&session_nextpage=data_edit&session_offset=50&session_start=601&session_dbkey=1255374433;591791;672_afghan_bios&dbkey=1255374433;591791;672_afghan_bios.
6. http://www.beyondthe11th.org/about.ourwork.php.
7. http://www.ips.org.pk/international-relation/pakistan-and-its-neighbours/1081.html.
8. See http://www.auaf.edu.af/ and http://www.auaf.edu.af/admissions/process for more information. According to its website, AUAF was Afghanistan's only not-for-profit, private, independent university in 2010. AUAF takes pride in being nonpolitical, nonsectarian, and committed to providing world-class higher education that will produce Afghanistan's future business, civic, and government leaders.

Chapter 5: The Political Is Personal

1. In 2005 Sajia was working on trafficked women and child marriage, among other issues, for Medica Mondiale. She was also founding organizer of the Women's Internet Café, a World Bank–initiated project providing Internet access and duplication services for students and faculty at Kabul University. In 2010 Sajia was a gender and policy adviser in the GTZ Gender Mainstreaming Project. She was responsible for issues as they relate to national gender policy and Islamic perspectives. See http://www.wisemuslimwomen.org/muslimwomen/bio/sajia_behgum/.

2. The SCA is active in eighteen eastern provinces of Afghanistan, focusing on education, health, and disability. According to the committee's website, their work began in the 1980s and has always focused on vulnerable groups in rural and underserved areas. Its goals include fighting poverty, "supporting economic and social development and strengthening democratic development and gender & human rights." See http://www.swedishcommittee.org/sca/index.html.

3. Afghanistan signed CEDAW in August 1980, but the reason the law was on Marzia's mind in 2010 is that the Afghan government did not ratify it until March 2003. The United States signed the treaty in 1980 as well, but the Senate has never ratified it. See http://treaties.un.org/Pages/ViewDetails.aspx?src=TREATY&mtdsg_no=IV-8&chapter=4&lang=en.

4. There are many origin stories for the *burqa* or *chador,* the full-body covering some Muslim women wear, but it is certainly more than one hundred years old. One story attributes its invention to the discreet concubines of the Ottoman emperor Suleiman the Magnificent, who was the sultan of Turkey from 1520 to 1566.

5. ASMA is a New York–based nonprofit organization founded in 1997 to "elevate the discourse on Islam and foster environments in which Muslims thrive." The organization is "dedicated to strengthening an authentic expression of Islam based on cultural and religious harmony through interfaith collaboration, youth and women's empowerment, and arts and cultural exchange." See http://www.asmasociety.org/home/.

6. The negotiations at the time of marriage are supposed to include the woman's "marriage portion," or *mahr,* which gives her some economic security in her marriage, especially in case of divorce. In practice, however, the marriage portion often gets lost in marriage negotiations, and the bride's family typically benefits from any money that changes hands. (For further discussion of this, see chapter 6.) Jamila's figures, though she expressed them in dollars, are just examples and may not reflect actual amounts featured in most marriage negotiations.

Chapter 6: Afghan Marriage Practices

1. Qadir fought the Taliban in the eastern part of the country. When the Taliban fell in 2001, he was made vice chairman of Afghanistan's interim administration after the Bonn Conference. He was assassinated in 2002, probably by the Taliban, although they have not taken credit for his murder. See http://www.zmong-afghanistan.com/profiles/qadir.asp. Qadir was never arrested or prosecuted for his daughter's murder, as far as I can tell.

2. According to Kaufman (2003), poverty caused by war, displacement, and drought is the primary motivation for selling young girls as brides. Most will be servants until they actually marry their owners, although their relationship to their husbands may hardly change with the marriage ceremony. Mullahs may advise against it, but the practicalities for poverty-stricken Afghans take precedence over religious principle.

3. Jamila's telling of the Zainab bint Jahsh story is not consistent with other versions. Others believe that the Prophet fell in love with her while she was still married to his adopted son, Zayed, and that Zayed divorced her so that the Prophet could marry her.

4. This right of repudiation predates Islam and does not, in Amina Wadud's interpretation, indicate an inequity in the Qur'an. Rather, the Qur'an simply allowed men a right they already had and did not initiate the idea that men had the power of repudiation (1999, 80).

5. Some sources say that Khadija was forty when she married the Prophet and produced no children during their fifteen-year marriage.

6. Whether gender equality is a central tenet of Islam is open to debate. Marzia and Jamila have spoken as if it were, at least with regard to rights. Wadud argues that men and women are equal in terms of their relationship to and status with Allah, but their social roles are complementary (1999, 73). Scholars such as Kecia Ali (2006) argue that overall, the prescribed relationship of men's and women's roles and rights is complementary rather than equal.

7. http://www.ncadv.org/files/DomesticViolenceFactSheet(National).pdf.

8. http://www.theatlantic.com/national/archive/2013/01/america-has-an-incest-problem/272459/.

9. Oliver Wendell Holmes (McCullough 2011, 7).

10. http://eh.net/encyclopedia/article/haines.demography. Race and location are big factors in many birthrate, child-mortality, and death-rate statistics in the United States. For example, child mortality rates for whites were 216.8 per 1,000 births in 1850 and 340 per 1,000 births for blacks in the same year. The respective numbers in 1900, when sanitary conditions and disease control were greatly improved, were still skewed by race: 110.8 and 170.3 per 1,000, respectively.

11. E-mail correspondence, April 29, 2013. Margaret Mills recounts the consequences of such suppression to those boys, who might be trafficked and shipped around, sometimes ending up drug addicted and far from home. Such an experience would not disqualify such boys for later marriage, she reports.

Chapter 7: Marriage Hits Home

1. Now Shahristan is a part of a new province called Daia Kiakondi.

2. According to sources on the Qur'an and science, *sultan* can also mean "utter force," which makes the verse signify "the possibility of piercing through the zones of the sky and the earth with the help of the force, i.e. that man can attain the desired force. This force could be attained with the progress of the knowledge and technology." See http://www.thequranandscience.com/display.php?article/12.

3. I have heard different versions of this story from other people, but I am restricting my report only to Jamila's version.

Part III: Uncertainty

1. These data are based on the Afghanistan Mortality Survey completed in 2010, which is considered the most comprehensive survey carried out in the country's history. For more details, see http://topnews.net.nz/content/220422-maternal-mortality-rate-afghanistan-decline; http://www.csmonitor.com/World/Asia-South-Central/2011/1216/Childbirth

-and-maternal-health-improve-in-Afghanistan; and http://www.bbc.co.uk/news/world-asia-15942940.

2. The poll contradicts Anatol Lieven's suggestion that the Taliban's views were not much different from those of rural Afghans. He said in 2012 that the Taliban's problem was in codifying into law what family practices and communities were used to controlling and in applying their rules to urban Afghan women, who had achieved real gains in their rights (2012, 31–32).

3. http://news.bbc.co.uk/2/shared/bsp/hi/pdfs/05_02_09afghan_poll_2009.pdf.

4. See also http://www.fefa.org.af/Eng_Pages/Reports/VRP_Rep/Women%20and%20Afghanistan's%202010%20Parliamentary%20Elections.pdf.

5. Such incidents would continue in the next several years. In May 2012, for example, 160 girls at the Aahan Dara Girls School in Taluqan were poisoned by a toxic material sprayed overnight in their classrooms. Fortunately, no one died in that incident, but it shows the lengths to which detractors will go to protest education for women. For more information, see http://articles.cnn.com/2012-05-29/asia/world_asia_afghanistan-girls-poisoned_1_afghan-girls-taliban-school-closure?_s=PM:ASIA; http://www.rawa.org/temp/runews/2011/01/21/who-benefits-from-taliban-revisionismo.html; and http://www.interaction.org/blog/schooling-afghanistan%E2%80%99s-50.

6. See http://www.washingtonpost.com/world/in-afghanistan-underground-girls-school-defies-taliban-after-earlier-efforts-failed/2012/04/24/gIQALBOVfT_story.html; and Heath 2011, 23.

7. http://news.bbc.co.uk/2/shared/bsp/hi/pdfs/05_02_09afghan_poll_2009.pdf.

8. Brodsky cites a 2000 report from Physicians for Human Rights.

Chapter 8: Addressing Afghanistan's Problems

1. According to the *International News,* Maulvi Hanif identified a would-be terrorist to the Crimes Investigation Department in Afghanistan in January 2010. His "pointation" led to the suspect's arrest and to the recovery of "60,000 US dollars, three satellite phones, laptop, computer software and important documents." See http://thenews.com.pk/TodaysPrintDetail.aspx?ID=26852&Cat=13&dt=1/24/2010.

2. Comments combine Marzia's testimony and observations in a *Los Angeles Times* article in December 2002. The article also contains Marzia's denial about being fired, as well as a statement by the deputy chief justice of the Supreme Court, Fazal Ahmad Manawi, about women's right to choose what they wear. See http://articles.latimes.com/pring/2002/dec/08/world/fg-chador8.

3. One example of what Marzia meant could be RAWA's unstinting opposition, since 2001, to U.S. support for Hamid Karzai and his "Northern Alliance criminal leaders who are as brutal and misogynist as the Taliban." See http://www.rawa.org/rawa.html.

4. Samar's description to reporters of her time in the Karzai cabinet points to some of the problems she encountered: "I didn't know that it would be this much difficult," she told one. After a month in office, "she still had no staff or budget, and the male ministers appeared to ignore her in cabinet meetings. But, as always, Samar refused to conform. 'After the meetings . . . people say I make too much noise, so I say: why did they appoint me? I am not confrontational . . . that doesn't work . . . but I have to say what I want for women.' She continued her calls for equality and justice, including demands for more female ministers in the government, schools for married women, and an end to arranged

marriages." She finally decided that her mistake was simply that she is an outspoken Hazara woman. "That is enough, I guess," she said. See http://www.answers.com/topic/sima-samar #ixzz1W43L6A2u.

5. As of August 2011, the parliamentary election of September 2010 was not fully resolved. Results were widely condemned as tainted by corruption. Karzai's attempt to circumvent the Independent Election Commission, which had constitutional authority to rule in contested elections, through the appointment of a special court was finally defeated when he abolished that court and affirmed early in August 2011 that the commission could be the final arbiter in the controversy. The eleven-month uncertainty paralyzed Karzai's government and prevented him from making permanent cabinet appointments or appointing Supreme Court justices. But even the commission's ruling in late August that nine candidates should be removed from Parliament and another nine should have their seats restored was unlikely to resolve the crisis, as many members of Parliament protested. Nordland and Wafa 2011.

6. The quotation is from the INLTC website, which also contains more information about the organization: http://inltc.af/home.htm.

7. http://www.nytimes.com/2010/06/14/world/asia/14minerals.html?adxnnl=1 &pagewanted=2&adxnnlx=1311285672-zOYc6pPUvObSHsN+krF9ZQ.

8. For a description of the state of Afghan law regarding marriage and family, see http://www .ecoi.net/188769::afghanistan/314491.312370.7893 . . . lk.312375/marriage-and-divorce-law .htm. For information about the Eliminate Violence against Women law, passed in 2011, see http://www.un.org/apps/news/story.asp?NewsID=37003 and http://unama.unmissions.org /Portals/UNAMA/Publication/HTP%20REPORT_ENG.pdf.

9. Barat and Sherzai 2009; http://www.globalpost.com/dispatch/news/regions/middle-east /120716/afghanistan-honor-killing-tamana-murder-spotlights-increase.

10. UN Women, UN Entity for Gender Equality and the Empowerment of Women, "Facts and Figures on VAW" (http://www.unifem.org/gender_issues/violence_against _women/facts_figures.php?page=4).

Chapter 9: Fast-Forward

1. Marzia first met Liz Brundige in 2004, when she was working as an intern at the International Association of Women Judges. Marzia spent time at their offices while she was at GW. Liz had graduated from Yale Law School and was working on Africa and Haiti. Liz introduced Marzia to Cynthia Bowman, who arranged for the fellowship at Cornell. "She was the one," Marzia says, "that you know sometimes when you are very, very sad, if she just write to you or talk to you, you will be healed. So she was the one. I love her too much."

2. Evidence of this is the help she has offered to Marzia since her move to Canada, including FedExing her documents she needed from the United States.

3. Marzia met Dobriansky in 2002 when she was on a mission to Afghanistan for a meeting of the U.S.-Afghanistan Women's Council. Her role in the Bush administration was to promote and defend "the administration's interventionist policies in the Middle East." See http://www.rightweb.irc-online.org/profile/Dobriansky_Paula. See also http://www .sourcewatch.org/index.php?title=Paula_J. Dobriansky.

4. For more information about the Tanenbaum Center and the prize, see https://www .tanenbaum.org/programs/peace/peacemakers-action-nominees-top-ten.

5. For more information about Jamila's relationship with WISE, see http://www.wisemuslimwomen.org/activism/casestudy/.

6. For more information about the fellowship, see http://www.soros.org/initiatives/scholarship/focus_areas/uk/durham-phd.

7. The Afghan National Council of Ulema (or Ulama) is the highest religious body in Afghanistan, comparable to the College of Cardinals at the Vatican. "It is a presidentially-appointed body of clerics and the members are paid by the Afghan Government. It is under Government control and supports President Karzai." The Ulema Council is headed by former Supreme Court Chief Justice Fazil Hadi Shinwari. It is composed of influential Sunni and Shia scholars, imams, and Islamic jurists from across the country. It reflects the network of provincial Ulema Councils. Members meet regularly with the president and advise him about Muslim moral, ethical, and legal issues. See http://www.afghan-bios.info/index.php?option=com_afghanbios&id=1218&task=view&total=2032&start=1238&Itemid=2.

8. https://afghanistananalysis.wordpress.com/2012/03/04/english-translation-of-ulema-councils-declaration-about-women/.

9. http://www.guardian.co.uk/world/2012/mar/06/hamid-karzai-restricive-code-women-afghanistan; http://www.guardian.co.uk/world/2012/mar/05/afghanistan-women.

10. Sally Armstrong quotes Elizabeth King, lead economist in the World Bank's Development Research Group, and the World Bank's chief economist, Nicholas Stern, both writing in 2001 (2002, 184).

Chapter 10: Future Prospects

1. Although some feminist theorists take issue in general with "governmentality," or the role of a strong central state in imposing standards and priorities (for example, Bedford and Rai 2010), Afghanistan may be a case they have not considered deeply. It currently presents a situation where local communities impose the most hardship on women.

2. For specific roles of the councils, see Lister and Nixon 2006, 211–13. The Interim Afghanistan National Development Strategy is the second guiding document along with the Afghanistan Compact adopted by interim planners post-Bonn in 2006.

3. "World Report, 2013: Afghanistan," *Human Rights Watch*, http://www.hrw.org/world-report/2013/country-chapters/afghanistan; "Afghanistan: Escalating Setbacks for Women," *Human Rights Watch*, http://www.hrw.org/news/2013/07/16/afghanistan-escalating-setbacks-women; "Afghan Women's Network and Civil Society's Statement on the Scrutiny of the EVAW Law in Afghan Parliament," *Afghan Women's Network*, http://afghanwomennetwork.af/EVAWStatement_FinalEnglish_.pdf.

4. *Islamic feminism* is a contested term. See Moghadam 2002, 1152–57, for objections and distortions sometimes associated with it, as well as for its positive contributions to "expanding legal literacy and gender consciousness" (1155). I use the term here as a constructive aspect of the women's work.

5. For a more detailed discussion of intersectionality, see Kitch 2009, 2–4.

6. For a full discussion of Young's ideas about seriality, see Kitch 2009, 240–41, and notes on 296–97.

REFERENCES

Abirafeh, Lina. 2005. "Lessons from Gender-Focused International Aid in Post-conflict Afghanistan . . . Learned?" In vol. 7 of *Gender in International Cooperation*. Bonn, Germany: Division for International Cooperation, Department for Development Policy.
Abu-Lughod, Lila. 2002. "Do Muslim Women Really Need Saving? Anthropological Reflections on Cultural Relativism and Its Others." *American Anthropologist* 104, no. 3: 783–90.
———. 2010. "Against Universals: The Dialects of (Women's) Human Rights and Human Capabilities." In *Rethinking the Human*, edited by J. Michelle Molina, Donald K. Swearer, Arthur Kleinman, and Veena Das, 78–84. Cambridge, Mass.: Harvard University Press.
Ahmed-Ghosh, Huma. 2003. "A History of Women in Afghanistan: Lessons Learnt for the Future; or, Yesterdays and Tomorrows: Women in Afghanistan." *Journal of International Women's Studies* 4, no. 3: 1–14.
———. 2006. "Voices of Afghan Women: Human Rights and Economic Development." *International Feminist Journal of Politics* 8, no. 1: 110–28.
Ali, Kecia. 2006. *Sexual Ethics and Islam: Feminist Reflections on Qur'an, Hadith, and Jurisprudence*. Oxford: Oneworld.
Alvi-Aziz, Hayat. 2008. "A Progress Report on Women's Education in Post-Taliban Afghanistan." *International Journal of Lifelong Education* 27, no. 2: 169–78.
Armstrong, Sally. 2002. *Veiled Threat: The Hidden Power of the Women of Afghanistan*. New York: Four Walls Eight Windows.
———. 2008. *Bitter Roots, Tender Shoots: The Uncertain Fate of Afghanistan's Women*. Ontario: Penguin Canada.
Azarbaijani-Moghaddam, Sippi. 2010. "Manly Honor and the Gendered Male in Afghanistan." In *Afghanistan, 1979–2009: In the Grip of Conflict*, edited by MEI, 184–87. Washington, D.C.: Middle East Institute.
Aziz, Nahid. 2011. "Psychological Impacts of War: Human Rights and Mental Health." In *Land of the Unconquerable: The Lives of Contemporary Afghan Women*, edited by Jennifer Heath and Ashraf Zahedi, 229–43. Berkeley: University of California Press.
Azoy, Whitney. 2010. "Post-buffer Afghanistan: A Nation-State Here to Stay?" In *Afghanistan, 1979–2009: In the Grip of Conflict*, edited by MEI, 14–16. Washington, D.C.: Middle East Institute.
Baker, Aryn. 2010. "Afghan Women and the Return of the Taliban." *Time*, July 29, 1–4.
Banerjee, Nipa. 2008. "Peace Building and Development in the Fragile State of Afghanistan: A Practitioner's Perspective." In *Afghanistan: Transition under Threat*, edited by Geoffrey Hayes and Mark Sedra, 241–62. Studies in International Governance. Ontario: Wilfrid Laurier University Press.

Barakat, Sultan, and Gareth Wardell. 2002. "Exploited by Whom? An Alternative Perspective on Humanitarian Assistance to Afghan Women." *Third World Quarterly* 23, no. 5: 909–30.

Barat, Mohammad, and Habib-ul-Rahman Sherzai. 2009. "Honor-Killing in Afghanistan: Father Kills His Daughter and Her Lover." *RAWA News*, June 21. http://www.rawa.org/temp/runews/2009/06/21/honor-killing-in-afghanistan-father-kills-his-daughter-and-her-lover.html.

Barfield, Thomas. 2010. *Afghanistan: A Cultural and Political History*. Princeton Studies in Muslim Politics. Princeton, N.J.: Princeton University Press.

———. 2011. "Afghanistan: The Local and the Global in the Practice of Shari'a." In *Shari'a Politics: Islamic Law and Society in the Modern World*, edited by Robert W. Hefner, 179–206. Bloomington: Indiana University Press.

Barlow, Rebecca, and Shahram Akbarzadeh. 2006. "Women's Rights in the Muslim World: Reform or Reconstruction?" *Third World Quarterly* 27, no. 8: 1480–94.

Bedford, Kate, and Shirin M. Rai. 2010. "Feminists Theorize International Political Economy." *Signs* 36, no. 1: 1–18.

Belluck, Pam. 2011. "Fatherhood Cuts Testosterone, Study Finds, for Good of the Family." *New York Times*, September 13, A1.

Benish, Abdul Jalil. 2010. "Impunity and Instability: An Unbroken Cycle." In *Afghanistan, 1979–2009: The Grip of Conflict*, edited by MEI, 46–48. Washington, D.C.: Middle East Institute.

Bergner, Gwen. 2011. "Veiled Motives: Women's Liberation and the War in Afghanistan." In *Globalizing Afghanistan: Terrorism, War, and the Rhetoric of Nation Building*, edited by Gilbert Joseph and Emily Rosenberg, 95–116. Durham, N.C.: Duke University Press.

Brodsky, Anne E. 2011. "Centuries of Threat, Centuries of Resistance: The Lessons of Afghan Women's Resilience." In *Land of the Unconquerable: The Lives of Contemporary Afghan Women*, edited by Jennifer Heath and Ashraf Zahedi, 74–89. Berkeley: University of California Press.

Brown, Elsa Barkley. 1992. "'What Has Happened Here': The Politics of Difference in Women's History and Feminist Politics." *Feminist Studies* 18, no. 2: 295–312.

Burki, Shireen Kahn. 2011. "The Politics of Zan from Ananullah to Karzai: Lessons for Improving Afghan Women's Status." In *Land of the Unconquerable: The Lives of Contemporary Afghan Women*, edited by Jennifer Heath and Ashraf Zahedi, 45–59. Berkeley: University of California Press.

Butler, Judith. 2004. *Precarious Life: The Powers of Mourning and Violence*. New York: Verso.

Canfield, Robert L. 2010. "Crisis in South Asia." In *Afghanistan, 1979–2009: In the Grip of Conflict*, edited by MEI, 87–89. Washington, D.C.: Middle East Institute.

Carastathis, Anna. 2013. "Identity Categories as Potential Coalitions." *Signs* 38, no. 4: 941–65.

Caton, Steven C. 1991. "*Rhetorics and Politics in Afghan Traditional Storytelling* by Margaret A. Mills: A Review." *Anthropological Linguistics* 33, no. 3: 329–30.

Centlivres, Pierre, and Micheline Centlivres-Demont. 2010. "The Invention of Afghan Nationalities, 1980–2004." In *Afghanistan, 1979–2009: In the Grip of Conflict*, edited by MEI, 37–39. Washington, D.C.: Middle East Institute.

Chakrabarty, Debjani. 2013. "Going Transnational: Politics of Transnational Feminist Exchange in India and the United States." Ph.D. diss., Arizona State University.

Chapman, Mary, and Angela Mills. 2011. *Treacherous Texts: U.S. Suffrage Literature, 1846–1946*. New Brunswick, N.J.: Rutgers University Press.

Cherlin, Andrew. 2013. "In the Season of Marriage, a Question. Why Bother?" *New York Times*, April 28, SR7.

Chishti, Maliha, and Cheshmak Farhoumand-Sims. 2011. "Transnational Feminism and the Women's Rights Agenda in Afghanistan." In *Globalizing Afghanistan: Terrorism, War, and the Rhetoric of Nation Building*, edited by Zubeda Jalalzai and David Jefferess, 117–43. Durham, N.C.: Duke University Press.

Chun, Jennifer Jihye, George Lipsitz, and Young Shin. 2013. "Intersectionality as a Social Movement Strategy: Asian Immigrant Women Advocates." *Signs* 38, no. 4: 917–40.

Clark, Kate. 2010. "How the Guests Became an Enemy: Afghan Attitudes towards Westerners since 2001." In *Afghanistan, 1979–2009: In the Grip of Conflict*, edited by MEI, 50–52. Washington, D.C.: Middle East Institute.

cooke, miriam. 2001. *Women Claim Islam: Creating Islamic Feminism through Literature*. New York: Routledge.

Crenshaw, Kimberlé. 1997. "Intersectionality and Identity Politics." In *Reconstructing Political Theory: Feminist Perspectives*, edited by Mary Lyndon Shanley and Uma Narayan, 178–93. University Park: Pennsylvania State University Press.

Crews, Robert D. 2010. "Liberating Afghanistan." In *Afghanistan, 1979–2009: In the Grip of Conflict*, edited by MEI, 75–78. Washington, D.C.: Middle East Institute.

Dharmapuri, Sahana. 2011. "Just Add Women and Stir?" *Parameters* 41, no. 1: 56–70.

Dupree, Nancy Hatch. 2002. "Cultural Heritage and National Identity in Afghanistan." *Third World Quarterly* 23, no. 5: 977–89.

Edwards, David B. 1994. "*Rhetorics and Politics in Afghan Traditional Storytelling* by Margaret A. Mills: A Review." *American Ethnologist* 21, no.4: 1123–24.

Faludi, Susan. 1991. *Backlash: The Undeclared War against American Women*. New York: Crown.

Fitzgerald, Paul, and Elizabeth Gould. 2009. *Invisible History: Afghanistan's Untold Story*. San Francisco: City Lights Books.

Franks, Mary Anne. 2003. "Obscene Undersides: Women and Evil between the Taliban and the United States." *Hypatia* 18, no. 11: 135–56.

Friedan, Betty. 1963. *The Feminine Mystique*. New York: Dell.

Gallagher, Nancy. 2004. "The Politics of Afghan Women's Liberation." *Middle East Studies* 38, no. 2: 201–4.

Grimké, Sarah Moore. 1837. "Letter #2, July 17." In *Letters on the Equality of the Sexes, and the Condition of Woman*, 9–14. Reprint, Charleston, S.C.: BiblioBazaar, 2008.

Guenther, Katja M. 2011. "The Possibilities and Pitfalls of NGO Feminism: Insights from Postsocialist Eastern Europe." *Signs* 36, no.4: 863–87.

Guy-Sheftall, Beverly, ed. 1995. *Words of Fire: An Anthology of African-American Feminist Thought*. New York: New Press.

Hanifi, M. Jamil. 2011. "Review Essay: Vending Distorted Afghanistan through Patriotic 'Anthropology.'" *Critique of Anthropology* 31, no. 3: 256–70.

Harrison, Robert Pogue. 2013. "A New Kind of Woman." *New York Review of Books*, April 25, 36–38.

Hassan, Palwasha. 2010. "Women's Agency in Afghanistan: From Survivors to Agents of Change." In *Afghanistan, 1979–2009: In the Grip of Conflict*, edited by MEI, 170–73. Washington, D.C.: Middle East Institute.

Hawley, John Stratton. 1999. "Fundamentalism." In *Religious Fundamentalism and the Human Rights of Women*, edited by Courtney W. Howland, 3–8. New York: Palgrave.

Heath, Jennifer. 2011. Introduction to *Land of the Unconquerable: The Lives of Contemporary Afghan Women*, edited by Jennifer Heath and Ashraf Zahedi, 1–35. Berkeley: University of California Press.

Ibrahimi, Niamatullah. 2010. "Charting a Course for a Better Future: Responding to the Crimes of the Past." In *Afghanistan, 1979–2009: In the Grip of Conflict*, edited by MEI, 43–45. Washington, D.C.: Middle East Institute.

Jabbra, Nancy W. 2013. "Women, Words, and War: Explaining 9/11 and Justifying US Military Action in Afghanistan and Iraq." *Journal of International Women's Studies* 8, no. 1: 236–55.

Jalali, Ali A. 2006. "The Legacy of War and the Challenge of Peacebuilding." In *Building a New Afghanistan*, edited by Robert I. Rotberg, 22–55. Washington, D.C.: Brookings Institution Press.

———. 2008. "Afghanistan: The Challenge of State Building." In *Afghanistan: Transition under Threat*, edited by Geoffrey Hayes and Mark Sedra, 25–50. Ontario: Wilfrid Laurier University Press.

Jalalzai, Zubeda, and David Jefferess. 2011. "Introduction: Globalizing Afghanistan." In *Globalizing Afghanistan: Terrorism, War, and the Rhetoric of Nation Building*, edited by Zubeda Jalalzai and David Jefferess, 1–30. Durham, N.C.: Duke University Press.

Johnson, Thomas H. 2007. "The Taliban and an Analysis of *Shabnamah* (Night Letters)." *Small Wars and Insurgencies* 18, no. 3: 317–44.

Kamrany, Taymor. 2010. "From Sustainable Jobs to Sustainable Peace and Prosperity." In *Afghanistan, 1979–2009: In the Grip of Conflict*, edited by MEI, 140–42. Washington, D.C.: Middle East Institute.

Kandiyoti, Deniz. 2005. *The Politics of Gender and Reconstruction in Afghanistan*. New York: United Nations Research Institute for Social Development.

Kaufman, Marc. 2003. "Young Girls Sold as Brides by Desperate Afghan Poor; Years of War, Drought Force Some to Give Up Daughters." *Washington Post*, February 23, A27.

Khan, Shanaz. 2001. "Between Here and There: Solidarity and Afghan Women." *Genders* 33: 1–26.

Kirkley, Evelyn A. 1990. "'This Work Is God's Cause': Religion in the Southern Woman Suffrage Movement, 1880–1920." *Church History* 59, no. 4: 507–22.

Kitch, Sally L. 2002. "Claiming Success: From Adversity to Responsibility in Women's Studies." *NWSA Journal* 14, no. 1: 160–81.

———. 2009. *The Specter of Sex: Gendered Foundations of Racial Formation in the United States*. Albany: State University of New York Press.

Kitch, Sally L., and Margaret A. Mills. 2004. "Appropriating Women's Agendas." *Peace Review* 16, no. 1: 65–73.

———. 2006. "Afghan Women Leaders Speak: An Activist Academic Conference." *National Women's Studies Association Journal* (Autumn): 191–201.

Kristoff, Nicholas, and Sheryl WuDunn. 2010. *Half the Sky: Turning Oppression into Opportunity*. New York: Vintage Books.

Larson, Anna. 2010. "Perspectives on Democracy and Democratization in Afghanistan." In *Afghanistan, 1979–2009: In the Grip of Conflict*, edited by MEI, 94–96. Washington, D.C.: Middle East Institute.

Levinson, Charles. 2012. "Afghan Women Seen Losing Ground." *Wall Street Journal*, March 7, A12.

Lewis, Reina. 2002. "Feminism and Orientalism." *Feminist Theory* 3, no. 2: 211–19.
Lieven, Anatol. 2012. "Afghanistan: The Best Way to Peace." *New York Review of Books*, January 11 (reprint, February 9), 30–32.
Lister, Sarah, and Hamish Nixon. 2006. "The Place of the Province in Afghanistan's Subnational Governance." In *Building a New Afghanistan*, edited by Robert Rotberg, 205–26. Medford, Mass.: World Peace Foundation.
MacKinnon, Catharine A. 2013. "Intersectionality as Method: A Note." *Signs* 38, no. 4: 1019–30.
Mahmood, Saba. 2001. "Feminist Theory, Embodiment, and the Docile Agent: Some Reflections on the Egyptian Islamic Revival." *Cultural Anthropology* 16, no. 2: 202–36.
Mayer, Ann Elizabeth. 1999. "Religious Reservations to the Convention on the Elimination of All Forms of Discrimination against Women: What Do They Really Mean?" In *Religious Fundamentalisms and the Human Rights of Women*, edited by Courtney Howland and Thomas Buergenthal, 105–6. New York: Palgrave.
McCullough, David. 2011. *The Greater Journey: Americans in Paris*. New York: Simon and Schuster.
Mehmet, Karen A., and Ozay Mehmet. 2004. "The Family during Crisis in Afghanistan." *Journal of Comparative Family Studies* 35: 311–31.
Mernissi, Fatima. 1987. *Beyond the Veil: Male-Female Dynamics in Modern Muslim Society*. Rev. ed. Bloomington: Indiana University Press.
———. 1991. *The Veil and the Male Elite: A Feminist Interpretation of Women's Rights in Islam*. Translated by Mary Jo Lakeland. Cambridge, Mass.: Perseus Books.
Merry, Sally Engle. 2006. *Human Rights and Gender Violence: Translating International Law into Local Justice*. Chicago: University of Chicago Press.
Mills, Margaret A. 1998. "Gender and Ethnography: A Report from the Twentieth International ISFNR Conference." In *FF Network*, no. 16, 8–13. Helsinki: Finnish National Academy/Folklore Fellows.
———. 1999. "Folklore." In *Encyclopedia of Women and World Religion*, edited by Serinity Young, 343–45. New York: Macmillan.
———. 2000. "Seven Steps Ahead of the Devil: A Misogynist Proverb in Context." In *Telling, Remembering, Interpreting, Guessing: Prof. Annikki Kaivola-Bregenhøj on Her 60th Birthday*, edited by Maria Vasenkari, Pasi Engers, and Anna-Leena Siikala, 449–58. Joensuu, Finland: Suomen Kansatietouden Tutkijain Seura.
———. 2001. "The Gender of the Trick: Female Tricksters and Male Narrators." *Asian Folklore Studies* 60, no. 2: 237–58.
———. 2003. "Women, Memory, and Community." In vol. 2 of *Encyclopedia of Women and Islamic Cultures: Family, Law, and Politics*, edited by Suad Joseph and Afsāna Iağmābādi. 478–79. Leiden: Brill.
———. 2011. "Between Covered and Covert: Traditions, Stereotypes, and Afghan Women's Agency." In *Land of the Unconquerable: The Lives of Contemporary Afghan Women*, edited by Jennifer Heath and Ashraf Zahedi, 60–73. Berkeley: University of California Press.
Moghadam, Valentine M. 2002. "Islamic Feminism and Its Discontents: Toward a Resolution of the Debate." *Signs* 27, no. 4: 1135–72.
———. 2003. *Modernizing Women: Gender and Social Change in the Middle East*. Boulder, Colo.: Lynne Rienner.
———. 2005. "Feminists versus Fundamentalists: Women Living under Muslim Laws and the Sisterhood Is Global Institute." In *Globalizing Women: Transnational Feminist Networks*, 142–72. Baltimore: Johns Hopkins University Press.

Mohanty, Chandra. 1986. "Under Western Eyes: Feminist Scholarship and Colonial Discourses." In *Feminism without Borders: Decolonizing Theory, Practicing Solidarity*, edited by Chandra Mohanty, 1–17. Reprint, Durham, N.C.: Duke University Press, 2003.

———. 2003. *Feminism without Borders: Decolonizing Theory, Practicing Solidarity.* Durham, N.C.: Duke University Press.

———. 2013. "Transnational Feminist Crossings: On Neoliberalism and Radical Critique." *Signs* 38, no. 4: 967–91.

Nemat, Orzala Ashraf. 2010. "Hamida's Story: Female Agents of Change." In *Afghanistan, 1979-2009: In the Grip of Conflict,* edited by MEI, 174–77. Washington, D.C.: Middle East Institute.

Nguyen, Mimi Thi. 2011. "The Biopower of Beauty: Humanitarian Imperialisms and Global Feminisms in an Age of Terror." *Signs* 36, no. 2: 359–83.

Nordland, Rod. 2010. "Lacking Money and Leadership, Push for Taliban Defectors Stalls." *New York Times,* September 6. http://www.nytimes.com/2010/09/07/world/asia/07taliban.html.

———. 2012. "Moral 'Crimes' Land Afghan Women in Jail." *New York Times,* March 29, A8.

———. 2014. "Taliban and Government Imperil Gains for Afghan Women, Advocates Say." *New York Times,* February 8, A5.

Nordland, Rod, and Abdul Waheed Wafa. 2011. "Seeking a Functioning Parliament, Afghan Panel Upends Vote Results." *New York Times,* August 22, A4.

Razack, Sherene. 2005. "Geopolitics, Culture Clash, and Gender after September 11." *Social Justice* 32, no. 4: 11–31.

Riphenburg, Carol. 2010. "Women's Prospects in Afghanistan: Oppression or Opportunity?" In *Afghanistan, 1979-2009: In the Grip of Conflict,* edited by MEI, 174–77. Washington, D.C.: Middle East Institute.

Ross-Sheriff, Fariyal. 2006. "Afghan Women in Exile and Repatriation: Passive Victims or Social Actors." *Affilia* 21, no. 2: 206–19.

Rostami-Povey, Elaheh. 2007. *Afghan Women: Identity and Invasion.* London: Zed Books.

Rotberg, Robert I. 2006. "Renewing the Afghan State." In *Building a New Afghanistan,* edited by Robert Rotberg, 1–21. Medford, Mass.: World Peace Foundation.

Rubin, Alissa J. 2010. "Taliban Overhaul Image to Win Allies." *New York Times,* January 21, A1, A6.

———. 2013. "Effort to Strengthen an Afghan Law on Women May Backfire." *New York Times,* May 19, A8.

Russo, Ann. 2006. "The Feminist Majority Foundation's Campaign to Stop Gender Apartheid: The Intersections of Feminism and Imperialism in the United States." *International Feminist Journal of Politics* 8, no. 4: 557–80.

Saktanber, Ayşe. 2006. "Women and the Iconography of Fear: Islamization in Post-Islamist Turkey." *Signs* 32, no. 1: 21–31.

Samar, Sima. 2011. "The Hidden War against Women: Health Care in Afghanistan." In *Land of the Unconquerable: The Lives of Contemporary Afghan Women,* edited by Jennifer Heath and Ashraf Zahedi, 179–87. Berkeley: University of California Press.

Semple, Michael. 2009. *Reconciliation in Afghanistan, Perspectives.* Washington, D.C.: United States Institute of Peace Press.

Shapiro, Susan. 2007. "Standing (Again) with Judith Plaskokw: A Selective Reading of Her Essays." *Journal of Feminist Studies in Religion* 23, no. 1: 25–29.

Singer, Michael. 1999. "Relativism, Culture, Religion, and Identity." In *Religious Fundamentalisms and the Human Rights of Women,* edited by Courtney W. Howland, 45–54. New York: Palgrave.

Sinha, Shakti. 2010. "Legitimacy or Credibility? The Case of the Afghan State." In *Afghanistan, 1979–2009: In the Grip of Conflict,* edited by MEI, 122–24. Washington, D.C.: Middle East Institute.

Skaine, Rosemarie. 2008. *Women of Afghanistan in the Post-Taliban Era: How Lives Have Changed and Where They Stand Today.* Jefferson, N.C.: McFarland.

Smith, Deborah J. 2011. "Between Choice and Force: Marriage Practices in Afghanistan." In *Land of the Unconquerable: The Lives of Contemporary Afghan Women,* edited by Jennifer Heath and Ashraf Zahedi, 162–76. Berkeley: University of California Press.

Spivak, Gayatri Chakravorty. 2010. *Can the Subaltern Speak? Reflections on the History of the Vanishing Present,* edited by Rosalind C. Morris. New York: Columbia University Press.

Trible, Phyllis. 1982. "Feminist Hermeneutics and Biblical Studies." *Christian Century,* February 3–10, 116. http://www.religion-online.org/showarticle.asp?title=1281.

Wadud, Amina. 1999 [1992]. *Qur'an and Woman.* New York: Oxford University Press.

Wali, Sima. 2002. "Afghan Women: Recovering, Rebuilding." *Ethics & International Affairs* 16, no. 2: 15–19.

Whitlock, Gillian. 2007. *Soft Weapons: Autobiography in Transit.* Chicago: University of Chicago Press. E-book.

Yeğenoğlu, Meyda. 1998. *Colonial Fantasies: Towards a Feminist Reading of Orientalism.* New York: Cambridge University Press.

Young, Iris Marion. 1997. *Intersecting Voices: Dilemmas of Gender, Political Philosophy, and Policy.* Princeton, N.J.: Princeton University Press.

Zahedi, Ashraf. 2011. "When the Picture Does Not Fit the Frame: Engaging Afghan Men in Women's Empowerment." In *Land of the Unconquerable: The Lives of Contemporary Afghan Women,* edited by Jennifer Heath and Ashraf Zahedi, 293–305. Berkeley: University of California Press.

INDEX

Abandon Child Marriage Workshop, 52
Abd, Imam (Abdul Rauf), 159
Abdullah Bin Masoud University, 88
Abu-Lughod, Lila, 11
Achakzai, Sitara, 75
Active Youth Foundation, 87–89
Afghan: anti-Soviet sentiment, 48, 70; basic rights, 53; contradictions, 62–63; generous spirit, 10, 45–46; illiteracy, 26, 237–38n3; mistrust of large organizations, 166–67; oral heritage and culture, 79–80; traumatized by war, 176
Afghan Bar Association's women's committee, 100
Afghani, Jamila: accomplishments, 50, 57–58; Active Youth Foundation, 87; Afghan Women's Professional Education Institute, 99; appearance, 53; asylum possibilities, 201–2; Basel commonalities, 49–50, 51–52; Basel differences, 124–25; children (her own), 55, 77–78, 114, 130, 144–47, 198, 200; children and education, 30, 31, 56–58, 87, 90–91; competitiveness in women's culture, 161–65; Constitution, 33; courage, 2, 12, 32, 83–84, 171–72, 198–99; current situation, 196–98, 230–32; despair and discouragement responses, 199–201; economic empowerment developments, 89, 93; education challenges, 19, 26, 30–33; education development organizations, 30, 32–33; election process challenges, 32; Elimination of Violence Against Women (EVAW) law, 85, 201; equal rights, 33; evolution of hope for Afghan women, 36, 42, 156–61, 176, 178, 199, 201, 232–33; family (husband and children), 77, 79, 83, 198; family background and support, 51–52; feminism, 146; focus, 27, 178–80; friendship roots and development, 10; future prospects, 200–202; Gender and Journalism (Islam training for media employees), 106–7; generosity, 10, 83; "good" v. "bad" Taliban characterizations, 172–73; gossip, 162–65; government commitment to progress for women, 94–95; health care challenges and developments, 32, 85–87; higher education in U. S. pursuit, 155, 196–97, 200; Humanitarian Country Team (HCT), 99; international media attention need, 92, 95–96, 110–12; Islamic education, 53, 103–7, 116–25; Karzai administration, 90–91, 92, 168–70; leadership development process, 54–62; marriage (her own), 124–25, 134–36, 143–47; marriage in Afghan culture, 116–17, 119–20, 242n3; NGO (international nongovernmental organization) assessments, 35–36, 93–94, 95–96, 157, 158–60; Pakistan exile, 50, 54–55, 74, 85; physical disability (previous polio), 53, 79; polygamy, 136–37; polygyny, 148; process required for women's rights progress in Afghanistan, 26, 40–41, 160–61; projects and activity development, 98–100; provincial and local governments, 92–93; security challenges, 82, 83–84, 171–72; sexual harassment-education relationship, 102–3; Taliban, 172–73, 198–99; Tanenbaum Peacemakers in Action Prize, 197–98; tradition and culture (rather than Islam) as source of women's oppression, 53, 103–7, 116–25; travels related to *Contested Terrain*, 12; urban environments importance, 53–54; violence survival, 83–84; violent conditions, 171–72; women's organizations failure to connect with ordinary Afghan women, 166; women's rights within teachings of Islam, 159. *See also* Afghan Women's Islamic Network (AWIN); Afghan Women's Network (AWN); education; Noor Educational and Capacity Development (NECDO); Noor Educational Center (NEC)
Afghan Independent Human Rights Commission, 73

Afghan Institute of Learning, 7
Afghanistan: British Afghanistan policy, 66–68, 239n1, 239n13; Communism impact and aftermath, 59–60, 167; contradictory nature of problems to be solved, 180; current reality, 178–80; divisions and factions, 236n1; economic factors, 23–24, 177; ethnic composition of, 236n1; foreign military withdrawal impact, 176; geopolitical significance, 3, 12; "good" v. "bad" dichotomy perspective, 45–46; history, 48–49; homosexuality, 128, 242n11; hospitals, 86–87, 240n3; international media attention, 31, 33, 35, 36, 91–92; maternal death rates (2010), 151; mineral deposits, 174–75; mortality survey (2010), 151, 242–43n1; neighboring countries' economic influence, 176–77; poverty, 20, 46, 174–76; process required for women's rights progress, 26, 40–41, 160–61; religions of, 236n1; Soviet (Communist) invasion and occupation, 48, 59–60, 66–67, 69–70; terrorist training ground, 176; tribal/patriarchal Afghan social structure, 19–20, 45–46, 236n1; "underprivileged majority," 236n3; women's rights struggle history, 62–63, 65–76; women's rights struggle pattern and variations, 62–68, 69, 97. *See also* prospects for Afghan future; Taliban; U.S. Afghanistan policy; war; *and specific aspects of social structure, government, and culture*
Afghanistan Human Rights and Democracy Organization, 74
Afghanistan Liberation Organization, 7
Afghanistan Mortality Survey, 242–43n1
Afghanistan Program for Vital Voices Global partnership, 37–38, 235n1, 238n9
Afghanistan Progressive Law Organization (APLO), 100
Afghanistan Research and Evaluation Unit on Family Dynamics and Family Violence, 133
Afghanistan Women's Council, 7
Afghan National Shura of Ulema, 200–201, 245n7
Afghan Supreme Court High Council, 165
Afghan women. *See* Afghan; Afghanistan; *and specific issues*
Afghan Women (newspaper), 75
Afghan Women Judges Association (AWJA), 2, 29–30, 50, 100, 169–70. *See also* legal reform
Afghan Women Lawyers and Professional Association, 75
Afghan Women Leaders Speak Conference (2005): activism commitment, 21; Afghan attendees, 19, 235n1; arrival of attendees, 1–2; attendee roles in Afghan society, 17, 19, 21–22, 235n1; characteristics of attendees, 48; disagreements and complexities, 33–35; economic empowerment conflicts, 33–35, 238n8; financial support, 9; hopes for progress expressed, 176; international intervention situations, 35–36; leadership development necessities, 17, 19, 48; Ohio State University financial support, 9; ongoing problems and difficulties, 25–27; overviews, 10, 42–43, 237n9; realities of women's lives, 19–24; recommendations, 26–27, 42–43; research and planning processes, 8–9; U.S. government relationship, 8–9, 235n6; women's rights struggle, 62–63. *See also* Afghani, Jamila; Basel, Marzia; *and individual attendees*
Afghan Women's Islamic Network (AWIN), 99, 103–4
Afghan Women's Leadership Project, 8, 81
Afghan Women's Network (AWN): Afghani role, 55–56, 102; collaborative efforts, 231; communications, 194; composition, 37; leaders, 75; limitations, 165, 168; ongoing activities and programs (2010–2013), 162; research and reporting about Afghanistan government, 212; sexual harassment and legal issues training, 102
Afghan Women's Organization, 230
Afghan Women's Professional Education Institute, 99, 102–3
Afghan Women's Resource Center (AWRC), 75
Afghan Women's Summit for Democracy, 237n1
Afkhami, Mahnaz, 8
Afzali, Amina, 237n1
Ahmadinejad, Mahmoud, 48
Ahmadyar, Aziza, 25, 235n1, 237n2
Albright, Madeleine, 71
Ali, Kecia, 242n6
al Qaeda, 4
American Institute of Afghanistan Studies, 9
American Society for Muslim Advancement (ASMA), 105, 197, 241n5
American University of Afghanistan (AUAF), 88, 240n8
Arghandiwal, Abdul Hadi, 212, 213
Arizona State University (ASU) Center for the Study of Religion and Conflict, 10
Arizona State University (ASU) Institute for Humanities Research, 10
Armstrong, Sally, 245n10
Asia Foundation, 9

Index

Asian Development Bank, 235n1
Avon Global Center, 183
Azarbaijani-Moghaddam, Sippi, 235n6
Azim, Afifa, 75
Aziz, Nahid, 153
Azizi, Farida, 37–38, 38, 235n1

baad, 73
badal, 73–74, 120, 219
Balkhi, Sediqa, 75, 237n1
Balouchi Afghans, 236n1
Barfield, Thomas, 209–10
Barr, Heather, 212
Basel, Marzia: accomplishments, 50–51, 59–60; Afghan bank directorship, 100; Afghan Bar Association's women's committee, 100; Afghani differences, 123–25; Afghanistan Progressive Law Organization (APLO), 100; Afghan marriage comments and ideas, 114–20; Afghan men judges, 28–29, 39, 58, 88, 93; Afghan women judges, 40, 41, 50, 59, 84, 100, 195–96; Afghan Women Judges Association (AWJA), 2, 29–30, 50, 100, 169–70; Afghan Women's Network (AWN), 102; Afghan Women's Organization, 230; appearance, 53; Australia exile, 181; Canada asylum, 184–96, 229; Canadian work for Afghan women, 195–96; childbearing, 121–22; child marriage, 95; commonalities with Afghani, 49–50, 51–52; Constitution, 27–28; Cornell professorship, 183; courage, 2, 12, 51, 83–84, 173, 181–82, 191–92; current and upcoming situation, 200–202, 229–30; dedication to women's causes, 60, 195–96; despair and frustration indications, 152, 155, 182, 191, 194; differences from Afghani, 52–54, 124–25; economic empowerment challenges, 33–35, 38–39; education, 50, 58–60, 87–88; election process, 27–28, 29, 169; Elimination of Violence Against Women (EVAW) law, 85, 201; factionalism and foreign intervention, 177–78; family background and support, 52, 58–60; family life structure, 120–21; focus, 27, 178–80; friendship roots and development, 10; generosity, 83; German Society for Technical Cooperation (GTZ), 100; gossip culture, 165; grief for Afghanistan, 155, 182, 191, 194; hope for her future, 192–93; hope for progress evolution, 156–61, 176, 178, 195; international media attention need, 39, 85, 91–92, 110, 111–12; Islamic principles, 29, 39–40, 41, 53; judges, 238n6; Karzai administration, 90–91, 167, 169–70, 173–74; lack of collaboration tradition, 29; leadership development, 60–61; legal system problems and developments, 28–29, 39, 60–61, 84; life changes and disruptions, 181–96; marriage, 52, 114–19, 121–24; marriage (her own), 124–25, 130–33, 137–43; Ministry of Justice projects, 100; Ministry of Women's Affairs, 169; need to develop informed public, 41; new idea evaluation, 47; New York exile, 183–84; NGO (international non-governmental organization) assessments, 35, 95–96, 157–58, 160–61; poverty, 175–76; process required for women's progress in Afghanistan, 26, 40–41, 160–61; project and activities development, 100–101; rule of law, 27–30, 92, 101–2; security need, 27, 84, 170–71; sexual harassment, 101–2; Sharia law instruction, 107–10; Supreme Court position loss, 165, 243n2; Taliban, 51, 60, 90–91, 173, 181–82, 191–92; teaching Islamic principles, 103, 107–10; tradition and culture (rather than Islam) as source of women's oppression, 40–41, 53, 93, 103, 107–10, 116–25; travels related to *Contested Terrain*, 11–12; universities, 88; urban (v. rural) environments, 84; U.S. immigration and asylum difficulties, 182–88; U.S. supporters, 182, 184, 189, 244n1, 244n2, 244n3; violence survival, 83–84; vocational education complexities, 33–35; women in leadership roles challenges and developments, 239n12; women leaders' challenges and developments, 26, 40, 84, 239n12; women's competition tradition, 29; women's rights organizations, 162
BBC poll (2009), 151–52, 153, 243n2
Begham, Sajia, 99, 241n1
Beyond the 11th, 87
bin Laden, Osama, 4, 70, 72
bint Jahsh, Zainab, 116, 119, 242n3
Bonn Agreement of 2001, 22–24, 73, 213, 237n1. *See also* Constitution
Bowman, Cynthia, 183, 189–90
British Afghanistan policy, 66–68, 239n13
Brodsky, Anne, 243n8
Brundige, Elizabeth, 183, 189, 243n1, 243n2, 244n2, 244n1
burqa issue, 7, 14, 40, 80, 208, 241n4
Bush, George W., administration, 4–5
Bush, Laura, 4, 5–6, 66, 202
Butler, Judith, 15

Cady, Linell, 182
Canadian Women for Women in Afghanistan (CW$_4$WA), 57, 239n4
Carastathis, Anna, 225

carpet weaving and embroidery "industries," 33–34
Center for the Study of Religion and Conflict, 154–55
chador, 53, 163, 208, 241
Chishti, Maliha, 217, 218
Clarke, Michael, 153
Clinton, Bill, 3–4
Clinton, Hillary, 212–13
Coca-Cola Critical Difference for Women program (OSU), 9
Cold War, 6
colonialism, 4–6. *See also* British Afghanistan policy; Soviet (Communist) invasion and occupation; U.S. Afghanistan policy; war
Columbus Council on World Affairs, 9
Communist Party, 59–60
Community Development Council, 152
Constitution, 22–23, 27–28, 33, 238n7
Contested Terrain (Kitch): Afghan oral heritage and culture, 79–80; author research training and review, 10–11, 235n8; author roles and responsibilities, 12–13, 16–17, 80–81; collaborative nature, 12; feminist theory and activism, 236n9; friendship roots and development, 17, 81; literary context, 14–15; narrators' privileged positions in Afghan society, 17; narrative challenges, 81–82, 236n11, 236n12; organization and structure, 16–17, 81–82, 156; potential value, 15; purposes, 11; terminology, 16, 236n11, 236n12; as transformational, 11–16
Convention on the Elimination of All Forms of Discrimination Against Women (CEDAW), 64, 101, 217, 239n1, 241n3
Crenshaw, Kimberlé, 225
Crimes Investigation Department, 243n1
Cure International, 86–87, 240n5
CW$_4$WA (Canadian Women for Women in Afghanistan), 57, 239n4

Dalil, Surya, 86, 162
Daly, Mary, 223
Department of Women and Reproductive Health, 151, 242–43n1
divorce, 116–19, 145–46, 239n13, 242n3, 242n4. *See also* legal reform
Dobriansky, Paula, 189, 244n3
Donini, Antonio, 218
Dorrani Pashtun, 23

economic empowerment, 33–35, 89, 238n8, 238n9

education: as basis for transformation hopes, 158–59; corruption effect, 32; higher education contradictions, 158; illiteracy, 26, 237n3; Islam misinterpretation effect, 31–32; progress evolution, 30–33, 87–89, 152; security, 32, 152–53; sexual harassment, 101–10; social issue and self-awareness training, 30; statistics, 30; textbooks, 32, 238n10; tribal/patriarchal culture impact, 31–32; universities, 88; violence, 32, 152–53, 243n5; vocational education complexities, 33–35. *See also* Islamic education; Noor Educational and Capacity Development Organization (NECDO); Noor Educational Center
elections and voting system. *See* political reform
Elimination of Violence Against Women (EVAW) law, 73, 85, 201, 212
Ensler, Eve, 80

Faludi, Susan, 224
family structure, 120–21. *See also* divorce; marriage; tribal/patriarchal Afghan social structure
Farhoumand-Sims, Cheshmak, 217, 218
Farsiwan Afghans, 236n1
feminism: Afghani on, 146; as Afghanistan survival factor, 204; author expertise and research, 8–10; *Contested Terrain* purpose, 11, 16, 80; contradictions and conflicts, 206, 216–18; future prospects and suggestions, 219–25; globalization relationship, 216–18, 221; as imperialism reinforcement, 216; Mills on, 64; transnational perspective, 156, 206, 216, 219–25; U.S. celebrities and misguided anti-*burqa* events, 3–4; Western v. Islamic, 64, 80, 81, 125, 205, 206
Feminist Majority Foundation (FMF), 3–4
Fiorenza, Elisabeth, 223
Foote, Julia, 222
"free market capitalism," 23–24, 237n9
Friedan, Betty, 224
Fuller, Margaret, 207
future. *See* prospects for Afghan future

Gailani, Fatana, 75
Gender and Journalism (Islam training for media employees), 106–7
Gender Mainstreaming Project, 241n1
German Society for Technical Cooperation (GTZ), 100, 241n2
Ghazanfar, Husn Banu, 75
Global Peace Mission of Malaysia, 56

government. *See* Karzai administration; Parliament; political reform
Grimké, Sarah, 222

hadith, 56, 63, 64, 170
Hamim, Mawlawi Muhammad Ibrahim, 136, 242n2
Hanif, Maulvi, 159, 243n1
Hanifi, M. Jamil, 237n8
Hassan, Palwasha, 22, 237n4
Hazara Afghans, 19, 35, 72, 177, 236n1
Heath, Jennifer, 209
health care developments, 75, 85–87, 151, 240n2, 242–43n1. *See also* Karzai administration
"Healthy Family, Happy Society" program, 75
Hekmatyar, Gulbeddin, 21
hijab, 2, 45, 69, 163, 201
Hizb-i-Islami faction, 212
Horn, Marian, 189
Humanitarian Assistance for the Women and Children of Afghanistan, 75
Humanitarian Country Team (HCT), 99
Human Rights Watch, 212

ijma, 159
imams, gender training program for, 31, 105, 106, 197–99, 208, 221, 230–33; challenges to gender training programs for, 108–9, 199; characterization as learned, 53, 105; comparisons of mullahs and, 53, 105, 144; internationals' need to incorporate perspectives of, 73, 105; importance of opinions, 105; women's and human rights, 159, 201. *See also* Islam; Islamic education
Imams for EVAW (Elimination of Violence Against Women), 201
imperialism. *See* colonialism; Orientalism
Independent Election Commission, 244n5
Independent National Legal Training Center, 169–70
Indira Gandhi Children's Hospital, 240n3
Interim Afghanistan National Development Strategy (2006), 211
international assistance need, 157–58. *See also* NGOs (nongovernmental organizations)
invasions. *See* war
Iran, 48, 75, 85, 177
Islam: Afghani studies and teaching, 31, 55, 56–57, 73–74, 104–5, 109, 159; divorce, 116–18; empowerment of women, 39–40, 41; gender equality, 242n6; Islamic fundamentalism compared to Christian fundamentalism, 222–24; legal reform, 108–9;
marriage, 105, 116–20, 241n6; misinterpretations and misuses, 53, 107–8, 131; outward appearances, 104; political relationship, 108–9; repressive practices relationship to, 29, 31–32, 38–39, 56–57, 103–8, 116–25, 160–61, 178–80; Western misinterpretation, 104; women leadership models, 39–40; women's progress relationship to, 26, 40–41, 160–61; women's rights awareness training for imams, 31, 73–74, 104–6, 108–9, 159. *See also* Afghani, Jamila; *burqa* issue; Islamic education; Sharia law
Islamic Center for Political and Cultural Activities of Afghan Women, 75
Islamic education: women's rights awareness training for imams, 31, 73–74, 104–5, 109, 159. *See also* Afghani, Jamila; Basel, Marzia; Islam; Sharia law; *and specific organizations*
Islamic feminism, 9, 222–23, 245n4
Islamic fundamentalism compared to Christian fundamentalism, 222–24
Islamic University, 88
Istanbul meeting (2010): Afghani project and activity changes, 98–100; author reflections, 111–12; author research training and review, 10–11, 235n8; background and preparations, 79; Basel project and activity changes, 100–101; commonalities and agreements, 110–12; culture v. tradition in Afghan rhetoric, 113; differences in perspective, 112–13; foundations, 10–11; logistics and complications, 77–79; overview of changes for Afghan women, 97–98; planning process, 76; terminology interpretations, 113
itjihad, 223

Jalal, Masuda, 237n1
Jalalzai, Zubeda, 219
Jan, Safia Ama, 76
Jefferess, David, 219
jihad, 40, 70, 71, 154, 174
Jinnah College for Women, 55
jirga, 25, 40, 109, 177, 240n5. *See also* Loya Jirga; Meshrani Jirga; Wolesi Jirga
justice. *See* legal reform
Justice Secular Support Program, 157–58

Kabul Beauty School, 24, 237n9. *See also* "free market capitalism"
"Kabul Bubble," 218
Kabul Museum, 215
Kabul University, 88, 102–3
Kakar, Fazal, 83, 143–46, 147, 148, 231
Kamal, Meena Keshwar, 40, 238–39n11

Kandiyoti, Deniz, 217
Karmanian, Susan, 189
Karzai, Hamid. *See* Karzai administration
Karzai administration: Bonn Agreement of 2001, 22; corruption, 169, 244n5; disconnect with women professionals, 169, 243–44n4; Elimination of Violence Against Women (EVAW), 168; failures, 47, 73, 240n7; immunity grant for all war crime suspects (2007), 73; international support, 23; manipulation of international aid donors, 92; messages from women's organizations to, 173–74; politics-Islam relationship, 108–9; power motivation and struggle, 170; relationship to professional women, 25, 47, 72, 73, 90, 168–69, 173; repressive "Islamic" guidelines for women, 200–201; Taliban, 90; tribal origins and alliances, 23, 237n8; women appointed to cabinet, 25, 237n1, 237n2; women's rights policies, 72–74, 167
Kaufman, Marc, 241n2
Khadija, 39, 44, 119, 122, 242n4, 242n5
Khail, Ashequllah Orya, 131, 138–40. *See also* Basel, Marzia
Khan, Amanullah, 65, 66–67
Khan, Daisy, 197
Khan, Daoud (Sardar Mohammed Daoud), 23, 48, 69, 239n3
Khan, Mohammad Hashim, 66
Khan, Shah Mahmud, 66
Kirghiz Afghans, 236n1
Koofi, Fawzia, 212
Kristoff, Nicholas, 209

"Law and Women" program, 75–76
Lawrence, T. E., 67
League of Women Voters (National and Ohio), 9
legal reform: competitiveness, 29; Crimes Investigation Department, 243n1; education relationship, 28–29; foreign support programs, 177; gender-based law enforcement, 179; international assistance coalition need, 158; Islam education projects, 107–10; Islam-repressive practices relationship, 29, 31–32, 38–39, 56–57, 103–8, 116–25, 178–80; judges, 28–29, 30, 238n6; judgeship opportunity developments, 84–85; Karzai administration effects, 169–70; legal rights training for women, 108–9; local and provincial governments, 25, 28, 76, 237n2; nepotism, 28; participation, 28; security relationship, 27; Sharia law instruction, 107–10; tribal/patriarchal Afghan social structure, 28–29, 177; women leaders, 27–28, 84–85. *See also* Afghan Women Judges Association (AWJA); Basel, Marzia; Sharia law; Supreme Court
Lehr, Rachel, 34–35
Leno, Mavis, 3, 13
Lewis, Reina, 226
Lieven, Anatol, 210, 243n2
Lister, Sarah, 210
local and provincial governments, 8, 25, 76, 237n2, 245n1. *See also* political reform
Loya Jirga (grand assembly): in 2002, 32, 51; in 2003, 22–23; in 2011, 194. *See also* Constitution; Parliament
Luce Foundation, 154–55

madrassa, 28, 71, 104, 199
mahr, 105, 116, 241n6
mahram, 6, 124, 132, 201
marriage: Afghani, 134–36, 143–47; author reflections, 147–49; Basel, 130–33, 143; children, 117–18; cultural rather than religious institution, 116–20; "culture-clash" perspective, 125–29, 147–49, 242n10; divorce, 116–18, 242n3, 242n4; economic factors, 116, 241n2; education relationship, 114–20, 121–24; family life structure, 120–21; inevitability, 114; inferiority attitude of women, 119; Islam teachings relationship, 116–20; legal reform, 118–19; personal experience narratives, 124–47; polygamy, 119–20, 136–37; polygyny, 148–49; poverty relationship, 116, 241n2; Qu'ran on, 116–20; statistics, 114; U.S. comparison, 147–49. *See also* tribal/patriarchal Afghan social structure
medical care. *See* health
Medica Mondiale, 241n1
Meena, Marzia, 235n1
Mernissi, Fatima, 222–23
Merry, Sally Engle, 211, 214, 221
Meshrano Jirga, 75. *See also* Parliament
military occupations. *See* war
Mills, Margaret, 242n11; Afghanistan visit (2013) findings, 15, 154; on Afghan oral heritage and culture, 79; Afghan Women Leadership Project founding, 81; Afghan Women Leaders Speak Conference (2005), 1–2, 43; feminist engagement concept, 219; on homosexuality in Afghanistan, 128; homosexuality in Afghanistan, 242n11; on international women's collaborative exchange of ideas, 219; qualifications and accomplishments, 7–8, 10, 235n5; on Taliban attitudes, 231; U.S. immigration and asylum difficulties for Afghans, 202; on Western

definitions and expectations v. realities of Afghan women's lives, 64
Ministry of Culture and Youth, 237n2
Ministry of Hajj, 73–74
Ministry of Health, 162
Ministry of Information, Culture, and Tourism, 235n1
Ministry of Information and Culture, 25
Ministry of Religious Affairs, 73–74
Ministry of the Interior, 102
Ministry of Women's Affairs (MWA), 22–23, 73–74, 75, 160, 169, 237n6
Mohanty, Chandra, 205, 222
mujahideen: Afghani on, 36, 50, 54, 115–16; Azizi on, 37; Basel on, 28, 59, 86–87, 123, 137, 177; civil wars, 65; education for women relationship, 71, 115–16, 123, 137; exiles necessitated by, 20, 50, 183–84, 215; factionalism and violence exacerbation, 177; impact on urban women, 20–21, 22, 123; international forces withdrawal effect, 155; Karzai administration, 73, 86–87; leaders, 239n3; NGOs (nongovernmental organizations) relationships, 86–87; Reagan misrepresentation, 6; restrictions on women, 6, 20, 25, 28, 37; Soviet (Communist) occupation period, 59; U.S. support for, 6, 21, 71; variations, 36; as weapons source for Taliban, 6, 60, 71. *See also* Karzai administration; Taliban; tribal/patriarchal Afghan social structure
mullahs, challenges for international community involvement with, 95, 104, 108; characterizations of, 28, 45, 53, 104, 109; comparison of mullahs and imams, 53, 144; differing viewpoints, 67, 109; discontent with Zahir Shah's rule, 68; internationals' need to incorporate perspectives of, 73; limitations of knowledge, 68, 104, 107, 212
Muslim Women Society, 7

namaz, 105
Napolitano, Janet, 91–92
National Archive, 215
Nemat, Orzala Ashraf, 75
NGOs (nongovernmental organizations): Afghani assessments, 35–36, 93–94, 96, 111–12, 157, 158–60; Basel assessments, 35, 95–96, 111–12, 157–58, 160–61; collaboration failures, 35, 159–60; difficulties and negatives, 35, 95–96; education impact, 71; factionalism and violence exacerbation, 35–36; genderization need, 206–9; improvement recommendations, 151–61, 157–58; intentions v. progress for Afghan women, 111–12; limitations of, 35, 95–96; medical, 86–87; misinterpretations of, 96; security problems for women employees, 25; women leaders, 1, 22; women's empowerment relationship to, 75; women's experience and hopes for, 111–12
Niazi, Mohammed Ayaz, 159
9/11, 1, 4, 5, 6, 72, 191. *See also* U.S. Afghanistan policy
Nixon, Hamish, 210
Noor Educational and Capacity Development Organization (NECDO): Afghani efforts against sexual harassment, 102–3; current activities and progress, 230–31; gossip impact on, 163; human rights issues inclusion, 98–99; progress since 2010, 199, 201; violence against women participants, 110–11; youth committees opposing violence against women (radio play), 110–11. *See also* Afghani, Jamila; Noor Educational Center (NEC)
Noor Educational Center (NEC): consciousness raising, 42; founding and early development, 2, 50, 56; leadership development projects, 30–32, 42; library, 30–31; rural Afghanistan activity, 84; self-dependency programs, 30–31; transformation hopes, 158–59; vocational education complexities, 30–31, 33–35; youth committees, 31. *See also* Afghani, Jamila; Noor Educational and Capacity Development (NECDO)
Northern Alliance warlords, 22, 24, 46–47. *See also* Karzai, Hamid; tribal/patriarchal Afghan social structure
Ntanda, Ntambo, 197

O'Connor, Sandra Day, 155
O'Hara, Rosanne, 189
Ohio State University Mershon Center for International Security Studies, 7, 9, 19
Organization for Liberation of People of Afghanistan, 7
Organization for Liberation of the Working Class of Afghanistan, 7
Orientalism, 5–6, 81, 111–12. *See also* British Afghanistan policy; U.S. Afghanistan policy

Paikan, Suraya, 75
Pakistan, 177
Pakistan exile, 85
Pakzad, Soriya, 75
Parliament: election corruption, 169; immunity grant for all war crime suspects (2007), 73; increase in women candidates in 2010 election, 152; Karzai administration failures, 169; women's presence (2005), 27–28, 75, 238n5; women's rights failures, 23

Pashtun Afghans, 19, 23, 68–69, 71–72, 145, 195, 215, 236n1
pashtunwali, 236n1
PASRA, 75
patriarchal/tribal social structure. *See* tribal/patriarchal Afghan social structure
People's Democratic Party of Afghanistan (PDPA), 6, 69–70
peshimam, 159
Physicians for Human Rights, 20
Plaskow, Judith, 223
political reform: election process, 27–29; elections and voting system corruption, 32; government participation developments, 25, 89–90, 237n1; provincial and local governments, 25, 28, 75, 76, 237n2; rule of law challenges, 27–30, 92, 100–101; women's leadership problems and progress, 26, 40. *See also* legal reform
polygamy, 119–20, 136–37, 201
polygyny, 148–49, 201
post-Istanbul meeting in 2010, 151–80
poverty, 20, 46, 174–76, 241n2. *See also* economic empowerment
predictions. *See* prospects for Afghan future
Prophet Muhammad, misinterpretations of Islam based on life of, 45, 63, 95, 103–4, 106–7, 120, 223; teachings and progressive attitudes about women, 44, 56, 63, 116–17, 119, 143; wives of, 39, 44–45, 56, 116, 119, 122, 242n3, 242n5
prospects for Afghan future: Afghan-run NGOs and women's networks, 208–9; author's suggestions, 218–27; comparative historical analysis, 221–26; conservative Afghan elements, 211–14; feminist analysis failure, 205; fundamentalist Islam and fundamentalist Christian parallels, 222–24; genderization of the international community, 206–9; globalization realities, 216–17, 221–22; "good governance" solution, 214; government alternatives for Afghanistan, 209–11, 245n1; international support improvement potential, 206–9; intersectionality, 224–25; limitations on working for democracy and women's rights, 219–20; models for potential solutions, 215–18; national unity v. tribalized society, 214–16; "neoliberal governmentalities" and feminist apparatus of NGO world, 217–18; NGO and international donor analysis, 205–6; reality-based collaboration, 226; serial coalitions, 226; strategy need, 204–5; terminology comprehension, 224–25; U.S.-Afghan interconnection utilization, 222–25; U.S. international policies impact, 224; women leaders' opposition to negotiation with Taliban, 213–14
provincial and local governments, 8, 25, 76, 237n2, 245n1. *See also* political reform
Provincial Development Committees, 211
Provincial Reconstruction Teams, 211

qabila, 20
Qadir, Haji Abdul, 115, 241n1
Qazilbash Afghans, 236n1
quam, 20
Qur'an. *See* Islam; Islamic education

Rabbani, Burhanuddin, 54–55, 185–88, 239n3
Razack, Sherene, 80, 222
Reagan, Ronald, 6
requirement for women's rights progress in Afghanistan, 26, 40–41, 160–61
Reuther, Rosemary Radford, 223
Revolutionary Association of the Women of Afghanistan (RAWA), 7, 40, 167–68, 238–39n11
Rhetorics and Politics in Afghan Traditional Storytelling (Mills), 7
Rostami-Povey, Elaheh, 72
Rubia International (RI), 34–35, 238n8
rule of law for Afghan women. *See* legal reform; political reform
Russia. *See* Communist Party; Soviet (Communist) invasion and occupation

safety. *See* security; violence
Safi, Hanifa, 76
Samar, Sima, 23, 237n6, 243–44n4
Saqib, Sabrina, 213
Sarabi, Habiba, 23
security, 27, 36, 170–76, 230. *See also* violence
Semple, Michael, 214
September 11, 2001, 1, 4, 5, 6, 72, 191
sexual harassment, 101–10
Shah, Mohammed Zahir, 48, 58
Shah, Nadir, 65–66, 67
Shah, Zafir, 66, 68–69
Shahristan, 132, 241n1
Sharia law: Communist era, 59; economic empowerment relationship to, 27; illiteracy relationship to, 107; Independent National Legal Training Center, 169; international ignorance, 93; judges, 169–70; Karzai administration, 201–2; marriage, 131; misinterpretations and misuse, 53, 71,

108, 131; sexual harassment, 101–3; varying interpretations, 131, 214, 219; women's education, 103, 107, 108; women's ignorance of, 27; women's rights guarantees in, 27. *See also* Islam
Shorish-Shamley, Zeiba, 3
Shuhada Organization, 75
shuras, 20, 48, 92, 109, 177, 211
Sisterhood is Global Institute, 8
Soft Weapons (Whitlock), 14
solutions envisioned by Afghan women leaders, 26, 40–41, 160–61
Sorush, Lisa, 235n1
Soviet (Communist) invasion and occupation, 48, 59–60, 66–67, 69–70
Spivak, Gayatri, 216, 222
Stapleton, Jenny, 190
Sultan, Masuda, 26, 38, 238n4
Supreme Court, 27, 29–30, 84–85, 100. *See also* legal reform
Swedish Committee for Afghanistan (SCA), 99, 111, 241n2

Tajik Afghans, 19, 23, 35, 72, 177, 236n1, 239n3
Taliban: Afghani encounters with, 172, 198–99, 232; Basel encounters with, 51, 132, 138, 173, 181–82, 191–92, 213–14; BBC poll measuring support for (2009), 151, 243n2; bin Laden connection, 4; difficulty of negotiating with, 65–66, 71–72, 90, 172–74, 189, 194, 212–14; economic factors, 174; election site violence, 173; "good" v. "bad" characterizations, 172–73; kidnapping of Basel colleague, 181–82; misinterpretation of Islam, 104; murder of women leaders (2006 and 2012), 76; origins and history, 71; power motive, 172; Rabbani murder, 189; repression of and violence against women, 23, 236n3; response to women's education efforts, 95–96, 111, 241n1; security impact, 170–74; United Nations support implication, 72; weapons acquisition, 172. *See also* mujahideen; tribal/patriarchal Afghan social structure; violence
Talibs. *See* Taliban
Tanenbaum Center for Interreligious Understanding, 197
Tanenbaum Peacemakers in Action Prize, 197–98, 199
Tempe, Arizona author meeting with Basel (2011), 154–55
Tolo TV, 85, 89, 240n1
Transitional Justice Plan, 73. *See also* Bonn Agreement of 2001

tribal/patriarchal Afghan social structure: competitiveness of women, 161–62; foreign intervention effect, 28–29, 177; impact on women's economic empowerment, 33–35, 89, 238n8, 238n9; Islam misinterpretation, 107–8; political and legal system impact, 19–20, 28–29, 236n1; pre-Islamic roots, 19–20. *See also* Karzai administration; Taliban; violence; *and specific effects on Afghan women*
Trible, Phyllis, 223

umma, 56, 154
UN-Habitat, 60, 239n5
UNICEF Afghanistan, 165
United Nations Afghanistan policy, 72
United Nations Assistance Mission in Afghanistan, 73
University of Dawat and Jihad, 88
University of Nebraska-Omaha Center for Afghanistan Studies, 238n10
U.S. Afghanistan policy: arrogance, 9, 11, 96; author recommendations, 202–3; *burqa* removal focus, 7, 14; Cold War mentality, 6, 70; colonialism, 4–5, 11; consultation failure, 9; culture-clash rhetoric, 4–5; democracy formation failure, 24; failed interventions, 23, 202; failure to support Afghan women's organizations, 7, 21; focus from 2002–2005, 9; "free market capitalism," 23–24, 237n9; "good" v. "bad" Taliban characterizations, 172–73; ignorance of Afghan history and culture, 6–7; inadvertent factionalism strengthening, 177; Karzai support, 22, 203; limitations on Afghan educational opportunities in the U.S., 202, 203; long-term capacity building failure, 9; misguided gender sensitivity of, 4–5; mujahideen warlord support, 21, 23, 47, 70–71; organizations impacting, 3–4; Orientalism, 5; public narratives, 3; revenge for 9/11, 72; Taliban support, 71–72; terminology misuse, 3; women's rights failures, 6–7, 66, 92–94; World War II and Cold War mentalities, 66–67, 70–71. *See also* Karzai administration
U.S. women, 5, 235n3; children, 126–27; family structure evolution, 126–27; feminist celebrities and misguided anti-*burqa* campaign, 3–4; judgeship appointments, 27, 50; women's rights struggle, 5. *See also* U.S. Afghanistan policy; *specific U.S. organizations; and specific U.S. women*
Uzbek Afghans, 215, 236n1

violence: elimination efforts, 111; "honor" killings, 179, 245n10; marriage practices, 115, 145–46, 153, 241n1; media attention need, 110–11; security failures, 26; sexual harassment aspect, 102–3; Sharia law misuse, 108; tribal/patriarchal Afghan social structure, 115; unrelenting presence, 83–84; women leaders, 76. *See also* Elimination of Violence Against Women (EVAW); family structure; Taliban

Vital Voices Global Partnership, 238n9

vocational education, 33–35, 238n8, 238n9

Voice of Women Organization, 75

Volunteer Network of Afghan Imams, 201

Wadud, Amina, 178, 222, 224, 242n4

Wali, Sima, 20, 22–23, 237n1, 237n6

war (and invasions and military occupations): destructive impact on women, 20; exiles and asylum, 20; factionalism and violence exacerbation, 35–36, 236n1; "good" v. "bad" Afghanistan characterizations, 46–47; Karzai administration, 23, 46–47; 9/11and Bush administration, 4–6, 12, 23; security impact, 22; traumatized population, 153, 176. *See also* colonialism; Soviet (Communist) invasion and occupation; U.S. Afghanistan policy

Western influences, 47–49. *See also* British Afghanistan policy; U.S. Afghanistan policy; war; *and specific NGOs*

Whalen, Patricia, 50

Whitlock, Gillian, 14, 80, 81

Williams, Delores S., 223

Winfrey, Oprah, 80

Winship, Joan, 189

Wolesi Jirga. *See* Parliament

Women for Afghan Women, 26, 238n4

Women's Alliance for Peace and Human Rights in Afghanistan (WAPHA), 3

Women's Internet Cafe, 241n1

Women's Islamic Initiative in Spirituality and Equality (WISE), 197

women's rights. *See* Afghanistan; economic empowerment; education; legal reform; political reform

women's vision for progress achievement, 26, 40–41, 160–61

WuDunn, Sheryl, 209

Yeğenoğlu, Meyda, 216, 222

Young, Iris Marion, 81, 226

SALLY L. KITCH is Regents' Professor of Women's and Gender Studies and the founding Director of the Institute for Humanities Research at Arizona State University. She is the author of *The Specter of Sex: Gendered Foundations of Racial Formation in the United States.*

Typeset in 10.5/13 Adobe Minion
Composed by Lisa Connery
at the University of Illinois Press
Manufactured by Sheridan Books, Inc.

University of Illinois Press
1325 South Oak Street
Champaign, IL 61820-6903
www.press.uillinois.edu

The University of Illinois Press
is a founding member of the
Association of American University Presses.